Reading between the Lines

Reading between the Lines

Annabel Patterson

The University of Wisconsin Press

The University of Wisconsin Press
114 North Murray Street
Madison, Wisconsin 53715

Printed in the United States of America

Library of Congress Cataloging-in-Publication Data
Patterson, Annabel M.
Reading between the lines / Annabel Patterson.
350 pp.   cm.
Includes bibliographical references and index.
ISBN 0-299-13540-3   ISBN 0-299-13544-6 (pbk.)
1. English literature—Early modern, 1500–1700—History and
criticism—Theory, etc. 2. Milton, John, 1608–1674—Criticism and
interpretation—History. 3. Authors and readers—Great Britain—
History. 4. Reader-response criticism. 5. Rhetoric—1500–1800.
6. Canon (Literature) I. Title.
PR421.P38   1993
821'.4—dc20   92-50257

The only direct link between philosophy and the citizens would be the trail the philosophic legislator blazes for a few of the young, who could discern between the lines of his legislation his invitation to question, in a suitably prudent way, all authority and law.
—Thomas Pangle, on Plato's *Laws*

"[Henry James] can't say what he means!" Hazel cried. "It's got to be between the lines! The things we learn about each other are like that! . . .He's got to represent those delicate things that are ruining lives."
—Nancy Price, *Sleeping with the Enemy*

If I know the truth, I have only to make it heard, in spite of all the between-the-lines censures, by the only signifier my acrobatics through the branches of the tree can constitute, provocative to the point of burlesque, or perceptible only to the practised eye, according to whether I wish to be heard by the mob or by the few.
—Jacques Lacan, *Ecrits*

Contents

Acknowledgments

There are a number of quite specific debts that I would like to recognize here, in addition to acknowledgments made in the text. I am particularly grateful to Michael Schoenfeldt, who read the manuscript for another publisher and provided a series of truly constructive suggestions whereby my chapter "The Good Old Cause," in particular, was substantially improved. The chapter on Spenser's Legend of Justice and *View of the Present State of Ireland* also greatly benefited from the suggestions of Cynthia Herrup, my colleague at Duke and editor of the *Journal of British Studies*, in which a shorter version appeared; as also from the skepticism of F. J. Levy, whose openness to literary scholars encroaching on historians' territory is well-known. Although this book was all but finished when I began to enjoy my fellowship at the National Humanities Center, I benefited generally during the last stages from the interest of Lawrence Stone and specifically from the classicist skills of Graeme Clarke, who helped me to translate Langbaine's preface to Longinus. Linda Levy Peck, who as editor of *The Mental World of the Jacobean Court* had sponsored an earlier version of my chapter on Donne, and at that stage prevented me from making some foolish historical mistakes, now became a constant support. As for Jonathan Lamb, another NCH colleague, he generously allowed me to appropriate part of his argument about the politics of the sublime and apply it to Milton's *Paradise Lost*, where its appearance of originality is, I fear, somewhat misleading.

This is the place, also, to thank the following for permission to reprint or rework material already published: University of Chicago Press, for overlapping parts of "All Donne," in *Soliciting Interpretation*, ed. Katharine Maus and Elizabeth Harvey; as mentioned above, for "The Egalitarian Giant," earlier seen condensed in the *Journal for British Studies*; and for "Couples, Canons and the Uncouth," which appeared in identical form in *Critical Inquiry* in 1990. Cambridge University Press, for a large part of "No Meer Amatorious Novel?" in *Politics, Poetics, and Hermeneutics in Milton's Prose*, ed. David Loewenstein and James Turner, which here reappears as one of the sections of "Sleeping with the Enemy"; as also for permission to incorporate "John Donne, Kingsman," from *The Mental World of the Jacobean Court* into the much longer chapter that now carries that title.

I have also been blessed, at the University of Wisconsin Press, by an acquisitions editor who does not let her work end and her interest die when one signs a contract, but continues to act as a humane and humorous guardian angel over all stages of a book's passage through design into print. Thank you, Barbara Hanrahan—as also for keeping all unwritten promises.

Finally, between the lines of this book I, at least, can read the support and marital prestidigitation of Lee Patterson, who has a lot to put up with, but continues, undeterred, to try and make me lead a normal life. And so, as a completely inadequate gesture of gratitude, I dedicate this one to him.

Reading between the Lines

Introduction

Things change. This collection of essays is my personal witness to the sheer volume of change, some of it disturbing, some liberating, all challenging to the mind, that have taken place in the profession to which I am vocationally indentured: in the educational and other priorities of institutions of advanced training; in the structuring of and communications between disciplines; in the kind of books people write and the styles in which they write them. While nobody but myself could conceivably be interested in the autobiographical implications of this testimony, it is abundantly clear to me that this book could not have been written thirty years ago, when I was first student, then teacher, of English literature at one of the older Canadian universities.

The conception of "literature" at that time and in that place was, though scarcely unsophisticated, relatively untroubled. One alternated between recalling the lives of "major" authors and their intellectual history as the primary contexts in which their writing was to be understood, and the "close reading" of texts (usually poems or prose fictions) authorized by the New Criticism. Though there must have been a contradiction even then between the first, with its emphasis on biography and personal evolution, and the second, with its decrees against the biographical "fallacy," it was one that did not infiltrate the classroom. It was an excellent education and a benign environment. As a beginning teacher, I was the beneficiary of a project, premature for its time, to hire young women; and if, in alluding (in Chapter 2) to that era as something to break away from, I imply its limitations, that oedipal gesture is trivial in comparison to my larger sense of empowerment.

We can see now that, those being the early sixties, we stood on the edge of a precipice. Like the protagonists of the iconoclastic feminist western *Thelma and Louise,* we sat in our automobiles on the lip of the Grand Canyon, and prepared, as an alternative to arrest and capital punishment, to launch into space. Some would say that, in the academy as in the motion picture, only the conventions of fiction permitted us to avoid inspection of the wreck at the bottom of the canyon. Literary studies was caught up in a series of paradigm shifts, in a whirlwind of larger ideas and projects: the philosophy of language (from Chomsky to Saussure); structuralist anthropology (from Lévi-Strauss to Northrop Frye); deconstructive critique of rationalism by Derrida and de Man; a revival of philosophical pragmatism by Richard Rorty; Marxist political philosophy as resuscitated by Althusser; a wave of academic feminism; the civil rights movement and its logical consequence, Afro-American studies; and the related though not identical movements for multiculturalism and interdisciplinary studies. It may later occur to analysts of the past half century as decidedly odd that literary study, rather than sinking into insignificance as a result, expanded to meet the challenge, became indeed so voracious of concepts and knowledge systems seemingly extraneous to its central concerns that it is now, as I write in the 1990s, and in certain quarters where these developments are deemed reprehensible, held responsible for the whole affair.

Things change; *plus ça change, plus c'est la même chose.* Each adage is as true as its converse. As Burton Bledstein showed in *The Culture of Professionalism,* two tendencies evident in academia today were also evident in North American colleges in the nineteenth century. On the one hand, they espoused a democratic ideal of higher education that was defined *against* Old World standards and compelled it "to be far more flexible and diversified than European systems." When "Mid-Victorians," as Bledstein calls them, "boldly defined such new subjects as sociology and American history, they only peeked at the possibilities of pluralism," but they established its logic nevertheless.[1] On the other hand, what appeared as bold idealism could equally appear as directionless floundering. Francis Wayland, president of Brown University in the 1840s, wrote that "the educational system has no necessary connexions with any thing else. In no

---

1. *The Culture of Professionalism: The Middle Class and the Development of Higher Education in America* (New York and London, 1978), 125–26.

other country is the whole plan for the instruction of the young so entirely dissevered from connexion with the business of subsequent life."[2]

Presumably the truth lay then, and still lies, somewhere between the positive and negative evaluations. And presumably now, as also in the mid-nineteenth century, universities and colleges are the scapegoats, in the fully ritual sense of the word, for a society experiencing massive social and cultural alteration. Precisely because institutions of higher education enable reflection in an unusually concentrated and continuous form, they experience the *agon* of change intensified disproportionately.

Although I never intended to write *about* professionalism, the essays collected here serendipitously record the effects of the changes in my sector of the profession. Perhaps it is only coincidence that, as an immigrant from England, who spent twenty years in Canadian universities on my way to the United States, I continually find myself in a mongrel position, halfway *between* theories, agendas, camps, whose oppositional quality makes them better able to explain themselves. But because I intuit a wider discomfort with the polarization of these issues that now confront us, I offer these essays, and the reflections on professional disagreements they contain, as a set of mediatorial options. Between laments for the death of "the Western Tradition" and holistic distaste for it, between neoconservative proponents of a "Great Books" approach to education and those who insist that "literature" is an empty category filled only contingently according to society's needs (which now have changed irretrievably), there clearly exist several positions of compromise.

This book reconsiders the rewards of reading white, male, canonical authors, from antiquity and from the English Renaissance, specifically Plato, Spenser, Shakespeare, Donne, and Milton; but it also deals with the "gendered" topics of rape and divorce, and with the maverick Puritan pamphleteer Job Throkmorton. The entire argument is framed by paperback novels by

2. Bledstein, *Culture of Professionalism* 242. Other criticisms which reverberate a century later include the charge that most colleges were made up of different "self-serving" groups, that faculty members "were defensive on all fronts," that students were alarmingly undisciplined and cynical, and that resources were "both maldistributed and irrationally dispersed," p. 246.

Joseph Heller and Nancy Price, and at its center is a long chapter on sixteenth-century popular culture, as represented in the 1587 edition of "Holinshed's" *Chronicles*. These interests are not on opposite sides of some theoretical Pale, but continuous with each other. For contrary to what we ourselves were taught (for reasons which themselves will occasionally be the subject of these inquiries), the canonical authors of early modern England were by no means themselves unthinking or deliberate promoters of political uniformity or the hierarchical status quo; on the contrary they subjected such notions to extremely critical scrutiny and even promoted alternatives. Among those alternatives was precisely that tradition to which my emigré status has sensitized me, and toward which these early modern writers and others contributed, in ways we ought to remain alert to: a tradition of various kinds of republican or egalitarian thinking, or, in terms of religious history, of toleration or latitudinarianism. It sometimes seems that intellectual developments in the United States, including movements that regard themselves as liberating, are insufficiently protective, if not actually contemptuous, of this tradition, which gave them both a Constitution and modern political liberalism. It is alarming to find the term "liberal" used as an insult, not only by conservative politicians but by left-wing intellectuals. In the double Chapter 7, therefore, an evolutionary and unskeptical account of Milton's republicanism is combined with a skeptical analysis of how that has affected the critical history of his writings; but the title of the chapter, "The Good Old Cause," is intended to have considerably wider application.

In Chapter 1, which describes a series of commentaries on Plato's *Laws*, Heller's *Picture This* introduces my plea on behalf of other would-be compromisers, that we not abandon the Great Books to those who claim to have determined their social function or the values promoted by their authors; especially when, as by Leo Strauss and Allan Bloom, they are claimed for an elitist politics and pedagogy inimical to the concept of a "liberal education," a concept, however, both Strauss and Bloom liberally deploy. As James Sloan Allen has argued, it is important to remember that the term "Great Books" was introduced into the American cultural vocabulary by John Erskine toward the end of the First World War, as part of his program for educating the huge numbers of young men to be discharged from the army, and subsequently aligned by Erskine's student Mortimer Adler with his own theory of liberal education, which retained that same principle of egalitarian outreach.[3]

There is, therefore, a strong theoretical connection between the debates on the canon and pedagogical priorities and the sociopolitical values for which, by synecdoche, literary values have come to stand. But there is also a strong connection between both of these disputes and the interpretive methods implied by *reading between the lines*. This is a hermeneutical strategy, as I show in this first chapter, most often associated with Leo Strauss and his disciples, but improperly so, since it is in fact implicit in all acts of interpretation, and in some kinds more than others. It is certainly implied in deconstruction as an exegetical practice, and also in psychoanalytic criticism (on which I shall touch in conclusion). And in the early modern period, reading between the lines, which unlike the last two practices was dependent on *writing* between the lines, was already clearly understood to be a political strategy with liberating consequences.

When in *Censorship and Interpretation*[4] I first defined a hermeneutics that reads between the lines to recover the opinions of those who wrote in censoring societies, I did not fully realize, as I now do, the vital importance of redeeming this principle and returning it to wider application. In this book, evidently, I apply it in the service of a more open society than Straussianism aims to promote. This principle was actually defined during the early eighteenth century by John Toland, the Whig editor of the republican thinkers Milton and Harrington, as a system of writing differently for different audiences. The definition occurs in a pamphlet entitled *Clidophorus* (1720) but whose subtitle is part of the argument that there are two styles: "The one open and public, accommodated to popular prejudices and the Religions establish'd by Law; and the other private and secret, wherein, to the

3. See James Sloan Allen, *The Romance of Commerce and Culture: Capitalism, Modernism, and the Chicago Bildungsideal* (Chicago, 1983), 78–109. I owe this reference to Peter Childers.

4. *Censorship and Interpretation* (Madison, 1984; rpt. with a new introduction 1990).

few capable and discrete, was taught the real Truth stript of all disguises." And, Toland continued within the pamphlet, even in Hanoverian England the strategies of writing so as to *appear* to be endorsing established beliefs and institutions "are as much now in use as ever, tho the distinction (between what appears to be said and what is actually meant) is not so openly and professedly approv'd, as among the Antients" (94). Despite the fact that in 1695 precensorship by licensing was formally abolished, Toland had no illusions about the constraints on freedom of expression that governed the age of Swift and Defoe; and he was also aware that political censorship is not the sole inhibitor of explicitness. "In this state of things," he continued,

> while liberty in its full extent is more to be wish'd than expected, and thro human weakness people will preferr their repose, fame, or preferments, before speaking of Truth, there is nevertheless one observation left us, whereby to make a probable judgement of the sincerity of others in declaring their opinion. 'Tis this. When a man maintains what's commonly believ'd, or professes what's publicly injoin'd, it is not always a sure rule that he speaks what he thinks: but when he seriously maintains the contrary of what's by law establish'd, and openly declares for what most others oppose, then there's a strong presumption that he utters his mind. (96)

In other words, while alert to the less admirable human impulses which promote self-censorship, ambition, and timidity, Toland was unambiguous as to the ethical superiority of those who dare to express minority or heterodox opinion.

Without such an understanding of how early modern writers are likely to have expressed themselves on the major sociopolitical issues of their time, modern assessments of what canonical writers can mean for us today must be damagingly ahistorical. Our profession has, evidently, taken much too literally the statements of orthodoxy and deference to rulers that, unsurprisingly, mark the pages of Spenser, Shakespeare, and Donne. Too often modern criticism has *reversed* Toland's canny insight that "when a man maintains what's commonly believ'd, or professes what's publicly injoin'd, it is not always a sure rule that he speaks what he thinks," and has assumed, rather, that "what's publicly injoin'd" was *necessarily* believed by every thinking person. I find that counterintuitive; and I read with dismay Alvin Kernan's statements in *The Death of Literature* that in the early modern period, "the courts and the aristocracy fostered the arts, and poetry was defined in ways that suited ruling-class interests and values . . . The crown controlled all writing, directly through censorship and patronage, and indirectly through a courtly poetics."[5] This is the old, simple story that literary criticism and literary history, always in the aggregate more conventional than their subjects, have seemed to prefer to the more complex record that emerges if we read between the lines. If this story were true, it might arguably justify *abandoning* the writings of Spenser, Shakespeare, and Donne, and, for that matter, Milton's *Paradise Lost*, as not only irrelevant but noxious to those concerned with how humanists may contribute, if at all, to solving the problems of the real world.

In this book, I apply the techniques of "close reading" that thirty years ago were central to a literary education, and which were subsequently given a philosophical twist by Derrida and de Man, in the spirit of a still earlier tradition of skepticism that was, we should now see, at least as liberating as New Criticism and deconstruction. Perhaps more so; because if, to return to Kernan's *The Death of Literature*, we recognize as some of the points "where literature and its poetics interact in day-to-day activity with the social world" political patronage in the arts, pornography, illiteracy, tax laws, and the ways in which advertising and image making have "captured the language," *all* of these problems identified by Kernan as within a humanist's purview are in fact explored by the writers I deal with here. Donne's entire career can now be seen as a struggle with the ethics of patronage. Illiteracy and its disempowerments are a central problem in Spenser's *Shepheardes Calender*. Shakespeare's *Rape of Lucrece* raises questions not only about rape but about the definition of pornography, and whether it can sometimes be produced by literary critics. The Jacobean tax conventions were a central issue for Donne and a circle of his friends, not least because of the relation between taxation and constitutional theory. Advertising and image making were as pervasive (though not, of course, as in-

5. *The Death of Literature* (New Haven, 1990), 11.

vasive of the home) in Tudor England as today, and, as "Holinshed's" *Chronicles* reveal, they were then capable of being seen
through. In addition, Spenser's *View of the Present State of Ireland*
raises troubling questions about what used to be called colonial-
ism, but which in the postcolonial world is now called "intervention in the affairs of a foreign country." Milton's *Doctrine and
Discipline of Divorce* is a complex exhibit of the devious ways in
which sexuality and gender politics intersect; and his other
writings, from his commonplace book through *Paradise Lost*, constitute a lifelong struggle to reconcile his belief in the transfer-
ability of classical republicanism to early modern England and
his preference for a meritocracy of the very highly educated,
which, like Tocqueville, he sometimes felt were mutually incompatible. Altogether, these early modern texts evince an enviable
degree of *comprehension* of the complex transformations already
occurring in that society and what further transformations might
be feared or hoped for.

Finally, these essays also record my own, if not lifelong, at least
decade-long struggle to operate *between* the boundaries, not only
of the clearly "literary" and the clearly "extraliterary," but also
between two academic disciplines, literary study and history, an
ambition which seems to be irresistibly expanding toward the
history of law. While Chapters 1, 2, and 8 address themselves
primarily to debates within literary studies, Chapters 3, 4, 5, 6,
and 7 envisage a mixed audience of literary scholars and historians of the sixteenth and seventeenth centuries. Chapter 5, on
the representation of popular culture in "Holinshed's" *Chronicles*,
is also an attempt to initiate a revaluation of that extraordinary
exercise in the writing, *avant la lettre*, of a modern cultural history. I would like the whole project to be thought of as an experiment in the new interdiscipline, cultural history; and, like all
intellectual experiments, especially if successful, its rough edges
and other failures will certainly be made apparent.

1

"Just Reading" or Reading Plato's Laws

In *Picture This*, his first major novel since *Catch-22*, Joseph Heller combines the story of Rembrandt's famous painting *Aristotle Contemplating the Bust of Homer* with the story of Aristotle, imagined as a man sitting without complacency for his portrait, contemplating meanwhile his own intellectual debts to Socrates and Plato.[1] The novel's topics are art and its production, from seventeenth-century Holland to today, and philosophy (especially political philosophy) and *its* production, from fourth-century Greece to twentieth-century America. Heller sees connections between the political history of the United States in the early 1960s, the sale of the Rembrandt for $2,300,000 to the Metropolitan Museum of Art in November 1961, and the immense publicity for the museum's acquisition, which resulted in a wave of popular enthusiasm for Greek philosophy. "Paperback editions of works by Aristotle appeared on bestseller lists, and publishers, underestimating demand, ran out of stock" (304). *Picture This* is packed with Heller's rewritings or dramatizations of Greek political history, and sardonic accounts of American political history; for example:

> The auction [of the Rembrandt] was held that autumn between the Berlin crisis and the Cuban missile crisis that brought the former allies Russia and the U.S. to the brink of war again. In less than three years, U.S. troops would be sent to Vietnam to protect American interests in an area that had none except these U.S. troops. (300)

1. *Picture This* (New York, 1988).

It is not my purpose here to explore these sallies per se, although the antimilitarism of *Picture This*, like *Catch-22* itself, has acquired a new topicality subsequent to publication. Instead, I wish to bring out the practical and theoretical value of the account of Plato that Heller produces for an audience and a context I imagine he did not envisage, for an academic audience embroiled in a "Great Books" debate and pondering its implications for intellectual freedom. In his flamboyant melange of ancient and modern cultures, his alignment of political philosophy, "real" politics, and the representational arts, and in particular in his reading of the *Laws*, the last and most unpopular of Plato's dialogues, for a popular audience, Heller provides an eccentric and therefore sharp focus on problems that have been obscured by disciplinary boundaries and institutional protocols. Specifically, the *Laws* is, among classical and canonical texts, a proposal for a society in which censorship is ubiquitous; and *Picture This* is only the most recent and most candid of a series of interpretations of and commentaries upon the *Laws* in our century, readings which, while normally made in an academic context and assuming scholarly objectivity, in fact appropriate Plato's dialogue, affirmatively or negatively, for an argument about what sort of society we ought to endorse. It matters, then, whether we continue to read this dialogue, and what we read *about* it. As Heller's novel creates a personality for Aristotle, the story I will tell involves biographical and autobiographical fictions of various kinds that have leached into a kind of discourse supposedly impervious to them; it leads eventually to Leo Strauss and his pupils, whose approaches to reading Plato have political motivations as strong as Heller's, though not so explicit; and eventually the *Laws* themselves will connect these modern perspectives, and the cautions I derive from them, to the early modern writers with which this study is primarily concerned.

For those not already familiar with the *Laws*, Heller's hostile summary of its contents has at least the advantage of not making or assuming the claim that a pandect of such a text can be objective and value free. (I am not here engaging the hermeneutical question as to whether *any* account of a classical text can be value free, still less the insoluble problem of what, theoretically, would be correct or accurate in translation of or commentary upon texts whose ancient semantics have all to be reconstructed in relation to other texts; but rather the narrower, though not less important issue of whether the claim or assumption of objective redescription has a mystifying function.) Heller, however, intends to shock, his primary tools being bluntness, terseness (not to be confused with reductiveness), and ironic juxtaposition. After the death of Socrates, wrote Heller, Plato lived another fifty years:

> He wrote his books. He founded his Academy. And he gradually abandoned hope in the potential of men and societies to improve themselves. . . . Convinced that knowledge is virtue and that all knowledge is innate in all men and could be uncovered through untiring search, he vested his faith for a model community in the concept of a "virtuous tyrant," a man with absolute power who was altruistic enough to become his philosopher king. And three times he went to Sicily when deluding himself into believing he had one. (259)

On each of those occasions, according to Diogenes Laertius, Plato found either himself or his sponsor in serious danger from precisely that arbitrary power that in theory he saw as the solution; and, at seventy, he returned to Athens and "refrained from meddling in politics ever again" (260). "One regrets," Heller continues,

> that he did not live long enough to finish the *Laws* and rewrite for coherence and clarity these garrulous instructions by an elderly Athenian Stranger to two listeners for a Model City in which the only freedom was the freedom to obey, and in which Plato would have been prohibited from making that same discourse, and all his earlier ones.
> All power in his new community of the *Laws* would be vested in the elderly, said the elderly Plato, because the elderly were conservatives.
> There were slaves. . . .
> Denouncing wealth, he gave power to the wealthy. (261)

Lest any of his readers should fail to observe the contemporary political allegory he is here constructing, Heller engages in radical anachronism. As a comment on Plato's endorsement of wealth as the criterion for political power, Heller introduces the figure of Cornelius Vanderbilt, "who in 1882 laid the foundation for the study of political science as an academic discipline," with the following laws of his own. Vanderbilt's First Law of Government: "Law? What do I care about the law? H'aint I got the power?" Vanderbilt's Second Law of Government: "The public be damned" (262–63).

This reincarnation of the spirit of Plato's *Laws* is parodic only at the level of idiom. At the level of political theory it faithfully transmits the message of the dialogue in which utopianism admitted, right back here at its beginnings, its dependence on coercion. "In Plato's *Laws*," wrote Heller, "which seek to remedy all ills, there are prescriptions by the score, and there are prescriptions for the punishment of those who flout them. . . . In comparison to the *Laws*, Jonathan Swift is Santa Claus" (263). Behind coercion lies paranoia. In addition to the sheer multiplication of laws, the massive bureaucratization of this society, a phenomenon that would later perplex Aristotle, Plato here introduced in absolute form what Michel Foucault would much later designate the society of surveillance. Censorship was to be ubiquitous. The complete merging of church and state (in effect, a theocracy not unlike Calvin's Geneva) required enforced submission to the state religion as handed down by ancestral tradition. Regulations for enforcing conformity included the supervision of children's games, which should always be identical to prevent the very idea of innovation. Left-handedness was forbidden. Women (and here is a thought for contemporary feminism) were *required* against their deepest instincts for privatization to be educated like men and to undergo military training. The new state was heavily militarized. The population was to be artificially stabilized at 5,040 citizens. And, most tellingly, despite the fact that at every level the figures of authority in military, religious, and civic organizations were to be elected by the citizens according to public standards of virtue, nobody could be trusted. The magistrates were to be watched over by another elected group of Scrutineers or Auditors, who in turn would be watched over by the mysterious and incompletely defined Nocturnal Council.

Heller clearly wishes to imply that Western civilization, at least in so far as represented by the United States of America, has inherited more from the *Laws* than from other parts of the Platonic tradition, whatever may be claimed to the contrary. This is a revision of intellectual history we would do well to heed. But beyond its contemporary application, we need to attend to the matter of its reliability. In fact, Heller's reading of the *Laws* as a serious proposal for a completely repressive society is supported in certain areas of both classical studies and political philosophy by an apologetic theory of Plato's development, which explains the apparent descent from the idealism of the *Republic* to the deep cynicism of the *Laws*. Actually there are two competing theses. In the first of these, it is argued, Plato became dubious about the capacity of man to derive the ground of virtuous behavior from rational argument; in the second, he became pessimistic about the capacity of man to behave in society according to principle. The first would seem to be a theoretical problem internal to philosophic thought; the second, a historical, biographical event, the consequence of Plato's observations of political life in the Greek world, which included the execution of Socrates, his own experiences with the tyrants of Sicily, and the decline of Athenian hegemony in relation first to Sparta and then to Philip of Macedon. Either thesis may be expressed as a hypothesis that Plato became a pessimist only in very old age— the term "dotage" is sometimes used—which somehow implies that the *Laws* can be ignored, that they do not count in our overall understanding of Platonism. The classical scholar Gregory Vlastos, for instance, committed to denying the appearance of metaphysical pessimism earlier in the canon, wrote in 1957:

> Now there is one hope which, as we know from the *Laws*, Plato did resign before his death: the one based on the belief that the office of the philosopher king was not above the capacities of human nature . . . Just when it crashed must be a guess. Mine would put it after Plato's final encounter with Dionysius the Younger, when he saw the ugly face of autocratic power at closer and more painful quarters than at any other time in his life.[2]

For Vlastos, the historical argument for Plato's pessimism *can* be admitted, provided it is restricted to the *Laws* and hence to Plato's

2. "Socratic Knowledge and Platonic "Pessimism," in *Platonic Studies* (Princeton, 1973, 1981), 212, 216. Originally published as a review of John Gould, *The Development of Plato's Ethics* (New York, 1955), *Philosophical Review* 66 (1957): 226–38.

senescence ("At that age one does not go about finding a new philosophy" [216]), and precisely because it protects Plato from the
theoretical move to disillusionment with the world of abstract
ideals.

E. R. Dodds, another classical scholar, also contributed to the
theory of negative maturation in a brilliant essay, first published
in 1945,[3] but revised in 1951 and then entitled "Plato, the Irrational Soul, and the Inherited Conglomerate."[4] This essay be-
haves much like Heller's *Picture This*, relating its view of Plato
to Dodds's own politico-historical environment from the late
1930s onward, a topicality increased in revision. Though without Heller's scathing irony, Dodds's account of the *Laws* was manifestly an indictment of Plato's closed society, and allegorically
also of the rise of Soviet totalitarianism and of the trials of dis-
sidents under Stalin. The addition of the term "Conglomerate"
to his vocabulary in 1951 ironically anticipates, though in geo-
political reverse, Heller's attack on military-industrial formations
on the other side of the world.

For Dodds, the bulk of the Platonic canon, though written in
the fourth century, needs to be understood as a form of nostalgia for "the golden years before the Great War." "The transition
from the fifth century to the fourth was marked (*as our own time
has been marked*) by events which might well induce any rationalist
to reconsider his faith" (208–9; italics added). The fate of imperial Athens, of Plato's kinsmen the tyrants Critias and Charmides,
as well as of Socrates himself, led Plato, in Dodds's view, not to
abandon rationalism but to modify it with a form of irrational-
ism ("magico-religious ideas") derived from Pythagoreanism—a
belief in guilt and self-purification. It was this belief that made
it possible to envisage the Guardians as human achievers of or
strivers toward the Forms. But under further historical disillusionment this irrational strain in Plato's thought developed into
the full-fledged cynicism of the *Laws*:

> Far from supposing, as his master had done, that "the unexam-
> ined life is no life for a human being," Plato now appears to hold
> that the majority of human beings can be kept in tolerable moral

3. As "Plato and the Irrational," *Journal of Hellenic Studies* 65 (1945): 16–25.
4. E. R. Dodds, *The Greeks and the Irrational* (Boston, 1951, 1957), 207–35.

health only by a carefully chosen diet of "incantations" (ἐπῳδαί)—
that is to say, edifying myths and bracing ethical slogans. We may
say that in principle he accepts Burckhardt's dichotomy—rationalism for the few, magic for the many. (212)[5]

What Dodds in 1951 called "edifying myths and bracing ethical
slogans," readers of Louis Althusser are more likely to recognize
as the apparatus of a state ideology. For Dodds, however, unlike
Vlastos, we are not to discount "all this as a senile aberration,
the sour pessimism of a tired and irritable old man" (215). The
cynicism expressed by the Athenian is only a more extreme version of remarks to be found in the *Republic* and the *Phaedo*. "No
doubt," wrote Dodds, again anticipating Joseph Heller, "this is
partly Plato's fun; but it is the sort of fun that would have appealed to Jonathan Swift" (p. 215).

The topical imperative in Dodds's reading of Plato culminates
in an attack on the society of the *Laws* as a censoring society.
Dodds compared the split in Plato's though to Arthur Koestler's
categories of the Yogi and the Commissar,[6] whom in earlier dialogues he believed could unite:

> But when that illusion faded, Plato's underlying despair came
> more and more to the surface, translating itself into religious
> terms, until it found its logical expression in his final proposals for
> a completely "closed" society. . . . The "Yogi" . . . did not wholly
> vanish even now, but he certainly retreated before the "Commis-
> sar," whose problem is the conditioning of human cattle. (216).

The term "closed society" was added in 1951, replacing the earlier "Servile State," and indicating that, in the interim, Dodds
had been reading Karl Popper, whose massive attack on Plato for
advocating a closed society had first been published in 1944.[7]

For Dodds, then, there is no incompatibility between the two
theses of Plato's development toward pessimism, the internal-

5. In 1945, this read merely "a carefully chosen diet of 'incantations' or
slogans (ἐπῳδαί) and myths" (18). The change indicates Dodds's continued
meditation on the role of ideology in political culture.

6. Arthur Koestler, *The Yogi and the Commissar and Other Essays* (New York
1946). The title essay was first published in *Horizon* in June 1942.

7. See Karl Popper, *The Open Society and Its Enemies*, 5th ed. rev., 2 vols.
(Princeton, 1966), especially 1:173–201.

theoretical and the external-empirical, since the latter produces the former; Plato's experiences with Greek politics led him to imagine what Dodds calls a "counter-reformation," a reaction against precisely that Enlightenment in which his own mind had been trained to speculate and to innovate. Karl Popper's *The Open Society and Its Enemies* had offered a similar historical argument, but with a psychoanalytic twist. According to Popper, Greece in the sixth and fifth centuries B.C. experienced the transition from the "closed society," defined as magical or tribal or collectivist, to the "open society," that in which "individuals are confronted with personal decisions" and social mobility leads to class struggle (173–77). And whereas Socrates was the avatar of the new world of individual decision making—a position that inevitably and fatally entangled him in that phase of the class struggle represented by the Thirty Tyrants, Plato, antidemocratic by birth and temperament, and perhaps sincerely feeling that the factionalism and self-destructiveness of the open society were appalling, betrayed Socrates by making him the spokesman for a society returned to closure by the inquiring mind itself. While using the *Laws* as the definitive statement of Plato's repressive tendencies, Popper assumed that in the earlier dialogues Plato adopted the speaking voice of Socrates as an expression of his own guilty conscience. "I cannot doubt," wrote Popper, "the fact of Plato's betrayal, nor that his use of Socrates as the main speaker of the *Republic* was the most successful attempt to implicate him. But it is another question whether this attempt was conscious" (195). Plato's own absence as a character in the dialogues was "a further expression of this Oedipal struggle"; the suppression of his personality that in other philosophic circles becomes a matter for praise, becomes for Popper only an "attempted suppression—for it is not at all difficult to read between the lines" (196).[8]

What was at stake in Popper's struggle with Plato in the 1940s and subsequently? The answer, or rather one answer designed

8. Other signs are to be found in his "evasiveness and his resort to scorn in combatting the equalitarian theory of justice, his hesitant preface to his defence of lying," and, in the *Menexenus*, "that sneering reply to Pericles' funeral oration," where, "in spite of his attempt to hide his feelings behind irony and scorn, he cannot but show how deeply he was impressed by Pericles' sentiments" (197).

by Popper for posterity, appears in the preface written for the second edition of *The Open Society* in 1951, where we are informed of the book's historical origins in the Second World War and its aftermath:

> Although much of what is contained in this book took shape at an earlier date, the final decision to write was made in March 1938, on the day I received the news of the invasion of Austria. The writing extended into 1943; and the fact that most of the book was written during the grave years when the outcome of the war was uncertain may help to explain why some of its criticism strikes me to-day as more emotional and harsher in tone that I could wish. . . . Neither the war nor any other contemporary event was explicitly mentioned in the book; but it was an attempt to understand those events and their background, and some of the issues which were likely to arise after the war was won. The expectation that Marxism would become a major problem was the reason for treating it at some length. (viii)

Popper had subsumed, then, a critique of communism under his hostility to Plato, and in 1951 offered his readers a psychological key (though not a psychoanalytic one) to reading "between the lines" of his *own* work. Indeed, he suggests, his psychological disposition had already altered; by the time this new preface was written, a visit to the United States, as the definitive site of the attempt "to build up an open society," had considerably lifted his spirits and ameliorated his own pessimism.

One should know of these distinctive modern accounts of the *Laws* (which though they diverge in accounting for the dialogue's reactionary content yet agree that that *is* the content) when reading Allan Bloom's passionate call for the return to Plato as a remedy for "the closing of the American mind." The *Closing* nowhere mentions Popper, but it presumably alludes to *The Open Society* in its title and elsewhere. Bloom asks us "to begin all over again, to try to figure out what Plato was talking about, because it might be the best thing available";[9] and he certainly assumes that he himself has successfully completed this exercise. On the one hand, there *is* no problem of interpretation. Bloom favors what he calls "the good old Great Books approach,"

9. *The Closing of the American Mind* (New York, 1987), 310.

in which a liberal education means reading certain generally recognized classic texts, *just reading them*, letting them dictate what
the questions are and the method of approaching them—not
forcing them into categories we make up, not treating them as historical products, but trying to read them as their authors wished
them to be read. (344; italics added)

On the other, we are told precisely how Plato can serve as a pro-
phylactic against the return of the 1960s (for that may be seen
as Bloom's unspoken agenda). He tells us a story about "the little
Greek Civilization Program" a group of Cornell professors "set
up against the currents," and how his students in this program,
who had been reading "Plato's *Republic* during the entire year,"
had learned to apply it to present circumstances:

These students were rather contemptuous of what was going on,
because it got in the way of what they thought it important to do.
They wanted to find out what had happened to Glaucon during
his wonderful night with Socrates. They really *looked down* from
the classroom on the frantic activity outside, thinking they were
privileged, hardly a one tempted to join the crowd. I later found
out that some of these students had indeed gone down from the
library seminar room into the agora, where the action was. They
had made copies of the following lines from the *Republic* and
handed them out, competing with the hawkers of other kinds of
tracts.

The lines in question were *Republic* 491e–492b, where Socrates
asserts that the corruption of young men by private education
by sophists is nothing compared with the sophistry of those who
make this charge, the demagogues who manipulate the youth
as a whole. "When many gathered together sit down in assemblies, courts, theaters, army camps, or any other common meeting of a multitude," the effect of public rhetoric and group opinion is such as to nullify that of private education. Plato is here
used (implicitly) to support Bloom's preference for "select universities" (90) and even more select programs ("the little Greek Civilization Program") within them. And so, Bloom draws the moral
from his anecdote, his students "had learned from this old book
what was going on and had gained real distance on it, had had
an experience of liberation. Socrates' magic still worked"
(332–33). Seemingly blind to the role of the teacher and the

teacher's beliefs, as well as to the stark contradiction between his contemporary application of Plato and his embargo against reading Great Books as "historical products," Bloom can claim to have been "just reading" the *Republic*.

I wonder, however, what would have happened if he and his students had been reading the *Laws*. The aristocratic tenor of Plato's thought, which Bloom himself, an admirer of Burke and Tocqueville, finds so congenial, and the nostalgic desire for the pre-Enlightenment closed society, which Bloom articulates in "Introduction: Our Virtue," can both be made to look attractive in the *Republic*; but even Bloom's student Thomas Pangle, whose translation of and commentary on the *Laws* is modeled on Bloom's *Republic* (and dedicated to him), was apparently incapable of massaging out of its text its most uncomfortable aspects. While philosophically coherent both with itself and with the *Republic*, Pangle is forced to admit that something has changed:

> The Athenian has tried to convey the peculiar mixture of openness and closedness to the truth that he hopes will characterize the city he is founding. The only direct link between philosophy and the citizens would be the trail the philosophic legislator blazes for *a few* of the young, *who could discern between the lines of his legislation his invitation to question, in a suitably prudent way, all authority and law.* The citizens *in general* could look up to the life which is the philosopher's goal, the life that partakes of the truth, but they could know of such a life only through the veil of a particular religious belief. . . . In short, the Athenian suggests that the citizens could be brought up in a belief which denies to them and their city great significance or hope, and which consoles them by awakening and responding to their capacity for a very austere, imitative reverence.[10]

We can recognize behind this language that Pangle agrees with Vlastos, Popper, and Dodds as to the *content* of the *Laws*; but that Plato's description, via the Athenian, of how coercive regulations are to be rendered acceptable to the citizens "in general" (which inspired Dodds to speak of "edifying myths and bracing ethical

---

10. Thomas L. Pangle, trans., *The Laws of Plato* (New York, 1980), 485–66 (italics added). The structure of this translation, with its concluding "Interpretive Essay," derives from Allan Bloom, trans., *The Republic of Plato* (New York, 1968).

slogans," or "rationalism for the few, magic for the many") is not obnoxious to Pangle, and is to be rendered acceptable to his readers by his own austere reverence for Plato and the paraphrase that conveys it.

But we can also recognize something more. In the notion that the philosophic legislator blazes a "trail" (in a sort of high-minded paper chase) for the young "who could discern *between the lines* of his legislation his invitation to question, *in a suitably prudent way,* all authority," Pangle offers the shadow of a theory as to how to read the *Laws* that contains a special twist; that is to say, the reactionary and repressive climate of the dialogue is not seamless; that there exists "between the lines" of its text another, alternate understanding, but one that is available only to selected readers, which constitutes, we might say, the residual trace of the Greek Enlightenment otherwise discarded. Although we have earlier encountered this phrase in Popper's psychological theory of Plato's betrayal of Socrates, the principle of "reading between the lines" is usually associated nowadays with the name of Leo Strauss, Allan Bloom's teacher, as Bloom was the teacher of Pangle.

In *Persecution and the Art of Writing,* published in 1952, Leo Strauss popularized a distinction between the exoteric text, which says what it means, and the esoteric text, which while appearing on the surface to be an orthodox treatise on morality or religion, actually contains a skeptical subtext directed only to a small group of like-minded intellectuals. As suggested in my preface, the true source of this distinction was probably John Toland, writing in the early eighteenth century about the problems of religious toleration and intellectual freedom, and whose odd pamphlet, *Clidophorus,* contained in its extended title the same distinction between the "Exoteric and Esoteric Philosophy" that Strauss is famous for.[11]

There is heavy irony involved in this debt, if debt it is, since Toland's theory of reading between the lines was evidently a

11. John Toland, *Clidophorus, or, of the Exoteric and Esoteric Philosophy; That is, Of the External and Internal Doctrine of the Ancients: The one open and public, accommodated to popular prejudices and the Religions establish'd by Law; and the other private and secret, wherein, to the few capable and discrete, was taught the real Truth stript of all disguises* (London, 1720).

response to English political censorship at the end of the seventeenth century. As Toland put it, esotericism is only a temporary resort; the desirable future is the open society. "Let all men freely speak what they think . . . leaving their speculative opinions to be confuted or approv'd by whoever pleases; then you are sure to hear the whole truth, and till then, but very scantily, or obscurely, if at all" (95–96). And in the service of the open society as he understood it, Toland became the biographer of Milton and the unacknowledged rewriter of the *Memoirs* of the regicide Edmund Ludlow, figures who will appear as allies in my chapter on "The Good Old Cause."[12] Strauss, on the other hand, created a hermeneutics of reading the ancients between the lines in order to reveal, beneath their surface idealism or piety, a message of such deep cynicism that it should *never* be made public, except "in a suitably prudent way" to a chosen group of acolytes. In *Persecution and the Art of Writing* and other essays Strauss argued that philosophy, especially political philosophy, has always told, to the chosen few, a terrible truth: that the world was constructed by chance, and that man, if not constrained by ideology, is motivated solely by lust, greed, and competition.[13] It is for this reason that Strauss believed that "philosophy must remain the preserve of a small minority,"[14] citing Plato's belief "that the gulf separating the 'wise' and the 'vulgar' was a basic fact of human nature,"[15] one that dictated not only the failure but the positive danger of popular, that is, widespread, education.

Strauss's own emphasis on the term "persecution" in *Persecution and the Art of Writing* is therefore highly misleading. Despite his own Jewish heritage, and the history of persecution of his

12. See A. B. Worden, ed., *Edmund Ludlow: A Voyce from the Watch Tower*, Camden Society, 4th ser., vol. 21 (London, 1987), 22–80. We should be wary, however, of idealizing Toland, who seems to have been at best a scamp, and at worst an arduous plagiarizer.

13. For a remarkably outspoken critique of Straussianism, see Shadia Drury, *The Political Ideas of Leo Strauss* (New York, 1988). See also Stephen Holmes, "Truths for Philosophers Alone?" *Times Literary Supplement* 1–7 (1989): 1319–24, which builds on Drury's critique but substitutes for her forthrightness a brilliant and blistering humor.

14. Strauss, "On a Forgotten Kind of Writing," in *What Is Political Philosophy? and Other Studies* (Glencoe, 1959), 222.

15. *Persecution and the Art of Writing* (Westport, Conn., 1952), 33.

people, Strauss aligned himself *not* with those heterodox philosophers of the early modern period, who, having themselves
suffered from political or theological repression, "desired to contribute to the abolition of persecution as such" (33), but rather
with Plato, who at least in the *Laws* appeared to have recommended a persecuting society.

The art of writing between the lines that Strauss described
in *Persecution and the Art of Writing* actually constituted an art
of reading. It focused especially on the phenomena of self-
contradiction or gratuitous error, taken to be signs that the author
in question was writing esoterically. So, too, an author's silences
may signal heterodox intention. Other esoteric strategies include
ambiguous passages, a painfully technical style or vocabulary,
the use of disreputable characters as one's own mouthpiece, pretending to critique what one really intends to defend (24), making
the view one really holds clear and articulate before hypocriti-
cally attacking it, placing the heart of one's argument not at the
beginning of a text but rather in the middle (to which only vet-
eran readers will penetrate) (13,25), and above all the deployment
of "the specific immunity of the commentator" or of the historian of ideas (14).

The "specific immunity of the commentator," that self-
protective appeal to academic objectivity, was of course available to Strauss in his last and posthumously published major
work, *The Argument and Action of Plato's Laws*, which consists of
a line-by-line paraphrase of and commentary upon the dialogue.[16] Despite his own insistence elsewhere on the irony of
Socrates, and on irony as a tool of esotericism generally, Strauss
discovered in the *Laws* a text which was not itself structurally
ironic (that is to say, we are not invited to question the thesis of

16. *The Argument and Action of Plato's Laws* (Chicago, 1975). Strauss's student
Joseph Cropsey, who provided a foreword, stated that the commentary was
completed in 1971, two years before Strauss's death at the age of eighty-four.
For a brief biography of Strauss, see Allan Bloom, "Leo Strauss: September 20,
1889–October 18, 1973," *Political Theory* 2, no. 4 (November 1974): 372–92. Strauss
was educated in Germany and received his degree of doctor of philosophy at
Hamburg in 1921. In 1932, with the rise of the National Socialists, he left Germany, first for France and England and then, in 1938, for the United States,
where he taught first at the New School for Social Research in New York and
then, from 1949 to 1968, at the University of Chicago, on which his influence
was profound.

Plato's cynicism) but rather an essay on political hypocrisy and double-speak. The classical text reveals, if you read it according to his own system, the final rationale for the arguments expressed in *Persecution and the Art of Writing.* Strauss discerned in the *Laws* an authoritative model not only for the anti-Enlightenment society he recommended, but also for Straussianism itself, as a mode of communication and social practice exempted from the rules that apply to others. For instance, Strauss underlined the implications of the "Dorian law of laws," which authorized the peculiar privileges of seniority, or gerontocracy, that are to be replicated in a different form in the new state. "Everyone must admit," the Athenian asserts (book 1, 634d–e),

> that one of [the Dorians'] finest laws is the one which forbids the young to criticize any of their institutions but stipulated that all should say with one voice that all their laws are fine since they were given by gods, and should not tolerate dissent on this point; yet one of their old men may make speeches of this sort when speaking to a ruler and men of his own age, provided no one young is present. (10–11)

Sometimes a salient paraphrase will suffice; sometimes the commentary will add, in a deceptively neutral tone, disturbing nuances. Consider, for example, the discussion of poetic justice in book 2 (660e–664a). "The possibility is therefore not completely excluded," Strauss adds at the end of his summary, "that the *logos* to which Kleinias had eventually assented is untrue":

> But even if it is untrue, a legislator who is not altogether useless must dare to teach an untruth for the benefit of the young; deliberately teaching a salutary untruth is an act of courage. . . . The Athenian does not answer Kleinias's question regarding the many other incredible things which people have been induced to believe; to do this might lead very far. Instead he goes on to say that the legislator has to consider nothing but whether his invented story is salutary to the city. (30–31)

Perhaps the most telling passage in Strauss's commentary, however, occurs at the moment where he shows how, in Plato's discussion of atheism in book 10 (889–890), the legislator must proceed by stating the case for his antagonists as clearly as possible (precisely the strategy Strauss recommended in *Persecution and the Art of Writing* for the esoterical writer). The atheists say

that whereas the physical world has come into existence by
nature and chance, through the "aimless and compulsory
motions" of the elements and the stars, "all legislation is by art,
not nature, for its positings are not true," and the gods also have
been constructed by art and law. "Hence there are different gods
for different places, as each group agreed when giving laws for
itself." Thus far, Strauss is paraphrasing Plato; but *not* present
in the original, and crucial for our understanding of Strauss's
motives in constructing his commentary, is the criticism of Plato
that follows:

> *One is tempted to say* that the Dorians and hence, in particular, the
> new colony are in no way threatened by the new-fangled and per-
> nicious wisdom, and that the Athenian contradicts himself by say-
> ing that the pernicious speeches have been broadcast, so to speak,
> among all men. . . . [For] does he not by restating those speeches
> contribute to their being spread still more widely than they
> already are? Does he not act the part of a "corrupter of the young"?
> (145–46; italics added)

The Athenian stranger himself becomes potentially a corrupter
of the young alongside the atheists whose case he has so persuasively stated; and Strauss himself becomes potentially a corrupter of the young not only by repeating the Athenian's words
but also drawing out their subversive implications, an intellectual temptation itself signaled by the phrase "One is tempted to
say." Yet so intricate is the relationship established in this new
text between the three speakers that no one could finally attribute
to Strauss the commentator, on the basis of this passage, the
corrupting (if anthropological) notion that belief in the gods is
purely conventional.

   The hints here of an autobiographical subtext are repeated in
Strauss's disagreement with Plato on the fairness of the distinction made in book 10 of the *Laws* (908e20) between two sorts of
atheist. As Strauss paraphrases this section, it certainly seems
to be peculiar, and illogical, in the original: Plato distinguished
between the essentially good but imprudent unbeliever, who "is
likely to be of utter frankness of speech regarding the gods . . .
and, by ridiculing others would perhaps make them, too, impi-
ous," and the more dangerous kind who "possess powerful
memories, and are quick at learning." The more dangerous kind,

"renowned as gifted, full of craft and guile, belongs to the class of men from which come many soothsayers and jugglers, sometimes also tyrants, public speakers, and generals, plotters of private mysteries and the devices of those called sophists"; in other words, you can find them everywhere, and often in important positions. "Of these two types," continued Strauss in his paraphrase, "the dissembling one (*the ironic one*) deserves not one death or two, but the other needs admonition with imprisonment" (155). Strauss then complained in his commentary that

> the disjunction made by the law is not complete: what happens to the atheist who is a just man and does not ridicule others because they sacrifice and pray and who to this extent is a dissembler? Is it literally true of him that he deserves not one death or two, i.e. no death at all, nor imprisonment? Also, why could not such an atheist not possess a good memory and be good at learning? One could say that he will become guilty only if he frankly expresses his unbelief—but what if he expresses it only to sensible friends? Can one imagine Socrates denouncing him to the authorities? (156)

From this extraordinary passage we can learn a good deal about Strauss's self-identification with the *Laws*. First, he has exploited the literal translation of οὐχ ἑνὸς οὐδὲ δυοῖν ἄξια θανάτοιν ἁμάρτανον, to produce "he deserves not one death or two," whereas a conventional translation would register that the Greek idiom was intended to intensify, not deny, the need for punishment. Second, he has confronted Plato on what he regards as an irrational distinction between two types of atheist, evidently wishing to conflate them. But why? Why should it matter to Strauss that the intellectual talents of the ironic or hypocritical atheist should also be permitted to the man of high principles, who is only "to this extent a dissembler" that he keeps his atheism within himself or the circle of his sensible friends? Without indulging in psychoanalytic hypothesis, one can fairly observe that, as compared with the colorless style of the commentary as a whole, the dramatic intensity of this intervention signals the presence of a strong intention; perhaps Strauss's own complex wish, at the end of his career, to both admit and deny his own role in the "corruption of the young" away from society's beliefs and conventions.

Apart from the circle of sensible friends, Plato also provided another model of the Straussian community, in the Nocturnal Council that Plato introduced at the end of the dialogue, as the final guarantee that the closed society would function. Here we need to shift gears from the Straussian beliefs or nonbeliefs to the extent to which those beliefs have become practices. As M. F. Burnyeat, Shadia Drury, and Stephen Holmes have all energetically protested, the influence of Leo Strauss, though enormous within the academic community, has not been restricted to academia. Burnyeat has called him a "guru of American conservatism,"[17] Drury has observed that the Claremont Graduate School in California, to which Strauss moved from the University of Chicago, "describes itself as an Institute for the Study of Statesmanship and Political Philosophy" (16). It does not require much insight to perceive that the Nocturnal Council is the model for such an institute; and that there are several comparable organizations throughout the United States, with close links to government, has been pointed out by Burnyeat and Holmes. Strauss did not need to make this point (explicitly or obliquely) in his commentary, because it had already been made for him by Glenn Morrow, whose own commentary on the *Laws*, while genuinely idealistic, had already suggested (not without a certain anxiety) that Plato "intends it to be a kind of institute of higher studies."[18] And, he added, "a little reflection will show us that there are many ways the Council could influence public policy in an interpretative and advisory capacity" (510). While Morrow somehow managed to assuage his own doubts, and to conclude that the relation of the Council to the state would be "a kind of compound sovereignty—of legal technique and scientific knowledge," so that in the *Laws* "the rule of law and the rule of philosophy" are at last reconciled, thirty years later we may not be so sanguine about the behind-the-scenes influence of privately funded think tanks.

But to return to the effects of Straussianism *within* the academy, my purpose here is not only to add to the growing body

17. "Sphinx without a Secret," *New York Review of Books* 32, no. 9 (May 30, 1985): 30.
18. *Plato's Cretan City* (Princeton, 1960), 576.

of dissent from its anti-Enlightenment arguments, its antidemocratic tendencies, and its elitist theory of higher education. The
point is to advocate the continuing importance of reading and
rereading Great Books like the *Laws* of Plato, and the impossibility of "just reading" them, which Straussianism, in the person of Allan Bloom, claims to recommend while doing something entirely different. If the examples of reading the *Laws* that
I have adduced here can tell us anything other than about themselves, they prove not only that no reading is innocent, not only
that each commentator brings to his chosen task a driving sense
of urgency arising out of his own historical circumstances, but
that our task (and freedom) is to choose. The fear of never being
able to determine the hermeneutical issue (which of these readings is closest to Plato's intentions) does not debar us from adju-
dication. Dismantling the assumption that disinterestedness pre-
vails in the transmission of the classics does not automatically
mean that interest alone must prevail instead; but the question
of whether a particular interpretation is benign or malign in its
effects on intellectual freedom is not only admissible but clearly
central to our current professional *agon*. In place of "just reading" like Allan Bloom—that is, offering a purportedly innocent
yet authoritative reading of a text whose meaning has in fact been
a matter of controversy for decades—I offer the alternative of a
"just reading" in a very different sense, one that attempts to be
judicious, fair to the text at issue, yet explicitly aimed at socially
equitable goals. And for those of us in the academy who wish
to continue teaching Great Books without being automatically
associated with neoconservatism, who believe that *among* the
definitions of "greatness" is the capacity of highly complex texts
to resist appropriation even as they provoke and demand it,
the story of the *Laws* and its modern reception is particularly
instructive.

The issue of intellectual freedom within literary studies, in particular, can be sharply focused by book 7 of the *Laws*, which deals
directly with literary and cultural censorship. Indeed, a major
Platonic point resides in the pun on the word *Nomoi*, which does
triple duty for "laws" as the rules of the imaginary polity, for cultural customs, which in certain instances the new laws may wish
to alter, and for "songs" or "tunes," thereby situating literature

at the heart of the philosophical problem which requires legislation. By cultural use, poems have become laws unto themselves, codified by tradition (799e), but for the Athenian the
ancient etymology was prophetic of the legislator's right to re-
arrange those laws and literary precedents as he sees fit. In one
instance, the Athenian lays it down as dogma that the use of
bodily movement contravenes the "public standards of song";
a few lines later he rejects the practice (*nomon*) of competing
in public lamentations, on the grounds that a well-ordered community only has need of "auspiciousness of language" (801).
But if literary laws, or canons, are only practices, accreted by
custom and capable of being dispensed with, why does that
not apply to the *Nomoi* that will constitute the State? This question, which produces the same result (law is convention) that
Strauss derived from Plato's discussion of atheism, is as per-
tinent when the focus is imaginative literature. And indeed,
the most astonishing moment in the entire dialogue occurs
when Megillus and Kleinias ask the Athenian, now that he has
laid down the law with respect to poetry, what does he recommend in the case of writings not set to music; what definition
can he offer of what children should or should not be permitted
to read? Fortunately, the Athenian says, he is not at loss for a
paradigm:

> As I look back on the discourse you and I have been holding ever
> since daybreak until this moment—and I really believe there has
> been some divine guiding about this matter—well, be that as it
> may, our conversation has been, to my mind, just like a kind of
> poem. I dare say there is nothing surprising in my having felt this
> keen pleasure in reviewing this compact formation, as I may call
> it, of discourse of my own composition. The fact is that of all the
> many compositions I have met with or listened to, in verse or in
> plain prose, I find it the most satisfactory and the most suitable
> for the ears of the young. So I really think I could not direct our
> curator of law and minister of education to a better standard, or
> bid him do better than instruct his schoolmasters to teach it to
> their pupils, and also if in his researches he should light upon con-
> nected and similar matter in the verse of our poets, in our prose
> literature, or even in the form of simple unwritten discourse of
> the same type as the present, by no means to neglect it, but get
> it put into writing. He should begin by making it compulsory on

the teachers themselves to learn this material and appreciate it. (811d, e.)[19]

If we are not to regard this passage as deliberately absurdist and hence ironic, we must take its extremism seriously: at the far end of the canonical process, when conceived as that which must support established beliefs and exclude both skeptical critique and innovation, lies absolute simplicity. We must be prepared to imagine that the literary canon of the new state could consist of a single text—the text of the *Laws* themselves.

To tie this modern debate about interpretative procedures and principles to a book about early modern writers is easier than one might think. In 1578, when Elizabeth I was formally welcomed into the city of Norwich, an oration honoring her arrival at the gates of Norwich hospital was made by Stephen Limbert, "publike schoolemaister," and its words were preserved for posterity by the 1587 edition of "Holinshed's" *Chronicles*. Limbert, of course, wished to assure the queen not only of the city's loyalty, but of their united acceptance of Elizabeth's highly Erastian church and state, which since 1572, when it was first officially challenged by the Puritan *Admonitions* to Parliament, had become increasingly tightly controlled. We can therefore recognize what Limbert intended by invoking Plato's *Laws*, and in particular book 11, which regulates trading practices and business dealings of all kinds. As a spokesman for the citizens of Norwich, a center of the cloth trade, he was willing to equate material prosperity with religious uniformity:

> For you are said for your singular wisdome and learning, to have studied that divine law of the most wise Plato, which he left written in the eleventh booke of Lawes. . . . We certeinlie now inhabit, and lead our lives in those most happie Ilands, of the which Hesiodus maketh mention, which not onlie abound with all maner of graine, wooll, cattell, and other aids of mans life; but much more with the most pretious treasure of true religion and the word of God, in the which onlie the minds of men have rest and peace.[20]

19. *The Collected Dialogues of Plato*, ed. Edith Hamilton and Huntington Cairns (New York, 1961), 1382.

20. *Holinshed's Chronicles of England, Scotland, and Ireland*, 6 vols. (London, 1808; rpt., New York, 1965), 4:396.

But in the 1587 edition of the *Chronicles*, the subject of my fifth chapter, there is plenty of evidence that this praise of the Elizabethan fusion of church and state, with the latter very much in the dominant position, was at best only one of a whole range of opinions. Indeed, a few pages later in the same remarkably inclusive chronicle, we are told that "Matthew Hamont, by his trade a ploughwrite of Hetharset three miles from Norwich," was summoned before the bishop for denying the divinity of Christ or the necessity of the doctrine of redemption; "and bicause he spake words of blasphemie (not to be recited) against the queenes maiestie and others of hir councell," he was first condemned to lose both his ears, and then "burned in the castell dich of Norwich" (4:406). The spirit of the *Laws* as a whole was stronger than Limbert's utopian rhetoric.

The "canonical" writers reconsidered in this study were no more convinced than the authors of the 1587 *Chronicles* that political and religious consensus was possible, still less that what was needed was the closed society of the *Laws*. In 1579, a year after the celebrations at Norwich took place, Edmund Spenser published his *Shepheardes Calender*, which was considerably closer in spirit to the authors of the Puritan *Admonitions* that it was to schoolmaster Limbert. In 1596 he published the second instalment of *The Faerie Queene*, and began to write his *View of the Present State of Ireland*, both of which, as I show in Chapter 4, debated a central premise of Plato's *Laws*, that the lawmaker must above all seek to inhibit societal and cultural change and innovation. Donne, as a law student and then as secretary to Sir Thomas Egerton, wrote a series of satires, unpublished in his lifetime, that indict the Elizabethan legal system and argue for its reform, while at the same indicating that, thanks to the wide reach of the Tudor treason laws, such thoughts are highly dangerous to their spokesman.

As for Milton, his interest in Plato's *Laws* was almost as intense as his interest in their polar opposite, the classical origins of republican thought; but he evidently grew suspicious of the former. In his 1638 letter to the Florentine priest Benedetto Buonmattei, he was willing to use *Laws* 7 (797), "the opinion of Plato that grave actions and mutations in the Republic are portended by changed custom and style in dressing," to support an argu-

ment that the Athenian democracy collapsed because of the corruption of Attic dialect.[21] In 1641, in *The Reason of Church Government*, the fourth of his pamphlets arguing in favor of further
reform of the English church and especially for its transformation away from a hierarchical system of bishops and archbishops
to something resembling the Scottish Presbyterian model, Milton
was again willing to employ the Plato of the *Laws* in the service
of his own, most un-Platonic agenda. Referring both to the arguments against atheism in *Laws* 10.887, which I have shown to have
been of particular interest to Leo Strauss, and also to *Laws* 9.859,
where Plato in effect authorized the role of ideological persuasion in the service of the state, Milton accepted Plato's suggestion that the legislator should always introduce his laws with
some well-written preface:

> In the publishing of humane lawes, which for the most part aime
> not beyond the good of civill society, to set them barely forth to
> the people without reason or Preface, like a physicall prescript,
> or only with threatenings, as it were a lordly command, in the
> judgement of Plato was thought to be done neither generously nor
> wisely. His advice was, seeing that persuasion certainly is a more
> winning and more manlike way to keepe men in obedience then
> feare, that to such lawes as were of principall moment, there
> should be us'd as an induction, some well temper'd discourse,
> shewing how good, how gainfull, how happy it must needs be
> to live according to honesty and justice, which being utter'd with
> those native colours and graces of speech, . . . would so incite, and
> in a manner, charme the multitude into the love of that which is
> really good as to imbrace it ever after, not of custome and awe,
> which most men do, but of choice and purpose. (1:747)

This proposition, that intellectuals and, particularly, men of
eloquence should serve the Law in a suasive capacity is clearly
at the heart of the arguments I am making and refuting, as to
whether indeed early modern literature, as Kernan conventionally put it, "was defined in ways that suited ruling-class interests and values." Even as Milton makes with Plato's authority
the proposition that good writing may persuade to obedience,
he makes it in the service of two notions incompatible with

21. *Complete Prose*, ed. D. M. Wolfe et al., 8 vols. (New Haven, 1953–82),
1:329.

Plato's—the first, that change in the practices and institutional structures of the established church is desirable; the second, that religion should be prevented from upholding a secular tyranny.[22]

But in *Areopagitica*, the pamphlet in which, of course, Milton addressed himself to the problem of censorship and recommended to the Long Parliament that they *undo* their own new law reestablishing prepublication licensing, he finally recognized precisely what it was that the Plato of the *Laws* stood for with respect to cultural uniformity. In a passage which anticipates later negative evaluations of the *Laws* as the least enlightening of the dialogues, and that focuses on *Laws* 7 as the place where Plato's repressive intentions are revealed, Milton wrote:

> Plato, a man of high autority indeed, but least of all for his Commonwealth, in the book of his laws, which no City ever yet receiv'd fed his fancie with making many edicts to his ayrie Burgomasters, which they who otherwise admire him, wish had bin rather buried and excus'd in the genial cups of an Academick night-sitting.[23]

This disrespectful reference to the Nocturnal Council is followed by an attack on a mind that "seems to tolerat no kind of learning, but by unalterable decree, consisting most of practicall traditions, to the attainment whereof a Library of smaller bulk then his own dialogues would be abundant." (Milton has noticed, and taken seriously, the Athenian's proposal that the literary canon of the new state should consist in a copy of the *Laws* themselves.) He ridicules the proposal "that no Poet should so much as read to any privat man, what he had writt'n, untill the Judges and Law-keepers had seen it, and allow'd it"; and his strategy throughout is to assume that Plato never meant these proposals to be taken seriously.

22. The conclusion of the pamphlet includes the following clearly republican outcry: "What will they do then in the name of God and Saints? . . . as they have done to your souls, they will sell your bodies, your wives, your children, your liberties, your Parlaments, all these things, and if there be ought else dearer than these, they will sell at an out-cry in their Pulpits to the arbitrary and illegall dispose of any one that may hereafter be call'd a King, whose mind shall serve him to listen to their bargain" (1:851).

23. *Complete Prose* 2:522.

It is, however, important to see that Milton himself understood the structural relation between law and literature, or, as he himself prefers to conceive of it here, though without using the modern term, between law and culture as much more widely conceived. Why, he asks, did Plato not apply these rules to himself? Why did he give the works of Aristophanes to the "Tyrant Dionysius" to read?

> But that he knew this licensing of Poems had reference and dependence to many other proviso's there set down in his fancied republic, which in this world could have no place: and so neither he himself, nor any Magistrat, or City ever imitated that course, which tak'n apart from those other collateral injunctions must needs be vain and fruitlesse. . . . If we think to regulat Printing, thereby to rectifie maners, we must regulat all recreations and pastimes, all that is delightfull to man. No musick must be heard, no song be set or sung, but what is grave and Dorick. There must be licencing dancers, that no gesture, motion, or deportment be taught our youth but what by their allowance shall be thought honest; for such Plato was provided of. (1:523–24)

Milton scholars assume that Milton was being facetious; but any extended observation of *our* contemporary cultural scene, of the absurdist spread of censorship and First Amendment issues, should persuade us rather that he was preternaturally sighted. Once cultural censorship starts, there can, logically, be no end to it. And by the same token, we could still use Milton's extraordinary eloquence in the service of open debate and the belief that the Enlightenment was not a one-time, one-era event but essentially continuous: "The light which we have gain'd, was giv'n us, not to be ever staring on, but by it to discover onward things more remote from our knowledge" (2:550). "Where there is much desire to learn, there of necessity will be much arguing, much writing, many opinions; for opinion in good men is but knowledge in the making" (2:554).

2

Couples, Canons, and the Uncouth: Spenser-and-Milton

Coupling

Among the processes of canon formation is the habit of coupling writers together; and among the most powerful of couples in the traditional English literary canon is Spenser-and-Milton. Much of my own professional life has probably been determined by my first teaching assignment in 1963, which included "Spenser-and-Milton," in those days at Toronto a famous cornerstone course carrying the stamp of the formidable Renaissance scholar A. S. P. Woodhouse, known affectionately if disrespectfully to his students as Professor Nature-and-Grace. For several years I labored mightily, though neither naturally nor, I suspect, gracefully, on Spenser-and-Milton, sensing all the time that the connections I made, the doctrines I was conveying, lacked persuasion; and no doubt the seed of this essay was sown in those days, although its angle of sight was not then available, obscured on all sides by institutional pillars.

When we couple writers together we usually imply a criterion of fit or at least explicable mating. While there is nothing to prohibit a merely comparativist curiosity, or coupling in the service of some other agenda, we presumably give greater authority to relationships that imply causality, even, or especially, if causality is defined as the influence of the one writer on the other. Most of such relationships are one-directional, from the earlier to the later dead, and a plausible coupling requires either the successor's own testimony that the influence relation existed, or other evidence that the influence relation was strong enough to be formative; or, preferably, both.

Of course there are two-way literary relationships between writers who actually knew each other, such as Milton and Marvell, or Milton and Dryden. One might suppose that the criteria of causation and documentation would lead us to privilege such natural economies in the House of Fame, with their added dramas of interdependence, whether it be the reciprocal support that Milton and Marvell gave each other, or the usually unspoken competition, with ideological overtones, that structures the Restoration works of Milton and Dryden. In fact, these real-life couples have been only minor themes of traditional literary studies, suggesting a systemic preference for the vertical or linear relationship over the horizontal force field that comes into play when contemporaries collaborate in or vie for the same cultural space. It is no accident that Dryden, one of the pioneers in defining the very concept of literary tradition, was himself instrumental in shaping the concept "Spenser-and-Milton," in a context that speaks volumes about how and why authors have themselves contributed to canon formation. In the preface to his *Fables*, a volume of translations that formally marks the boundary between the seventeenth and eighteenth centuries, not only by appearing in 1700, Dryden remarked:

> Milton was the Poetical son of Spencer, and Mr. Waller of Fairfax; for we have our Lineal Descents and Clans as well as other Families: Spencer more than once insinuates, that the Soul of Chaucer was transfus'd into his Body, and that he was begotten by him Two hundred years after his Decease. Milton has acknowledg'd to me, that Spencer was his Original; and many besides myself have heard our famous Waller own, that he deriv'd the Harmony of his Numbers from . . . Mr. Fairfax.[1]

However, while Dryden, marking the turn of the century by summarizing its literary achievements, appears to be offering a choice of traditions, in fact he proceeds in *Fables* to conflate them by translating Chaucer "into our Language, as it is now refin'd,"

---

1. *Fables Ancient and Modern* (1700), in *The Poems*, ed. John Kinsley, 4 vols. (Oxford, 1958), 4:1445.

and therefore incorporating Chaucer's rough soul into his own Augustan (Wallerian) poetics. Two lineal descents merge in Dryden himself, who has subsequently been presented more often as Milton's successor than as his rival in Restoration culture; and, significantly, literary influence is conceived in terms of early modern English laws of inheritance. When poetic souls pass down they pass as property, to a single son only. The story of literary relationship is that of a mysterious primogeniture, one that may skip "Two hundred years" if necessary; and the more strenuous synchronic relations between Dryden and Milton, one the beleaguered exponent of a failed Restoration and the other the sublime analyst of a failed Revolution, are smoothed away in the aura of personal testimony ("Milton has acknowledged to *me*") that familiarizes (literally) and so legitimates an otherwise debatable theory.

To quote this passage reveals also the unsurprising news that famous couples are only segments of longer (but not wider) dynasties. Wordsworth, whose expressed acts of allegiance to Milton might seem to justify a "Milton-and-Wordsworth" dyad, also defined a longer canonical series that he would himself enter at the proper time. In *The Prelude* he recalled his first year at Cambridge as that stage in his education when he discovered the unmistakably major English poets, and, by implication, how very few they were:

> Beside the pleasant Mill of Trompington
> I laughed with Chaucer; in the hawthorn shade
> Heard him, while birds were warbling, tell his tales
> Of amorous passion. And that gentle Bard,
> Chosen by the Muses for their Page of State—
> Sweet Spenser, moving through his clouded heaven
> With the moon's beauty and the moon's soft pace.
> I called him brother, Englishman, and friend.
> Yea, our blind poet, uttering odious truth,
> Darkness before, and danger's voice behind—
> Soul awful—if the earth had ever lodged
> An awful soul—I seemed to see him here
> Familiarly, and in his scholar's dress
> Bounding before me, yet a stripling youth,
> A boy, no better, with his rosy cheeks

Angelical, keen eye, courageous look,
And conscious step of purity and pride.[2]

Wordsworth here proposes that he can resurrect as his friends the most famous of the literary dead and restore to the influence relation that aura of personal testimony that vibrates (however disingenuously) in Dryden's account of Milton; but what is resurrected has been rather carefully selected. Chaucer is not even the "rough diamond" cherished by Dryden "who must be polished before he shines," but merely ludic and romantic. Spenser, though embraced as brother and friend, is feminized by way of "the moon's beauty and the moon's soft pace"; and Milton, secretly admitted a threat by way of the epithets "odious" and "awful" (the latter repeated) is then infantilized: imagined "familiarly" a boy again, a boy "no better," and for good measure "bounding." Was Milton ever a bounder? Although Wordsworth's responses elsewhere to both Spenser and Milton are in a far deeper and more candid register, the very act of canonization, and implicitly of self-canonization, produces an account of literary relationship that is manifestly not to be trusted.

But if authorial motives will often include self-interest, it is supposedly excluded from the august processes of academic canon formation. The coupling of "Spenser-and-Milton," as an instance of those processes, might appear to support that supposition. It has achieved its exceptional power by being based on a statement of Milton's own that has seemed to satisfy the criteria for coupling outlined above: causality (the influence relation existed) and significance (it was formative). In *Areopagitica* Milton asserted that Spenser, at least in the Cave of Mammon episode, is "a better teacher than Scotus or Aquinas."[3] The effect of this statement on the academic canon was pronounced in 1950 by Ernest Sirluck, who called it "one of the most famous tributes by one great poet to another." "The importance of this passage as furnishing the clue," he continued, "to one of the major sources of Milton's literary inspiration has long been recognized,

2. *The Prelude 1799, 1805, 1850*, ed. Jonathan Wordsworth, M. Abrams, and Stephen Gill (New York, 1979), 105-7.
3. *Complete Prose Works*, ed. D. M. Wolfe et al., 8 vols. (New Haven, 1953–82), 2:516.

and many studies of one or both poets have taken it as their point of departure."[4] These remarks introduce, however, an essay designed to explain away an uncomfortable fact—that Milton misremembered what Spenser actually wrote about Guyon in the Cave of Mammon and on his own authority brought the Palmer along to keep an eye on things. For Sirluck, the "mistake" was actually a strategic if unconscious revision, bringing Spenser into line with Milton's own ethics.[5] A skeptical or deconstructive reader might see this as a Freudian slip, revealing Milton's resistance to Spenser's pedagogy, or remember that Duns Scotus was the butt of Renaissance humanists in their attack on scholasticism, his name the origin of all subsequent dunces. Yet until recently skepticism of this or any other kind (and mine will be of another kind) has been inadmissible in Renaissance studies. For much of this century, the Spenser-and-Milton construct has supported, and itself been supported by, a pedagogic tradition that might justly be called Christian humanism, and not only because some of its greatest scholars were instrumental in explicating the Christian humanist scholarship of the Renaissance. Sirluck spoke for the profession, taking the comment in *Areopagitica* as grounds for establishing Milton as Spenser's pupil in classical ethics, Christian Neoplatonism, and Reformation nationalism. But the value of this connection resides in a particular view of the function of literature, one that is itself a product of classical ethics, Christian Neoplatonism, and Reformation nationalism. As a better teacher than Scotus or Aquinas, Spenser appears in the position that, for Sir Philip Sidney, poetry occupied with respect to philosophy, and which in turn Spenser-and-Milton as a couple have come to occupy in the academic canon—that is to say, an effective conveyance of certain traditional values, including the value of tradition itself.

We are now, however, in a position to see this coupling as the site of fundamental beliefs about what English literature is and

4. "Milton Revises *The Faerie Queene*," *Modern Philology* 48 (1950): 90.

5. "Deposited in Milton's memory, warmed by his general approbation of the poem and the poet, the Mammon episode appears to have grown pliant and malleable, to have lost those features which distinguished it from Milton's own ethic . . . When Milton calls upon his memory for Spenser's Legend of Temperance, it emerges as he would himself have written it: with the personification of Reason always present because always needed" (96).

what it is good for, beliefs which may be contested; not least because Spenser and Milton have recently been linked, by David Norbrook, as inheritors of a quite different estate, the line of radical social critique that in the late fourteenth century in England began to acquire a cultural or literary dimension.[6] This discovery of Norbrook's, which implicitly retains the Spenser-and-Milton relationship in the service of a different agenda, converges with broader competitions for the political soul of Milton, which in turn are connected to competing definitions of the English Revolution and its consequences for the modern world, topics to which this chapter can only beckon. But I will attempt methodically to test the claims of the "sage and serious" couple as against those of the radical and reformist one; and in the process I hope to broaden the implications of this competition and to suggest that it tells a story about how we conceive of what we are doing when we persuade our students to read such texts. In short, the dyad Spenser-and-Milton and what we say about it may function as a key to a politics of education.

Uncoupling

Editors of Milton have certainly assumed that one of their tasks, given what Sirluck called "the clue" to a formative influence, was to follow its trail. But if one looks carefully, they have filled their footnotes to Milton's poetry and prose *not* with actual Miltonic quotations or echoes of Spenser, but with shared mythological commonplaces (such as the genetically coded appearance of the serpent women, Milton's Sin and Spenser's Error), accidental convergences of vocabulary, or analogous subject matter. At least 90 percent of Spenser's appearances in the footnotes and indices to the Yale Prose or the Merritt Hughes's textbook edition[7] are of this kind. The fact is, Milton's actual allusions to or quotations from Spenser are extremely few, and they are not consistent with the image of one Christian humanist writer following the footsteps of another. Even in *Areopagitica* itself Spenser may be merely a tool that Milton reaches for, of no more authority in the argument than Bacon, for example, who is quoted twice

6. *Poetry and Politics in the English Renaissance* (London, 1984).

7. M. Y. Hughes, ed., *John Milton: Complete Poems and Major Prose* (New York, 1957).

as many times as Spenser (that is, twice) and whose wise words on the unwisdom of censorship are more integral to the pamphlet's purpose. Yet we do not, I think, find many keystone courses on Milton and Francis Bacon, or much scholarly effort devoted to deepening their relationship.

If there were a formative influence relationship, one might reasonably have supposed that Spenser's Legend of Holiness would have played a substantial role in Milton's campaign for a more enlightened government of the English church. Yet at precisely the point where one would look for a strong allusion to "our old patron Saint George" the dragonslayer, Milton invokes rather the authorship of Peter Heylyn and his Caroline history of the saint, published in 1633 (*Reason of Church Government*, 1:857). And although there are references in *Animadversions* to "Faery Land" and the cave of Mammon (1:674, 719), nowhere in his critique of Anglicanism does Milton acknowledge Spenser as a guide. He surely remembered Spenser's "star-read" "Wizards" from the prologue to *Faerie Queene*, book 5, and reproduced them as the "star-led Wizards" of the *Nativity Ode*; but that is the only unmistakable *verbal* echo that Merritt Hughes discovered in all his long list of likenesses. There is not a single "quotation" from *The Faerie Queene* in *Paradise Lost*, although, as Paul Stevens has shown, Milton clearly alludes to *A Midsummer Night's Dream* in his account of the creation of Pandemonium,[8] and Hughes himself believes that Adam, weeping after the Fall, "though not of Woman born," is Milton's echo of *Macbeth* 5.8.37–39. Milton *may* have intended his readers to find Spenser the source of the "Forests, and enchantments drear" that Il Penseroso reimagines, although it is Chaucer who receives the real compliment of having the *Squire's Tale* unmistakably synopsized. Spenser *may* be among the other romancers who is banished in the invocation to *Paradise Lost*, book 9, and in *Paradise Regained* (3:335–44), although it is Boiardo, there, who receives the inverted tribute of detailed dismissal. Neither Spenser nor Chaucer is named by Il Penseroso, although L'Allegro had no such reticence with respect to Shakespeare and Jonson. Tasso is named, but no other

8. *Imagination and the Presence of Shakespeare in Paradise Lost* (Madison, 1985), 83–84.

Modern, as a model for the vernacular epic writer in *The Reason of Church Government*. And if the Ludlow masque is, as I concede, Milton's most Spenserian production, *A Midsummer Night's Dream* and *The Tempest* (the most masque-like of Shakespeare's plays) compete strongly for its ambience with Spenser's Legend of Chastity. Comus' echo of Ariel's "Come unto these yellow sands," for instance, is *textually* entangled with Shakespeare, whereas the Attendant Spirit's vision of Cupid, Psyche, and their children is not necessarily dependent on Spenser's Garden of Adonis for its access to the myth.

And as for Milton's commonplace book, perhaps the most reliable account of his reading that we have, it contains two references to Spenser, but he is numerically at a disadvantage compared with Chaucer (four allusions), Boiardo (four allusions), Sidney (four allusions), Dante (eight allusions), and conceptually he is placed in a different category, since the text cited is not *The Faerie Queene* but *A View of the Present State of Ireland* (1:465, 496). There is no evidence that Milton suppressed overt allusions to Spenser in some version of an influence anxiety. On the contrary, it appears that Spenser was, to Milton, only one among many influences. And there *is* considerable evidence that the Spenser whom Milton chose to evoke in his own work was not always and only the "sage and serious" Spenser whom Christian humanism could admire. More often, indeed, he was a very different fellow.

Recoupling

For Spenser *is* named and the *Faerie Queene* explicitly invoked in *Eikonoklastes*, to help Milton trample on the grave of Charles I and to undermine posthumously the king's protests against the violent alteration of public institutions. Milton, in this pamphlet, is in favor of such violent alteration and of unconstitutional change:

> If there were a man of iron, such as Talus, by our Poet Spencer, is fain'd to be the page of Justice, who with his iron flaile could doe all this, and expeditiously, without those deceitfull formes and circumstances of Law . . . I say God send it don, whether by one Talus, or by a thousand. (3:390)

This Spenser is scarcely an authority on temperance, and quite incompatible also with Wordsworth's sweet one, "moving through his clouded heaven with . . . the moon's soft pace." And when Milton returns in *The History of Britain* to the legend of Guyon and to the British chronicles, he does so, apparently, still in the spirit of Talus. He makes no reference to Spenser in rehearsing again the story of Sabrina whose legend he selectively mined for the Ludlow *Maske*; but at the very next episode in the chronicles he reproduces a Spenserian stanza (*Faerie Queene* 2.10.24) distinguished only by its bloodthirstiness:

> Let Scaldis tell, and let tell Hania,
> And let the Marsh of Esthambruges tell
> What colour were thir Waters that same day,
> And all the Moar twixt Elversham and Dell,
> With blood of Henalois which therein fell;
> How oft that day did sad Brunchildis see
> The Greenshield dy'd in dolorous Vermeil.

"It is difficult to see," French Fogle comments in the Yale edition, "why Milton chose to quote this stanza from out of the nearly 63 that Spenser devoted to recounting the legendary history of Britain" (5 [1]: 20)

There can be no doubt, however, about why Milton cited Spenser, with admiration, in *Animadversions*. Deep into his tirade against the Anglican bishops of his own generation, Milton remembered "the false Shepheard Palinode in the Eclogue of *May*, under whom the Poet lively personates our Prelates." Claiming that "our admired Spenser inveighs against them, not without some presage of these reforming times," Milton proceeded to copy out accurately (as compared with his faulty memory in relation to Guyon and the Palmer) twenty-nine lines from the *May* eclogue in Spenser's *Shepheardes Calender*. And those lines were carefully chosen to demonstrate Spenser's prophetic powers by virtue of beginning with one of prophecy's deepest convictions:

> The time was once, and may again returne
> (For oft may happen that hath been biforn).
> (*Complete Prose Works* 1:722–23)

Milton thereby coupled the *Shepheardes Calender* with *Lycidas*, his own antiprelatical pastoral; or rather with the tendentious headnote to *Lycidas,* which claimed that a poem written in 1637 was capable of foretelling "the ruin of our corrupted Clergy then in their height," that is to say, the expulsion of the bishops from the House of Lords, an event which Milton himself could only have prophesied when he wrote *Animadversions* but which had in fact occurred when he republished *Lycidas* in the collected *Poems* of 1645.

The bonds that Milton himself chooses to make explicit between Spenser and himself, therefore, are predominantly political, polemical, and full of hostilities—not between Spenser and himself, but between them both and their mutual opponents. More frequently and more emphatically than he remembers his advice on Temperance, Milton perceives Spenser as a harsh exponent of the problems in Ireland, of the violent national history that preceded the Tudor era, of the need for drastic reforms in the Elizabethan church, in a phrase, of the *lex talionis.* I do not mean to argue that Spenser was *not* a significant figure to Milton. But once one reviews the evidence as I have just done, it certainly looks as though the extent of his influence has been overstated, and that the structure of that influence has been more wishfully distorted by the Christian humanists than by the politico-culturalists.

To recognize how Milton constructed his Spenser in this way does not require one to follow David Norbrook, Christopher Hill,[9] and most recently Michael Wilding[10] in their attempts to construct their own Milton, one who was, in Wilding's terms, a radical from start to finish. The story of Milton's political stance is a great deal more complicated than any that has yet been told, and we will all, no doubt, continue the struggle for his political soul for quite a while. In my own view (which will open out in Chapter 7) Milton was by instinct anti-authoritarian, but he wanted freedom from authority for himself primarily, or at best a small group which decreased in proportion as his political

---

9. *Milton and the English Revolution* (London, 1977). This powerful biography did its best to undermine the "prevalent donnish assumption that ideas are transmitted principally by books," taking Milton out of his study and setting him "in permanent dialogue with the plebeian radical thinkers of the English Revolution" in their "free-for-all discussions" in the "underworld of thought" (5).

10. *Dragons Teeth: Literature in the English Revolution* (Oxford, 1987).

experience lengthened. He was by instinct also a meritocrat, and perhaps a *cultural* aristocrat, who found that the social structure of his day provided no fit company for him other than a courtly elite whose liabilities he could certainly fathom. He was a member of an emergent class who sought to enter the class above him by acquiring mastery over the traditional culture. Because he was not born into the gentry, he was not protected by the sealed envelope of ideology, and experienced occasional intimations of social contradiction, as in the famous admission, in *Reason of Church Government*, that "ease and leasure was given [him] for . . . retired thoughts out of the sweat of other men" (1:804).[11] But precisely because he was working, in the early and late poems, in conventional literary forms (some of whose social function he intuited), he *was* to some extent protected from full confrontation with his own inconsistencies, his own desire to speak for change, but to speak of it only, as the *Reason* also puts it, to "the elegant & learned reader" (1:807). In this predicament, Spenser served most often for Milton not as an author a learned and elegant person would read but as a more primitive force, an avatar of change and rough justice, a voice from the past that spoke of an even older past in order to reimagine the future.

And in thinking of Spenser in this way, he forged one more link between them, made one more allusion to his "original" (Dryden's term); one that has barely made its way into traditional Spenser-and-Milton criticism, but that ought to carry at least as much force as the "sage and serious" connection to which we have been accustomed.

The Uncouth

"Uncouth unkiste." The first words of the *Shepheardes Calender* are not poetry but academic literary criticism, or possibly part of its parody. They are the words of E. K., semi-anonymous, self-appointed commentator on the *Calender*, quoting Chaucer, and engaged in the process of canon formation.[12] " 'Uncouth un-

11. See also his *Apology against a Pamphlet*, where he thanks Providence for having "ever bred [him] up in plenty, although [his] life hath not bin unexpensive in learning" (1:929).

12. Edmund Spenser, *The Poetical Works*, ed. J. C. Smith and E. de Selincourt (Oxford, 1912), 416.

kiste,' sayde the olde famous Poete Chaucer."[13] In fact, E. K. *misquotes* Pandarus' "unknowe, unkiste," whose proverbial meaning, "The kiss of greeting is not given to strangers," served to encourage in Troilus a bolder approach to seduction. In the *Calender* the term "uncouth" as E. K. provides it seems initially merely a strategy for introducing the unknown, a new poet, a cultural stranger, who will nevertheless become part of the native tradition in poetry that begins with Chaucer. He will then, presumably, be no longer uncouth; although, as Joseph Wittreich pointed out, his identity *remained* unknown to many. George Puttenham (himself a putative author only of an anonymous *Arte of English Poesie*) had not heard the secret in 1589.[14] But as E. K.'s preface continues, the substitution of "uncouth" for "unknowe" begins to appear strategic. The uncouth quickly develops a deeper semantic range, encompassing the history of literary forms, philology, and sociology; and as the *Calender* itself proceeds, the very secret of the *Calender*'s authorship, or rather the need for secrecy, is perceived as one of the uncouth's own meanings.

Generically or formally, what is uncouth is affiliated to "pastoral rudenesse," "rough sounde," "rymes more ragged and rustical" than is to be expected in Elizabethan poetry. Philologically, the "uncouth" denotes the *Calender*'s linguistic archeology or primitivism, "the words them selves being so ancient" but "so grave for the straungenesse." In E. K.'s opinion, this anonymous poet is especially to be commended "that he hath laboured to restore, as to theyr rightfull heritage such good and naturall English words, as have ben long time out of use and almost cleane disherited" (417). Note the implication of an alternative poetic lineage, an alternative theory of *inheritance*. The philological meaning of "uncouth" derives (with important differences) from Richard Mulcaster, Spenser's own teacher, whose enthusiasm for his native language Spenser must have absorbed, although its formal statement in Mulcaster's *Elementarie* was not published until 1582. Defending English as the language of education, Mulcaster wrote:

13. See Geoffrey Chaucer, *Troilus and Criseyde*, 1. 809: "Unknowe, unkist, and lost, that is unsought."

14. Wittreich, *Visionary Poetics: Milton's Tradition and His Legacy* (San Marino, Cal., 1979), 105–6.

But ye will saie it is *uncouth*, in dede being unused. And so was it in Latin, and so is it in each language . . . [but] our English wits be verie wel able, thanks be to God, if their wils were as good, to make those *uncouth* & unknown learnings verie familiar to our peple, even in our own tung.[15]

But by his own commitment to a historical and progressive linguistics Mulcaster was opposed to archaism for its own sake,[16] or as a way to recuperate the past in the image of the vernacular; he would, in other words, have strongly disapproved of the *Calender*'s intentions as E. K. describes them.

Sociologically, "the rusticall rudeness of shepheards" is not only a pastoral convention but an economic fact, and connects to the *Calender*'s linguistic program by way of the conservative tendencies of rural dialect, "such olde and obsolete words . . . most used of country folke." There is also, or especially, an aesthetic dimension to the uncouth; or at least E. K. presents the *Calender*'s central program in an aesthetic register:

> Yet neither every where must old words be stuffed in, nor the common Dialecte and maner of speaking so corrupted therby, that as in old buildings it seme disorderly and ruinous. But all as in most exquisite pictures they use to blaze and portraict not onely the daintie lineaments of beautye, but also rounde about it to shadow the rude thickets and craggy clifts, that by the baseness of such parts, more excellency may accrew to the principall . . . Even so doe those rough and harsh termes enlumine and make more clearly to appeare the brightness of brave and glorious words. (417)

Yet the metaphor also suggests the strategic virtues of a controlled and negotiated populism, increasing the value of the high by contrast with the low, the superstructure by the base, learned acquisition by the habits of the folk, the patriarchal language of humanist tradition by renewed contact with the "Mother tonge." And if the principle of "disorderly order" here articulated seems to favor the higher term in each case, the new poet himself must

15. *Elementarie*, ed. E. T. Campagnac (Oxford, 1925), 270–71 (italics added).

16. To venerate the old for its antiquity was, in Mulcaster's view, to resist progress for the sake of a hard (Arcadian) primitivism: "If this opinion had bene alwaie maintained, we had allwaie worn old Adams pelts, we must still have eaten the poets akecorns, & never have sought corn, we must cleve to the eldest and not the best" (274).

be situated, by the "basenesse" of his pseudonym, Colin Clout, on the side of the disorderly element. And at the very end of the work, its commitment to a popular audience is made as explicit as it could be:

> Goe lyttle Calender, thou hast a free passeporte,
> Goe but a lowly gate emongste the meaner sorte.
> Dare not to match thy pype with Tityrus hys style,
> Nor with the Pilgrim that the Ploughman playde a whyle.
>
> (467)

In this final strategy, as David Norbrook has explained, Spenser aligned himself with the popular reformism that led from *Piers Plowman* (adopted as a symbolic text by the leaders of the Peasants' Revolt in 1381), through the fifteenth-century *Plowman's Tale* attributed to Chaucer, to those who, in negotiating the weathercock state religion of the sixteenth century, recuperated and transmitted the texts of Wyclifflite and other early reformers for use in their own Protestant campaigns.

I differ from Norbrook, however, in guessing how the emphasis on popular and learned culture was distributed through the *Calender*, and how it was intended to be understood. The *Calender*'s mission overall might better be stated as itself a cultural compromise, designed to broaden the audience for poetry and to bridge, without blurring, the obvious distinctions between readers of different social and economic status. The learned, indeed pedantic, introduction and glosses stand for the scholarly, humanist program; the *April* and *November* eclogues clearly represent the domain of courtly pastoral which would shortly become the dominant fashion; the secretive (Aesopian) polemics of *February*, *May*, and *September* point to an engagement with ecclesiastical and secular politics that would have drawn its own audience; and the *appearance* of the *Calender*, with its blackletter type and woodcuts appealing, like those of Sebastian Brant, to the *indocti* or uneducated,[17] asks important questions about the relation between literacy and popular culture.

But I do not wish to suggest that Spenser's method was merely to offer something for everyone. On the contrary, there is an

---

17. For a fuller discussion of this issue, see my *Pastoral and Ideology* (Berkeley, Los Angeles, and Oxford, 1987), 92–105.

implied argument for improved communication and sympathy between different social groups, education from below and tolerance from above. As E. K. explains that the choice of the January opening was "according to the simplicitie of commen understanding" (420), so one of his notes reminds us that, at least in the religious sphere, illiteracy among the common people has been a tool of oppression. In the bad old days of medieval superstition, "Friers and knavish shavelings . . . sought to nousell the comen people in ignoraunce, least being once acquainted with the truth of things, they woulde in tyme smell out the untruth of theyr packed pelfe and Massepenie religion" (443). The *Calender*'s populism, then, is in the liberating spirit of the Reformation itself; and it assumes, though not naively, that the *docti* are entitled, indeed required, to speak to and for the "comen people," that literature can indeed be a pedagogy, but a pedagogy of outreach.

In one of his eclogues Spenser himself summed up the relation between his social revaluation of the uncouth and the problems of recuperating the alternative tradition. In *September*, Diggon Davy speaks for reform in the church, for socio-economic protest, and even for the many-headed monster itself. But he also speaks to the confusions and fears that render that voice unstable. And at one telling moment he reproaches himself for instability, for desire for change, using the word that E. K. so dramatically brought to our attention:

> To leave the good, that I had in honde,
> In hope of better, that was *uncouth*:
> So lost the Dogge the flesh in his mouth.
>
> (453)

In opening his mouth, like the dog in the fable, in pursuit of an imagined improvement, Diggon may worsen his condition; yet the very statement of this predicament reminds us that the uncouth is also, in the strongest sense, Aesopian. As Hegel put it in his *Aesthetics* (a text that gave philosophical authority to the tradition that the fable originated in a slave culture),[18] the Aesopian speaker speaks in fables "because he dare not speak his

---

18. *Asthetik*, ed. G. Lukács (Frankfurt am Main, 1955), 1:376: "Im Sklaven fangt die Prosa an." For an earlier insistence that the fable cannot be properly

teaching openly, and can only make it intelligible in a kind of riddle which is at the same time always being solved."

In view of the *Calender*'s claim to be launching not only a new poet but also a new or renewed English tradition in poetry, it is striking to observe the difference between its social assumptions and those of George Puttenham, literary critic and spokesman for the art of courtly self-fashioning. In Puttenham's *Arte of English Poesie*, published a decade after the *Calender*, the uncouth as a rhetorical term is derived from *acyron*, which in Greek means that which is invalid, without authority, not dominant—of persons, having no right or power; of bodily members, unimportant. It is further glossed by Puttenham as what happens "when we use an obscure and darke word"; but it is illustrated by an "uncouth speech [of] the Tanner of Tamworth . . . to king Edward the fourth," whom he had signally failed to recognize—when he discovered his mistake, he cried out, "I hope I shall be hanged tonight," an archaic and/or rural expression of "hope" meaning "expect" that appears also in Chaucer's *Reeve's Tale*.[19] In other words, all of the meanings that were gathered under the Spenserian uncouth are gathered here also—linguistic archaism, the association of archaism with dialect, the association of dialect with the uneducated lower classes and with the problem of unintelligibility or restricted communication that the reformist speaker shares with those who have no effective voice in the system. Yet in Puttenham's courtly poetics the uncouth is not revalued upward as it is in Spenser's; rather, it is grouped in the last section of the *Arte* with the vices of expression, several of which read style, as does Spenser in the *Calender*, as a metaphor for class, but with markedly different sympathies. Closely connected to *acyron*, for example, is *tapinosis*, or "the abaser," illustrated by the tale of a sergeant who approached Queen Elizabeth's coachman, crying "Stay thy cart good fellow. . . . that

---

understood without locating it in ancient slave cultures, see Samuel Croxall, *Fables of Aesop and Others* (London, 1722), where the status of both Aesop and Phaedrus as emancipated slaves is reinforced by a Whig reading of history. See also my *Fables of Power: Aesopian Writing and Political History* (Durham, 1990).

19. Chaucer, *The Canterbury Tales*, "The Reeve's Tale," line 4029: "Oure manciple, I hope he will be deed." I owe this reference to Ann Middleton.

I may speake to the Queene" (217). In both episodes, Puttenham understands the linguistic indecorum as a failure of proper social deference. And although he records that Edward IV laughed at the Tanner of Tamworth, and gave him "for recompense of his good sport" a considerable estate, and that Elizabeth was "tickled" by Sergeant Benlowes' tapinosis, Puttenham himself does not seem amused, nor approve the royal condescension. "These and such other base words," he insisted, "do greatly disgrace the thing and the speaker" (217).

Approximately fifty years later, Milton wrote a pastoral elegy, *Lycidas;* began it with mysterious statements of compulsion and impropriety (his fingers are both "forc'd" and "rude"); and closed it down by identifying himself as an "uncouth swain." The E. K.'s of our profession have been glossing *Lycidas* ever since, but the energy expended in that exercise has not been equally distributed. More than one hundred notes and short articles have been devoted to the "two-handed engine," and several to the apocalyptic inferences of "yet once more"; but Miltonists have not, apparently, concerned themselves with the deeper semantics of the "uncouth," although two chose "Milton's Uncouth Swain" for their titles.[20] Nor, when the Spenser-Milton connection is made for *Lycidas*, is the convergence made at the point of the uncouth; although even the poem's title probably derives from the *May* eclogue, which existed in a Latin translation by Theodore Bathurst in which Piers, the bearer of the radical tradition, was actually renamed "Lycidas."[21] In Patrides' invaluable casebook,[22] the gloss is merely "unknown or rustic." In 1908 T. K. Sidney, declaring that "boorish [or] awkward" is "a force certainly not intended here," directed attention to Virgil's *indocte*, "untaught," "unskilled," a gloss that, by its recourse to

20. Stewart A. Baker, "Milton's Uncouth Swain," *Milton Studies* 3 (1971): 35–53; Emory Elliot, "Milton's Uncouth Swain: The Speaker in *Lycidas*," in *Milton Reconsidered* (Salzburg, 1976), 1–21. A partial exception is David Norbrook (*Poetry and Politics* 284), who admitted a semantics combining " 'clumsy' . . . a conventional pastoral gesture of humility", "the harsh language of religious prophecy"; and the one meaning he saw in E. K.'s preface—"that this new poet was as yet 'regarded but of few' but would soon be universally known."

21. Although not printed until 1653, Bathurst's translation of *The Shepherds Calender* was completed ca. 1608. See Wittreich, *Visionary Poetics*, 257–58.

22. C. A. Patrides, ed., *Milton's Lycidas: The Tradition and the Poem* (New York, 1961, rev. 1983).

Latinity, immediately reestablishes the *indocti* as the *docti*.[23] Although Milton uses *uncouth* elsewhere,[24] the Columbia edition of Milton's works somehow omits the word from its index. The *Milton Variorum* (2[2]:731) prefers "unknown," as appropriate to a poem "signed only with initials," and mentions E. K.'s "Uncouthe, unkiste" to suggest only that the word was already "somewhat archaic," a very different matter from itself *signifying* the archaic. And in Josephine Miles's account of "The Primary Language of *Lycidas*,"[25] "uncouth" is distinguished by its absence, and we are told that *"fresh, high, new, pure, sacred* are the especial terms of value" (88), and, even more significant, that "the liberal and natural Protestant spirit continued its poetizing in these terms of scope and sacred feeling, one of the most characteristic American poetic adjectives being the *pure* of *Lycidas*" (91). And indeed, the Protestant spirit carried in that version of English literary tradition defined by Dryden, Wordsworth, and their academic heirs has continued to regard its values as both "liberal" and "natural," unknowing of the repressed politics of the former term and the Romantic idealism of the latter.

Which brings me back, at last, to the question of pedagogy and theories of education. It is no coincidence that the term "liberal" as defining a certain theory of education appears in the opening pages of Mulcaster's *Elementarie*, a theory that explains his belief that the uncouthness of English as a language of scholarly exchange could be smoothed away by a grammar school education. Despite (or because of) the commitment of Merchant Taylors to providing free education for a third of their pupils, Mulcaster was certainly opposed to the leveling implied by the *Calender*, with its appeal to the rustic, uneducated, and simple reader. The goal of Mulcaster's linguistic nationalism was entirely compatible with Elizabethan policy—the support of public peace (which included the peace of the church) and maintenance of

23. Sidney, "The 'Uncouth Swain' in Milton's *Lycidas*," *Modern Language Notes* 23 (1908): 92.

24. He uses it five times in *Paradise Lost*, three to describe a dangerous voyage into the unknown (2.407, 827; 8.230); to define as previously inexperienced Eve's dream and Moloch's pain; and in *L'Allegro* to characterize pejoratively the cell where the darker Melancholy resides.

25. "The Primary Language of *Lycidas*," in Patrides, *Milton's Lycidas*, 86–91.

social stratification.[26] He wished to restrict education to the governing classes, to avoid "too manie bookmen," and above all to keep "learning liberall, where learners be no slaves" (19), by which remarkable phrase he meant the reverse, where no slaves be learners; that is to say, education should be available only to those who are financially independent. Although technically, of course, there were no slaves in England, Mulcaster is here using the term to denote that class defined by Sir Thomas Smith in his *De republica anglorum*, published in 1583 but describing the structure of English society as he saw it in the middle of the century. Both constitutionally and socially, Smith recognized that the largest section of the population had "no voice or authoritie in our common wealth, and no account is made of them but onlie to be ruled"; and he included in this voiceless class "day labourers, poore husbandmen, yea marchantes or retailers which have no free lande, copiholders, and all artificers," as well as apprentices, whose condition Smith himself defined as a *vera servitus*, a virtual slavery.[27]

Mulcaster's own terminology, however, requires him to deal with what might have seemed a counterexample, the example of Aesop, in whose story the Renaissance reader learned that intelligence could empower the disenfranchised. "And tho slaves be sometimes learned," wrote Mulcaster, "yet learning is not slavish, Neither when the parties demeanor doth procure his fredom, is learning manumised, which was never bond." "If you look but

26. Compare Kenneth Charlton, *Education in Renaissance England* (London, 1965), 130: "The grammar schools of Renaissance England had become to the nation what the voluntary elementary schools of the nineteenth century were to their various denominational sponsors, instruments for maintaining the *status quo*. It was not until the age of Thomas Arnold that a further attempt was made at the humanist study of the classics, and even later, into the twentieth century, that the grammar schools came to be regarded as instruments of social change, as a ladder up which those 'capable of profiting' could ascend."

27. *De republica anglorum* (1583), ed. L. Alston and F. W. Maitland (Cambridge, 1906), 46, 137. In one of the first glosses to *The Shepheardes Calender*, on the word *couth* (the uncouth's mirror image), E. K. remarks that "it commeth of the verbe Conne, that is, to know or to have skill"; but he also remarks, with seeming irrelevance, that he derived that self-evident gloss from "the worthy Sir Tho[mas] Smith in his booke of government," which he claims to have seen in manuscript, in the library of Gabriel Harvey. The fact that Spenser and his friends had been reading it prior to publication supports my claim that the *Calender* connected its theory of education to political theory also.

to Aesop among slaves, & Plato among writers," he continued,
you will see that Plato had a better conception of intelligence,
transcending social conditions: "Aesop fought still for the fredom
against servilitie, & Plato for nature against mutable fortun, measuring not even princes by their place, but by their . . . naturall
power" (19–21). Yet at the same time Mulcaster proclaimed that
since learning has "the best voice in anie estate," it should be
entrusted to only such an "utterer, as is part of the state and capable of best state," whereas slaves, having "no voice nor part in
the state, being held but for catle, tho reasonable withall," have
no claims on education that will serve the general interest (20).
At the heart of this passage, then, lies a crucial distinction between two theories of pedagogy, one the Aesopian, which
assumes that education ought to liberate, to be a weapon against
economic bondage, the other the Platonic, which assumes that
education transcends (in the sense of ignoring rather than oblit-
erating) social distinctions. This debate is still with us. Mulcaster's concern that the state should not produce "too manie
bookmen" was singled out by E. T. Campagnac, Mulcaster's
modern editor, in 1925, citing the view of Stanley Baldwin, Conservative prime minister of Britain, that a liberal education
worked in the interests of "the unity of Society and Government," and adding his own concern that the educational currency
not be devalued by too wide circulation, since while "the State
needs some learned men . . . learned men need the help of the
unlearned" (xix).

Although Spenser did not directly refute Mulcaster's contention that we ought to agree in keeping "learning liberall" in this
restricted sense, the *Shepheardes Calender* certainly implied a
wish for a more inclusive national culture. As for Milton, he was
well aware that "liberal," as a term in the philosophy of education, was actually a sociological distinction. The term appears
in *Of Education*, where he speaks of "manly, and liberall exer-
cises" (2:385); and his editors observe: "Originally 'worthy of
a free man,' as opposed to 'servile' or 'mechanical,' by Milton's
time 'liberal' applied to pursuits or occupations becoming to a
gentleman" (3:385). In fact Milton finesses this issue. He also
speaks of a "compleate and generous Education" (2:378), another
phrase in which etymology implies, but does not insist on, social
specification. "Generous," from Latin *generosus*, "of good or

noble birth," matches the Renaissance semantics of "liberal," and both are confirmed by the subsequent reference to the "noble and gentle youth" (2:406) whom Milton imagines as his ideal clientele. Milton never (how could he, as one who had with his father's support climbed Aesop's ladder?) explicitly restricted access to the humanist-scientist program he proposed for the schools of the new republic; but the very terms in which he critiqued the educational practices of his day reinstated the absolute difference between "a learned man" and "any yeoman or tradesman competently wise in his mother dialect only" (2:370).

But at least in *Lycidas*, the poem that seems in its closure to signify Milton's farewell to his own privileged period of education in pastoral Cambridge and Horton, we hear also the prickly, self-conscious voice of the bright but difficult boy (perhaps not so very different after all from Wordsworth's bounder) whose desire for incorporation in the great tradition was driven by his sense of being an outsider; and vice versa. The ambition thematized in the poem was the force that, in Milton's hands, made the pastoral surpass itself and then, at the crucial moments, turn and rend itself for being a false surmise. And when, at the very end, the entire poem is framed (in the colloquial sense also) as the product of an "uncouth" brain, we ought, if apprised of "uncouth's" relation to the *other*, radical tradition, have some profound rethinking to do. More personal and hence less socially critical than Spenser's uncouth, Milton's was nonetheless connected to that side of his own personality that led him from *Lycidas* to the church reform pamphlets and from there to political iconoclasm. And whereas Spenser's populism was subsequently greatly complicated (though not, I shall argue, abandoned), Milton's uncouth, with Spenser as its genius, remained with him throughout his polemical career, eventually to be subsumed, as we shall see, by the sublime.

3

A Petitioning Society

In Shakespeare's *Henry VI, Part 2*, which may be the first of his plays to have appeared on the Elizabethan stage, he retells the history of a weak, if pious, king and the struggles for power between leading aristocrats that are the consequence of royal otherworldliness. Illustrating the effect of these struggles on the nation below, there is an early scene designed to establish the disreputable character of the duke of Suffolk, as against the benevolence of the Lord Protector, Humphrey, duke of Gloucester. There "enter three or four Petitioners," (we are told in a stage direction) who hope to "deliver [their] supplications" to the Lord Protector. Unfortunately for them, there is a confusion of identities, and the petition "Against the Duke of Suffolk, for enclosing the commons of Long Melford," is handed to Suffolk himself instead of to Gloucester. Enclosing the commons, taking away from the villagers the open land they have traditionally been allowed to use for grazing, and fencing it in as one's private property, all represent here the feudal divide between the propertied and the landless that could either be exacerbated by aristocratic greed or mediated by aristocratic concern for the common people, something for which Gloucester was famous. This small scene had no basis in the chronicles from which Shakespeare was working. It was presumably added to make a special point. Apart from giving a local, sixteenth-century flavor to a fifteenth-century conflict,[1] we might infer from it the inadequacy of a proce-

1. As Harold Brooks points out in the Arden edition, the name of Long Melford would have had associations in Stratford in 1590/1, since the Clopton

dure for seeking redress of grievances that is dependent on the good will of a particular nobleman and vulnerable to the malice of another.

In the first scene of *Coriolanus*, which retells a famous story about the formative early years of the Roman republic, the military hero Coriolanus is self-defined as the enemy of the Roman plebeians. From that perspective, Coriolanus takes a jaundiced view of "a petition granted" to the plebeians, "a strange one/to break the heart of generosity/And make bold power look pale," (1.1.209–211). Again, there is no mandate in Shakespeare's source, North's translation of Plutarch, for the use of the term "petition" to describe this incident, which is presented both by North and by Shakespeare as a successful food riot, successful in the sense that the Senate responded by granting the plebeians political representation. The uprising results in the creation of new state officers, the tribunes of the people.[2] Coriolanus' language may appear to support the view of some contempo rary social historians that riots in early modern England should really be seen as "an extreme form of petitioning."[3] Yet the constitutional innovation here would conflict with their further assumption, that such violent demonstrations did not have as their goal social disruption, still less a major social reconstruction, but only intended a *return* to previous understandings about land use or the price of bread.

---

family, often mentioned in the corporation records, were descended from the fifteenth-century owners of Long Melford. These included William Clopton, esquire, and his wife, listed in the recusancy returns instigated by Whitgift in 1591 as confessed Romanists who "paid their fines monthly." See *Minutes and Accounts of the Corporation of Stratford-upon-Avon*, 1553–1620, introd. Edgar Fripp, vol. 4: 1586–1592 (London, 1929), xxxv.

2. After the story of Menenius Agrippa's intervention with the belly fable, North merely reports: "These persuasions pacified the people, conditionally, that the Senate would graunte there should be yerely chosen five magistrates, which they now call *Tribuni Plebis*, whose office should be to defend the poore people from violence and oppression."

3. The phrase is taken from Buchanan Sharp, *In Contempt of All Authority: Rural Artisans and Riot in the West of England, 1586–1660* (Berkeley and Los Angeles, 1980), 42. The position, however, has been quite widely accepted. See my essay on the historiography of popular protest in *Literature and the Civil War*, ed. Thomas Healy and Jonathan Sawday (Cambridge, 1988), 21–36.

It is typical of Shakespeare's ironic sense of structure, however, that the sociopolitical move of petitioning, half ritual demonstration, half effective lobby, (and all the more effective, obviously, when accompanied by a show of force) will be symbolically reversed in terms of the power-relations of Roman society when Coriolanus, seeking the consulship, must engage in the *petitio consulatus*, the formal move of requesting the plebeians to endorse his candidacy. It will be their failure to complete *this* ritual in his favor that will drive Coriolanus to leave his own city and join forces with its enemies. More subtly still, the term "petition" itself, so clearly politicized at the play's opening, will be echoed three times in the last act in the attempts of Cominius, Menenius, and finally Volumnia (respectively colleague, father-figure, and mother) to persuade Coriolanus not to attack his own nation.[4] Thus a mediatory process that has been shown capable of effecting political change is replaced, at the play's ending, by an increasingly personal, emotional and apolitical form of influence, without which, we must suppose, the city would have fallen.

In the second scene of *Henry VIII*, which was almost certainly Shakespeare's last play (the sense of an ending provided by *The Tempest* notwithstanding), there is a slightly different relationship between these two aspects of the petition. Early in the play, as a figure of social benevolence opposed to the rapacity of Cardinal Wolsey, Queen Katherine kneels as a suitor to her husband, yet presenting her own "petition" on behalf of others. "I am solicited," she says,

> not by a few,
> And those of true condition, that your subjects
> Are in great grievance: there have been commissions
> Sent down among 'em, which hath flaw'd the heart
> Of all their loyalties. (1.2.18–22)

She refers to the new "exactions" or taxes ordered by Wolsey, recorded in "Holinshed's" *Chronicles* as "the sixt part of everie

---

4. See Cominius: "He replied / It was a bare petition of a state / To one whom they had punish'd" (5.1.19–21); Menenius: "I have been blown out of your gates with sighs, and conjure thee to pardon Rome and thy petitionary countrymen," (5.2.73–75); Volumnia: "This boy . . . Does reason our petition with more strength / than thou hast to deny't . . ." (5.3.174–77).

mans substance." Once again, although the source-text recounts in some detail the political process whereby the magnates of the clothing industry agreed to the tax, but then began to protect their own financial interests by laying off "spinners, carders, fullers, weavers and other artificers" in great numbers, producing an armed and potentially rebellious group of four thousand unemployed men, it makes no mention of Queen Katherine's "petition." One would scarcely notice this small addition unless in the series I am here creating. In this context, Shakespeare's insistence that the new tax is liable, if the petition is not granted, to produce an armed rebellion reverberates both with the anti-enclosure protest of *Henry VI, Part 2*, however timid, and with the food riot of *Coriolanus*, which is either accompanied by or interpreted as (the difference is salient) a formal petition. Yet what makes Katherine's petition work is neither the show of force, nor its threat precisely, but rather her status as an especially privileged mediator. Again, there may be an intentional structural irony in the fact that, just before her death, the now cast-off Katherine sends a written and entirely personal petition to her ex-husband asking for kindness for her daughter, husbands for her waiting-women, and wages for her men ("they are the poorest") (4.2.131–51). It would certainly be possible to argue that, though he subjected his society to an increasingly skeptical sociopolitical analysis, Shakespeare ultimately fell back on the subtler (though scarcely more hopeful) sphere of interpersonal relations. Yet by bringing its audience almost up to date, so to speak, on the history of petitions, *Henry VIII* provided a vantage point from which to observe what had been happening to this peculiar form of intervention in the world—a form which we still use, perhaps without reflection, and often quixotically, as a way of transmitting an otherwise blocked or resourceless minority opinion.

In fact, Shakespeare is only on the periphery of my argument here. I propose that these plays emerge from, and speak to, a petitioning society, that is to say, to a society that still employed a feudal and in many ways unsatisfactory procedure whereby those without power could appeal against a perceived unjustice. Some of the ways in which it was unsatisfactory are indicated above. A successful petition depended entirely on the good will of the person or group to whom it was addressed, or on the influence of a benevolent mediator. There was no law that required a petition to be granted, but it was undoubtedly the case that the fear of force, riot or rebellion constituted a strong rationale for granting it. Yet in the opening decades of the seventeenth century, the context of *Coriolanus* and *Henry VIII*, there was already emerging another, more assertive concept of petitioning, one in which physical force in the background was represented or preempted (the distinction is a nice one) by legal-constitutional reasoning. And there are earlier signs, earlier even than *Henry VI, Part 2*, of an emergent theory of petitioning as a more assertive practice than is implied by the term "petition," its supporting rhetoric of humility, its gestures of genuflection. Central to the transition from deference to demand, I suggest, was the increased weight on *written* petitions, on *signatures* (which imply both a degree of literacy and a ritual of self-determination), and on the *number* of signatures attached to any petition: the greater the number, the closer we come to majoritarianism.

This proposal constitutes a change from, and (I hope) an advance upon my earlier, incomplete response to that premise of revisionist social history mentioned above—that active social protest should really be seen, in Buchanan Sharp's words, as "an extreme form of petitioning." Because my earlier concern was to rescue early modern popular protest from revisionist *historiography*, I missed the *historical* issue. I had dismissed the idea of petitioning itself without further thought. The discovery of two unrelated and seemingly eccentric texts that staged or theorized petitions reopened for me the central question: what kinds of intervention in the sociopolitical process were available to the seemingly powerless citizen—the majority—in early modern England? Neither of these texts is "literary" in the modern sense. However, since they both thematize the act of writing as a crucial aspect of effective intervention, they encourage the framing of a hypothesis: that at the other end of the spectrum from an extreme form of petitioning we might find literature, in the literal sense of writing. But before turning to that more tenuous hypothesis, I must first justify my claim that England in the late sixteenth and early seventeenth century could properly be described as a petitioning society.

At every level of authority the petition, by the individual or the group, direct or via an intercessor, was the acceptable form in which requests for social reordering were made. In the county quarter rolls (the records of quarter sessions before the justice of the peace) there are petitions about paternity suits, about the right to erect cottages, about the maintenance of disabled or indigent persons, about the control of unruly or malevolent neighbors. In June 1608 there was a petition to the justices of Morland, to be relieved of the charge of maintaining the sea wall; another, signed by ten of the "parishioners and poor of East Chinnock" complaining that the profits from local lands have been wrongfully diverted by Richard Tayler and George Slade, "that by means thereof divers of our poor weak aged and impotent people are like to famish in this great time of dearth." In the Wells sessions of 1610 there was a petition by John Saffin on behalf of his servants, Matthew Beale and Jane Long, wrongfully accused by the vicar of Stogumber and Bicknaller before the ecclesiastical court "for lookinge on players at tyme of dyvine service wherof noe proofe could be made."[5] Note that the group petitions were signed by each member of the group, implying their literacy.

These quarter session records are a wonderful record of what the popular voice actually sounded like. As E. H. Bates, who edited the Somerset records, remarked (gratuitously, since his work was supposedly purely archival recovery) after perusing "the very acts and words of the parties in all ranks of society" contained in the sessions rolls:

> the lives of these plain English folk are the fountain from which the crowd of Shakespeare's characters is derived. Every one of his squires, constables, serving men, labourers, clowns, drunkards and other picturesque villains, have their real prototype in these pages.[6]

And he went on to quote Hamlet on theatrical mimesis, concluding that these minor legal records deliver up to a modern reader "the very age and body of the time, his form and pressure."

5. *Quarter Sessions Records for the County of Somerset*, vol. 1 (James I. 1607–1625), ed. E. H. Bates (Taunton, Somerset, 1907), 23:25–27, 60.
   6. *Quarter Sessions Records* 23:li.

At a higher level of appeal, a local entity could petition the monarch directly. In July 1587 the mayor and burgesses of Leicester drafted and redrafted a petition to the queen asking her to reincorporate the borough and to grant them the fee farm of certain lands, whose revenues were to go to municipal upkeep and support of the poor.[7] Sadly (and amusingly), in September 1597, a decade after the fee farm was granted, there was a petition to the queen against the mayor and burgesses of Leicester by the "poore commonalitie," complaining that since the town officials had appropriated for themselves all the revenue so generated, "not five poore people are the beter for your moste gracious gift, nether the towne any whit amended." At the end of the petition is a note by the major and burgesses, as follows: "The matter and contentes within wrytten, wee whose names are hereunder wrytten, doe thincke in our own consciences, to be most untrue."[8]

If petitions were the staple of regional government during Shakespeare's lifetime, they had already become equally important at the center. As Ronald Butt defines this development in his history of Parliament:

> By the beginning of the reign of Edward III, the Commons themselves were established as an actual petitioning body, putting forward what came to be called "common petitions." These were so described, however, not because they emanated from the Commons in Parliament but because, as it was expressed in a petition of 1346, they were petitions made "for the common profit." Some of these petitions may have been inspired by interested bodies or people outside Parliament, but their essential characteristic was their request to the king for action on a matter which was said to affect the general interest of the community. Such petitions often began with the words *"preint les communes"* (the Commons pray . . .). By now, "common interest" petitions were recognized as a category separate from "singular" petitions and were being

7. *Records of the Borough of Leicester . . . 1509–1603*, ed. Mary Bateson (Cambridge, 1905), 3:232–38. The care with which these drafts were constructed is instructive. On the last, the clause asking for the whole town in fee farm is canceled and in the margin "The naming of the whole towne in fee farme wilbe a great thing in shew and take hede how you put it in."

8. *Records of the Borough of Leicester* 3:286–87.

gathered on a single roll, which by the end of the fourteenth century was often headed with the title "common petitions."[9]

At the far end of the evolutionary history of "common petitions" in this sense lie those documents presented by the Commons to James I and Charles I, culminating in the 1628 Petition of Right. As Elizabeth Read Foster has persuasively argued, the great petition of 1628 should be seen, in both form and name, as the culmination of a process whereby Parliament developed an instrument, so it was believed, of constitutional validity.[10] Parliamentary petitions of right,[11] which required an answer from the monarch, were increasingly carefully distinguished from petitions of grace, which did not. In 1661 William Prynne, lecturing at the Inns of Court on the 1628 petition, called it a "law originally framed, prosecuted and passed according to the ancientest and most usual parliamentary way; to wit not by bill, as of late times, but by petition," and related it to the first English petition of right, that by the magnates to King John, which, together with his answer, constituted Magna Carta. Whereas Elizabeth I encouraged her parliaments to proceed by petition rather than by legislation, the concept of the petition of right as an instrument of constitutional remedy did not develop until James's reign, when there also developed a conviction that all significant and lasting negotiation between crown and Parliament required written record; in effect, codification. As Foster explained:

> More and more, parliament, particularly the House of Commons, had come to insist on written, formal communication with the crown. Members not only distrusted the Speaker of the House of Commons and the privy councillors in both Houses, but the King himself. They sought security in the written record. "I think it best," said a member in 1621 during the discussion concerning freedom of debate, "to recommend it to the King by petition in

---

9. *A History of Parliament: The Middle Ages* (London: 1989), 268–69. See also G. L. Harriss, "The Formation of Parliament, 1272–1377," in *The English Parliament in the Middle Ages*, ed. R. G. Davies and J. H. Denton (Philadephia, 1981), 63–78.

10. "Petitions and the Petition of Right," *Journal of British Studies* 14 (1974): 21–45.

11. Also called petitions of right were the private bills by which an individual initiated an action against the crown.

writing, for that which is done by word the manner may be forgotten, but *litera scripta manet*." Another added, "If we go by message we can have but a verbal answer, which cannot be a precedent, neither can it equal an act of parliament."[12]

Following the "ancient precedents," the rolls of Parliament stored in the Tower, where petitions and the answers to them were inscribed together, the Commons attempted, not always successfully, to have their petitions and the royal replies to each article enrolled in the Parliament rolls. A sense of how much these formalities mattered can be gathered from the petition on temporal grievances presented to the king in July 1610, on a piece of vellum measuring forty-one by thirty-two inches, which James later complained was "big enough to hang a little room."[13]

This petition, less well known than the 1628 Petition of Right, was remarkably outspoken in its correction of the royal prerogative, especially on the matter of the spate of proclamations which had followed James's accession (and to which Shakespeare adverts in *Measure for Measure*):

> By reason whereof there is a general fear conceived and spread amongst your Majesty's people, that proclamations will by degrees grow up and increase to the strength and nature of laws, whereby not only the ancient happiness and freedom will be much blemished, if not quite taken away, which their ancestors have so long enjoyed, but the same may also in process of time bring a new form of arbitrary government upon the realm. And this their fear is the more increased by occasion as well of certain books lately published which ascribe a greater power to proclamations than heretofore hath been conceived to belong unto them, as also of the care taken to reduce all the proclamations made since your Majesty's reign into one volume, and to print them in such form as acts of parliament have been, and still are used to be, which seemeth to imply a purpose to give them more reputation and more establishment than heretofore they have had.[14]

12. "Petitions and the Petition of Right" p. 37, citing *Commons Debates 1621*, ed. Wallace Notestein, Frances Relf, Hartley Simpson (New Haven, 1935), 2:58–59.

13. See *Proceedings in Parliament 1610*, ed. Elizabeth Read Foster, 2 vols. (New Haven, 1966), 2:253, 273.

14. *Proceedings in Parliament* 2:259.

In other words, as the Parliamentarians sought to have their own petitions acquire the force of law by formal inscription, so they were increasingly alarmed by the corresponding strategy when employed unilaterally by the crown.

The daring of this early Jacobean petition, which may be almost contemporaneous with *Coriolanus*, makes an interesting comparison with the first of the two texts that, as I earlier indicated, inspired this argument. At first sight it seems to belong to another world from that of parliamentary resistance to arbitrary government. Richard Mulcaster's *Elementarie*, published in 1582, was, in C. S. Lewis' term, "a glorified spelling book." Yet in the center of this work, as Lewis himself noted, was a defence against proposed phonetic reforms of English spelling, which "takes the form of an allegorical history of Old King Sound."[15] What Lewis does *not* mention is that this allegorical fantasy is actually an evolutionary political history, the account of an absolute monarch who was forced by his subjects to limit his prerogative. Despite the fact that Mulcaster's educational program as a whole was designed to consolidate the governing class, he could in the 1580s imagine the monarch as "a restrained not banished Tarquinius" (64), that is to say, one who, under pressure from his/her subjects, avoided a rebellion by appropriate constitutional change. At the birth of writing, Mulcaster imagined, phoneticism must have seemed the appropriate model for spelling; but as society became more complex and pronunciation was seen to be variable, phonetics had to give way to convention, paradoxically more stable because capable of fixation. When transformed into allegory, however, evolutionary linguistics became a politics. The rule of Sound, Mulcaster wrote, became imperious and unjust, "without anie mercie or pitie, but death for disobedience, no pardon, no forgivenesse, no misericordia, what equitie soever the contrarie side had": to the point that a group of his subjects, "men of good wit, & great understanding," "assembled themselves together to *common* [commune] upon so *common* a good . . . & told him in plane terms, that he must be content to refer himself to order, and so much the rather, bycause their meaning was not to seke either his deprivation, or his resigna-

---

15. Lewis, *English Literature in the Sixteenth Century Excluding Drama* (Oxford, 1954), p. 350.

tion, but that it wold please him to qualify his government, and
to use the assistance of a further councell" (66–67). The constitutional change proposed, if not revolutionary, carried a Roman
flavor:

> Neither yet, (which had ben contrarie to their promis) deprived
> theie Sound of all his rialtie, which was dictatorlike before, but
> theie joyned Reason with him, & Custom, to begin then in right,
> and not in corruption after, as a Caesar and a Pompeie, to be his
> colleges in a triumvirate. From that time forward Sound could do
> much, but nothing so much, as he could do before, being verie
> manie times, verie justlie overruled by his confederat compan-
> ions, and fellowes in office. Thus ended the monarchie of Sound
> alone. (70–71)[16]

The story Mulcaster tells of a political intervention in the kingdom of sound may be read as a metaphor for the writerly function
of petitioning—on behalf of the community by an intellectual
intercessor—which is a stronger function than that of the advice
to princes. Mulcaster's petition is carried to the monarch by "men
of good wit," for the "common good," lobbying for constitutional
change. And although it is represented as oral persuasion, the
emphasis on writing is both the frame of the allegory and, as we
shall see, its narrative conclusion. This is no passing metaphor
but a full thirteen pages of complex narrative. The narrative
begins in terms considerably more radical than those eventually
agreed upon: "Sound upon great cause, was deposed from his
monarchie, as no fit person to rule the pen alone" (66). And
among the arguments the men of good wit use to persuade him
to limit the prerogative is that "even great potentates, and con-
siderat princes, for the generall weall of their naturall states (his
being but voluntarie, and of their election) were verie well content . . . to admit such a councell." But there is a third phase of
the action, in which Reason and Custom fear a return of arbitrary government, because "Sounds malcontented frinds did
never rest . . . , ever bussing into the ignorant ears that of Sounds
authoritie, and his right to his own deliverie" (73). So they find
a good notary, and the terms of the agreement are set down in

16. I have deitalicized, and instead capitalized, the names of the main protagonists in this allegory.

writing and "the conditions subscribed by all their consents, for a *perpetuall evidence* against the repiner[s]" (74; italics added).

There is some irony in the fact that the *Elementarie* became interesting to postmodern criticism. I refer to Jonathan Goldberg's inquiry into how handwriting was actually conceived, taught, and practiced in early modern England, a project conducted, however, under the influence of Jacques Derrida's deconstructive theory of writing.[17] Goldberg devoted a few lines to the thirteen-page allegory of King Sound's enforced restriction of his prerogative (195), and was evidently more attracted to the implications of Mulcaster's single phrase "prerogative's power, a great princesse in proces" and to the possibility that *E*, the letter that makes the greatest difference in pronunciation, might stand for Elizabeth. Mulcaster's version of petitioning makes such a difference of emphasis possible—although I would have to say, barely possible—because he is both a careful advocate of limited monarchy and an unremitting antipopulist. As he distinguished the Platonic concept of education from the Aesopian one, Mulcaster was also careful to separate his concept of a mixed government from anything approaching democracy. The *Elementarie* provides a strong critique of the plebiscite, which he associates with the oral/aural transmission of policy:

> what reason had [writing] to follow everie mans ear, as a master scrivener, and leave everie mans pen to his own sound, where such difference was, as theie could not agree . . . where the right was, everie one laing clame to it? why not my ear best? Again why should ignorance in anie respect be taken for a gide in a case of knowledge? bycause of their *voices*? [i.e., votes] that were to *popular*, where the argument is singular. Bycause of their *wills*? that were to *willful*, where wisdom should warrant.

By the same token, however, Mulcaster's argument *against* a popular state and the extension of the franchise to "everie one" indicates that such radical alteration of the political structure was not theoretically inconceivable.

By the time Mulcaster's *Elementarie* was published, the concept of the petition had already been appropriated by social groups, and in the service of agendas, of which Mulcaster would surely

17. Goldberg, *Writing Matter: From the Hands of the English Renaissance* (Stanford, 1990).

have disapproved. From 1572 onward, when John Field and Thomas Wilcox directed the first *Admonition to Parliament*, the Puritan community learned to adapt the petition to two new functions: the first, to lobby Parliament in the direction of a more reformed church; the second, to indicate, by the number of signatories, the size of the lobby. The political implications of this gesture were not lost on the government. "Surely if this fond faction be applauded to," Archbishop Matthew Parker wrote to Cecil in 1573, " . . . it will fall out to a popularity, and as wise men think, it will be the overthrow of all the nobility."[18] During 1584–85, when Whitgift launched his campaign against nonconformity and imposed on the clergy the system of "subscription" to three articles (confirming the royal supremacy and agreeing that the Book of Common Prayer and the thirty-nine articles were consistent with the Word of God), the Puritan strategy was to muster petitions addressed to Parliament, which were worked over by a Commons committee so that they might be presented as a single coherent document.[19] But when Elizabeth intervened to cut off any further debate within Parliament on ecclesiastical matters, yet another strategy was required. The nonconformists, or rather some of their more reckless spokesmen, directed their appeal to the public at large.

I refer to the series of scurrilous but highly amusing pamphlets issued in 1589/90 by the fictional persona Martin Marprelate. Leland Carlson's massive study of the Marprelate controversy seems to have established the author of those pamphlets as Job Throkmorton,[20] member of Parliament in 1572, Oxford-educated

18. Quoted in D. M. Loades, *Politics and the Nation, 1450–1660* (Brighton, 1974), 291.

19. See Foster, "Petitions and the Petition of Right," 29.

20. *Martin Marprelate, Gentleman: Master Job Throkmorton Laid Open in His Colors* (San Marino, 1981). See also, however, the sensible caveats of Ritchie Kendall, *The Drama of Dissent: The Radical Poetics of Nonconformity, 1380–1590* (Chapel Hill, 1986), 258–59: "Carlson's own arguments for Throkmorton [versus Donald McGinn's for Penry] are persuasive; less convincing is his attempt to attribute virtually every satiric piece from the 1570s through the 1590s to the same hand . . . it is not necessary to insist upon a single artist as being responsible for this work; we may well be dealing, particularly in the satires of Martin Junior and Martin Senior, with a committee of authors. Nonetheless, the remarkable coherence of the whole Marprelate series suggests that even if different hands participated in their creation, there was a marked unity of purpose and method in their work."

Puritan, and, notoriously, again elected for Warwick in 1586. This highly contentious election in Shakespeare's home territory was itself an instance of unconventional and perhaps antigovernmental feeling, as well as being part of an extensive and well-organized national election campaign by the Puritans. *The Black Book of Warwick* recorded that "Mr. Job Throkmorton made very great labor to many of the inhabitants of this borough for their voyces," and was supported by "the worst sort of the inhabitants."[21] According to J. H. Plumb, Throkmorton forced his election by "threatening to invoke the rights of the commonalty to vote."[22] Throkmorton is listed as among the "Gentlemen and Freeholders in the countye of Warwicke 1580," along with Roger Wigston, whose wife harbored a Martinist press at Woolston Priory in July 1589; John Greene, Puritan host of the Crown Inn at Warwick, a strong supporter of Throkmorton for the 1586 election; and John Shakespeare, the playwright's father. The last two were kinsmen.[23] According to Edgar Thripp, editor of the Stratford Corporation records, both Throkmorton and Thomas Cartwright were popular figures in Warwickshire, and Whitgift was intensely disliked, not least for his persecution of Cartwright, who was imprisoned in 1590 for refusing the take the ex officio oath. In 1591 John Shakespeare was himself listed recusant by the commissioners whom Whitgift had sent out into Warwickshire, as elsewhere, to report on all those who were not attending church.[24]

Throkmorton was so staunch and imprudent a supporter of free speech in Parliament that, shortly after his election, he delivered in quick succession three inflammatory speeches, one attacking Mary, Queen of Scots, the second attacking Charles IX of France and Philip II of Spain, and the third, on February 27, 1587, supporting Sir Anthony Cope's bill proposing the establishment of Presbyterianism in England. In this third speech, "The Bill and the Book," Throkmorton fully anticipated the cause

---

21. *The Black Book of Warwick*, ed. Thomas Kemp (Warwick, 1898), 387, 389.

22. "The Growth of the Electorate in England from 1600 to 1715," *Past and Present*, no. 45 (1969): 94. See also J. E. Neale, *The Elizabethan House of Commons* (London, 1949, 1963), 240–45.

23. See *Minutes and Accounts of the Corporation of Stratford-upon-Avon* 3:55, 57, 64.

24. *Minutes and Accounts of the Corporation of Stratford-upon-Avon* 4:161.

that would subsequently be taken up by the opposition leaders in the Commons in the parliaments of James I and Charles I, connecting parliamentary freedom of speech to that of the pulpit, both of which, he ironically suggested, were currently a fiction:

> This freedom of ours, as yt is now handeled heere amongst us, I can very well lyken to a certaine lycense graunted to a preachere to preache the gospell freely, provided allwayes that he medle neyther with the doctryne of the prophetes nor the apostles. Pardon mee (right Honorable), is not this, I praye you, the very image of our freedom in this House at this day? Ye shall speake in the Parleamente House freely, provided all wayes that ye medle neyther with the reformation of religion nor the establishment of succession, the verie pillers and grounde workes of all our blisse and happinesse. . . .[25]

Throkmorton proved his point about the lack of freedom of speech by having to flee London to escape imprisonment in the Tower, and went into hiding in the country. Deprived of a parliamentary forum, he turned to a wider audience, to anonymous, illicit, and prolific publication.

At the heart of this publishing project lay a radical theory of petitioning. In *The just censure and reproofe of Martin Junior*, familiarly known as *Martin Senior* (and printed at Roger Wigston's house in July 1589), Throkmorton had pleaded for equal justice for the would-be reformers of the English church, that they might have their "remedie at the Kings bench" against molestations by the prelates, and urged "al the Puritans in the land, both lordes, knights, gentlemen, ministers, and people, to become joint suiters in one supplication unto her Majestie, and the Lords of her honorable privie counsell in these petitions" (C3r, v). And, he adds, "I can tell thee there would be gotten an hundreth thousand hands to this supplication, of knowen men in the land, all her Majesties most loyall and trustie loving subjects. Thou mayest then well thinke what a stroke so many woulde strike together, especiallie in so reasonable and just a suite" (C4r). Here one can see emerging a theory of the *mass* petition, along with a complex (and, as we shall see, ambiguous) pun on "hands," as a sign of corporate literacy. There may also be a still more esoteric pun

25. Carlson, *Martin Marprelate, Gentleman*, 104–6.

in the phrase "knowen men," on the one hand simply a reference to the well-known or established, on the other an ironic recuperation of a phrase that from the late fourteenth century, when it designated the Lollard followers of John Wyclif, signified paradoxically those who attempted to remain unknown except to each other, a clandestine because persecuted reformist minority.[26]

Throkmorton was also probably the author of an anonymous pamphlet actually entitled *A Petition directed to her Majestie*,[27] imported from Middelburg in 1592, to which Matthew Sutcliffe, dean of Exeter, who had replaced the unfortunate bishop Thomas Cooper as the episcopal spokesman, wrote a heavy-artillery reply.[28] Sutcliffe's *Answere* was dedicated to Sir Edmund Anderson, Lord chief justice of the court of common pleas. Its premise was that those who had recently published a petition for the release from prison of certain dissenters were, by the mere fact of that publication, not merely scofflaws but aiming at complete political reconstruction. This also involved, in Sutcliffe's rhetoric, a deconstruction by language:

> the lawes are not onely contemned, but most boldly oppugned: yea with such confidencie, that law is now accounted disorder, and faction and tumult, termed reformation: and libellers in evil time called reformers, what resteth for them to worke, but that al wise, and learned men being put from government, the seely sots which these call elders, and certaine famous authors of popular faction should be placed in the highest offices. . . . (A3r)

Sutcliffe was quick to conflate the Puritan pamphleteers with actual rebels from the past. "Jacke Straw and Wat Tyler, and Kett of Norffolke, and all rebels pretend reformation as well as these,"

26. See Anne Hudson, *The Premature Reformation: Wycliffite Texts and Lollard History* (Oxford, 1988), 57, 143, 478, 482–83.

27. [Job Throkmorton], *A Petition directed to her Most Excellent Majestie, wherein Is Delivered 1. A Meane Howe to Compound the Civill Dissention in the Church of England. 2. A Proofe that They Who Write for Reformation Doe Not Offend against the Statute of 23 Elizabeth, c. [2], and Therefore till Matters Bee Compounded, Deserve More Favour* (Middelburg, 1592).

28. Matthew Sutcliffe, *An Answere to a Certaine Libel Supplicatorie, or rather Diffamatory, and also to certaine Calumnious Articles, and Interrogatories, both printed and scattered in secret corners, to the slaunder of the Ecclesiasticall state, and put forth under the name and title of a Petition directed to her Majestie* (London, 1592).

(55); and throughout the pamphlet he speaks with undisguised class consciousness: "every man let him goe to his occupation, clownes to the plowe, marchants to their shops, Clarkes & scribes to their penne & ynkehorn, and this petitioner to Bedlem" (67). Petitioning is to be seen not as a traditional practice of social adjustment, but rather as a delirium; and the pen and inkhorn are to be reserved for professionals.

But what comes to the surface in this debate between Sutcliffe and Throkmorton nevertheless is the social power of the published petition. For Sutcliffe, *any* act of publication is an appeal for popular support, and a petition directed to a general readership via the press, instead of to the appropriate authority figure, is a contradiction in terms, an offence against the humility petitioning used to entail:

> seeing this petition is directed to her Majestie, to what ende is the same put in print? belike the mans purpose is, so much as the Queene by wisdome shall denie, the people by force, and furie shall establish, which in deede is his drift, for the same was never presented to her Maiestie, but onely to the people. (B3r)

Finally, Sutcliffe's attack assumes that the Martinists intended, by publication, to create a climate conducive to insurgency—an assumption that subsumes extensive popular literacy and attributes to the writer considerably more power than we usually do today. In the *Petition* Throkmorton had denied that his hundred thousand hands carried any intimation of physical violence, and invoked in his self-defence an early theory of authorial intention:

> We ought not bring newe sences unto words, but take that sence onely which the author bringeth. . . . Whereas Martin Senior speaketh of a hundred thousand handes and of striking, his wordes be carried (as I am perswaded) altogither from his sence & meaning. . . . These are his words. For opening of which I propounde this question, whether any man doeth knowe the meaning of these wordes better then the authour himself, which no man will affirme as I thinke. . . . That an hundred thousand handes would *strike a great stroke in this sute*, hath no other sence than this, that if hir Maiestie should understand, that an hundred thousand of hir most loving & loyall subjects should *subscribe* to such a petition, it would greatly move hir Highness to accept the same.[29]

29. *A Petition directed to her Majestie*, 46.

Glossing his "hundred thousand handes" as signatures, Throkmorton therefore underlined the significance of literacy in the campaign that he was currently spearheading and at the same time ironically matched the hated "subscriptions" imposed by Whitgift on the ministry with "subscriptions" an hundred thousandfold for the other side.[30] It was the new phenomenon of the many signing the petition that disturbed Dean Sutcliffe, who complained of "those vagrant rogues that came downe into all shires with bills craving subscriptions, which is nothing but the beginning of a conjuration. For never did so many joyne but in rebellion; nor can such a nomber confederate themselves without danger to the state," (p. 79). "God forbid," Throkmorton responded, "that a Tropologicall or Metaphoricall speach without intendement of anie harme, should come within the compasse of treason or rebellion."

Was Throkmorton disingenuous? For Sutcliffe, there was no doubt that he was. He dismissed Throkmorton's previous argument that the *Petition* had to be widely circulated to instruct the members of parliament by way of their constituents, "that the burgesses of Parliament are thither sent by all the people, which cannot understand what to desire, unlesse they be taught before." For, replied Sutcliffe, "if they meant onely to obtaine it by parliament, and not by force and faction of the people, it had bene sufficient to teach her Majestie, or the parliament: or any one burgesse. For so lawes are framed." He was equally contemptuous of Throkmorton's claim "that if they pretended rebellion, then they would rise up and reforme things themselves, rather then write bookes to the purpose. As if it were not madness to rise before they had prepared the peoples mindes to rebellion. Nay first a side must be made, and then matters must be executed" (74–75). In other words, Dean Sutcliffe seems to have anticipated in reverse the position of revisionist social history that riots might be regarded as an extreme form of petitioning,

---

30. The point is made by Sutcliffe himself: "But what reason hath this petifogger, or the scrivano his suggestor to condemne subscriptions, seeing both of them win more by scribling and subscribing, then any ecclesiastical person I know in England," (113). For the Martinist attack on Whitgift's required subscriptions as illegal, see especially the first of the Martin Marprelate series, *Oh Read over D. John Bridges,* familiarly known as the *Epistle,* published in East Molesey by Waldegrave in October 1588 (21–22).

arguing instead that certain extreme forms of petitioning were the preamble and incentive to uprisings.

In a review of late-sixteenth- and early-seventeenth-century history in England that he wove into the complex pages of the *Rehearsal Transpros'd* in 1672, Andrew Marvell drew an analogy between Christian passivity in the face of persecution and political obedience in the face of tyranny. "The Arms of the Church," he wrote, "are Prayers and Tears, the Arms of the Subjects are Patience and Petitions."[31] Marvell's implication, that the petitioning function is an expression of *patience* on the part of the improperly governed subject, is almost certainly ironic. It is no coincidence that the *Rehearsal Transpros'd* was also a defence of religious nonconformity against clerical intolerance, and that Marvell was recognized by Dryden as a later Martin Marprelate. He was certainly a loyal admirer of those who produced the 1628 Petition of Right, whom he called "an Assembly of the most Loyal, Prudent, and Upright English spirits that any age could have produced." "Their actions," Marvell continued, continuing also our theme of the connection between petitioning and written records, "are upon Record, and by them . . . will posterity judge them. And if we had not other effects and Laws from them but *the Petition of Right*, it were sufficient to eternize their memory among all men that wear an English heart in their bosome."[32] As Marvell surely knew, both inside and outside Parliament petitions had evolved not as expressions of patience but rather of energy, of social vision ahead of its time, of self-sacrificial commitment, and of impressive organizational skills. With respect to vision, it is striking how far the Elizabethan texts I have here exhibited anticipate convictions that we are more likely to think of as typical of the late Jacobean or Caroline period, convictions fully institutionalized in the 1628 Petition of Right. With respect to organizational skills, also, the Puritan "machine," as we might now anachronistically call it, was more effective in the 1580s than one might imagine; its descendants were the massive petitions of the early 1640s, when London was flooded and Parliament presented with mass petitions, including *The hum-*

31. *The Rehearsal Transpros'd and The Rehearsal Transpros'd: The Second Part*, ed. D. I. B. Smith (Oxford, 1971), 135.
32. *The Rehearsal Transpros'd*, 223 (italics original).

ble Petition of 150000. poore labouringmen, known by the name of Porters, and *the Petition of the Gentelwomen and Tradesmens-wives*, both of which emerged from the same press as Milton's *Of Reformation* and *Of Prelatical Episcopacy.*[33] Bishop Joseph Hall then attacked the petitioners, just as Dean Sutcliffe had attacked the Martinists, as "a tumultuarie" and compared them to "Jack Straws, and Cades, and Watt Tylers of former-times."[34] In contrast, we find Milton, in the *Apology* of April 1642, making an impassioned defense of the ordinary working man (and even of the working woman). It is a tribute to the openness of the Long Parliament, he maintains, that London has become a petitioning society:

> Insomuch that the meanest artizans and labourers, at other times also women, and often the younger sort of servants assembling with their complaints, and that sometimes in a less humble guise then for petitioners, have gone with confidence, that neither their meannesse would be rejected nor their simplicity condemned, nor yet their urgency distasted; . . . nor did they depart unsatisfi'd.
> (1:926)

By the time he came to write *Eikonoklastes*, his attack on the already executed King Charles I, Milton had clearly developed a fully fledged concept of the petition as a ritual within political society that masks rhetorically an infinitely stronger move. This idea is smoothly positioned within the republican constitutional theory that his pamphlets from 1649 onwards were defending. Specifically, Milton rejected the claim made in *Eikon Basilike* that, precisely by petitioning him in the famous Nineteen Propositions, the Parliamentarians had confessed their "inferioritie" in constitutional law to the king: "and that obliges them to rest, if not satisfi'd, yet quieted with such an Answer as the will and reason of their Superior thinks fit to give." In response, Milton

33. See Bradford F. Swan, *Gregory Dexter of London and New England: 1610–1700* (Rochester, N.Y., 1949), 26, 18–19. See also D. M. Wolfe, ed., in Milton, *Complete Prose Works* (New Haven, 1953–82), 1:191–92, who mentions also *The Humble Petition of Many Thousand Poore People*, and observes that "for the first time . . . the least literate workers of London had grown vocal and emphatic enough to be received with respect by the Commons."

34. Hall, "A Speech in Parliament," in *The Shaking of the Olive Tree. The Remaining Works of . . . Joseph Hall* (1660), 426–27. Cited in Milton, *Complete Prose Works* 1:689.

advanced the practice of the commons' petition to a theoretical level where it could not be denied. "First," wrote Milton,

> Petitioning, in better English, is no more then requesting or requiring, and men require not favours onely, *but thir due*; and that not onely from Superiors, but from Equals, and Inferiors also. The noblest Romans, when they stood for that which was a kind of Regal honour, the Consulship, were wont in a submissive manner to goe about and begg that highest Dignity of the meanest Plebeians, naming them man by man; which in their tongue was call'd *Petitio consulatus*. And the Parlement of England Petition'd the King, not because all of them were inferior to him, but because he was superior to any one of them, which they did of civil custom, and for fashions sake, more then of duty; for by plaine Law cited before, the *Parlament is his Superiour.* (3:461; italics added)[35]

We are suddenly back in the world of *Coriolanus*, observing the reversal that Shakespeare had dramatized, that for the highest office in the republic (the condition that Milton's England had now obtained) the candidate must seek permission from the "meanest Plebeians"—that is to say, through an early version of electoral process.

If, then, this chapter has persuasively sketched (for a sketch is all it can be) a petitioning society, we should also see that development, whether we like the results or not, as an evolution. From a ritualized practice that implied a deeply hierarchical system and whose effects in mediating social injustice were at best unpredictable, the petition gradually acquired a political and ideological force that caused it, through the new machinery of organized protest and more informed lobbies, to reverse its own semantics. Petitioning became, as Milton put it, the act of claiming one's due.

Since Milton has returned us to *Coriolanus* and the *petitio consulatus* we can now return to the presence of petitions in Shakespeare, with a sharper focus on the problems made visible

---

35. Milton, however, soon altered his opinion of petitions. In the *Second Defence of the English People*, published in 1654, he testified to the vast number of petitions that were directed to the Long Parliament between 1647 and 1649, demanding that Charles I be punished; but he distanced himself from this process as irrational and just as likely to have been mustered in *support* of the king: "What stability would there be among such petitions from so many giddy heads? (*Complete Prose Works* 4.1:635).

by his labile and ironic references to this form of social intervention. If Milton's pamphlets gradually reveal the rebarbative force of petitioning, Shakespeare's plays throw up a different kind of question. Could literature in the restricted sense itself constitute a form of petitioning, and if so, what would constitute a sign of such intention? The Shakespearean plays I began with include representations of petitions, and even, as in Queen Katherine's speech, the threat of "language unmannerly, yea, such which breaks / The sides of loyalty, and *almost* appears / In loud rebellion" (1.2.26–29; italics added). Do the relations between these scenes imply that Shakespeare was questioning the usefulness of the petition as a social force, or warning against its tendency to tip over the edge, by way of Queen Katherine's "almost," into dangerous militancy? Or could he imagine writing, *playwrighting*, as a form of petitioning that organized the views of the London citizenry and conveyed them effectively to the appropriate authorities? Were plays designed for the public stage another version of the "Tropologicall or Metaphoricall speach" for which Job Throkmorton, a celebrity in Shakespeare's neighborhood, claimed political immunity? Where did Shakespeare stand on petitioning? And how can we tell?

I mentioned above that Shakespeare seems to respond, in *Measure for Measure*, to James I's penchant for proclamations. *Measure for Measure* begins and ends with proclamations, but it also features petitions. In act 1, scene 2, Pompey asks Mistress Overdone, "You have not heard of the proclamation, have you?" referring to Angelo's new attack on immorality, including the proclamation that "all houses in the suburbs of Vienna must be plucked down," and Overdone replies, "Why, here's a change in the commonwealth!" In act 4, scene 4, when the Duke is about to return, he instructs Escalus and Angelo by letter to "*proclaim it in an hour before his entering, that if any crave redress of injustice, they should exhibit their petitions in the street.*" This convergence of proclamation and petition, which would emerge later in James's reign as opposing writs for change (one from above, the other from below) may or may not be perceived as ironic, depending on one's response to the Duke's idea of justice. But precisely what the Duke here encourages, that the people "should exhibit their petitions in the street," had in *Julius Caesar* five years earlier been rejected as a breach of protocol. "What," says Caesar, when Artemidorus tries to thrust upon him a written warning of the conspiracy, "urge you your petitions in the street? / Come to the Capitol" (3.1.11–12). Presumably, when urged at the Capitol, the place of government, the petitions would be given a just hearing. But Caesar's inflexibility turns out to be fatal to himself. By ignoring Artemidorus, Caesar walks straight towards his own assassination. If in the tropological leanings of these two plays towards political allegory we can recognize something of James I in the Duke, and something of Elizabeth I in Julius Caesar, it would follow that James receives a slight advantage in terms of his openness to messages from the street.

Everything I have written about Shakespeare and the popular voice leads me to believe that his allusions to petitions, in the street as well as in the Capitol, constitute a coherent and sympathetic argument for their necessity as well as for their limitations, and perhaps even for that *aufhebung* performed by Milton, whereby petitioning became (ideally) a legitimate procedure, neither arbitrary nor quixotic, through which the people's representatives could *claim* the people's due. As for the more tenuous hypothesis, that plays for the public theater might participate in, by imagining, that ideal practice, of course I cannot prove it. Like any other petitioner, I can only hope, by writing, to persuade.

4

The Egalitarian Giant: Representations of Justice in History/Literature

In Franz Kafka's *The Trial*, a horrifying fable of human alienation from human institutions, there is a central encounter between Kafka's persona K. and the painter Titorelli, whose task is to reproduce endlessly the icons of the judicial system—arbitrary, logically absurd, yet cruel and inescapable—of which K. has become the latest victim. Approaching a painting in progress, K. recognized its subject as a Judge, but could not identify a large figure rising in the middle of the picture from the high back of the judicial seat.

> "It is Justice," said the painter at last. "Now I can recognize it," said K. "There's the bandage over the eyes, and here are the scales. But aren't there wings on the figure's heels, and isn't it flying." "Yes," said the painter, "my instructions were to paint it like that; actually it is Justice and the goddess of Victory in one." "Not a very good combination, surely," said K., smiling. "Justice must stand quite still, or else the scales will waver and a just verdict will become impossible." "I had to follow my client's instructions," said the painter. "Of course," said K., who had not wished to give any offense by his remark. "You have painted the figure as it actually stands above the high seat." "No," said the painter, "I have neither seen the figure nor the high seat, that is all invention, but I am told what to paint and I paint it."[1]

Economically suggested by this conversation are two radical propositions: the first, that a society's cultural icons are designed

1. *The Trial* (New York, 1968), 145–46.

not by those who produce them (the artists) but by those who have power and influence; and the second, that their conceptual message is "all invention," that it bears no relation to what might provisionally be called fact or the truth. There is either unconscious self-mockery or official shamelessness in the fact that, as K. points out, the traditional symbols of justice's integrity and impartiality have been rendered ridiculous when combined with others from a competing set of social priorities—Victory, meaning the control of others by political or military force. And indeed, by the time the painter has added some highlights to his portrait, surrounding the judge's head with "a halo or high mark of distinction," the change in the chiaroscuro brought the allegorical figure "sweeping right into the foreground and it no longer suggested the goddess of Victory, but looked exactly like the goddess of the Hunt in full cry" (147).

While no reader of Kafka has any difficulty recognizing his impenetrable skepticism and attributing it in part to his experience as a Jew in a German-speaking corner of the dying Hapsburg empire, there exists no comparable set of assumptions with which to approach an early modern writer. The cultural reproduction of justice and other related abstractions is a topic on which, for want of hard information, we are often forced to speculate. While it is self-evident that a society's official values must somehow acquire reverence through symbolization, there is no way of determining, in the absence of authorial statement (and sometimes even when we have it), whether any given artist or writer is more likely, like Titorelli, to assist in that inculcation or, like Kafka, to mock, to question, to resist. Obviously, the further into the past our speculation on this topic must reach, the scantier our hard information is likely to be. But in addition to the problems of thinner documentation, academic thought, when it is turned on earlier cultures, evinces a mysterious desire to believe that skepticism is a product only of our own belated vision. Hence the enormous authority that has accrued to Lucien Febvre's *Le problème de l'incroyance*, with its *denial* of the possibility of atheism in early modern France;[2] or the success of

2. See Febvre, *The Problem of Unbelief in the Sixteenth Century: The Religion of Rabelais*, trans. Beatrice Gottlieb (Cambridge, Mass., 1982). As Gottlieb points

revisionist accounts of seventeenth-century English political history, with their denial of the possibility of any coherent political opposition.

The case I am here investigating is one that connects these two historical problems, skepticism and political unorthodoxy, by way of the issue with which we began, the representation of Justice: a pair of documents written by Edmund Spenser that both speak to, or rather interrogate, the representation of Justice in Elizabethan England and Ireland. Although one of these documents is an allegorical poem, or part of one, and the other a political tract recommending to the British government a major reconstruction of one of its colonies, there is intellectual traffic between them, and their relationship has become something of a cause célèbre among historians of Tudor Ireland. The poem in question is *The Faerie Queene* (the quintessential Elizabethan epic), whose fifth book is devoted to the topic of Justice. The tract is Spenser's *View of the Present State of Ireland*, written apparently to persuade Elizabeth I to subdue the perpetually rebellious Irish by violent repression followed by sociopolitical engineering, yet beginning with a complex discussion of the relation between Justice as we imagine it in the abstract and law as we know it of necessity.

Spenser and the Historians

Historians, especially if themselves of Irish origin, have developed a consensus that the tract is a disgraceful instance of colonial prejudice, although they disagree as to the motives and contexts, intellectual or sociohistorical, that gave rise to it. Nicholas Canny has argued that Spenser in the *View* was, in effect, acting as the spokesman for the New English settlers who were as critical of the English crown's fluctuating and parsimonious policy toward Ireland as they were of the degenerate and partly assimilated Old English, who continued to believe that reform

---

out, "the book is really about *croyance*" (xxix). "What Febvre wanted to demonstrate was that the mental equipment available in the sixteenth century made it as good as impossible for anyone to be an atheist." Originally published in 1942 as one of the cornerstones of *Annales* school historiography, Febvre's work has only very recently itself been subjected to skepticism.

of the Gaelic Irish was feasible.[3] Canny saw the tract as only the most notorious of a group of statements put out by the New English advising a more rigorous and holistic policy, whose proponents included Barnaby Rich, Andrew Trollope, Richard Beacon, and Sir Herbert Croft, an agenda culminating in the two pamphlets of Sir John Davies addressed to James I.[4] Canny's account of Spenser's motives conflicts with that of Father Brendan Bradshaw, who perceived the Irish question in terms of the Reformation, and argued that from the regime of Thomas Cromwell onward religious reform was advanced by a severe policy combining the word (persuasion) with the sword (violent repression).[5] Unlike Canny, who emphasized the socio-economic and political context, Bradshaw was convinced that Spenser's tract could be explained finally only by intellectual history, by the rival philosophical principles that underlay the conflict between *strategies* (persuasion versus force). Thus Lodowick Bryskett's *Discourse of civill life containing the ethike part of morall philosophie* is, we are told, "of special relevance to this discussion" (491),[6] and so too is Thomas Starkey's *Dialogue between Pole and Lupset* which invoked Aristotle and Plato, especially the Plato of the *Laws*, as a basis for arguments about law, persuasion, and social control (494).[7]

3. *The Elizabethan Conquest of Ireland: A Pattern Established, 1565–76* (London, 1976), which contains several references to Spenser's *View*; and, more specifically, "Edmund Spenser and the Development of an Anglo-Irish Identity," *Yearbook of English Studies* 13 (1983): 1–19.

4. Sir John Davies, *Discovery of the True Causes why Ireland was Never Entirely Subdued, and Brought under Obedience of the Crown of England, until the Beginning of His Majestie's Happy Reign* (London, 1612); *A Survey of the present Estate of Ireland, Anno 1615, Addressed to His Most Excellent Majesty James the First . . . by His Most Humble Subject E. S.* (San Marino, Cal., Huntington Library, EL 1746).

5. Bradshaw, "Sword, Word and Strategy in the Reformation in Ireland," *Historical Journal* 21, no. 3 (1978): 475–502. See also Bradshaw, *The Irish Constitutional Revolution of the Sixteenth Century* (Cambridge, 1979); and "Robe and Sword in the Conquest of Ireland," in *Law and Government under the Tudors: Essays Presented to Sir Geoffrey Elton*, ed. Claire Cross, David Loades, and J. J. Scarisbrick (Cambridge, 1988), 139–230.

6. Since Bryskett was Spenser's friend and superior in the Grey administration, this connection is plausible, even though Bryskett's treatise was not published until 1606.

7. For a study which offers itself as an alternative to both Bradshaw's approach via intellectual history and Canny's "anthropological view of social

The ongoing debate between Canny and Bradshaw was interestingly intercepted by Ciaran Brady, who, while agreeing with both that Spenser had "dark and bloody feelings towards Ireland," denied either that Spenser's Protestantism could account for his colonialist policy or that Spenser was merely a spokesman for a group position.[8] Brady inserted a new premise, that the *View* was incoherent: only the central section, he claimed, where the new ruthlessness is defended, is exceptional or original. The opening ethnological account of the Gaelic Irish that, he assumes, was intended to justify the proposed violence was "by the time Spenser wrote . . . the standard analysis" (28); and the closing section, where specific proposals for the reconstructed colony are outlined, amount "to little more than a reiteration of the principal objectives of English government in Ireland since the 1540s" (33). In other words, Spenser strove to be both ruthless and ameliorist, both "humanist and pessimist" (33). The *View*, Brady concludes, "is riddled with ambiguity." The source of this ambiguity is to be found in Spenser's personal circumstances, plagued by lawsuits, illness, and extreme disappointment of his hopes for personal advancement as the author of *The Faerie Queene*.

Partly in order to refute the claim that the *View* is an incoherent document, Brendan Bradshaw turned to *The Faerie Queene* for support, arguing that book 5 provides the "moral and philo-

---

development," see Hans S. Pawlisch, *Sir John Davies and the Conquest of Ireland: A Study in Legal Imperialism* (Cambridge, 1985). Pawlisch investigates the collision between common law and Gaelic customs such as gavelkind and tanistry in a way that may clarify some issues in the *View*, but his focus is on the next stage of English policy in Ireland, on Davies and the Jacobean strategy of using judicial procedures to consolidate the Tudor conquest.

8. "Spenser's Irish Crisis: Humanism and Experience in the 1950s," *Past and Present*, no. 111 (1986): 17–49. See also Brady, "Court, Castle and Country: The Framework of Government in Tudor Ireland," in *Natives and Newcomers: Essays on the Making of Irish Colonial Society, 1534–1641*, ed. Brady and Raymond Gillespie (Bungay, Suffolk, 1986), 22–49. In the most recent stages of this controversy, Canny and Brady squared off in *Past and Present*, no. 120 (1988): 201–15; and then reappeared in *Spenser and Ireland: An Interdisciplinary Perspective*, ed. Patricia Coughlan (Cork, 1989). See Canny, "Spenser and the Reform of Ireland" (9–24); Brady, "The Road to the *View*: On the Decline of Reform Thought in Tudor Ireland" (25–45).

sophical vindications of Spenser's radical programme" in the *View*.[9] But Brady himself had already invoked the poem as the positivist test against which his reading of the tract could be measured. In *Faerie Queene* 5, he declared, Spenser "not only defended the violent conduct of his former patron Lord Grey, but attempted, through the adventures of the book's main protagonist, Artegall, and his iron-clad steward Talus, to provide a moral justification for the relentless use of force and terror in bringing Ireland to order" (18). Moreover, the Legend of Justice can anchor interpretation of the *View* because here, we are told, Spenser renounced "the subtle intimations" of earlier parts of the poem and replaced them with scarcely mediated historical material and with "the simple means of assertion and didacticism" (45). We are thus offered an unusual inversion: a poem, or rather that part of it which is deemed to be unambiguous, is offered as the factual control for a prose tract rendered, in this new interpretation, unstable and hence poetic. Brady's conclusion is worth quoting in full for its methodological topsy-turvydom:

> The *View of the Present State of Ireland* is at once a far less useful and far more interesting document than it has been considered to be. Because its argument is so clotted and ambiguous it defeats all attempts to claim it as a contribution to the development of English political thought and eludes efforts to bracket it as a representative statement of a particular interest group. Its subtly occlusive polemic, moreover, renders it entirely unsuitable for use, as so many historians have used it, as a cache of interesting descriptions and observations concerning the state of Ireland. Yet because it is, deliberately and inadvertently, an eloquent expression of an acute sense of crisis by one who was supremely aware of the metahistorical possibilities of his age, it is a statement of remarkable import. It encapsulates the increasing bewilderment and mounting fear of catastrophe which was characteristic of so many Elizabethan responses to Ireland. But it gives expression to these feelings not in the banal and ephemeral diatribes of the publicists and men of action, but in a form shaped by a deep poetic vision. . . . In a sense, therefore, the *View* is the quintessential

9. "Edmund Spenser on Justice and Mercy," in *The Writer as Witness: Literature as Historical Evidence*, ed. Tom Dunne, *Historical Studies* 16 (1985): 76–89.

expression of the Tudor experience in Ireland as it declined from the uncritical self-confidence of the reformist 1540s to the bitter disillusion of the 1590s. But if it is representative, it is so only in the special, consummate manner of that emblem of Elizabethan aspirations and anxieties, the *Faerie Queene*. (49)

That is to say, in the consummate manner of the *other* books of *The Faerie Queene*. From the category of complex representation, from being an emblem of Elizabethan aspirations *and* anxieties in the 1590s, book 5 is excluded. This conclusion is of great theoretical interest, marking as it does not just a convergence but a complete exchange between the two disciplines of literary and historical study. Yet it also marks, in my view, one of the dangers inherent in crossing a disciplinary boundary. Brady accepted at face value the accounts of *Faerie Queene* 5 that he found in "standard" works of literary criticism; the danger is that one who crosses over is likely to be unduly influenced by (inadequately skeptical of) verdicts on the other side of the boundary that are, after all, only opinions.

Nonreverential Reading

It is, first, too easy an assumption that Spenser in the 1590s was deeply pessimistic about Ireland, yet still full of nationalist enthusiasm about Tudor England. Whether or not his Irish domicile represented, in any strict sense, a political exile,[10] Spenser left ambiguous the question of whether it should be seen as cultural exile, and whether he felt it to be voluntary. In the autobiographical *Colin Clout's Come Home Againe* (1595) he described how Sir Walter Ralegh had found him there in Kilcolman and persuaded him to return (at least temporarily) to London:

> [He felt] dislyking to my lucklesse lot:
> That banisht had my selfe, like wight forlore,
> Into that waste, where I was quite forgot.
>   (Lines 180–82)

10. While his employment by Lord Grey offered financial security and entrepreneurial opportunities, there exists a strong and still not disproved inference that the publication of his *Shepheardes Calender* in the winter of 1579, with its obvious allusions to the queen's quarrel with Archbishop Grindal and less obvious ones to her unpopular marriage negotiations with Alençon, might well have endangered at least his prospects in England.

This judgment is, significantly, attributed to Ralegh. And the complex pastoral premise of this poem, that Ireland may at one moment seem barbaric beside English courtly sophistication and at the next seem refreshingly innocent beside the English courtly rat race, the "enormities" (line 665) Spenser/Colin witnessed during his 1590 visit, indicates that Spenser's views of Ireland were at very least ambivalent.

The Faerie Queene, though written in that cultural exile, explicitly claims to be a celebration of the Elizabethan moment and continually invokes the queen as its primary reader. The second three books of the poem (published in 1596) are, however, considerably less optimistic than the first three (published in 1590) about the possibilities for national and religious unification, for an ethical or effective international policy, and even about the ethics and efficacy of literary interventions in contemporary culture. Book 5, entitled "The Legend of Justice," but in fact an allegorical account of the relations between law, politics, and economics in sixteenth-century Europe, has indeed proved such a problem for readers who believe that Spenser was an idealist and eulogist of his nation that it has suffered from "almost universal critical disesteem."[11] In the "standard" accounts on which Brady relied, book 5 has been disparaged not only for its brutality, unacceptable to modern readers, but as a falling away of talent and inspiration. For the latter charge, read resistance to its historical density, its insistence on referring to "real" events. Book 5 was an offense against the New Critical taboo (effective for half a century) which denied that historical knowledge was compatible with, let alone necessary to, a literary hermeneutics. Yet even as that doctrine attempted to control the value system of literary studies, criticism revealed its own permeability to historical circumstances. For the modern complaint against brutality, or rather a complaint against that complaint which registers both cultural change and its discontents, one might cite Graham Hough, who remarked in 1962 that "Justice is not a popular virtue in our age and a more or less conscious resentment against

11. T. K. Dunseath, *Spenser's Allegory of Justice in Book V of* The Faerie Queene (Princeton, 1968), 8. This book attempts to recuperate the poem by replacing the interest in the historical allegory ("the solving of historical equations") with a genuinely literary focus on "organic wholeness and thematic unity" (4, 14).

some of its classical forms is one of the current social derangements."[12] The term "derangement" is a particularly interesting substitution (for "arrangement"); and, Hough continued,

> what leaves us disgusted or dissatisfied is that so often *Artegall's* decisions seem harshly mechanical, lacking in insight and clemency. Yet it is idle to pretend that Spenser's Justice is not confronting a real problem. We have seen so much of the appalling corruptions of power in recent years that for us the whole field of executive authority is enveloped in confusion. There are many who deny the legitimacy of punishment altogether. Politically speaking the very words "police action" stink in the nostrils. Yet we all know that without penal authority the operation of justice is a mockery. How much slaughter and misery in the Congo might have been avoided by an early application of the old crude, outmoded colonial whiff of grapeshot? . . . We do not deny the facts, but we feel that Spenser ought to have been more embarrassed by them. It is quite clear that he was not embarrassed by them. He is an unhesitating exponent of the necessity for swift and relentless punishment. This is a point of view that is not in itself disreputable; and there is more to be said for it than is commonly said today. (197)

As contemporary Irish historians wrestle with the *View* in the light of their own preoccupations, so the British critic surveying *The Faerie Queene* in his own time, with a postcolonial dismay enhanced by the unruly 1960s, finds himself divided between different imperatives.

It is probably impossible to operate without a prejudice of one's own. Mine is for assuming less difference between Spenser and ourselves, by postulating both that he might have been embarrassed by the ethical conflicts posed by the colonial experience, and that he was strong-minded enough to give expression—troubling expression—to the contradictions he perceived. Artegall, the chivalric hero of this book, functions both as the Representation of Justice, British style, in the less civilized world surrounding that bossy, upstanding island and, in a series of achronological montages, as the fictional embodiment of several all-too-human representatives of that program: Arthur, Lord Grey, Spenser's employer, accused of excessive violence in Ireland in

---

12. See *A Preface to* The Faerie Queene (London, 1962), 193.

1580–82; Robert Dudley, earl of Leicester, in the Netherlands campaign in 1585, an act of self-aggrandizement for which (in life but not in the poem) he was forced to do public penance; Sir Francis Drake, decimating the Spanish Armada in 1588; and in at least the early stages of his military career (the 1591 campaign in Normandy in support of Henry of Navarre) Robert Devereux, second earl of Essex. In addition, in an episode central to the definition of Justice, the trial of Mary, Queen of Scots, is staged, with Elizabeth herself as Mercilla, the merciful judge, who "would not let just vengeance on her light";[13] yet after a couple of stanzas on the superiority of Mercy to Justice, on how it is "better to reforme, then to cut off the ill" (5.10.2), we learn *en passant* that Elizabeth has bowed to necessity ("strong constraint") and agreed to Mary's execution. At the very least, Spenser's handling of this episode shows that he notices the contradiction between principle and practice. And Artegall experiences enough difficulties and embarrassments in the course of his adventures to make visible, we might say, the gap between Justice in its ideal form and actual political experience; or, to put the same possibility in the terms invoked by Kafka, by the time Spenser finished with her, Astraea, the supernatural patron of this book, "no longer suggested the goddess of Justice, or even the goddess of Victory, but looked exactly like the goddess of the Hunt in full cry." The result *might* be to mark the distance between a sixteenth-century sensibility and our own; or it might, on the contrary, make visible even to sixteenth-century readers the need for Justification, the cultural practice of invoking fictional versions of events when the facts prove difficult to swallow.[14]

It is here that allegory itself comes under interrogation. Those responsible for the regulation of societies usually rely on allegory—that is to say, a stated belief in abstract principles and a

13. Spenser, *The Faerie Queene*, in *The Poetical Works*, ed. E. de Selincourt (Oxford, 1912), 5.9.50.

14. This point is made more conventionally by Jane Aptekar, *Ikons of Justice: Iconography and Thematic Imagery in Book V of* The Faerie Queene (New York and London, 1969), which finds "dubious, ironic undertones" in the Legend of Justice, and produces "iconographical evidence" to suggest we are meant to find Artegall objectionable (6–7). By iconography, however, Aptekar means not political icons employed by the Elizabethan state, but the more academic and esoteric emblem tradition.

system of iconographical representation of those principles—to assist them in their task. Evidently, public symbols are capable not only of standing for but of generating feelings of consensus and loyalty (flags, anthems, the Statue of Liberty, and even modern monarchs are obvious examples). But societies may invoke such symbols *more* frequently when experiencing painful transitions from one belief system to another; subgroups (like teenagers) will knowingly construct their group identity in terms of rival icons; and individuals when threatened will observe the corporate sign system with skepticism, and even subject them to deconstructive analysis. In the opening paragraph of *Amerika* Kafka replaced the torch in the hand of the Statue of Liberty with a sword. I would argue that Spenser, too, was from the start conscious of the limitations of abstract principle as an intellectual response to life in the early modern world, and alert to the tendency noted by Kafka to hand the task of producing the icons of political and judicial theory over to artists, with instructions given or implied. Spenser assumed that role, but not naively. With growing intensity he inspected the distance between abstract ideal and concrete instance; and in book 5 the problem comes to a head. Book 5 is the hard core of Spenser's inquiry into the ideological moves a society makes when it encodes as Platonic Forms necessary protocols and procedures, from organized religion, through socialized sexuality, to ordinary politeness; and in one early episode in book 5, the problematics of the cultural icon itself comes under skeptical scrutiny.

Artegall, as the knight of Justice, has actually been instructed in its principles by the goddess Astraea herself, and his adventures represent, more or less, his attempts to live up to his mandate. His inspiration (one could not call it a tool, for reasons that will appear) is precisely that icon of Justice that Kafka represented as absurd, the balance or scales, and Artegall is trained in its use only in highly abstract terms:

> There she him taught to weigh both right and wrong
> In equall ballance with due recompence,
> And equitie to measure out along,
> According to the line of conscience,
> When so it needs with rigour to dispence.
>
> (5.1.7)

So abstract, indeed, that we are prevented from finding any historically specific content, such as the evolution of the Court of Chancery as an equity court, or the problematic extension of the doctrine of equity during the sixteenth century to the point where it could be seen as infringing on Parliament's role as the supreme lawmaker.[15] In the history of Chancery, "equity" and "conscience" were often used as synonyms, as meaning a corrective, often subjective, to the rigors of rule-based law, and it appears therefore that Artegall has been equipped only with an attractive-sounding but vague doctrine immediately ironized by Spenser's statement that the only opportunity Artegall has had to put it into practice is in the forest, where, "for want there of mankind / She caused him to make experience / Upon wyld beasts" (5.1.7).

It is therefore much to the point, given the *principle* of "equall ballance" in these instructions, that one of the first of Artegall's adventures is an encounter with a figure who has come to be known as the Egalitarian Giant. The challenge the Giant presents to the knight of Justice is that he, too, stands for, argues for, a sort of justice. He actually holds "An huge great paire of ballance in his hand," and intends to wield it in the service of an egalitarian system that he, presumably lacking instruction, has imagined for himself.

If we wish to visualize the giant, we might do so by recalling the fantastic figure on the frontispiece of Hobbes's *Leviathan*, the giant composed of hundreds of tiny human figures; we need only remove his crown and substitute the scales for the raised sword that, in Hobbes's absolutist politics, is the final guarantee of social stability. It appears that Spenser's Giant also represents the Many, though the way in which he represents them is entirely different from the symbolic incorporation proposed by Hollar's engraving.[16] When Artegall and his robot servant Talus arrive at the seashore,

15. For a brief introduction to the relation between "conscience" and "equity," see J. H. Baker, *An Introduction to English Legal History* (London, 1979), 83–95. For the debates over "equity" or judicial construction versus strict adherence to the letter of the statutes, see Baker, ed., *The Reports of Sir John Spelman*, 2 vols. (London, 1978), 2:37–56; *A Discourse upon the Exposicion & Understandinge of Statutes With Sir Thomas Egerton's Additions*, ed. Samuel E. Thorne (San Marino, 1942), 54–67, 76–85.

16. For a summary of the argument in favor of Wenceslaus Hollar as the

> They saw before them, far as they could vew,
> Full many people gathered in a crew;
> Whose great assembly they did much admire.
> For never there the like resort they knew.
> So towards them they coasted, to enquire
> What thing so many nations met, did there desire.
> (5.2.29)

And his project is indeed a *popular* one, in the early modern and usually pejorative sense of that term. He intends to reweigh "equallie" everything in the world, from the natural components of earth and sea to the political entities of "realmes and nations." "For why, he sayd they all unequall were, / And had encroached uppon others share" (5.2.32):

> Tyrants that make men subject to their law,
> I will suppresse, that they no more may raine;
> And Lordings curbe, that commons over-aw;
> And all the wealth of rich men to the poore will draw.
> (5.2.38)

"*Therefore,*" wrote Spenser, "the *vulgar* did about him flocke":

> And cluster thicke unto his leasings vaine,
> Like foolish flies about an hony crocke,
> In hope by him great benefite to gaine,
> And uncontrolled freedome to obtaine.
> (5.2.33)

This emphasis on "great assembly" and a topic of international desire indicates that the confrontation between Knight and Giant is one of the more important in the Legend of Justice, and that we should be wary (though not reverent) in our approach. The task of the reader here (as in many other episodes in *The Faerie Queene*) will be to listen to the arguments of both the knight and the antagonist and to learn from their encounter how to distinguish true justice from its simulacrum. In brief, the Giant will argue that things need to be returned to their original state of equality (the guiding principle of radical movements since the late Middle Ages), and Artegall will argue for the hierarchical

---

engraver, see Arnold A. Rogow, *Thomas Hobbes: Radical in the Service of Reaction* (New York, 1986), 156–59.

status quo. As Thomas Cooper, bishop of Winchester, wrote in 1589 in the first official reply to the Martin Marprelate pamphlets, in the Peasants' Revolt of 1381 those pernicious leveling ideas were already articulate: "At the beginning (say they), when God had first made the world, all men were alike, there was no principality, then was no bondage or villeinage."[17] That is to say, Bishop Cooper and Artegall belong together; both were engaged in debating their adversaries on the structure and sanctions of all social institutions. Yet unlike some of the other episodes where an intellectual temptation is presented in the form of a debate, the knight of Justice is himself incapable of keeping the encounter at the level of persuasion, and in frustration falls back on simple force, permitting his robot servant Talus (the sign of talionic justice) to throw the Giant over a cliff.

From the middle of the nineteenth century onward literary criticism has averred that here Spenser's politics, or at least one aspect of his political theory, is unequivocally displayed. The Giant represents, we have been told, a false, demagogic, and restless populism, an image of the many-headed monster that so many of Spenser's contemporaries invoked as the specter of democracy,[18] against which Spenser would have been all the more resolute as a result of his experiences with the insubordinate Irish.

There is evidence, however, that this assessment has been influenced by the subsequent political history of England and, perhaps more important, France. For example, Artegall's argument for retaining the status quo, that "All change is perillous, and all chaunce unsound," was taken out of context by William Wordsworth in his late, fully reactionary phase, and incorporated into one of the political sonnets written in the late 1830s and in the climate of proposed electoral reform in England: "Perilous

17. Cooper, *An Admonition to the People of England* (London, 1589), ed. R. Arber (1895), 118.

18. See Christopher Hill, "The Many-Headed Monster," in *Change and Continuity in Seventeenth-Century England* (Cambridge, Mass., 1975), 181–204; and Graham Hough, *A Preface*, who finds "a tone of somewhat confused indignation" which "suggests a contemporary target" (194); Hough's own suggestion for the target is the Anabaptists at Munster, who "attracted unfavourable attention in England in 1575." But Spenser himself makes no such connection.

is sweeping change, all chance unsound."[19] In 1845 the Spenserian scholar G. L. Craik first observed:

> If this had been published in the end of the eighteenth instead of the sixteenth century—in the year 1796 instead of in the year 1596—the allegory could not have been more perfect, taken as a poetical representation or reflection of recent events, and of a passage in which the political and social history of the world was generally held to be not more memorable than entirely novel and unexampled. Here is the liberty and equality system of philosophy and government—the portentous birth of the French Revolution—described to the life two hundred years before the French Revolution broke out; described both in its magnificent but hollow show, and its sudden explosion or evaporation.[20]

In other words, Craik too read Spenser's episode retroactively in terms of British anti-Jacobin feeling.[21] It is worth noting, however, that, for Craik, Spenser was *capable* of ideas that, some have argued, were not conceivable until two centuries later. "This," he continues, "is probably one of the instances in which we overrate the advance of modern speculation":

> The system in question was never indeed before attempted to be carried into practice on so large a scale, or so conspicuous a platform, as in the end of the last century in France; but its spirit, though not perhaps its distinct shape, had appeared before in many popular outbreaks, and as an idea it must long have been familiar to thinking men. The principles not only of political philosophy but even of what is called political economy, generally assumed to be wholly a modern science, were the subject of much more attention, and were much more profoundly investigated, in Spenser's age than is commonly supposed.

19. William Wordsworth, "Blest Statesman He," in *Poems*, ed. John Hayden (Harmondsworth, 1977), 819.

20. *Spenser and His Poetry*, 3 vols. (London, 1845, 1871; rpt., New York, 1971), 2:194–95.

21. Compare also H. J. Todd's remark on this episode: "This fiction is an admirable picture of the absurdity of those levelling principles, which have lately made such a noise in the world. See *The Patriot*, a periodical Paper, published in Ireland in the year 1793, and written (it is supposed) by Baron Smith." Cited in *Edmund Spenser: A Variorum Edition*, ed. Edwin Greenlaw et al. (Baltimore, 1932–57), 177.

But modern criticism of Spenser has not adopted this insight about Spenser's foresight; rather, it has retained from Craik's account only the narrower view that the Giant's egalitarianism is intended to be seen as disastrous. To cite just two examples, for Angus Fletcher (literary critic) in 1971 the Giant "misunderstands the basis for a just representation of wealth, which is, according to ancient and Elizabethan thought alike, proportional rather than egalitarian." He "rebels against a constitution[al] authority which is already coherent, logical, and legitimate." And Spenser, Fletcher is confident, "wants to have nothing to do with him."[22] And Brendan Bradshaw (historian), though hostile to what he sees as Spenser's intellectual defense of a "severe" justice, nevertheless defines the Giant dismissively as "a popular demagogue" representing "the forces of anarchy."[23]

Yet while there are clear editorial instructions that the Giant's position is unacceptable—his message is defined as "leasing vaine" and the people "foolish" and misled—there are equally clear narrative and iconic indications that the confrontation between Knight and Giant is not simply a case of right versus wrong. Indeed, one of the central points of the debate is to establish how difficult it is to distinguish *between* right and wrong. At the heart of the interpretative problem here lies the nature of the scales as an icon of justice, or rather the existence of competing versions of the scales, one associated with Artegall and his patron Astraea, the other held by the Giant. Artegall's version is not *held* at all, but is only a symbol out of reach, transcending a fallen world; the Virgin, that is, Astraea, appears as an astrological sign after her departure from earth, "And next her selfe her righteous ballance hanging bee" (5.1.11). When the Giant gets hold of a scales, however, the metaphor of weighing is taken at its word, with disastrous effects on the ideology it supports. The Giant has taken his scales in a fully materialist sense, believing that, since God created the world in number, weight, and measure, it could be reweighed to determine if the original fairness of things was capable of being restored. In so doing, however, the

22. *The Prophetic Moment: An Essay on Spenser* (Chicago and London, 1971), 242–45.
23. "Edmund Spenser on Justice and Mercy," 78.

Giant demonstrates that at root justice is a matter of matter; if at the cosmic level it embraces geography and oceanography, at the social level it encounters economics.

Here the strains within justice as a theory are exhibited as strains on the allegorical system itself, an internal critique of the way allegory, by setting static emblems in narrative motion, is bound to reveal their inherent failures of logic or truthfulness. As Titorelli, by making his Justice winged at the heel, destabilizes the principle of *balance* expressed in the scales, so Spenser, by making his scales material, renders visible the screening of the economic that, starting with Aristotle, the move to abstraction permitted. And, although Spenser does not state the problem in quite this way, he makes it clear that the confrontation between Artegall and the Giant also stands for a confrontation between two ways of conceptualizing justice, the abstract and the applied. Although it is Artegall who delivers the antiliteralist lines "Be not upon thy balance wroken: / For they doe nought but right or wrong *betoken*" (5.2.47), and states that "the eare must be the ballance," it is also Artegall who demands that the Giant weigh abstractions (truth and falsehood, right and wrong) in his materialist scale—a blurring of registers that drives the Giant to distraction in trying to combine incompatible categories.

A reader who does *not* begin with a political bias against the Giant can find this episode destabilizing. With respect to the icon of the scales and the usually unexamined vocabulary we use to conceive justice—as weighing right against wrong, truth against falsehood—old conventions are suddenly rendered inane. This reader finds herself, along with the Giant and Kafka's K, struggling to make sense of an incoherent sign system; and therefore experiences frustration rather than satisfaction when Artegall and Talus break the rules of debate and solve the intellectual problem by using brute force:

> Like as a ship, whom cruell tempest drives
> Upon a rocke with horrible dismay,
> Her shattered ribs in thousand peeces rives,
> And spoyling all her geares and goodly ray,
> Does make her self misfortunes piteous pray.
> So downe the cliffe the wretched Gyant tumbled.
>
> (5.2.50)

Moreover, the simile patently *mourns* the Giant before the official, editorial comment ("So was the high aspyring with huge ruine humbled") can condemn him; more remarkably, the very choice of this image aligns the Giant with Spenser's own project, which at the end of books 1 (12.42) and 6 (12.1) is described as a feat of adventurous and often dangerous navigation, with the poem and its poet themselves represented as the "vessell" of the imagination.[24]

I see this debate about where Justice resides, how it can be determined, and what role symbols play in our conceptualization of these issues, as continued in Spenser's *View of the Present State of Ireland*, which he wrote immediately after delivering the second half of his poem to the press.[25] It is true that the most obvious connection between the two texts occurs at the point where Irenius, in the central part of the tract, advises a campaign

24. At the end of book 1 Spenser wrote:

> Now strike your sailes ye jolly Mariners,
> For we be come unto a quiet rode,
> Where we must land some of our passengers,
> And light this wearie vessell of her lode.
> . . . And then againe abroad
> On the long voyage whereto she is bent:
> Well may she speede and fairely finish her intent.

Book 6, canto 12, begins with another version of the same simile:

> Like as a ship, that through the Ocean wyde
> Directs her course unto one certaine cost,
> Is met of many a counter winde and tyde,
> With which her winged speed is let and crost,
> And she her selfe in stormie surges tost;
> Yet making many a borde, and many a bay,
> Still winneth way, ne hath her compasse lost:
> Right so it fares with me in this long way,
> Whose course is often stayd, yet never is astray.

25. W. L. Renwick, ed., *A View of the Present State of Ireland* (Oxford, 1970), 171, points out that the *View* identifies itself as having been written in England "with a consistency difficult to preserve if the placing were imaginary," and that of the seven dated manuscripts, five give 1596 as the date. It was entered in the Stationers' Register on April 14, 1598, but not published until the Dublin edition of 1633 dedicated to Wentworth, then Charles I's deputy general in Ireland. See *The Historie of Ireland collected by three learned authors*, ed. Sir James Ware (Dublin, 1633), which also contains the tracts of Meredith Hanmer and Edmund Campion.

of extreme military severity to reduce the rebellious Irish, and where book 5 of *The Faerie Queene* turns, in its last canto, to Artegall's attempts to rescue Irena (Ireland) from Grantorto (Great Wrong), "to reforme that ragged common-weale," and "To search out those, that used to rob and steale, / Or did rebell gainst lawfull government" (5.12.26). But if the episode of the Egalitarian Giant destabilizes our definition of Justice early in the book devoted to its exploration, the introductory sections of the *View* (which its detractors tend to ignore or minimize) make fully explicit the conceptual problems which the poem renders fantastic: the uneasy relation between abstract principle and concrete application. And if the egalitarianism of the Giant opens up a larger conceptual frame for what Justice might include, one that represents popular rather than Aristotelian concepts of redistribution and fairness, that too is intimated in the *View*'s anthropological account of the Irish, who corporately might be thought of as the Giant's adherents.

The *View*'s chief speaker, Irenius, is ironically allegorical himself, since his name is an etymological fusion of the ancient name of Ireland with the Greek word for "peace," but his mission is to argue for the complete subjugation of the Irish, if necessary by the sword, a program which involves also the cancellation of their history and culture. But, as is not always remembered, he is not the only speaker. Both Nicholas Canny and Brendan Bradshaw write of the *View* as if Irenius were identical with Spenser; and Ciaran Brady, while acknowledging that it is structured formally as a debate, does everything possible to undo that acknowledgment. Despite the fact that it is Irenius who is responsible for articulating the "Scythianism" of the Gaelic Irish, Brady refers to this section as "Spenser's ethnological views" (29). The other speaker, Eudoxius, is referred to as "the relatively passive partner in the dialogue" (37), and, later and more damagingly, as not a partner at all, as a "straw man," "an artificial construct deployed by Spenser to convince his readers that serious objections to his case had been considered and refuted" (41). "The dialogue form," Brady concludes, "was a decoy." But it is worth noticing the route by which this conclusion is reached, in which Brady lists a series of successful points scored by Eudoxius, of "damaging concessions" admitted by Irenius; and his assumption, finally, that "when this useful creature came too close to wrecking his maker's plan, he was silenced" (41). Given Brady's assumption that Irenius is really Spenser, this *would* be the only possible explanation; but if one were to assume, alternatively, that Spenser himself was genuinely ambivalent about his Irish experiences, then the very existence of these two voices becomes profoundly important,[26] and the concept of "silencing" acquires a different valence. If one reads the dialogue without preconceptions of what Spenser's views *must* have been, the less clear it becomes that Irenius is the only conveyor of authorial opinion, or that he conveys that opinion transparently. Eudoxius (sometimes Eudoxus) is identified by his name as a man of good judgment and/or of good reputation, and he alternates between straight man, feeding Irenius the necessary questions, and independent thinker, who asserts the value of many aspects of Irish culture that Irenius means to suppress.

Folkmotes

One of the Irish customs that Irenius would eradicate is the use of folkmotes, ancient places for public meetings carved out of the landscape or erected of giant stones:[27]

> Iren: There is great use among the Irish to make *great assemblies* together upon a Rath or hill, there to parly (as they say) about matters and wrongs between township and township, or one private person and another, but well I wot and true it hath been oftentimes approved, that in these meetings many mischiefs have been both practised and wrought. For to them do commonly resort all the scum of loose people, where they may freely meet and con-

26. But compare Patricia Coughlan, "Ireland and Incivility in Spenser," in Coughlan, *Spenser and Ireland*, 46–74, who holds that Spenser always maintains a double vision of Ireland, and that this ambivalence *is* expressed in the dialogue form, in which Eudoxius and Irenius "represent the two sides of an *interior* debate Spenser is conducting with himself" (65). This essay was brought to my attention by Thomas Scanlan when my argument was complete; but it is interesting to see that, in a single paragraph (66), Coughlan corroborates the importance of several of the issues I analyze below.

27. Although the *OED* defines *folkmote* as a meeting (event), it seems that Spenser believes, probably following local lore, that the name was given to these places from their ancient purpose. As a result, the topography of Ireland is marked, if you will, with democratic icons built into the landscape.

fer of what they list, which else they could not do without suspicion or knowledge of others. . . . (77; italics added)

It is surely significant that Irenius here uses the same phrase ("great assemblies") that Spenser chose to introduce the Egalitarian Giant, who, we remember, is introduced as surrounded by "Full many people gathered in a crew; / Whose great assembly" Artegal and Talus "did much admire." Eudoxius, true to form, admits that there may have been some abuse of the custom of these public meetings, but questions whether the ancient purpose does not justify the survival of folkmotes—"that people might assemble themselves thereon . . . which seemeth yet to me very requisite." In order to develop his position, Irenius then turns to historical anthropology, distinguishing between the folkmote proper, the square embankments built by the Saxons, and "danerathes," the round fortresses built by the Danes "to gather into in troublesome times" (78). The latter, of course, implies not social mediation but resistance. Eudoxius replies by enhancing the scientific account with the imaginative, in terms that would fit naturally into the opening cantos of *Faerie Queene* 5:

> Ye have very well declared the original of these mounts and great stones encompassed, which some vainly term the old Giants trivets, and think that those huge stones would not else be brought into order or reared up without the strength of Giants, and others as vainly think that they were never placed there by man's hand or art, but only remained there so since the beginning, and were afterwards discovered by the deluge, and laid open by the washing of the waters or other like casualty. But let them dream their own imaginations to please themselves, but ye have satisfied me much better. . . . (79; punctuation mine)

Eudoxius makes it clear, however, that his satisfaction resides in the euhemeral explanation, whereby the work of giants (dreamwork) is explained as a sociohistorical construction, the work of many hands in the service of cultural identity; he continues to insist on the value of places and occasions for self-government, significantly adding the concept of taxation by mutual consent: "it is very needful . . . for the country to gather together when there is any imposition laid upon them, to the which they then all agree," provided that "at those assemblies . . . there be any officers, as constables, bailiffs, or such like, among them" (79).

And Irenius continues to insist on the opposite. The dialogue remains on this issue a standoff; but the democratic position has at least been articulated.

Mantles and Glibs

Two other related Irish customs that Eudoxius defends and Irenius wishes to eradicate are the wearing of mantles and glibs ("a thick curled bush of hair hanging down over their eyes, and monstrously disguising them"). According to Irenius, these habits are related *as* disguises, as covers of subversive activity that prevent the lawmaker from seeing what the Irish are up to. While Eudoxius traces the origin of mantles to antiquity, mentioning the biblical fact that Elijah wore one (which was passed on at his apotheosis to Elisha) and that when Aeneas visited Evander he was entertained in pastoral simplicity by being seated on mantles on the ground, Irenius argues that the mantle is "a house for an outlaw, a meet bed for a rebel, and an apt cloak for a thief." The outlaw "under it covereth himself from the wrath of heaven." The rebel "*wrappeth* his self round and ensconceth himself strongly" in his mantle, and sometimes, "being *wrapped* about their left arm instead of a target," acts as a means of self-defense. The thief can "in his mantle pass through any town or company, being close hooded over his head as he useth from knowledge of any to whom he is endangered"; the wandering Irish woman of ill repute can use her mantle as "a coverlet for hir lewd exercise, and when she hath filled her vessel, under it she can hide both her burden and her blame." As for the hairy glibs, undeterred by Eudoxius' ironic comment that the English these days are wearing their hair longer than the Irish, Irenius complains that "they are fit masks as a mantle is for a thief, for whensoever he hath run himself into that peril of law that he will not be known, he either cutteth off his glib quite, by which he becometh nothing like himself, or pulleth it so low down over his eyes that it is very hard to discern his thievish countenance" (50–53).

One might detect in this argument not only the legislator's instincts for surveillance and dislike of anything that provides cover (the closed society must also be transparent), but also a figurative debate on the merits of censorship versus the strategies used to evade it. In his 1590 preface, Spenser had offered *The Faerie Queene* to the public as a "darke conceit . . . clowdily *enwrapped* in Allegorical devises," that is to say, as a commentary on the Elizabethan regime mantled in an intricate chivalric fashion, and hence "furthest from the daunger of envy, and suspition of present time"; and the very figure to whom that statement was addressed, Sir Walter Ralegh, himself appears in the poem wearing allegorically the name of Sir Timias, the squire who falls hopelessly in love with Belphoebe (Elizabeth) and who responds to her anger by becoming a wild Irishman and appearing "in wretched weeds disguiz'd, / With heary glib deform'd" (4.8.12). It is typical of the poem to enter this startling idea *en passant*, almost as a joke, and it is typical of the tract that Eudoxius expresses his reluctant persuasion against the Gaelic customs in a similar high-spirited manner: "O evil minded man, that having reckoned up so many uses of mantles, will yet wish it to be abandoned. Sure I think Diogenes' dish did never serve his master more turns, notwithstanding that he made his dish his cup, his measure, his waterpot, then a mantle doth an Irishman, but I see they be all to bad intents, and therefore I will join with you in abolishing it" (53).

Bards

It is odd, given Spenser's vocation, that so little attention has been paid to the section in the *View* that deals with the Gaelic poetic tradition. True to form, Irenius attacks the Irish bards and the high esteem in which their society holds them, and Eudoxius replies, in surprise:

> Do you blame this in them, which I would otherwise have thought to have been worthy of good account, and rather to have been maintained and augmented amongst them, than to have been disliked? For I have read that in all ages, poets have been had in special reputation, and that meseemes not without great cause, for besides their sweet inventions and most witty lays, they are always used to set forth the praises of the good and virtuous, and to beat down and disgrace the bad and vicious. . . . So they say that the Lacedemonians were more inclined to desire of honour with the excellent verses of the poet Tyrtaeus, than with all the exhortations of their captains, or authority of their rulers and magistrates. (73)

But it is perhaps no surprise (by now) to discover the direction of Irenius' refutation of this otherwise inarguable point; for the Irish bards, he claims, use their influence in precisely the wrong direction: "whomsoever they find to be most licentious of life, most bold and lawless in his doings, and most dangerous and desperate in all parts of disobedience and rebellious disposition, him they set up and glorify in their rhymes, him they praise to the people, and to young men make an example to follow" (75). One man's rebel is another man's hero. So complex is the representation here that Irenius, in his hopeless endeavor to create a mode of aesthetic evaluation that would not be subject to political relativism, feels called upon to recapitulate an entire lay, so effectively that he seems carried away by the stark energy of the original. "Do you not think, Eudoxus," he asks, "that many of these praises might be applied to men of best desert? Yet are they all yielded to a most notable traitor." This song, he complained, was first sung "unto a person of high degree" and "bought as their manner is for forty crowns" (74–75). Yet in recycling it for a larger audience, Spenser (as distinct from Irenius) is engaged in a curious act of ventriloquism, offering to publish precisely that rebellious message Irenius wishes to silence.

Jus Politicum

At the very least, then, Eudoxius is allowed to articulate an intelligent sympathy for Gaelic culture, and is shown to be capable of identifying its politics as in some sense right and fair. The fact that he is usually persuaded to change his mind under "strong constraint" does not necessarily eradicate from the reader's mind the justice of his position. Admitting this, we can better understand the purpose of the opening sections of the *View*, where Irenius explains that because it is impossible to embody an abstract ideal of justice in a working political system, especially where the governed energetically resist the governors, idealism must give way to pragmatism, absolute principle to local contingency. For example, Irenius is himself capable of describing Brehon law (now to be supplanted) as "a certain rule of right unwritten, but delivered by tradition from one to another, in which there often appeareth great show of *equity* in determining the right between party and party" (5; italics added);[28] that is to say, a *competing* "rule of right" to the one he favors. And he will later make the point brutally explicit:

> for no laws of man *according to the strait rule of right*, are just, but as in regard of the evils they prevent, and the safety of the common weale they provide for. As for example, in the true *balancing* of justice, it is a flat wrong to punish the thought or purpose of any before it be enacted; for true justice punisheth nothing but the evil act or wicked word. Yet by the laws of all kingdoms it is a capital crime to devise or purpose the death of the king. The reason is for that when such a purpose is effected it should be too late to devise of the punishment thereof, and should turn that common weal to more hurt by such loss of their prince, than such punishment of the malefactors; and therefore the law in that case punisheth his thought: for better is a mischief than an inconvenience,[29] so that Jus Politicum, though it be not of itself just, yet by application, or rather necessity, is made just, and this only respect maketh all laws just (21–22; italics added)

As the italicized phrases indicate, this is the logical extension of Artegall's claim that the "doome of right" can take place only "in the mind", and that "the eare must be the ballance, to decree / And judge" the evidence (5.2.47). The pamphlet explains more darkly that "the straight rule of right" is never straight in the real world, but bent to the needs of the situation; and that "in the mind" means at the level of Platonic idealism, whereas what rules in the world as we actually know it is *Jus Politicum*, "not of itself just" but "made just" by necessity. In fact, Irenius himself has no time for the cerebral processing of law. Where Eudoxus suggests that the judge, when an ambiguous case "cometh before him to trial, may easily decide this doubt and lay open the intent of the law by his better discretion" (that is to say, by applying the notions of equity and conscience), Irenius replies that "it is dangerous to leave the sense of law unto the reason or will of the judges who are men and may be miscarried by affections

28. To a modern reader, it is tempting to see a certain irony in his subsequent complaint that Brehon law is "repugning quite both to God's law and man's" in permitting a financial compounding for murder instead of capital punishment.

29. "Inconvenience" is a legal term for the social or public cost of a given law; it is to be distinguished from a "mischief," a cost to an individual, and is ubiquitous in the *View*. I owe this information to Thomas Scanlan.

and many other means, but the laws ought to be like to stony tables, plain, steadfast, and unmoveable" (33).

This word "unmoveable" establishes another connection between the two debates we are conflating, for the concept of (re)distributive justice must structurally be linked to the problem of change. When Artegall prohibits the Egalitarian Giant from daring to weigh the world anew in his all-too-material scales, he insists that "All change is perillous, and all chaunce unsound." The origin of this statement is, surely, the seventh book of Plato's *Laws*,[30] where, in the context of regulating children's games, the first item in the program of cultural surveillance that will ultimately embrace all literature and drama, the Athenian delivers his position on change:

> Change—except when it is change from what is bad—is always, we shall find, highly perilous [σφαλερώτατον], whether it be change of seasons, of prevailing winds, of bodily regimen, of mental habit, or, in a word, change of anything whatever without exception, except in the case I have just mentioned, change from bad. . . . When men have been brought up under any system of laws and that system has, by some happy providence, persisted unchanged for long ages, so that no one remembers or has ever heard of a time when things were otherwise than as they are, the whole soul is filled with reverence and afraid to make any innovation on what was once established. A lawgiver, then, must contrive one device or another to secure this advantage.[31]

These convictions Spenser gives to Artegall, whom, however, he clearly represents as distorting the empirical evidence in the world around him. Artegall rejects the Giant's premise that change has occurred since the first divine measurements were taken. Not only is the earth "immoveable" in the center of the universe, he claims, but all the other elements know "their certaine bounde. . . . And mongst them al no change hath yet beene found" (5.2.35, 36). From this premise Artegall draws a sociopolitical conclusion. As part of his immutable plan, God "maketh

30. I agree with Bradshaw that Plato's *Laws* is part of Spenser's intellectual building material; I do not agree that to find a source is to find *agreement* with the source. One may just as likely encounter adaptation or serious critique.

31. Plato, *Laws* 7.797e–798b, from *The Collected Dialogues of Plato*, ed. Edith Hamilton and Huntington Cairns (New York, 1961), 1369–70.

Kings to sit in sovereignty; / He maketh subjects to their powre obay" (5.2.41). Yet this position flagrantly contradicts the narrator's clear statements in the Proem (stanza 4):

> Me seemes the world is runne quite out of square,
> From the first point of his appointed sourse,
> And being once amisse growes daily wourse and wourse.
> . . .
> Right now is wrong, and wrong that was is right,
> As all things else in time are chaunged quite.

If Artegall cites Plato's *Laws* on the subject of avoiding change, the *View* implies that the *Laws* provides the harsh model for Irenius' social engineering. Indeed, Irenius seems to allude explicitly to early phases of that dialogue when stating the pragmatic basis of law and the impossibility of establishing absolute principles:

> laws ought to be fashioned unto the matters and condition of the people to whom they are meant, and not to be imposed upon them according to the simple rule of right, for then as I said instead of good they may work ill, and pervert justice to extreme injustice: For he that would transfer the laws of the Lacedemonians to the people of Athens should find a great absurdity and inconvenience: For those laws of Lacedemon were devised by Lycurgus, as most proper and best agreeing with that people, whom he knew to be inclined altogether to wars, and therefore wholly trained them up even from their cradles in arms and military exercises clean contrary to the institution of Solon, who in his laws to the Athenians laboured by all means to temper their warlike courages with sweet delights of learning and sciences. (11)[32]

But Spenser also raises the problem of change in relation to legal reconstruction in a way that recalls and ironizes (pun intended) the Athenian lawgiver's adamancy. Irenius opens the topic with the innocuous statement that structural change, for which he

32. This is a condensed version of the debate that occupies *Laws* 1.625e–630. Similarly, the reference to Tyrtaeus in the discussion of the Irish bards is probably an ironic allusion to *Laws* 9.858e, where an analogy is drawn between the "bad precepts" for living that are derived from "Homer, or Tyrtaeus," and the good rules (which, however, need to be alluringly written) of the legislator.

uses the usually stigmatic term "innovation," is required when the laws no longer fit the times, when it is necessary to change *back* to an earlier order. Eudoxius, however, warning against too much or too violent social engineering, suggests instead an ameliorist approach: "not as ye suppose to begin all as it were anew and to alter the whole form of the government, which how dangerous a thing it is to attempt, you yourself must needs confess. . . . For all *innovation is perilous*" (94). The views of these two dialogians therefore repeat, but in unexpected combinations, those of the two antagonists in *Faerie Queene* 5, canto 2. While Eudoxius shares with the Giant a belief in the political principles of public discussion and self-determination, it is he who repeats Artegall's statement that "all change is perillous" and rejects the possibility that one could "alter the whole form of the government." Eudoxius therefore identifies himself as a liberal reformer. On the other hand, Irenius' commitment to what he regards as a necessary "innovation" (complete sociopolitical reconstruction) connects him linguistically but paradoxically (since his own social theory is anything but egalitarian) to the Giant, whose followers, deprived of his leadership,

> gan to gather in tumultuous rout,
> And mutining, to stirre up civill faction,
> For certaine losse of so great expectation.
> For well they hoped to have got great good,
> And wondrous riches by his *innovation*.
> (5.2.51; italics added)

The witty exchange that Spenser here accomplishes suggests at the least that *terms* like "innovation" are unreliable as the ground of political theory; one man's dangerous innovation is another's urgently needed reform. More important, it connects the specifically Irish argument to the broader sociopolitical one. The distinction Irenius draws between the now-civilized English and the barbarous Irish is really no distinction. The English have reached the calm that they have "by how many civil brawls, by how many tumultuous rebellions, that even hazard oftentimes the whole safety of the kingdom" (12). The Irish, still rebellious, are not insensate. They have their own political principles: "the laws themselves they do specially rage at and rend in pieces as most repugnant to their liberty and natural freedom" (12).

Eudoxius, by further generalization, destroys the last distinction between the rebellious Irish and popular, class-based protest:

> It is then a very unseasonable time to plead law, when swords are in the hands of the vulgar, or to think to retain them with fear of punishments, when they look after liberty and shake off all government. (12)

Spenser and the Postmodernists

It might be supposed that recent changes in literary studies would have proved more receptive to the complex message that, I argue, Spenser was transmitting in the later 1590s. Not so. Ironically, when contemporary critics pick up the same disturbing signals that led Brady to call the *View* incoherent and Hough to call Spenser inept in dealing with the Egalitarian Giant, they seem to work even harder, to provide only more sophisticated reasons, why we should not imagine the disturbance intentional. Thus David Baker has argued that Spenser did not get permission to publish the *View* in 1598 because "he misjudged the effect his text would have on its intended readers—and those readers, for their part, misread (or disregarded) his intent."[33] For Baker, the *View* was intended to be read as royalist polemic, but it failed because the authorities were suspicious readers and detected in it "a tacit critique of English legal verities." Citing Irenius on the need for "stony tables," Baker remarks:

> If these lines are ironic—and I do not think they are intentionally so—it is because the dialogue they are set within can be read as a circuitous demonstration that law in Elizabeth's colony cannot be plain, steadfast, and unmoveable, that, for the English, Ireland has become a chaos of legal ambiguity, subversive equivocation, and pervasive uncertainty. (152)

For Baker, Spenser "did not distrust his ideological language and could not have 'spoken' any other, but he could sense, and lead his suspicious readers to sense, that in Ireland another tongue was spoken and another truth given voice" (161). This is the furthest that Baker will go in admitting that Spenser's official readers were right to be suspicious; and his argument may be recognized

---

33. " 'Some Quirk, Some Subtle Evasion': Legal Subversion in Spenser's *A View of the Present State of Ireland,*" *Spenser Studies* 6 (1985): 150.

as another version of Brady's formula for the *View,* that it is "deliberately and inadvertently, an eloquent expression of an acute
sense of crisis." But where does inadvertence end and delibera-
tion begin? Baker correctly intuited that the *View* is a troublesome
and far from transparent document (and his essay is a refresh-
ing shift away from critical orthodoxy); but he fell victim, apparently, to a fashionable shibboleth derived ultimately from
Marx—that individuals are incapable of penetrating the sealed
dome of ideology under which they are born.

By the same token, the problems evident in Spenser's treatment of the Giant versus Artegall were placed by Stephen Greenblatt in the general context of "peasant rebellions" and disposed
of in what has come to be known as the theory of containment.[34] Taking for granted that "the great ruling class night-
mare in the Renaissance" was "the marauding horde, the many-
headed multitude, the insatiate, giddy, and murderous crown"
(5), Greenblatt tried to come to terms with evidence to the contrary. He acknowledged "the uncanny resemblance between the
Giant's iconographic sign and Artegall's" and "the still more uncanny resemblance between the Giant's rhetoric and Spenser's
own." But this perplexity, we are told, "is not an embarrassment
but a positive achievement, for Spenser's narrative can function
as a kind of training in the rejection of subversive conclusions
drawn from licensed moral outrage" (22). Freud's "uncanny" is
offered as a vaguely psychological substitute for ambivalence,
let alone for a theory of conscious intention. Quoting with satisfaction Spenser's image of the Giant tossed over the cliff by
Talus, Greenblatt decided that Talus' violence "exorcises" "the
potentially dangerous social consequences—the praxis—that
might follow from Spenser's own eloquent social criticism." It
would be so much simpler, I aver, to imagine that Spenser's own
eloquent social criticism was being expressed, all the more elo-
quently for its symptomatic evasion of censorship, in the enigmatic forms he thought he could get away with. It is not for nothing that the last stanza of *The Faerie Queene* refers to "a mighty
Peres displeasure" and concludes with an ironic piece of advice
to himself:

34. "Murdering Peasants: Status, Genre, and the Representation of
Rebellion," *Representations* 1 (1983): 1–29.

Therfore do you my rimes keep better measure,
And seeke to please, that now is counted wiseman's
threasure.

I am not suggesting that Spenser was opposed to the policy
of Irish subjugation that the *View* as a whole promotes. There is
ample evidence in his defense of Lord Grey and the *Brief Note
of Ireland* (if indeed correctly attributed to him)[35] that he saw no
other alternative. The colony was in too much danger. But it is
a mistake to believe he was *comfortable* with this final solution,
or only inadvertently revelatory of the contradictions in the ideology of Justice that appear in both the Legend of Justice and the
View. He is prepared to argue for violent suppression, but only
on the naked grounds of necessity. When Eudoxius asks how his
reforms are to be begun, Irenius replies, "Even by the sword"
(95); and when questioned as to whether such "violent redress"
is necessary, he backs away into allegory:

> by the sword which I named I do not mean the cutting off of all
> that nation with the sword, which far be it from me that ever I
> should think so desperately or wish so uncharitably, but by the
> sword I mean the royal power of the prince, which ought to stretch
> itself forth in her chief strength, to the redressing and cutting off
> of those evils which I before blamed, and not of the people which
> are evil; for evil people by good ordinance and government may
> be made good, but *the evil that is of itself evil will never become good*.
> (95; italics added)

This sudden relapse into allegory and emblem indicates the ulti-
mate dilemma of all serious inquiry into the nature of justice;
when pragmatic thinking throws up into consciousness the
naked realities of opposed interests and unequal power relations,

35. Like the *View*, the *Note* was submitted to the Privy Council, but it requests
the queen to take pity on the English colonists rather than on the Irish: "our
feare is leste your Maiestes wonted mercifull minde should againe be wrought
to your wonted milde courses." See *The Works of Edmund Spenser*, ed. Edwin
Greenlaw et al. (Baltimore, 1932–57), 9:241–2. Jean Brink has pointed out to
me that both Violet Hulbert ("Spenser's Relation to Certain Documents on
Ireland," *MP* 34 [1936–37]: 345–53) and W. L. Renwick doubted Spenser's
authorship, the first on the grounds of discrepancies of attitude between the
Note and the *View*, the second on the grounds of style.

the impulse is to invoke some supervening and essentialist system of value ("the evil that is of itself evil") to shield oneself from the full implications of pragmatism and realism.[36] The heart of the matter, however, is whether one is capable of self-consciousness about that temptation, especially when it is also the practice of one's government, and if so, whether that skeptical self- and social consciousness was available in early modern England. I believe that it was. What *Spenser* showed in the *View* was the spectacle of Irenius caught in the act of apologetic icon making; it is not quite as explicit as K.'s encounter with Titorelli, but given Spenser's circumstances it is more iconoclastic than we have been taught to expect.

If the subordinate icon of the *View*, then, is the folkmote, the "old Giants trivets," the dominant icon remains the sword.[37] But even this is problematic. For reasons of gender Elizabethan iconography did not permit such a representation in the strong visual terms available to Hobbes.[38] As John King has shown in his study of Tudor political iconography, Elizabeth herself,

36. Contrast, however, Ciaran Brady's interpretation of this passage: The sword "served symbolically to represent the power of the magistrate or indeed the divine order, as a metaphor for rigour, a cutting edge, as an image of sheer power unrestrained by convention, and of course it also denoted an instrument of mortal violence . . . . It is through such a subtle process of assertion, qualification, abstraction and reaffirmation that Spenser seeks to induce his readers to accept the violence which is about to be proposed, while allowing them to evade the moral consequences of such acceptance" "Reply," *Past and Present*, no. 120 (1988): 215.

37. It was this aspect of the *View* which Milton invoked against the Irish who "by their endlesse treasons and revolts have deserv'd to hold no Parlament at all, but to be govern'd by Edicts and Garrisons." See his *Articles of Peace made and concluded with the Irish Rebels* (1649), in *Complete Prose Works*, ed. D. M. Wolfe et al., 8 vols. (New Haven, 1953–80), 3:303. But it was also this Spenser whom Milton appropriated for *Eikonoklastes*, in wishing for "a man of iron, such as Talus, by our Poet Spencer, . . . fain'd to be the page of Justice" (3:390) to assist him in his own campaign *against* the institution of monarchy.

38. Some have argued that *Leviathan*'s frontispiece tactically combined the features of Charles II and Cromwell. See Keith Brown, "The Artist of the *Leviathan* Title-Page," *British Library Journal* 4, no. 9 (1978): 34; and Rogow, *Thomas Hobbes* 159–60. The theory that Cromwell was represented was first introduced in 1842 by W. Whewell, in his *Lectures on the History of Moral Philosophy* (London, 1841), 21.

though sometimes accompanied in portraits by the sword of Justice, is not actually represented as holding it.[39] When Spenser himself represents her as Mercilla in *Faerie Queene* 5, he describes that same sword, rusted, underneath her feet (5.9.30); though he adds the possibility that "when as foes enforst, or friends sought ayde, / She could it sternely draw." In the *View*, however, Spenser acknowledged that those lines were inevitably a metaphor for the military agency of others. The pamphlet requires the existence of a male figure who would wield the sword of victory and pursue the hunt if the queen would only let him: Robert Devereux, second earl of Essex, who, though unnamed, is clearly indicated: "being himself most steadfast to his sovereign Queen, his country coasting upon the South Sea, stoppeth the ingate of all that evil which is looked for, and holdeth in all those which are at his back with the terror of his greatness" (94).[40] But Essex is unnamed for a reason. As Richard McCoy reminds us, Elizabeth was already disturbed by the large number of knighthoods Essex conferred on those who accompanied him on the Cadiz expedition, thereby increasing his own popularity; and in October 1596 Francis Bacon had already defined the earl as a "man of nature not to be ruled; of an estate not grounded to his greatness; of a popular reputation; of a military dependence." "I demand," Bacon continued, "whether there can be a more dangerous image than this represented to any monarch living, much more to a lady, and of her Majesty's apprehensions?"[41] It is highly likely that Spenser already knew of her displeasure when he published (in the fall of 1596, in the wake

39. *Tudor Royal Iconography: Literature and Art in an Age of Religious Crisis* (Princeton, 1989), 263–65.

40. Renwick "takes it"that Spenser means the earl of Ormond, bu the phrase "coasting upon the South Sea" can only refer to Essex, who in 1596, when the *View* was written, achieved the capture of Cadiz and established himself as a popular military hero. Renwick does acknowledge that the concluding reference to "such an one . . . upon whom the eye of all England is fixed and our last hopes now rest" is probably Essex. Most important, he acknowledges that in 1596 another invasion by Spain was daily expected in Ireland, "until it was forestalled by the Cadiz expedition" (182).

41. McCoy, *The Rites of Knighthood: The Literature and Politics of Elizabethan Chivalry* (Berkeley and Los Angeles, 1989), 88.

of Cadiz)[42] the penultimate and gratuitous stanza of *Prothalamion*, with its praise of "a noble Peer, / Great *Englands* and the Worlds wide wonder, / Whose dreadfull name, late through all Spaine did thunder." If not yet unambiguously of a rebellious disposition, there were already aspects of gigantism in Essex's campaign for the popular imagination that rendered him a risky hero for this bard to extoll.

The Sword or the Pen

In conclusion, I propose that Spenser's Legend of Justice and his *View* were participating in a contemporary struggle for control over the idea of Justice that went far beyond Ireland in its implications. At the center of that struggle was the question with which we began: what could be thought, spoken, and published in early modern England, and especially in the last, increasingly tense years of Elizabeth's reign? Nothing sharpened that issue more than the Martin Marprelate controversy of 1589/90, which when Spenser returned to London in the winter of 1589 to offer the first instalment of his epic to the queen and see it through the press would have been the talk of the town.

In the previous chapter I established at least a home-county connection between Shakespeare and Job Throkmorton, the leading writer and entrepreneur in the Marprelate campaign. There are other interesting Throkmorton connections. Job's uncle was Sir Nicholas Throkmorton, who successfully defended himself, showing great (and skeptical) legal expertise, against charges of complicity in Sir Thomas Wyatt's rebellion against Mary in 1553, and whose trial became a classic case in the theory of jury independence. Job Throkmorton was, moreover, a cousin of Elizabeth Throkmorton, whose secret marriage to Sir Walter Ralegh led to his banishment from court (and so to Spenser's representation of this episode in *The Faerie Queene*, where Ralegh appears wearing his Irish glib); Job Throkmorton shared Spenser's admi-

---

42. William A. Oram et al., eds., *Shorter Poems of Edmund Spenser* (New Haven and London, 1989), 755, point out that the double wedding of Elizabeth and Katherine Somerset took place on November 8, 1596, and that the double betrothal must have been celebrated at Essex House after Essex's return from Spain on August 7, and before the court moved from Greenwich on October 1.

ration for, and perhaps connections with, the Leicester family.[43] And in *The just censure and reproofe of Martin Junior* (July 1589), familiarly known as *Martin Senior*,[44] Throkmorton interestingly, and amusingly, represents John Aylmer, bishop of London, who had been one of Spenser's targets in *The Shepheardes Calender*,[45] as setting on his pursuivants to ever more rigorous pursuit of the Martinists and their supporters, among whom, rumor has it, is the earl of Essex. Alymer himself will "take order also, that the Court may be watching to disperse, or reade these libelles there":

> And in faith I thinke they doe my Lord of Essex great wrong, that say, he favours Martin: I do not think he will be so unwise, as to favour these, who are enemies unto the state. For if hee doe, her majestie, I can tell him, will withdraw her gratious favour from him. (A4r)[46]

There were thus a number of strong reasons why Spenser would have been more than ordinarily interested in the Marprelate controversy; and he may even have known, through the Ralegh connection, the identity of Martin himself.

As I have shown, Throkmorton was instrumental in developing a *theory* of the petition signed by many hands as a new and powerful expression of the popular voice. His appeal to "al the Puritans in the land, both lordes, knights, gentlemen, ministers,

---

43. See Carlson, *Martin Marprelate, Gentleman*, 238: "He was an admirer of Robert Dudley, the earl of Leicester, and of his older brother, Ambrose Dudley, earl of Warwick."

44. [Job Throkmorton], *The Just Censure and Reproofe of Martin Junior. Wherein the Rash and Undiscreete Headines of the Foolish Youth, Is Sharply Mette with, and the Boy Hath His Lesson Taught Him, I Warrant You, by His Reverend and Elder Brother, Martin Senior, Sonne and Heire unto the Renowmed Martin Mar-prelate the Great* (Wolston, Warwickshire, 1589).

45. Aylmer is represented in the *July* eclogue as the shepherd Morrell, and we are told the poem is written in "disprayse of proude and ambitious Pastours. Such as Morell is here imagined to bee."

46. Robert Codrington, the seventeenth-century biographer of Essex, records an event, perhaps legend, perhaps true, whereby, when the queen was inveighing against one of the first Martinist pamphlets, Essex plucked the offending book from under his cloak, exclaiming, "Why, then, what will become of me?" See Codrington, *The Life and Death of the Illustrious Robert, Earl of Essex*, in *The Harleian Miscellany*, ed. William Oldys and Thomas Park (London, 1808), 1:219. Cited in Ritchie Kendall, *The Drama of Dissent: The Radical Poetics of Nonconformity, 1380–1590* (Chapel Hill, 1986), 173.

and people, to become joint suiters in one supplication unto her Majestie, and the Lords of her honorable privie counsell" (C3r, v) imagines unanimity across class boundaries and an intervention by a "great assembly" in the interest of a new system of justice. This imagination is, as it were, given human form in Spenser's vision of the Egalitarian Giant. Likewise, Matthew Sutcliffe's complaint that "law is now accounted disorder, and faction and tumult, termed reformation" matches, from the opposite viewpoint, Spenser's destabilization of the language of justice in both *Faerie Queene* 5 and the *View*. Indeed, Sutcliffe attempted to maintain control over the crucial Spenserian term "innovation," which in the program of Elizabeth's higher clergy on the defensive must be stigmatically differentiated from "true" reformation:

> By these I doe see, that it sorteth well, that men that desire *innovation* shoulde speake against lawes. . . . which cannot be without a dangerous *innovation* of state . . . Good men desire reformation of manners by execution of good lawes, and supplie of imperfect: They stand for the state, they withstand all *innovations*, they proceede orderly. These fellowes contrariwise seeke the overthrowe of infinite lawes, of infinite officers: and that by revelling and disorder.[47]

Like Artegall, Sutcliffe accuses his opponent of planning destabilization: "of a certaine state to make a most uncertaine and wavering state, and to overthrowe the most excellent studie of the civill lawes, yea civilitie it selfe; to bring in barbarisme." In most contemporary criticism, Spenser is identified with Artegall, and, it must therefore follow, with Sutcliffe. Myself, I prefer to believe that Spenser was, in his view of the function of writing, closer to the canny petitioner (who was fully aware of the ambiguity inhering in the great stroke to be accomplished by the hundred thousand hands) than he was to the vituperative dean. As for Throkmorton's alternative icon—a hundred thousand hands signing the petition, a hundred thousand *writers* condensed into

47. Matthew Sutcliffe, *An Answere to a Certaine Libel Supplicatorie, or rather Diffamatory, and also to certaine Calumnious Articles, and Interrogatories, both printed and scattered in secret corners, to the slaunder of the Ecclesiasticall state, and put forth under the name and title of a Petition directed to her Majestie* (London, 1592), 47, 68, 76–77; italics added.

a single "great stroke" of the pen—it is a great image from the 1590s, one to be superimposed on the kingly giant from *Leviathan* who stands in our minds as the emblem of absolutist theory, an uplifted sword in his right but not his writing hand. In our own time, it is an image entirely consistent with that from the 1990s, of the huge crowds, led by intellectuals, who peaceably demanded the complete reconstruction of their societies, and who have given us, for all the enormous difficulty of the task, an Eastern Europe about which Kafka might have written differently.

5

The Small Cat Massacre: Popular Culture in the 1587 "Holinshed"

More then ten Hollensheads, or Halls, or Stowes,
Of triviall household trash he knowes.
>   John Donne, *Satire 4*, ca. 1597

Vast, vulgar Tomes . . . recover'd from out of innumerable Ruins.
>   Edmund Bolton, *Hypercritica*, ca. 1610

Voluminous Holingshead . . . full of confusion, and commixture of unworthy relations.
>   Peter Heylyn, *Microcosmus*, 1639

In the 1587 edition of "Holinshed's" *Chronicles*, in a section subsequently excised by order of the Privy Council, there is a description of the celebrations in London that followed the apprehension of the Babington Plot conspirators. The chronicler (who at this point in the narrative seems to have been Abraham Fleming) puts great emphasis on the popular consensus against the conspirators, and claims the occasion as a moment of social harmony, a festival of which the government would approve:

> Beyond this the well affected of the citie did passe certeine degrees: for besides that some wearied themselves with pulling at the bellropes, which were roong both daie and night, as upon the daie of hir maiesties coronation; so other devised a further testification of joie, insomuch that although wood was then at a sore extent of price, yet they spared not their stacks or piles, were the same little or great; but brought (we thinke in conscience)

117

everie house a portion, where fires might conveniently be made and without danger. Memorandum that none were more forward herein than *the meaner sort of people,* who rather than they would omit to ad little or much to a fire, being unprovided of fuell, parted with a penie or two to buie a few stiks by retaile. Insomuch that now *by common consent this action grew to be generall.*[1] (italics added)

An important part of the effect here is that of personal reportage and eyewitness testimony; the "generall" distribution of the bonfires is "by count of the writer hereof, who went of purpose to view them, and indeed did note them all." As is well known, this technique is of great antiquity in claiming authenticity for a historical work. It is used throughout those parts of the *Chronicles* that deal with the reigns of recent monarchs, Henry VIII, Edward VI, Mary Tudor, and Elizabeth. And since many eyewitnesses were involved, either the author-compilers themselves or the original authors of documents the chroniclers chose to include, the total effect of all these first-person testimonies is highly complex and interesting. In contemporary critical terminology we would call this effect "multivocality."

Another marked feature of this passage, however, is that of editorial foregrounding (with a literal "Memorandum") what is especially to be noted. There is, as has often been observed with disapproval, a great deal of editorializing in the *Chronicles,* and its general tenor (the delivery of lessons on political obedience) has not unreasonably given the impression that this, the most ambitious of the Tudor chronicles, was designed primarily in the service of the Elizabethan state. We need, however, to look a great deal closer at the relationship between what we might call the "official" position represented by the editorial interventions, and the many other voices whose intonations and opinions the *Chronicles* have recorded for posterity. In this case, the editorial voice wishes the reader especially to note the concurrence in these festivities of "the meaner sort of people."

This is to be seen, then, as an event of popular culture in the early modern sense of the term "popular," which was usually

1. *Holinshed's Chronicles of England, Scotland, and Ireland,* 6 vols. (London, 1808; rpt., New York, 1965), 4:899–900. For the reader's convenience, I shall cite this edition rather than the three-volume sixteenth-century one.

stigmatic. The central message is carried by the traditional phrase "by common consent," which, along with the similar "with one consent," had since the late Middle Ages carried a strong valence of self-determination by the people at large, a possibility which the conservative forces in government and society were determined at all costs to avoid. Literary and extraliterary documents abundantly testify to the hostile pressure *against* the popular, to the extent that modern readers have all too often been persuaded, not only that popular culture was insignificant as a political force, but that those who disparaged it themselves represented a consensus; for a majority, statistically, they clearly could not. Yet here, in the 1587 *Chronicles*, popular culture and its capacity for producing group action is, we might say, held harmless: invoked to support the chronicler's claim (at least on the surface of his text) that the nation is united in concern for the safety of the queen and the Protestant religion, and that it benefits from the natural expressions of exuberance of the underclasses. This sector of society is to be included in the climax to which the 1587 *Chronicles* drew, the executions of the Babington conspirators and, for conspiring with them against Elizabeth, the trial of Mary, Queen of Scots. Without this "common consent," which would also, at another level, be demonstrated in the petitions presented by the House of Commons to Elizabeth for the maximum sentence upon Mary, the story will not work.

I shall argue in this chapter that we need to pay much more attention than scholarly protocols have hitherto permitted to the role of popular culture in the 1587 *Chronicles*, which itself pays close and even obsessive attention to material (as my three epigraphs indicate) others regarded or professed to regard as vulgar, trivial, and unworthy. The result should be doubly beneficial: both in producing a better understanding of what "Holinshed's" *Chronicles*, that leviathan of the press, really contributed to Elizabethan cultural statement; and also in revealing some of the gaps and biases in our own academic enterprises.

The representation of popular culture in the 1587 *Chronicles* is important on several accounts. In the first place, it suggests an anthropological concern shared by several of the compilers that bears interesting comparison to contemporary work in cultural anthropology; in particular, the theories of "thick description" articulated by Clifford Geertz[2] and of underclass codes of resistance by James C. Scott.[3] Many of the passages added to the 1587 edition of the *Chronicles* have the effect both of thickening the description of events under inspection with a rich brew of mundane detail, including demotic humor, and of showing that "the meaner sort of people" developed their own forms of resistance to governmental controls and official ideology. For if in the public celebrations when the Babington conspirators were apprehended the emphasis falls on consensus, elsewhere the *Chronicles* more often preserve the record of popular dissent. We need to look with respectful eyes at this record, which can give substance to the belief that doing "cultural history" for the early modern period is both possible (without invoking analogies from premodern cultures in exotic parts of the word) and, as compared to other forms of historical inquiry, likely to give different results.

Second, and as part of the same corrective, a fresh look at what the author-compilers chose to include should result in a new evaluation of the work and its principles of construction. Judged by the standards of modern historiography, both editions of the *Chronicles*, appearing in 1577 and 1587 respectively, have usually been regarded as baggy and undisciplined, erratic in their coverage, overzealous in their inclusion of the full texts of primary documents, lacking the analytical and structural skills of the continental historians, and overtly propagandistic and moralizing. As F. J. Levy put it, in what is still our major study of Tudor historiography:

> There was no conception of history writing as selective: a historian did not remake the past in his own image or in any other but instead reported the events of the past in the order in which they occurred. The criterion by which a historian was judged was the quantity of information he managed to cram between the covers of his book; if the matter of quality arose at all, it was relevant to

2. See "Thick Description: Toward an Interpretive Theory of Culture," in his *The Interpretation of Cultures* (New York, 1973), 3–30.

3. See *Weapons of the Weak: Everyday Forms of Peasant Resistance* (New Haven and London, 1985).

accuracy. Once facts could be established as equal in authenticity, they were assumed to be equal in all other ways as well.[4]

In a more recent unpublished paper (which I am grateful to have been allowed to see, and to push against) Levy still sees Holinshed's *Chronicles* as the product of a transition between providential history and the new, humanist methods, which results in incoherence. Holinshed was "plagued with discordant, almost irreconcilable authorities," an excess of source material, and, it is implied, a level of interpretative indecision that "came close to abdicating [moral] responsibility altogether." "This was to leave the reader to be his own historian." Abraham Fleming, the source of the most evident moralizations added in 1587, "exacerbated the situation, for he insisted on the importance of understanding the whole picture while simultaneously blurring its outlines." "Thus," Levy concluded, "the book which goes by the name of Holinshed—and especially its 1587 edition—may be seen as a palimpsest, with each layer written over the incomplete erasure of the one below." And he cites in support of this position both Peter Heylyn's and Edmund Bolton's later assessments: Heylyn's "voluminous Holingshead . . . full of confusion, and commixture of unworthy relations," and Bolton's more generalized critique of the Tudor chronicles: "Vast, vulgar Tomes [which] seem to resemble some huge disproportionable Temple . . . in which store of rich Marble, and many most goodly Statues, Columns, Arks, and antique Peices, recover'd from out of innumerable Ruins, are here and there in greater Number then commendable order erected."

There are several problems with this evaluation, not least in their reliance on the negative judgments of seventeenth-century commentators. While Donne's allusion to the "triviall household trash" that Elizabethan chronicles contain is almost certainly ironic, for reasons that will appear in my next chapter, Heylyn's is a rhetorical gesture clearing the historiographical field of competitors, and Bolton's is riddled with class prejudice. Following a lament that the Tudor chronicles had been initiated by commercial printers, rather than by royal commission, Bolton cited with approval Sir Henry Savile's epistle dedicating his own translation of Tacitus to Elizabeth. "Our Historians (saith the Knight) being of the Dregs of the Common People, while they have

4. See *Tudor Historical Thought* (San Marino, 1967), 168.

endeavourd to adorn the Majesty of so great a Work, have stain'd and defiled it with most fusty foolerys."[5]

This is not the place for a full sociological analysis of the "authors" of the *Chronicles*, but some explanation as to what Savile and Bolton were disdaining is in order. The conception of this massive work is credited to a printer, Reginald or Reyner Wolfe, originally from Strassburg, who planned to produce a universal history. Raphael Holinshed, who was university educated and had entered the clergy, was employed by Wolfe as a translator; and when Wolfe died in 1573, the project was taken over by three publishers, George Bishop and John and Luke Harrison, who employed Holinshed to finish it with the assistance of William Harrison and Richard Stanihurst. The first edition appeared in 1577. When Holinshed himself died in 1580, the publishers' team expanded, in order to produce a new edition, to include Ralph Newberie, Henry Denham, and Thomas Woodcock, and the team of historians or antiquaries now contained John Hooker, alias Vowell, Abraham Fleming, Francis Boteville, otherwise known as Thynne, and John Stow. The new edition appeared in January 1587.[6] In addition to a formal "Continuation" of the history from the point where the first edition had left off (1572) up to the very moment of publication, there now appeared many long supplements and smaller interpolations in earlier parts of the *Chronicles*.

There is disagreement as to who was responsible for most of it, the *Dictionary of National Biography* stating that Hooker/Vowell was the editor in chief,[7] Stephen Booth supporting the claim of Abraham Fleming, who certainly signed the preface to the "Continuation,"[8] and Elizabeth Story Donno believing, as the title

---

5. Edmund Bolton, *Hypercritica; or A Rule of Judgement, for writing, or reading our Historys* (Oxford, 1722), rpt. in Joseph Hazlewood, ed., *Ancient Critical Essays*, 2 vols. (London, 1815), 2:237. In Savile's Latin the insults are even worse: for "the Dregs of the common People," read "*ex faece plebis.*"

6. Publication had been planned since 1584, when it was twice entered in the *Stationers' Register*, on October 6 and December 30. It is evident, though, that the revision kept being expanded to give it up-to-the-minute topicality.

7. This view is supported by Vernon Snow in his introduction to the 1965 reprint (viii).

8. Booth, *The Book Called Holinshed's Chronicles* (Berkeley, 1968), 61–71. He based his assessment on the arguments of Sarah C. Dodson, "Abraham

page of the "Continuation" asserted, that the major figure was John Stow, who had provided Holinshed with material for the first edition, whose own *Chronicle* had been published in 1580, and whose qualifications as a historian were greatly superior to those of Fleming.[9]

Of the five collaborators on the 1587 edition, only John Stow could conceivably have deserved the charge of being of "the Dregs of the Common People." Hooker/Vowell was educated at Oxford and a member of the Irish parliament; Thynne was the son of the famous editor of Chaucer, a member of Lincoln's Inn, and a friend of Sir Thomas Egerton; Fleming was also university educated and became chaplain to the countess of Nottingham; Harrison, likewise, graduated from Oxford and became chaplain to Lord Cobham; but Stow, significantly, was a tailor. He appears to have been an autodidact, and became both a great antiquary, purchasing Reyner Wolfe's collection of manuscripts, and a member of the Society of Antiquaries founded in the 1580s. From his own independent historiographical projects, the *Chronicles* or *Annales* (1580, 1592) and the *Survay of London* (1598), as well as from the character of the manuscripts he collected, it can be inferred that Stow was unusually interested in political protest and resistance.[10] Stow had some early record of trouble with the authorities. In 1568 he was examined by the Privy Coun-

---

Fleming, Writer and Editor," *University of Texas Studies in English* 34 (1955): 51–66, and William E. Miller, "Abraham Fleming: Editor of Shakespeare's *Holinshed*," *Texas Studies in Language and Literature* 1 (1959–60): 89–100. See also Anne Castanien, "Censorship and Historiography in Elizabethan England: The Expurgation of Holinshed's *Chronicles*," Ph.D. diss., University of California, Davis, 26–27. Castanien maintains that Fleming was, in effect, the editor of the 1587 text throughout, both before and after the censorship.

9. Donno, "Some Aspects of Shakespeare's *Holinshed*," *Huntington Library Quarterly* 50 (1987): 231.

10. See Barrett Beer, "John Stow and Tudor Rebellions, 1549–1569," *Journal of British Studies* 27 (1958): 352–74. For Stow's collections, see J. Gairdner, ed., *Three Fifteenth-Century Chronicles*, Camden Society, 3d ser., vol. 28 (1880), which contains "Historical Memoranda in the Handwriting of John Stowe," i.e., the demands of Jack Cade's rebellion in 1450. Stow included a version of these demands in his *Chronicles* (1580), along with a document which he called "The complaint of the commons of Kent, and causes of the assembly on the Blackheath" (654–58) for which there is no contemporary manuscript witness. Both documents, significantly, were inserted by Abraham Fleming into the 1587

cil on the charge of possessing Roman Catholic propaganda against Elizabeth; and his house, being searched, revealed "old fantastical books" with papist tendencies.[11] In the preface to his *Abridgement* (1570), and as an aspect of their rivalry as producers of condensed chronicles for wider audiences, Richard Grafton had complained that Stow's *Summarie of Englyshe Chronicles* (1565) had contributed "to the defacing of Princes doinges," and that in his historiography "the gates are rather opened for crooked subjectes to enter into the fielde of Rebellion, then the hedges or gaps of the same stopped."[12]

---

edition of the *Chronicles*, with attribution to Stow in the margin. I owe this information to Ellen Caldwell. The *Chronicles* contain other evidence of Stow's taste in antiquities. For the reign of Richard II, under 1397, the *Chronicles* record a story "Out of an old French pamphlet belonging to John Stow, about a "vision" received by a prior of St. Alban's, "that the realme of England should be destroied through the misgovernment of King Richard." For the reign of Mary, Stow possessed a manuscript diary, Harleian MS 194, which covers the period July 1553 to October 1554, material from which was included in his *Annales*, as also in "Holinshed's" *Chronicles*. The diary was subsequently edited by J. G. Nichols for the Camden Society as *The Chronicle of Queen Jane, and of Two Years of Queen Mary* (London, 1850). The main subject of the diary, however, is the rebellion of Sir Thomas Wyatt the younger, to which the diarist is notably sympathetic. For example: "And as [Wyatt] marched towardes Kingeston he mett by chaunce a merchaunt Christopher Dorrell, whom he called, saying, 'Cosen Dorrell, I praie you comende me unto your cetezens the Londonours, and saie unto theym from me, that when libertie and freedome was offered theym they wolde not receyve yt, neither wolde they admytt me to enter within their gates, who for their fredome, and the dysburdenyng of their grefes and opression by straundgers, wolde have franclie spente my bloode in that their cause and quarrell; but nowe well apperith their unthanckfullnes to us their frendes . . . and therefore they are the lesse to be moned hereafter, when the myserable tyrannye of straundgers shall oppresse theym' " (46).

11. See *Tudor Royal Proclamations*, ed. Paul L. Hughes and James F. Larkin, 3 vols. (New Haven and London, 1969), 2:312, where it is recorded that on February 24, 1569, the bishop of London sent to the Privy Council a list of thirty-eight "unlawful books" found in Stow's possession, including recent recusant works by Thomas Dorman, Thomas Heskyns, Robert Pointz, John Rastell, Richard Shacklock, and Thomas Stapleton.

12. This tends to undermine the transparency of Stow's claim, in the preface to his *Annales* (1592), that the primary function of chronicles is the "discouragement of unnatural subjects from wicked treasons, pernicious rebellions, and damnable doctrines." I owe the Grafton reference to David Kastan; but I draw from it additional support for the suspicion that the prefatory announcements of the Tudor chronicles are not to be taken at face value.

And if we are looking for evidence of Stow's thinking, we might very well ask why he took the trouble to publish, and to dedicate to Edmund Spenser, an unusual translation of a story out of Boccaccio, which, in the translation he chose, contains a remarkable attack on social hierarchy:

> Then should they remember who were of noblesse,
> Who might intitle him to the blood royall:
> They should see how Nature whith her besinesse,
> Brings forth her effect & wondrous gifts all,
> Being as in her birth, to every man egall;
> For as naked is a King borne as I understond
> As is the lowist borne that never had house ne lond.
>
> For when our moder Eve brought forth Abell and Caine,
> Who couth prefer himselfe for birth or linage,
> Or of these two infants who couth the title
> Of gentle blood of noblesse or parage?
> That time no difference was twixt gentle & page,
> But every one was fayn to endevour
> His living to get with sweat and labour.
>
> Of all this time was none bond in servage,
> Was none by service under subjection,
> Till that the people gan to rule and rage
> Guiding themselfe by will and not by reason
> Offending their lawes by their transgression:
> Then of right and Justice they must be correct
> Of one their soveraigne, and they to him subject.

If one expects that this unusual account of the origins of sovereignty was designed to lead the reader away from a primitive egalitarianism back to monarchical theory, one is quickly disabused; for after a conventional warning that "he that should bee ruler and have regency" must himself abide by the law, the examples cited are not of monarchs, but rather of the biblical patriarchs and judges, Moses, Joshua, and Gideon, who stand for the principle of meritocracy:

> Which though for their virtue were poore & deject
> Yet were they for their vertue chosed to direct
> And guide the people. So shortly it is true,
> There is no gentleman save only by vertue.[13]

13. John Stow, "The Statelie Tragedie of Guistard and Sismond," in *Certaine*

As the dedication to Spenser is interesting in its own right, a response, perhaps, to the second instalment of *The Faerie Queene* the previous year, so the mere publication of this provocative poem in 1597, its provocation safely contained by the double envelope of its archaism and "only being a translation," helps to counteract the impression that Stow might otherwise have given (by dedicating his 1592 *Chronicles* to Archbishop Whitgift) of capitulating to the authorities.

This curious record might tempt one to believe that Stow, who happened to live on Throkmorton Street, was, like Job Throkmorton in the case of the Martin Marprelate pamphlets, the leading spirit of the 1587 *Chronicles;* but if he was indeed a closet sympathizer with the old religion, his principles were certainly not shared by the other members of this project, which was markedly Protestant, sometimes (in Fleming's contributions) rabidly anti-Catholic. And in any case the interest of the *Chronicles* in popular culture, as we shall see, seems to come from more than one source, from more than one ideological direction. If Savile's and Bolton's strictures against "the Dregs of the Common People" are intelligible, it must be as a response to the involvement of the printers and publishers as sponsors of the project, to an improper confusion between business entrepreneurialism and historical antiquarianism, and especially to the texture of the history so produced, with its multiple layers of social consciousness.

My general thesis about *both* editions, but especially the second, is that the *Chronicles* were not the muddle of which later historians have disapproved. Rather, Holinshed initiated a procedure whereby, indeed, as Levy put it, the reader was left to be his own historian, not because the historian had abrogated his interpretative task, but because he wished to register how extraordinarily complicated, even dangerous, life had become in post-Reformation England, when every change of regime initiated a change in the official religion, and hence in the meaning

---

Worthy Manuscript Poems of great Antiquitie Reserved long in the Studie of a North-folke Gentleman (London, 1597), D2v–3v. A comparison with the translation by William Walter, published by Wynkyn de Worde in 1532, indicates that the Walter translation contains no such political argument. The dedication to Spenser in 1597 is exceedingly interesting.

and value of acts and allegiances. What at one moment was loyalty, obedience, and piety could at the next be redefined as treason or heresy.

Consider this comment on the execution of Northumberland, whose head was buried in the Tower by the body of Protector Somerset. "So that there," the chronicler added, "lieth before the high alter two dukes between two queenes, to wit, the duke of Summerset and the duke of Northumberland betweene queene Anne and queene Katharine, all foure beheaded" (4:4). That irony was conceivable on this topic is confirmed by Roger Williams in a pamphlet attacking religious intolerance. *Christenings Make not Christians* was published in 1645 as an argument against the Massachusetts Puritans and their hold on the New World; but he pointed, by analogy, at the insincerity, the political motivation, of England's unstable religious history at home, which unfortunately was transportable to the New World:

> When England was all Popish under Henry the seventh, how esie is conversion wrought to half Papist halfe-Protestant under Henry the eighth? From halfe-Protestantisme halfe Popery under Henry the eight, to absolute Protestantisme under Edward, the sixth; from absolute Protestation under Edward the sixt to absolute popery under Quegne Mary, and from absolute Popery under Queen Mary, (just like the Weathercocke, with the breath of every Prince) to absolute Protestantisme under Queene Elizabeth. [14]

The result of such "weathercock" religion was, to say the least, diversity of opinion, which it was the responsibility of the *Chronicles* to record. This historiographical practice was therefore even *more* sophisticated than that recommended by Jean Bodin and gradually absorbed into English practice, for example by Samuel Daniel, [15] whereby the old moralizing was to be replaced by his-

14. Williams, *Complete Writings*, 7 vols. (New York, 1963), 7:36. I owe this reference to Thomas Scanlan.

15. See Daniel, "Certaine Advertisements to the Reader," prefatory to his *Collection of the History of England* (1612), in *Complete Works*, ed. A. B. Grosart, 5 vols. (London, 1896; rpt. New York, 1963), 4:83: "For the Worke it selfe, I can Challenge nothing therein but onely the sowing it together . . . holding it fittest and best agreeing with Integrity (the chiefest duty of a Writer) to leave things to their owne Fame, and the Censure thereof to the Reader, as being his part rather then mine, who am onely to recite things done, not to rule them."

torical "objectivity," a concept which Holinshed had already, in 1577, perceived to be theoretically impossible. When the second edition was planned, this agenda was understood by the group of five who carried it out, although they had different and quite distinctive preoccupations. That the principle of multivocality *was* a principle is confirmed even by Francis Thynne, whose own calm and judicious narrative style contrasts strongly with Abraham Fleming's far from disinterested interventions. Toward the end of Thynne's catalogue of the archbishops of Canterbury, a catalogue which would culminate with Edmund Grindall and his successor Whitgift (and would, significantly, be removed by censorship), Thynne remarks, in relation to the history of Grimsby, Whitgift's birthplace:

> Which matter being set downe in manie of our chronicles, as in Caxton, Henrie Knighton, Eulogium, Scala chronicon, Campden, and others, I will deliver the words of the said Authors, least I might seeme (in being ambitious in names) to bring emptie casks without anie wine. The words of which authors, although they be long and to some maie seeme needlesse to be so often remembred, *yet I have not refused to give everie author leave to tell his owne tale,* for that I would not seeme to wrong them in misreporting thereof; and for that I desire to make common by manie copies (as occasion may serve) the writings of former ages remaining in private hands. (4:773; italics added)

Most of Thynne's contributions, being long catalogues of office-holders in church and state, do not lend themselves to anthropological reportage; but thanks to his colleagues, this concern that "everie author" should be permitted "to tell his owne tale" results not only in an extremely *dramatic* narrative, where the distinctive voices of human authors are indeed audible, but in the reporting of voices not normally recorded at all—the subliterary, if not illiterate, sounds of popular culture.

There is one other aspect of the 1587 *Chronicles* that pertains to my inquiry here—the fact that it constituted perhaps the most striking and intricate exhibit we possess of active, reconstructive, governmental censorship. Because the second edition was continued through the alarming events of 1586, the Babington conspiracy and the trial of Mary, Queen of Scots, the chroniclers literally writing up-to-the-minute journalism, it caused, not surprisingly, a governmental panic. When the *Chronicles* appeared at the booksellers in January 1587, and the Privy Council became aware of its contents, there was an immediate governmental intervention. On February 1 Whitgift, as archbishop of Canterbury, was ordered to recall and reform the work.[16] Unsold copies were collected from the booksellers; but instead of merely suppressing them, a committee was appointed to revise (the original term was "castrate") the text, according to certain principles of which there is no remaining record.[17] When the edition was called in, Thynne's monumental catalogues of ecclesiastical officeholders or genealogical inserts simply disappeared, and sections of his continuation of the history of Scotland were rewritten. The material on the Sidney family, which had been contributed by Edmund Molyneux, was severely truncated. Also much condensed was John Stow's account of Leicester's visit to the Netherlands; and the detailed description of the Babington Plot and its consequences, which Fleming, in a marginal note, had claimed as his own, was replaced by a very much briefer and less colorful version of those events. On the basis of the few copies that survived uncastrated, a nineteenth-century edition replaced what had been deleted, permitting us to speculate about the censors' reasoning.[18] From the fact of revision alone, we must infer both that the authorities tolerated the project in principle, and that they took a highly *textualized* interest in the representation of recent history. It was not merely a question of what facts or events could be recounted but the manner of their recounting

16. See *Acts of the Privy Council, 1586–87*, ed. J. R. Dasent (London, 1901), 311–12.

17. For a description of the so-called Fleming papers, which included Fleming's personal account "de Modo Castrandi, Reformandique Chronica," advertised but never published by Francis Peck in 1732, and now presumed lost, see Anne Castanien, "Censorship and Historiography in Elizabethan England, 26–27.

18. The most important attempts to describe and analyze the revisions are Castanien's painstaking thesis; Donno, "Some Aspects of Shakespeare's Holinshed," *Huntington Library Quarterly* 50 (1987): 229–47; and Stephen Booth's *The Book Called Holinshed's Chronicles*, which, however, adopted the position that there are "no common denominators among the materials removed and there is nothing in any of the excised pages that looks obviously dangerous to governmental policy" (60).

that mattered. But *nothing* was altered in those sections of the history that had been covered in the first edition, despite the fact that they had been much amplified in the interim. Presumably the government was no longer interested in the texture of the *Chronicles* for the reigns of the earlier Tudors.

This chapter will not discuss the censorship of the 1587 *Chronicles*, except to suggest that there is a connection between that official intervention and what we may now be able to say about the nature of the project as a whole. But as a frame of expectation, as a shaping condition of the stories the chroniclers chose to tell (some of which, as we shall see, are *about* censorship), the eventual castration of the project should not be forgotten. It is only one of the many ironies later readers may experience that the interpolations in earlier reigns went unnoticed by Whitgift and the Privy Council; for had it not been so, the basis of my argument here might have largely disappeared.

> In time of this rebellion, a priest that by a butcher dwelling within five miles of Windsor had been procured to preach in favor of the rebels, and the butcher (as well for procuring the priest thereto, as for words spoken as he sold his meat in Windsor) were hanged: the priest on a tree at the foot of Windsor bridge, and the butcher on a paire of new gallowes set up before the castell gate, at the end of the same bridge. The words which the butcher spake were these. When one bad him lesse for the carcasse of a sheepe than he thought he could make of it: Naie by Gods soule (said he) I had rather the good fellowes of the north had it, and a score more of the best I have, than I would so sell it. This priest and butcher being accused on a mondaie in the morning whilest the kings armie was in the field, and the king himselfe lieng at Windsor, they confessed their faults upon their examinations, and by the law martiall they were adjudged to death, and suffered as before is mentioned. (3:802)

The source of this anecdote, which took place in 1536, is the Henry VIII section of the *Chronicles*. The context of the episode is the Pilgrimage of Grace, which represented the only major organized threat to the Henrician Reformation. Its tone is, I suggest, ambiguous, the "words" which the butcher spoke, conceivably in jest but certainly casually in the course of his daily trade, being scarcely a justification for capital punishment. Even the most threatening clauses of the new treason legislation enacted in Henry VIII's reign, which, according to Bellamy, "was regarded for the greater part of the remaining years of the century as the zenith of severity,"[19] especially for its specific inclusion of "words," would seem to have required more than this as a pretext for an exemplary execution. It is true, of course, that it was also for "procuring" the priest's sermon that the butcher was executed. But Holinshed's account differs in interesting ways from an earlier version of this anecdote recorded by Edward Hall, by including that legalistic phrase "for words spoken," thereby intimating that he has in mind precisely this extension of the treason law that was subsequently repudiated by, of all persons, Mary Tudor; whereas Hall not only uses the word "treason" as if it were inarguable but states that both priest and butcher confessed "there treason,"[20] a rather different matter from "confessed their faults." In fact the butcher was executed not under treason law but under martial law, which exempted the authorities from all due process.

Part of the story's point, evidently, is its sense of place, with the name of Windsor four times insisted upon, the executions being symbolically carried out "at the foot of Windsor bridge" and upon a pair of new gallows constructed for the purpose at the other end of that same bridge. Why the prominence of

19. John Bellamy, *The Tudor Law of Treason* (London, 1979), 37.

20. Edward Hall, *Union of the two Noble and Illustre Famelies of Lancaster and Yorke*, ed. Henry Ellis (London, 1809; rpt. New York, 1965), 823: "In this tyme of insurrection, and in the rage of horley borley, even when the kynges armie and the rebelles were ready to joyne, the kynges banner being displaid, & the kynges majestie then liying at Winsore, ther was a boocher dwelling within v. myle of Winsore which caused a priest to preach that all such as toke parte with the Yorkeshiremen whome he named Goddes people, did fight and defend Goddes quarel & farther the saied bocher in sellyng of his meat, one did bid him a lesse price of a shepe than he made of it, he answered nay by Godes soul, I had rather ye the good felowes of the north had it among them and askore more of ye best I have; this priest & bocher abovesaid on the Monday in the mornyng, and the same day were both sent for, which confessed there treason, and so accordyng to the law mershal they were adjudged to die: & so the saied Monday, there were both examined, condempned and hanged, the boocher was hanged on a new paire of Gallowes set at the bridge ende before the castel gate: and the priest was hanged on a tree at the foote of Winsore bridge."

Windsor, if not that it was the king's residence, the place of royal power and supposedly immune from such manifestations of disobedience? Roger Manning, who found another version of the story in Hall's *Chronicle,* suggested that "the severity of the punishment may also be related to the fact that [the offense] was committed within the verge (i.e. within twelve miles) of royal palaces while the king's banner was displayed in time of rebellion."[21] In his own use of the word "severity" Manning was recording the *effect* the story had on him; but he nevertheless saw nothing in it to disturb his belief that martial law was taken for granted by the public at large and became problematic only fifty years later, when it appeared as one of the major grievances in the Petition of Right in 1629 (108–9).[22] I, however, see the anecdote, especially as transplanted and revised by Holinshed, as *intending* to produce a meditation on severity; only one of many signs that the *Chronicles* played a part, and a major one, in the long, slow, but continuous process of public education on issues of the law, politics, constitutional theory, and social policy more generally; a process that the chroniclers themselves imagined began with Magna Carta, that took a big step forward in the reign of Richard II, and that led not only to other symbolic moments like the Petition of Right but ultimately to the replacement of rulers by governments.

While the supplements to the reign of Henry VIII deserve analysis in other contexts, I am concerned here primarily with what was interpolated, and from what source, in the reigns of Edward VI and Mary Tudor. Here the story of the English Reformation was continued, not as an international drama, the emphasis of the Henrician section and of Fleming's additions to it, but as one of a nation divided against itself. The account of Edward's reign is dominated by two interrelated events: the protests generated all over the country by the Edwardian Reformation and the social policies of Protector Somerset; and, as their consequence, the trial and execution of Somerset. We do not ourselves need to sentimentalize Somerset to recognize that the *Chronicles,* especially in the 1587 version, make him the hero of the story. They do so

21. "The Origins of the Doctrine of Sedition," *Albion* 12 (1980): 107.
22. See also Lindsay Boynton, "Martial Law and the Petition of Right," *English Historical Review* 89 (1964): 255–84.

by simplifying the various branches of the Edwardian reform program and by deemphasizing the factionalism of the court, as well as by focusing on the popular response to his program.[23] Whereas his protectorate was, according to John King, "the only time during the Tudor age when no one was executed on grounds of heresy,"[24] the *Chronicles* tend rather to emphasize social and economic issues. Holinshed had given an evenhanded account of Somerset's 1549 proclamation against enclosures, "tending to the benefit and releefe of the poore," but added that "how well soever the setters forth of this proclamation meant . . . yet verelie it turned not to the wished effect, but rather ministred occasion of a foule and dangerous disorder" (3:916). Anti-enclosure riots, he reported, broke out in Somerset, Buckinghamshire, Northamptonshire, Kent, Essex, and Lincolnshire. At the same time a more religiously motivated rebellion broke out in Devon and Cornwall, and the *Chronicles* record the "articles" or demands of these rebels, who insisted upon a return in their local churches to the doctrine of transubstantiation, complaining about those who "rudely presuming unworthilie to receive the same, put no difference betweene the Lords bodie & other kind of meat; some saieng that it is bread before and after" (3:918-19). Here the common people themselves insist on the more esoteric and mystical interpretation of the sacrament; but their protest is in part against the materialist thinking of popular Protestantism, as represented, for example, by Luke Shepherd's dialogue *John Bon and Mast Parson*, written in support of the Edwardian Reformation and published in 1548.[25] In this black-letter pamphlet, printed "by John Daye and William Seres, dwelling in Sep-

23. For an excellent brief account of the reign and Somerset's policies, as well as his "fundamental administrative error and his overbearing circumvention of the Privy Council," see John N. King, *English Reformation Literature: The Tudor Origins of the Protestant Tradition* (Princeton, 1982), 25–30.

24. *English Reformation Literature*, 26. He also points out that Somerset permitted and encouraged an unprecedented degree of freedom of speech and the press.

25. Practically nothing is known of Luke Shepherd. He is mentioned by John Strype, *Ecclesiastical Memorials* 2:116, who states that he was imprisoned in the Fleet for former pamphlets written in Henry VIII's reign. Edward Underhill mentions Shepherd in his autobiography. His editor remarks that Underhill "does not say that his imprisonment was in Henry's reign, and from the context it may rather be concluded that it occurred in the reign of Mary" (325).

ulchres Parish at the sign of the resurrection," John Bon represents not only the newly theological Protestantism, with its clear opposition to the doctrine of transubstantiation, but also a grass-roots common sense, focusing on the material fact that the Host "is but a cake."[26]

It is typical of the *Chronicles* that these articles, which are not only strictly and perhaps strategically limited to anti-Reformation issues, but also quite coherent, are preceded by a derogatory, antipopulist statement derived from Foxe's *Actes and Monuments*, which denies to the Devon and Cornwall rebels precisely that crucial political achievement, "consent." For we are told, in language anticipatory of Shakespeare's *Coriolanus*, that

> herein such diversitie of heads and wits was among them, that for everie kind of braine there was one maner of article: so that neither appeared any *consent* in their diversitie, nor yet any con-

26. *Parson:* Thou hast even knowen the sacramente to be the body of
   Christ
   John: Ye sir ye say true, all that I know in dede
   And yet as I remember it is not in my crede
   But as for Copsi Cursty (Corpus Christi) to be a man or no
   I knewe not tyll this day. . . .
   Parson: Why folishe felowe, I tel the it is so
   For it was so determined by the Church longe ago
   It is both the sacramente and very Christ himself
   . . . .
   It is not possible his manhode for to se
   John: Why sir ye tell me it is even very he
   And if it be not his manhode, his ghost it must be
   Parson: I tell ye none of both. . . .
   John: Then is it but a cake, but I pray ye be not wroth.
   Parson: Wroth quod he, by the masse ye makes me swere an othe
   I had rather wyth a docter of divinitie to reason
   Than wyth a stubble cur that eateth beanes and peason
   John: I crie ye mercy Mast Parson pacience for a season
   In all this cumlicacion (complication) is nother felony or treason.

Compare also the "Dialogue between Truth and Custom" that Foxe inserted into his account of Edward's reign, where Truth cites the Church Fathers to the effect that holy communion involves a spiritual consumption only ("Non accumus dentem, nec ventrem paramus. we sharpen not oure tooth nor prepare our bellie"); and then adds the materialist, commonsense critique: "And for a proofe, if you consecrate a whole loafe, it will feede you so well as your table bread. And if a little Mouse get an host, he will crave no more meate to hys dinner." See John Foxe, *Actes and Monuments* (1583), 1390.

stancie in their agreement. Some seemed more tolerable, others altogither unreasonable, some would have no justices, some no state of gentlemen. (3:918)[27]

It is easy to be persuaded by such statements (and there are plenty of them) that the author-compilers of the *Chronicles* were actively hostile to the underclasses, especially, of course, when engaged in some form of riot and rebellion. It is all the easier to be so persuaded if one has a predisposition to believe that that must have been their mission and opinion. As with Shakespeare's play, however, another reading is available; not so much between the lines as in the interstices between historical events on the traditionally grander scale and between the passages of editorial moralizing on the dangers of sedition. For instance, Holinshed had found in Richard Grafton's *Chronicle* (1569) another anecdote, this from the uprisings of 1549, of the workings of martial law—the tale of a miller "that had been a great dooer in that rebellion," who was being pursued by Sir Anthony Kingston. "But the miller being thereof warned," Holinshed had written, "called a good tall fellow that he had to his servant, and said unto him:

> I have businesse to go from home, if anie therefore come to aske for me, saie thou art the owner of the mill and . . . that thou hast kept this mill for the space of three years, but in no wise name me.

The inevitable occurred; Kingston arrived to arrest the miller, and finding the servant ready to own to ownership of the mill, had him hauled away to the nearest tree, saying, "Thou has beene a busie knave, and therefore here thou shalt hang." When the servant, in panic, reclaimed his real status, nothing availed:

27. Compare Shakespeare, *Coriolanus* 2.3.15ff.:

> *First Citizen:* for once we stood up about the corn, [Coriolanus] himself stuck not to call us the many-headed multitude.
> *Third Citizen:* We have been called so of many; not that our heads are some brown, some black, some abram, some bald, but that our wits are so diversely coloured; and truly I think, if all our wits were to issue out of one skull, they would fly east, west, north, south, and their consent of one direct way should be at once to all the points of the compass.

The similarity of language (although the speaker is mocking the class prejudice he repeats) is marked enough to suggest that the *Chronicles* are here too an actual "source."

Well then, said Sir Anthonie, thou art a false knave to be in two tales, therefore said he, hang him up; and so incontinentlie hanged he was in deed. After he was dead, one that was present told Sir Anthonie; Suerlie sir this was but the millers man. What then, said he, could he ever have doone his maister better service than to hang for him. (3:925-96)

We might be able to infer the social purpose of this real-life fable from that "incontinentlie" that puts up its own small resistance to the summary judgments of martial law, not to mention the brutal joke at the end; but the *Chronicles* helps the watchful interpreter by adding a marginal note: "This was a hard proceeding, though the partie had been nocent."[28]

In 1587 this section of this history received a massive insertion of new material: the story of the siege of Exeter, as told by John Hooker.[29] As Abraham Fleming was to insist on eyewitness testimony in his account of the Babington conspiracy, so, we are told, "I John Hooker the writer herof was present, and *Testis oculatus* of things then doone" (3:939). Hooker's relation to his regional narrative was, however, completely different from Fleming's perspective on London almost forty years later, and whether knowingly or not, his story (like Holinshed's fable of naive peasant and callous knight) indicates that though Edward's attempts to enforce a genuinely reformed liturgy were the primary cause of the unrest, there were local instances of class conflict in which the gentry gave the provocation.

One episode in particular should be not without interest to those who follow the adventures of Spenser and Sir Walter Ralegh. For here, it turns out, Ralegh's father was the troublemaker. "It happened," wrote Hooker,

that a certeine gentleman named Walter Raleigh dwelling not far from thense, as he was upon a side holie daie riding from his house to Excester, overtooke an old woman going to the parish church of Saint Marie Clift, who had a paire of beads in hir hands,

28. Depending on how good a reader of the *Chronicles* one were, one might have found some satisfaction in a later report of Sir Anthony Kingston. In summer 1555 a conspiracy against Queen Mary was discovered, and "sir Anthony Kingston was accused and apprehended for the same, and died in the waie comming to London" (4:84). How precisely he died we are left to imagine. The source of this information is John Stow (*Chronicle* 1100).

29. Compare *The discription of the cittie of Excester, collected and gathered by John Vowel* (London, 1575).

and asked hir what she did with those beads? And entring into further speeches with her concerning religion, which was reformed, and as then by order of law to be put into execution, he did persuade with hir that she should as a good Christian woman and an obedient subject yeeld thereunto; saieng further, that there was a punishment by law appointed against hir, and all such as would not obeie and follow the same, and which would be put in execution upon them. (3:492)

It is easy to imagine this episode being conveyed by the younger Ralegh to Spenser, and transformed by him into one in *The Faerie Queene* (1.3.13–14) whereby Una, symbol of a united Protestant church, encounters the old woman Corceca, "blind Devotion," telling her beads in the darkness of a cave. "But now for feare," wrote Spenser, figuring the English Reformation, "her beads she did forget. / Whose needlesse dread for to remove away, / Faire Una framed words and count'nance fit." Hooker's tale not being an allegory, however, but a local memory of misunderstanding between classes, such overzealous behavior on the part of Ralegh senior makes matters considerably worse:

This woman nothing liking, nor well digesting this matter, went foorth to the parish church, where all the parishioners were then at the service: and being unpatient, and in an agonie with the speeches before passed betweene hir and the gentleman, beginneth to upbraid in the open church verie hard and unseemlie speeches concerning religion, saieng that she was threatened by the gentleman, that except she would leave her beads, and give over holie bread and holie water, the gentlemen would burne them out of their houses and spoile them, with manie other speeches verie false and untrue, and whereof no talke at all had passed betweene the gentleman and hir. Notwithstanding she had not so soon spoken, but that she was beleeved: and in all hast like a sort of wasps they fling out of the church, and get them to the towne which is not far from thense, and there began to intrench and fortifie the towne. (3:942)

Ralegh himself was captured and kept prisoner in a local church tower, "being manie times threatened to be executed to death," but survived. While I certainly would not claim that Hooker's account *favors* the old woman and her colleagues, his attention to psychological detail (her "agonie" at the conversation with Ralegh) is remarkable. It seems clear, despite his statement to the contrary, that no falsehood is involved in *her* account, only exaggeration of Ralegh's warnings (whose tone—sympathetic, paternalistic, or threatening—we are left to imagine).

Hooker remarks on the fact that in Exeter in 1549 there were "two sorts of people," those willing to accept the Edwardian Reformation and those, "the greater number," of "the olde stampe, and of the Romish religion . . . addicted to their own fantasies, and their bottels were so far seasoned with the old wines, that they cannot abide to heare of anie other religion" (3:947). In Hooker's view, the conservatism of the majority in Exeter was strong enough to be antinationalist: "they regarded not king nor Keisar, passed not for kin nor freendship, regarded not countrie nor commonwealth, but were wholie of the opinion of the rebels, and would have no reformation in religion" (3:947).

But in the siege of Exeter, another, irresistible motivation develops: hunger. Here a theme that is always close to the surface in popular culture rises to the surface; and whereas in the story of the butcher who wished he could donate his meat to the northern rebels in 1536 food is the secondary issue, and in the articles of Devon and Cornwall in 1549 bread is to remain symbolic, in the siege it is primary:

> For no force is feared, no lawes observed, no magistrate obeied, nor common societies esteemed, where famine ruleth. For as the poet saith: *Nescit plebs jejuna timere.* . . . And albeit there were good store of drie fish, rise, prunes, rasins, and wine, at verie reasonable prices, yet bread which as the prophet saith, *Confirmat cor hominis,* Strengtheneth man's heart, that wanted: neither was anie to be had. And in this extremitie the bakers and householders were drive to seeke up their old store of puffins and bran, wherewith they in times past were woont to make horsebread, and to feed their swine and poultrie, and this they moulded up in clothes, for otherwise it would not hold togither, and so did bake it up and the people well contented therewith. For (as Plutarch writeth) *Fames reddit omnia dulcia, nihilque contemnit esuriens:* Hunger maketh all things sweet, and the hungrie bellie shunneth nothing. (3:952)

While it might be possible to scorn this description as "triviall household trash," an anthropological perspective must treasure it; not only for the data on baking in hard times (the Exeter inhabitants would be amused at our current obsession with bran, and the expensive forms in which it is processed); not only for the rare word "puffins," which the compilers of the *Oxford English Dictionary* encountered only here; but also for the clarity with which it renders the clash of cultures: the classically educated historian trading in quotations,[30] the life of the mind, yet alert to the recalcitrant social truth of "the hungrie bellie" elsewhere, a material fact which the canny bakers knew how to assuage, molding their bran in cloth to make it, like the social fabric of the besieged town, "hold togither." We might infer that Hooker intends this as a metaphor; for he explains that the common people would have readily surrendered, had not the magistrates insisted on a rigorously equitable food distribution.

There is some ironic reverberation, therefore, between this long interpolation in the 1587 edition and Holinshed's previous inclusion, in 1577, of the complete text of Sir John Cheke's *The Hurt of Sedicion*. Cheke's tract had been published in the immediate aftermath of the 1549 uprisings, and was presumably intended in part to insulate from the policies of Somerset, which were thereby discredited, Cheke and the other learned humanists assembled by Catherine Parr to educate the young king. Cheke's strategy was to deny validity to both the religious and social causes of the unrest. Particularly to the Norfolk rebels who had assembled under the leadership of Robert Ket at Mousehold, and who had held a series of trials of gentlemen under the "Tree of Reformation," Cheke had written as follows:

> Ye pretend a common-wealth. How amend ye it? by killing of gentlemen, by spoiling of gentlemen, by imprisoning of gentlemen? A marvellous tanned common-wealth. Whie should ye thus hate them? For their riches or for their rule? . . . In countries some must rule, some must obeie. . . . And therefore not they that know their own case as everie man doth, but they that understand the common-wealth's state, ought to have in countries the preferment of ruling. (3:989)

---

30. The source of the first quotation, inaccurately quoted, is Lucan, *Civil War* 3.58, "nescit *plebes* jejuna timere." The wider context is important. Caesar, having just driven Pompey out of Italy, turns his attention to the task of "winning the fickle favour of the populace; for he knew that the causes of hatred and mainsprings of popularity are determined by the price of food. Hunger alone makes cities free; and when men in power feed the idle mob, they buy subservience; a starving people is incapable of fear." *Lucan: The Civil War*, trans. J. D. Duff (Cambridge, Mass., 1928), 119.

But after this standard appeal to irremediable social difference (precisely that which Stow's "translation" of the Boccaccio story denied), Cheke cannily appealed to the economic aspirations of the rebels themselves, and invoked the possibility of personal social mobility through the market as a defense against political readjustment of the power relations:

> And to have no gentlemen, bicause ye be none your selves, is to bring down an estate, and to mend none. Would ye have all alike rich: That is the overthrow of labour, and utter decay of worke in this realme. For who will labour more, if when he hath gotten more, the idle shall by lust without right take what him lust from him, under pretense of equalitie with him. . . . If there should be such equalitie, then ye take awaie all hope from yours to come to anie better estate than you now leave them. (3:989)

But we do not leave Edward's reign with the voice of hegemony ringing in our ears. The last section of the story, which deals in detail with Somerset's trial and execution in 1552, offered in 1587 *two* different eyewitness reports of the execution. Both focus, one more skeptically than the other, on a local "hurly-burly" that occurred just before the execution. Holinshed was responsible for the inclusion of the first one, along with its attribution: "Wherefore I thinke it good to write what I saw (saith John Stow)":

> The people of a certeine hamlet which were warned to be there by seaven of the clocke to give their attendance on the lieutenant, now came thorough the posterne, and perceiving the duke to be alreadie on the Scaffold, the foremost began to run, crieng to their fellowes to follow fast after. Which suddennes of these men, being weaponed with bils and halberds, & this running caused the people which first saw them, to thinke some power had come downe to have rescued the duke from execution, and therefore cried Awaie, awaie; Thereupon the people ran, some one waie some an other, manie fell into the tower ditch, and they which tarried, thought some pardon had beene brought. Some said it thundered, some that the ground mooved, but there was no such matter. (3:1034)

In Stow's account, the entire commotion was caused by tardiness, the local constabulary arriving late for the job of superintending the crowds around the scaffold, and the crowd's misconception that their hasty, last-minute arrival constituted an insurrectionary "power." The tone is comedic, but the comedy is black; and although Stow's presence at the scene in one sense makes him an ordinary member of the crowd, his rejection of the superstitious interpretations of the "great noise" creates some intellectual distance.

For the second edition, Fleming chose to supplement Stow's response, or to contrast it, with that of Foxe, "ex martyrologio," a significant context for the ethical interpretation of Somerset's fall. "This amazement of the people," Fleming added, "is in other words recorded by John Fox . . . which because they be *effectuall* I thinke good to interlace." What he means by "effectuall," the reader is left to deduce:

> When the duke had ended his speech (saith he) suddenlie there was a terrible noise heard: whereupon there came a great feare on all men. This noise was as it had beene the noise of a great storme or tempest, which to some seemed to be heard from above: like as if a great deale of gunpowder being inclosed in an armorie, and having caught fire, had violentlie broken out. But to some againe it seemed as though it had beene a great multitude of horssemen running togither, or comming upon them; . . . Whereby it happened, that all the people being amazed without any evident cause, and without anie violence or stroke stricken, they ranne awaie, some into the ditches and puddles, and some into the houses thereabout. Other some being affraid with the horrour and noise, fell downe groveling into the ground with their pollaxes & halberds, and most part of them cried out: Jesus save us, Jesus save us. . . . And I myselfe [margin: Namelie John Fox the writer of this report] which was there present among the rest, being also affraid in this hurlie burlie, stood still altogither amazed, looking when anie man would knocke me on the head. (3:1034)

The "effectuall" strategy of Foxe's account and of its quotation is to merge the historian completely with the common people, and to subject him to the same comedic point of view.

But there is another significant difference of perspective. Whereas Stow records the popular voice as crying in unison, "Awaie, awaie," what Foxe remembers is a corporate "Jesus save us, Jesus save us." And in accordance with Foxe's mission in the *Actes and Monuments*, he supplies a typological interpretation of the "great noise," which is here accepted as a portent: "It happened here, as the evangelists write, it did to Christ, when the officers of the high priests & Phariseis comming with wepons to take him, being astonied ran backe, & fell to the ground." And, most important to the historiographical mission in which Fleming has now enrolled his predecessor, Foxe provides the final assessment of Somerset's importance to England, and the meaning of his demise. Seeing Sir Anthony Browne riding up to the scaffold, the people "conjectured that which was not true, but notwithstanding which they all wished for, that the king by that messenger had sent his uncle pardon":

> And therefore with great rejoising and casting up their caps, they cried out; Pardon, Pardon is come: God save the king. Thus this good duke, though he was destitute of all mans helpe, yet he saw before his departure, in how great love and favour he was with all men. (3:1035)

Like Fleming's account of the celebrations in London in 1586, this too is a moment of popular consensus and celebration, of *national* enthusiasm ("God save the king"), but one, it turns out, that is illusory. There is to be no last-minute reprieve. On the contrary, Somerset's popularity with the common people merely underscores the gratuitousness of his removal from the political scene. The *Chronicles* look through Foxe's eyes at a past which shows no rationale for such horrific events, whose very frequency indicates that governments are run by faction rather than principle, and toward a future made only more threatening by the removal of one figure who seemed concerned with something other than his own advancement:

And trulie I doo not thinke, that in so great slaughter of dukes as hath beene in England within this few yeares, there was so manie weeping eies at one time: and not without cause. For all men did see in the decaie of this duke, the publike ruine of all England, except such as indeed perceived nothing. (3:1035)

If the *Chronicles* represented the reign of Edward ultimately as a tragedy with occasional traces of social comedy, its account of Mary Tudor's reign was closer to a farce with tragic undertones. The nature of the transition between the two reigns is set, tonally, by John Stow, in an anecdote which was added in 1587, and which, in little, illustrates several of the themes of the expanded *Chronicles*: the dangers of outspokenness; the constant resurgence nevertheless of a popular voice with something to say about large public issues; and a mysterious pattern in events, which has very little to do with the providentialism often attributed to the Tudor chroniclers. For the year 1553, squeezed between the account of Edward's death and the letter from Mary Tudor to the Council claiming the crown, we find the following:

> The eleaventh of Julie. Gilbert Pot, drawer to Ninion Sanders Vintener, dwelling at S. Johns head within Ludgate, who was accused by the said Sanders his maister, was set upon the pillorie in Cheape, with both his eares nailed, and cleane cut off, for words speaking at time of the proclamation of ladie Jane. At the which execution was a trumpet blowne, and a herald read his offense, in presence of one of the shiriffes. & About five of the clocke the same daie in the afternoone, Ninion Sanders, master to the said Gilbert Pot, and John Owen a gunner, comming from the tower of London, by water in a wherrie, . . . were drowned at Saint Marie Locke, and the whirriemen saved by their ores. (3:1065)

In Mary's reign too the theme of emergent nationalism in conflict with religious conviction is a central part of the story, but now, of course, the resistance is to the forced reimposition of Catholicism, and resistance has been broadened to include the aristocracy and gentry. Where, then, is the "nation" to be found? This question is implicit in the event that marks the beginning of the reign, the rebellion of Sir Thomas Wyatt the younger. Holinshed had described how a band of the London militia sent out against Wyatt had instead revolted in his favor, crying out as they did so, "We are all Englishmen, we are all Englishmen" (4:13). And subsequently he had described their execution, in terms that make it quite clear that he deplored it:

> a great multitude of their said poore caitifs were brought foorth, being so manie in number, that all the prisons in London sufficed not to receive them: so that for lacke of place they were faine to bestow them in diverse churches of the said citie. And shortlie after were set up in London for a terrour to the common sort (bicause the white cotes being sent out of the citie, as before ye have heard, revolted from the queens part to the aid of Wiat) twentie pair of gallowes, on the which were hanged in severall places to the number of fiftie persons, which gallows remained standing

there a great part of the summer following to the great griefe of good citizens, and for example to the commotioners. (4:21)[31]

Interaction between high and popular forms of resistance continues as a recognizable theme, both of the original and of its supplementation. In describing the execution of Lady Jane Grey, Fleming turned again to Foxe's *Actes and Monuments* and produced the story of how Lady Jane had lost Mary's sympathy some years before, by casually demonstrating disbelief in the Real Presence in the Eucharist. "Touching this ladie Jane in the high commendation of her goodlie mind," wrote Fleming, "I find this report in maister Foxes appendix":

> namelie that being on a time when she was verie yoong at Newhall in Essex at the ladie Maries, was by one ladie Anne Wharton desired to walke, and they passing by the chapell, the ladie Wharton made low curtsie to the popish sacrament hanging on the altar: Which when the ladie Jane saw [she] marvelled why she did so, and asked hir whether the ladie Marie were there or not? [i.e., watching them]. Unto whome the ladie Wharton answered no, but she said that she made hir curtsie to him that made us all. Why quoth the ladie Jane, how can he be there that made us all, and the baker made him. This hir answer coming to the ladie Maries eares, she did never love hir after, as is credibly reported. (4:23)

This anecdote connects retroactively to the articles of the Devon and Cornwall rebels in 1549, to Luke Shepherd's *John Bon and Mast Parson*, as well as to the resourceful bakers of Hooker's account of the siege of Exeter. Can it be merely coincidence that, in summing up Mary's reign and providing a catalogue of the "learned men" who distinguished the reign and sometimes suffered for it, Holinshed listed "Lucas Shepherd . . . an English

31. This passage is based on the *Chronicle of Queen Jane* (59), which gives, however, different figures: 400 condemned to death, 26 hanged one day and "a greate nombre" the next. For other estimates of the executions in London and elsewhere, see David Loades, *Two Tudor Conspiracies* (Cambridge, 1965), 113–27. There was a mass pardon issued on June 4, 1558, containing 245 names. Loades concludes that "the total number who suffered in body or estate was less than five per cent of the number involved." But he also suggests that in London and in Kent the punishments were clearly irrational and "lacked any constructive value for the stability of the regime. For a few days the government acted as though it intended to pursue a course of terror, but then abandoned this approach in favour of indiscriminate mercy" (126–27).

poet" (4:153) and immediately followed this surprising entry with this, equally surprising: "Jane Dudleie daughter unto Henrie Greie duke of Suffolke, wrote diverse things highlie to her commendation, of whome yee have heard more before heere in this historie" (4:153).[32] And Fleming's insertion of *this* anecdote, hidden away in Foxe's appendix, rather than the more solemn dialogue between Lady Jane and Dr. Feckenham, Queen Mary's personal confessor, whose mission was to "reduce" her to Catholicism before her execution, is indicative of his practice in this section of the *Chronicles*. Fleming quarries the all too homogenous pages of the *Actes and Monuments*, with their obsession with theological debate, for the unusual, the telling, and the irreverent moment.

It appears that demystification is, for the chroniclers, at least as characteristic of popular culture as is superstition; it is equally clear that in certain circumstances they do not disapprove. One of the sections most augmented in 1587 deals with the plans for Mary's marriage to Philip II of Spain, a union for which Fleming has the most profound contempt, and which he spares no opportunity to deride, not least for its childlessness. Mary's first parliament has no difficulty in agreeing to the marriage, a complaisance that Fleming rebukes by inserting a fable (presumably of his own authorship) which imagines a national will to the contrary, expressed in the "whole bodie of the parlement";

> Howbeit, it was to be wished, even to the disappointing of that mariage (if God in counsell had so provided) that the whole bodie

32. Not only did she write, but her writings were published, posthumously. In 1554, immediately after her execution, there appeared a small collection of what she had written in the Tower, under the title *Here in this booke ye have a godly epistle made by a faithful Christian*, including several letters, a prayer, and the account of her debate with Feckenham, which she may or may not have written up herself. Other sixteenth-century editions, and one in 1615, were published at home and abroad, and Foxe included Lady Jane's writings in the *Actes and Monuments*. John King considered these publications "the most powerful contemporary Protestant attack on the Marian regime." See his *English Reformation Literature* (Princeton, 1982), 419. As a sign of her impact on popular culture, a broadside ballad purporting to be Lady Jane's last words went through more than one edition in London. See Carole Levin, "Lady Jane Grey: Protestant Queen and Martyr," in *Silent but for the Word: Tudor Women as Patrons, Translators, and Writers of Religious Works*, ed. Margaret Hannay (Kent, Ohio, 1985), 97–98, 273.

of the parlement had beene semblablie affected, as it is said, that all the nations of the world were, when the sunne would needs be maried. Against which purpose of the sun the people of all regions assembling, humblie besought Jupiter to cast in a blocke and impediment against that wedding. But Jupiter demanding of them why they would not have the sun married; one stepping up made answer for the rest, and said: Thou knowest well enough Jupiter that there is but one sun, and yet he burneth us all: who, if he be maried and have children, as the number of suns must needs increase; so must their heat and ferventnesse be multiplied, whereupon a generall destruction of all things in their kind will ensue. Hereupon that match was overthrowne. (4:27)

But immediately following this literary reproach to absolutism Fleming *also* inserts, with an abruptness easily mistaken for inconsequence, an anecdote attributed in the margin to John Stow:

On the eight of Aprill, then being sundaie, a cat with hir head shorne, and the likeness of a vestment cast over her, with hir fore feet tied togither, and a round peece of paper like a singing cake betwixt them, was hanged on a gallows in Cheape. (4:28)

Again, the disputed "cake" is at the heart of a countercultural message, whose materialist impact is enhanced by its economy of reference. Fleming/Stow assume that the "cat" is female, and therefore make available the demotic meaning of the word as denoting a prostitute (as in cathouse) and perhaps also food ("cates"). Shakespeare makes these puns ricochet around his Kate in *The Taming of the Shrew*.[33] Here the symbol of the cat resonates to implicate the queen and the debate over the Eucharist in a hostile and antifeminist, albeit carnivalesque, gesture of defiance.[34]

33. Shakespeare, *The Taming of the Shrew*: "she shall have no more eyes to see withal than a cat" (1.2.109); "but will you woo this wildcat?" (1.2.189); "for dainties are all Kates [cates]" (2.1.185); "For I am he am born to tame you, Kate, / And bring you from a wild Kate to a Kate / Conformable with other household Kates" (2.1.265–67). For the Kate/cat pun, see Helge Kökeritz, *Shakespeare's Pronunciation* (New Haven, 1953), 98.

34. There is another version of this story in Foxe, *Actes and Monuments*, 1469: "The VIII of Aprill, there was a Cat hanged upon a gallowes at the Crosse in Cheape, apparelled like a Priest, ready to say Masse, with a shaven crowne. Her two forefeet were tyed over her head, with a round paper lyke a wafer cake

Like Hooker/Vowell on the subject of Exeter in 1549, Fleming insists that the nation was divided by the prospect of the Spanish marriage; although "some supposed that this land would have become a golden world," others "were of a contrarie opinion, supposing (as it came to passe indeed) that the peoples minds would be alienated" (4:61). The optimistic "some" developed their idyllic hypothesis in propaganda, which Fleming, again quoting from Foxe, represents as both excessive consumption and excretion: "Maister White then bishop of Lincolne in his poetical veine, being droonke with joie of the marriage, spued out certeine verses" (4:61).[35] So too, he imports Foxe's description of the official celebrations to honor the Spanish king. At London bridge "was a vaine great spectacle set up, two images representing two giants, one named Corineus, and the other Gogmagog holding betweene them certeine Latine verses, which for the vaine ostentation of flatterie I overpasse" (4:62). Against this "vaine ostentation," Fleming, following Foxe, offers the power of demotic humor in putting official ritual in its place, describing the setting up of a public "rood" or crucifix in St. Paul's church as part of the welcome to King Philip— "as good a pageant as the best," but one not intended as such. We are treated to a sardonic picture of how Bishop Bonner "in his roialtie, and all his prebendaries about him . . . anointed the rood with oile in divers places, and after the annointing crept unto it and kissed it." Foxe, of course, intended this cer-

---

put betweene them: whereon arose great evil will against the Citie of London. For the Queene and the Byshops were very angry withall: and therefore the same after noone, there was a Proclamation, that who soever could bring foorth the partie that did hang up the Cat, should have xx nobles, which reward was afterwardes increased to xx markes, but none could, or would earne it."

35. This metaphor would very shortly be adopted by the Martin Marprelate pamphlets. See, for example, *Read over D. John Bridges*, where the bishop of Gloucester is said to have announced in a sermon that "beefe and brewesse had made him a papist" (32); *The Just Censure and Reproofe of Martin Junior*, where it is recommended to Whitgift that "Bancroft and drunken Gravate should be the yeomen of his Cellar" (18); and especially in the organizing metaphor of the response to Bishop Thomas Cooper's *Admonition to the People of England* (1589): *Hay any worke for Cooper . . . wherein worthy Martin quits himself like a man . . . and makes the Coopers hoopes to flye off and the Bishops Tubs to leake*, where the equation is between Anglican propaganda and spilled beer.

emony to be read as an act of idolatry; and its demotic parody follows:

> Not long after this, a merrie fellow came into Pauls, and spied the rood with Marie and John new set up, wherto (among a great sort of people) he made low curtsie and said: Sir, your maistership is welcome to towne. I had thought to have talked further with your maistership, but that ye be heere clothed in the queenes colours. I hope ye be but a summers bird, for that ye be dressed in white and greene. (4:63)

Here today and gone tomorrow. This is the comic version of the message the *Chronicles* carry in tragic form, as the story of the four Tudors unrolls, each determined to erase the traces of his or her predecessor.

In considerable glee the *Chronicles* (via Foxe) mock the rumor of Queen Mary's pregnancy: "Thus we see then how man dooth purpose, but God disposeth as pleaseth him. For all this great labor, provision, and order taken in the parlement house for their yoong maister long looked for, comming so surelie into the world; in the end appeered neither yoong maister nor yoong maistresse that anie man yet to this daie can heare of" (4:70). But the skepticism of popular opinion is also invoked (and approved) on this topic:

> In the middest of this great adoo, there was a simple man (this I speake but on information) dwelling within foure miles of Barwike, that neer had beene before halfe waie to London, which said concerning the bonefires made for queene Maries child; Here is a joifull triumph, but at length all will not prove worth a messe of pottage. . . . For the people were certified, that the queene neither was as then delivered, nor after was in hope to have anie child. At this time manie talked diverselie. Some said this rumour of the queenes conception was spread for a policie: some other affirmed that she was deceived by a tympanie or some other like disease, to thinke hirselfe with child, and was not . . . but what was the truth thereof, the Lord knoweth, to whome nothing is secret. (4:82)

And when Mary proclaimed war against France and Philip left for the campaign in Flanders, "there was great talk among the common people, muttering that the king making small account of the queene, sought occasions to be absent from hir" (4:87).

The result of this campaign was the loss of Calais to the French, the greatest disaster of the reign and a sign, for the chroniclers, of its wrongheadedness.[36]

When we turn to the reign of Elizabeth, it must first be acknowledged that the chroniclers were, in large part, willing to tell a more optimistic story. Whether or not they were *bound* to is an important question nevertheless. They were working, evidently, with the narrative premise of a return to Protestantism that was satisfactory to the majority of their countrymen, a premise which alone could justify the emphasis on Catholic conspiracy, on the trials of Edmund Campion and William Parry. The trial for treason of Sir Nicholas Throkmorton in Mary's reign, which had been transcribed with evident sympathy for the accused and for the jurors who acquitted him, is now balanced by the trial of Sir Francis Throkmorton, the nephew of Nicholas, for whom not a trace of sympathy is discernible. Or rather, by the omission of the trial itself and the transcription only of Throkmorton's confession, along with official documents denying the public rumors that the confession had been obtained through torture. The troublesome matter of the queen's plans to marry the French duc d'Alençon in 1579, which so disturbed Edmund Spenser and the Leicester faction, makes no appearance at all in the narrative until Alençon *departs*, with much accompanying ceremony, in 1581; and her troubles on the other end of the theological scale with the Puritan polemicists are unrepresented.

Yet from time to time, thanks to the reportorial procedure adopted throughout, we can hear, alongside the expression of loyalty or the excoriation of traitors, other more mundane and humane intonations. For instance, we can compare Fleming's sardonic reprise of the official pageants designed to celebrate the Spanish marriage in 1554 with his treatment of Elizabeth's reception into Suffolk and Norfolk in 1578. He chose to insert, verba-

36. "The said towne was woon from the French king by K. Edward the third, in the time of Philip de Valois then French king: and being in possession of the kings of England two hundred and eleven years, was in the time of Philip and Marie . . . lost within lesse than eight daies: being the most notable fort that England had" (4:93).

tim, the entire account by T.[homas] C.[hurchyard] of these festivities[37], unwilling, he tells us, to "let it perish in three halfepenie pamphlets, and so die in oblivion" (4:375). The comment is valuable as a key to the chroniclers' own concept of their task—creating a permanent public archive in relation to transient or popular consumption. Not that popular culture is ignored. When the queen entered Norwich, "the acclamations and cries of the people to the almightie God for the preservation of her majestie ratled so lowd, as hardlie for a great time could anie thing be heard" (4:377), and on Sunday, when a mysterious coach containing "Mercury" approached the court, the people "followed it in such flocks and multitudes, that scarse in a great greene (where the preaching place is) might be found roome for anie more people" (4:386). But since we are once again reading a first-person, on-the-spot reportage, the human element, with its tendency to demystification, tends to jar with the idealizing texts of the Latin orations and English poems. Even "Mercury's" speech, which contains its own description of these pageants, is surprisingly candid about the organization that at every level underwrites such a show:

> With that a swarme of people everie waie
> Like little ants about the fields gan run,
> Some to provide for pompe and triumph well,
> Some for good fare, yea houshold cates and meate,
> And some they ran to seeke where poets dwell,
> To pen foorth shews and paint out trifles well.
>
> (6:387)

Without the worker ants, neither the literal consumption of provisions ("cates") by the royal party nor the metaphorical consumption of literary sweetmeats ("trifles") would have been possible.

Nor is there any mistaking the mixture of humor and chagrin with which the reporter is forced to acknowledge the gap between the ideal and the real. The pageants are plagued by material circumstances. The queen does not come when she is expected: "there having althings in readinesse, they hoovered on

37. Thomas Churchyard, *A Discourse of the Queenes Maiesties entertainment in Suffolk and Norfolk* (1579).

the water three long houres, by which meanes the night came on, and so they were faine to withdraw themselves and go homeward, trusting for a better time and occasion" (4:394); speeches are not delivered because they are cut off by rain (4:379); shows are not what they should be because of economic constraints ("by meane of some crossing causes in the citie"); and at one point we are told directly what the real costs are to a community of having to put on such entertainments:

> But now note what befell after this great businesse and preparation. For as the queenes highnesse was appointed to come unto hir coch, and the lords and courtiers were readie to mount on horsseback, there fell such a showre of raine (and in the necke thereof came such a terrible thunder) that everie one of us were driven to seeke for covert and most comfort, insomuch that some of us in bote stood under a bridge and were all so dashed and washed, that it was a greater pastime to see us looke like drowned rats, than to have beheld the uttermost of the shewes rehearsed. Thus you see, a shew in the open field is alwaies subject to the sudden change of weather, and a number of more inconveniences. But what should be said of what the citie lost by this cause; velvets, silkes, tinsels, and some cloth of gold being cut out for these purposes, that could not serve to anie great effect after? (4:401)

In fact, the question of what should be said is deliberately rephrased as what *could* be said by prudent recorders, who fall back on common wisdom or tactful silence:

> Well, there was no more to saie, but an old adage, that Man dooth purpose, but God dooth dispose, to whose disposition and pleasure the guide of greater maters is committed. So this thursdaie tooke his leave from the actors, and left them looking one upon another, and he that thought he had received most injurie, kept greatest silence, and lapping up (among a bundle of other misfortunes) this evill chance, everie person quietlie passed to his lodging. (4:401)

It is difficult not to believe that an intelligent sixteenth-century reader might observe the connections between this passage and Fleming's earlier comments. Courtiers like drowned rats, or bishops crawling to kiss the rood, are likewise "as good a pageant as the best," "a greater pastime . . . than to have beheld the uttermost of the shewes rehearsed." Both in respect of Queen Mary's pregnancy and Norfolk's pomp, "we see . . . how man dooth purpose, but God disposeth." In the "bundle of other misfortunes" besides the weather itself that Elizabeth's courtiers experienced were weathercock politics and economic distress.

And there is something truly startling in what immediately follows this long and florid account of the progress—the anecdote of the ploughwright Matthew Hamont, who in early 1579 was tried and convicted for heresy before the bishop of Norwich, having "published" his belief that "the new testament and gospell of Christ are but meere foolishnesse, a storie of man, or rather a meere fable," and that God will save a repentant sinner by mere mercy, without any need of this fabulous redemption. This anecdote bears comparison with that of the radical butcher in 1536; the crime for which the ploughwright is executed is not in fact heresy, but sedition: "bicause he spake words of blasphemie (not to be recited) against the queenes majestie and others of hir councell," his ears were cut off and he was "burned in the castell dich of Norwich" (4:405–6).

That there was a will in the 1587 *Chronicles* to optimism can be deduced from the insertion of a large chunk of what might be called industrial history—the account of the rebuilding of the port of Dover. Despite the fact that this project began, at the queen's instigation, in 1583, this account is chronologically deferred until 1586, when the story of the reign as the chroniclers conceive it is already drawing to a close. Dover had been allowed to fall into disrepair at the time of the loss of Calais, and its state was therefore a matter of national confidence and prestige. Here we are given, verbatim, the words of Reginald Scot, a kinsman of Sir Thomas Scot, chief supervisor of the reconstruction. Reginald, himself an expert surveyor of Romney marshworks, becomes another of the many eyewitnesses whose testimony both enlivens and complicates the *Chronicles*. From Scot we learn everything we could possibly want to know about the technology of construction on sand against water: what "provision of stuffe should be made, to wit, of timber, thorne, faggots, needles, keies, beetels, piles, pasture, earth"; how between April and harvest, when they were not needed in the fields, hundreds of workmen, carts and oxen were summoned from the market-towns by proclamation. Since Scot had a personal and family interest in promoting a positive account of this project, he decided to "omit all contentions and factions concerning these proceedings, as also all injurious practices against those works" (4:857), a declaration which, by summoning up the specter of sabotage, accomplishes rather the opposite. We also learn that the Romney marshmen were the preferred workmen and what they were paid (eight to sixteen pence per day for a ten-hour day, from six in the morning to six at night, with a two-hour midday break) (4:862). However, it also emerges that the workers had to report at 5 A.M., "and such as were absent had no allowance that daie: if they came late, their wages was totted at the expenditors good discretion" (4:863). These figures may or may not be qualified by the unquantifiable statement that Sir Thomas Scott and his officers "did (not seldome times) bestow rewards bountifullye upon the poore workmen, who upon sundrie occasions were driven to worke longer than the rest, and with more difficultie; for some at some times wrought in danger of life, and offtimes in the waters up to the wast or shoulders" (4:861–62). But the suggestion that danger money was paid is surely in conflict with Scot's other statement, that the writing of this industrial history is (in some mysterious territory where psychology merges with public relations) reparation for inadequate material compensation:

> In the declaration hereof also, the parties which have deserved commendation or consideration maie perhaps in some sort have a kind of recompense: for other reward was not looked after, or sought for by the best executioners hereof, sith the better sort imploied their travell with great charges, the meaner sort their readie furtherance to their power, the poorer people their labor at a small rate to the preferring and performance of this worke; and all with such forwardnesse and willingnes of mind, as the like hath not beene knowne or seene in this age. (4:858)

The reconstruction of Dover, then, was presented by Scot and reproduced in the *Chronicles* as an instance of high-minded collaboration between classes, of benevolent industrial relations. Yet precisely because Scot shares the anthropological impulse of the project as a whole, tensions and contradictions in his narrative reveal the presence of a counterculture. There is one astonishing passage, in which Scot records how the workers responded to the issue of timekeeping:

For they never ceased working the whole daie, saving that at eleven of the clocke before noone, as also at six of the clocke in the evening, there was a flag usuallie held up by the sargent of the towne, in the top of a tower, except the tide or extraordinarie busines forced the officers to prevent the houre, or to make some small delaie and staie thereof. And presentlie upon the signe given, there was a generall shout made by all the workers: and wheresoever anie court (cart) was at that instant either emptie or loden, there was it left, till one of the clocke after noone or six of the clocke in the morning, when they returned to their businesse. But by the space of half an houre before the flag of libertie was hanged out, all the court drivers entered into a song, wherof although the dittie was barbarous, and the note rusticall, the matter of no moment, and all but a jest, yet it is not unworthie of some briefe note of remembrance; because the tune or rather the noise therof was extraordinarie and (being delivered with the continuall voice of such a multitude) was verie strange. In this and some other respect, I will set downe their dittie, the words wherof were these:

> O Harrie hold up thy hat, t'is eleven a clocke,
>   and a little, little, little, little past:
> My bow is broke, I would unyoke,
>   my foote is sore, I can worke no more.

Here, then, is yet another instance of popular culture as consensus, raising "a generall shout," as in Fleming's account of the Babington Plot the celebratory bonfires "grew to be generall." On this occasion, however, the anthropologist experiences it with a slight unease, as "extraordinarie" and "strange." Here too the literal consumption of food is at issue—the workers must demand a lunch and dinner break—but there can be no real sense of community when the many singing as one do so in order to bring pressure on their overseers. An inevitable prejudice, whether social or cultural, produces condescension ("the dittie was barbarous, and the note rusticall, the matter of no moment, and all but a jest"); but the observer is not blind to the ethical content of the scene. The fact that the workmen begin to sing half an hour *before* their break is expected indicates that they expect "extraordinarie business" will delay it; the ritual complaint economically suggests their endurance, their skepticism, and their humor ("t'is eleven a clocke, and a little, little, little, little past"). And Scot explicitly located this practice within a broader cultural poetics, in which that which is "extraordinarie" (worthy of historical note) may also be potentially unruly:

> The song was made and set in Romneie marsh, where their best making is making of wals and dikes, and their best setting is to set a needle or a stake in a hedge: howbeit this is a more civill call than the brutish call at the theater for the comming awaie of the plaiers to the stage. (4:865–66)

We can now return to that opening anecdote, the description of the popular celebrations in London at the discovery of the Babington Plot and the arrest of the conspirators; part of a large block of material written by Abraham Fleming, with himself as the primary witness. In the whole design of the supplement, this will lead in terms of both historical causation and emotional affect to the trial of Mary, Queen of Scots. There seems to be no doubt that Fleming was straightforward in his intentions, which were to present the conspiracy in the darkest possible light, to justify the executions in all their severity, and ultimately to justify the conviction and execution of the Scottish queen, whose complicity in the plot (he may or may not have known) had been partially engineered by Sir Francis Walsingham. At the same time, as I have argued elsewhere,[38] the historiographical principle of the *Chronicles* ("to give everie author leave to tell his owne tale") resulted in Fleming's recording (in the uncensored text) of the unpublished or illegally published statements of the conspirators in the Tower. The effect of *this* imprudent multivocality would have been, at the very least, to unsettle the readers' sympathy and allegiance, which, at the end of this long story of changing religions, must already have been a complex construction. It was scarcely surprising, then, that this section of the text was strenuously pruned in the censored version.

In Fleming's original, uncensored account of the festivities, along with the bells and the bonfires, the ritual, we are told, expanded into a public picnic, which could also be perceived as a sociopolitical, secular, eucharist:

> The people . . . did not so staie their inward rejoising; but bringing out their square and round tables into the open streets, like

---

38. In *Writing and Censorship*, ed. Paul Hyland and Neil Sammells (London, 1992).

neighbors sitting togither, and furnishing the boords with such
provision as the present time afforded, made merrie in comelie
and honest sort. Where (by the waie) this is notewoorthie, that
manie times an evill thing doth effectuat a good. For by the breaking out of this conspiracie . . . it so came to passe, that many a
privat reconciliation was procured by this mutuall meeting of
neighbours between diverse that before had beene at overthwarts
and in secret grudge, all which was washed awaie with a cup of
merrie go downe for hir sake, that *Secundum Deum est columen
salutis nostrae.* (4:900)[39]

In this passage, it is almost impossible to resist the ritual allure
of the scene, the impression of verisimilitude, the utopian
hypothesis of social harmony, with the queen, the secular
redeemer, as the ritual's central object of reverence. But a suspicious reader—rendered suspicious by earlier sections of the
Chronicles—might now notice that Fleming qualifies his own theory of consensus by the phrase "the well affected of the citie,"
which, like Scot's refusal to discuss any hostility to the Dover
project, immediately summons up the thought of the ill affected;
that the parenthetical motivation ("we thinke in conscience")
makes one wonder what other motivations (social pressure, or
simple carnival impulse) might have been operative on such an
occasion; and that the sacrificial gestures of "the meaner sort"
were memorable (that is, of historical significance) precisely
because of economic hardship, because "wood was then at a sore
extent of price."

These intimations of strain reappear in a more easily recognizable form when Fleming addresses the problem of verbal testimony, and offers his own version of the popular voice raised in
consensus:

people thronged togither to see the unnaturall beasts that were
attached, . . . which how damnable it was, the whisperings, communications, and lowd speeches of the multitude, pointing at
them with the finger of infamie as traitors of singular note (some
saeing, Looke, looke, yonder go the errant traitors that would have

39. This phenomenon is confirmed by Thomas Nelson, *A Short Discourse
Expressing the substaunce of all the late pretended Treasons* (London, 1586), which
describes how the people "set their Tables in the streates, with meates of every
kinde, where was preparde all signes of joye, that could be had in mind" (Aiiir).

killed our queene, yonder goe the wretches that would have burnt
our citie, that would have alienated the state of the land, that would
have laid all open unto bloudshed, slaughter, desolation, and spoile:
yonder they go whome heaven above dooth abhorre, the earth
below detest, the sun, moone, and starres be ashamed of, all creatures doo cursse and count unworthie of breath and life) . . . whome
none can pitie without suspicion of impietie, none lament but
with lacke of loialtie, none favorablie speak of but with great note
of ingratitude and privie trecherie? To this effect tended the interchangeable speeches of the people, all with one voice disclosing
the conceipts of their mind against these eminent traitors. (4:898–99)

This certainly sounds at first reading like the unimpeachable
voice of hegemony. On second thought, however, it appears that
the chronicler was conscious of the fictionality of his task—that
is to say, the production of univocality, or political consensus,
by ventriloquism. Leave alone for the moment the question of
whether the "people" (a problem of political and socio-economic
definition) "really" responded in this way (a problem of historical verifiability), and attend simply to the rhetorical strategy.
The quotation that begins with an air of dramatic realism (some
saieng, Looke, looke . . .) gradually modulates into high-cultural
rhetoric ("yonder they go whome . . . the sun, moone, and starres
be ashamed of") and ends by admitting that unanimity is *required*,
since "none can pitie" the conspirators "without suspicion of
impietie . . . none favorablie speak" of them "without great note
of ingratitude and privie trecherie."

And lest we should have any doubt as to how this official
version of popular culture has been constructed, Fleming
proceeded, a few pages later, to show the mechanism at work:

the people were in dailie expectation and desire to heare some
report of the conspirators now by their owne confessions suffi-
ciently convicted: whereupon a preacher at Pauls crosse *was commanded from authoritie,* to deliver some notice to the assemblie,
answerable to the knowledge which he himselfe received by eare
at the best hand; namelie, that diverse of the traitors were apprehended, and without anie torture or torment confessed their trea-
sonable intentions; which were, to murther her majestie, and
procure meanes for the arrivall of forren powers, whereby the land
might be overrun, heaven and earth confounded, and all things
turned topsie turvie. (4:909)

The redefinition of the carnival impulse ("topsie turvie") as apocalypse ("heaven and earth confounded") shows how far the editorial account of this crisis was incompatible with the demystifying spirit of the *Chronicles* elsewhere. Whether or not Fleming felt himself, also, "commanded from authoritie"; whether he misjudged that mandate and went too far in developing a punitive rhetoric which discredited itself; whether he understood the gap between that rhetoric and the "facts"; he was here evidently struggling, caught between his own anti-Catholic impulses and the anthropological logic of the project as a whole.

In conclusion, I would like to recall, and to wrest to opposite purpose, Levy's words of reproach to the *Chronicles* for putting everything in, no matter how trivial, vulgar, or unworthy, by some standards, it might seem. "Once facts could be established as equal in authenticity," Levy wrote, "they were assumed to be *equal* in all other ways as well." Just so; an egalitarian principle, however, that traditional historiography, often accused of being exclusively concerned with the history of elites, is bound to see rather as *lack* of principle. Cultural history, however, can take comfort from the self-definitions of cultural anthropology, which, in Clifford Geertz's words, is concerned with the following: "construing social expressions on their surface enigmatical"; learning to distinguish between involuntary gestures (a twitch) and conspiratorial signals (a wink); disentangling "a multiplicity of complex conceptual structures, many of them superimposed upon or knotted into one another, which are at once strange, irregular, and inexplicit" (phrases which coincidentally replicate Levy's critique of the *Chronicles*). All of these types of interpretation are justified, finally, by remembering that they are *just* interpretations, and hence debatable; and by their saving relation to the small things of this world, rather than the large concepts. The anthropological approach to culture is, in Geertz's word, necessarily "microscopic." The cultural anthropologist

confronts the same grand realities that others—historians, economists, political scientists, sociologists—confront in more fateful settings: Power, Change, Faith, Oppression, Work, Passion, Authority, Beauty, Violence, Love, Prestige; but he confronts them in contexts obscure enough . . . to take the capital letters off them. These all-too-human constancies, "those big words that make us all afraid," take a homely form in such homely contexts. But that is exactly the advantage. There are enough profundities in the world already. (5, 6, 10, 21)

In the 1587 edition of "Holinshed's" *Chronicles*, this microscopic vision recognizes radical butchers, canny bakers, naive miller's men and iconoclastic ploughwrights, dead cats thrown into the street in symbolic fancy dress, old women "in an agonie" misconstruing the advice of officious gentlemen, puffins and bran baked in cloths to hold the loaves together, square and round tables brought out into the streets, soaked pageanters ("drowned rats") taking shelter under a bridge, the wherrymen saved by their oars. As Geertz would say, "another country heard from" (23).

Yet the obvious fact remains that reading the *Chronicles* from an anthropological perspective is a very different matter from doing fieldwork. We are getting this information easily, vicariously. It was the chroniclers themselves who did the work, who were the original ethnographers. As Geertz puts it, "the ethnographer 'inscribes' social discourse; *he writes it down*. In so doing, he turns it from a passing event, which exists only in its own moment of occurrence, into an account, which exists in its inscriptions and can be reconsulted" (19). We owe them our gratitude for having been there before us (often as on-the-spot reporters), and for leaving us so rich an archive. And we owe the archive itself another inspection.

6

Quod oportet *versus* quod convenit: *John Donne, Kingsman?*

The much of privileg'd kingsmen, and the store
Of fresh protections make the rest all poore.
                                                    Elegy 14

All the great eulogists—Spenser, Donne, Jonson, Dryden—were
profoundly conservative in their politics.
                            Lauro Martines, *Society and History in*
                            English Renaissance Verse

Encapsulated here in the quotation from Lauro Martines is the
myth I continue to wrestle with—that most "canonical" writers
from the early modern period were "profoundly conservative
in their politics," by which Martines means, specifically, monarchical in terms of constitutional theory and elitist in terms of
class. In the case of Donne, this legend was given its strong form
at the end of the nineteenth century. In 1899 Edmund Gosse
delivered his own assessment of Donne as a preacher, which
locked him into a class attitude:

> He belonged to an age in which the aristocratic element exercised
> a domination which was apparently unquestioned. Although of
> middle-class birth, the temperament, manners, and society of
> Donne were of the most distinguished order. The religious power
> of democracy had been discovered. . . . The Rebellion, and still
> more the success of the Rebellion, driving men and women of
> incongruous classes close to one another in the instinct of self-
> protection against the results of a common catastrophe, began

the democratization of the pulpit. But of Donne we must think as untouched by a least warning of such a political upheaval. He belonged, through and through, to the old order; was, indeed, in some ways, its most magnificent and minatory clerical embodiment. . . . This unity of purpose, this exaltation of a sovereign individuality, made to command in any sphere, gave to the sermons of Donne their extraordinary vital power; and if this particular charm has evaporated. . . . it is that the elements in ourselves are lacking, that we no longer breathe the aristocratic Jacobean atmosphere.[1]

We know now, of course, that as a member on his mother's side of a recusant family that included Sir Thomas More, his grandfather William Rastell, who fled to Louvain, two maternal uncles who became Jesuits, one of whom was captured in 1583 and sentenced to death, though not executed, Donne would have had, at the very least, some complicated feelings about what "the old order" was. Gosse's relocation of Donne in terms of class calmly substitutes "belonging" (which can here be only a matter of sensibility or style) for the recalcitrant fact of middle-class birth. But even in psychological terms, Gosse's construction of his subject as a pillar of the establishment can be accomplished only by ignoring everything that makes Donne interesting, paradigmatic of a culture marked by social mobility and contested religious affiliations. Nevertheless, ex cathedra statements like these tend to retain their subliminal effect, even after their bias has been noted.

In the wake of Gosse's portrait (behind which lay the hagiographical *Life* by Isaac Walton, published in 1640 as a sign of the "old order" in a time of political upheaval), the picture of Donne has changed considerably—and yet, in crucial respects, not changed at all. First came Donne's recuperation by Grierson in 1921, and then, more influentially, by T. S. Eliot.[2] It was no coincidence that Eliot chose to elevate Gosse's Donne while demoting Milton, the literary hero of the Whigs. Then came the modern biography by R. C. Bald, which revealed all too clearly

1. Gosse, *The Life and Letters of John Donne*, 2 vols. (London, 1899), 2:236–37.

2. Eliot's interest in Donne was sparked by the appearance in 1921 of H. J. C. Grierson's anthology *Metaphysical Lyrics and Poems* (Oxford, 1921) which Eliot reviewed.

Donne's absorption by the Jacobean patronage system.[3] And this was followed by John Carey's iconoclastic study,[4] which boldly converted to a post-Freudian analysis materials that for Bald were simply the occasion for moral evaluation. This more subtle phase of the legend of Donne's "conservatism," though the terms Carey used were "ambition" and "apostasy," requires a more complex refutation. Looking at the middle period of Donne's life, the period immediately before his decision to take orders, Bald was forced to admit that it did not present "a particularly edifying spectacle"; from his letters, especially, Donne appeared to Bald "as one who had mastered the arts of the courtier, and it is clear, even when he finally turned to the Church, that he did not intend to abandon those arts, but to rise by them" (301). Here lies the origin of John Carey's thesis, complete with the term—arts—that he would make structural. Bald struggled with the evidence, and wished to give Donne the benefit of the doubt—"the truth seems to be," he wrote, "that these qualities in him were not essential and permanent traits of his character; rather, they were symptoms of his despair" (301); but he (and Gosse behind him) nevertheless created the premises on which Carey (and after him Jonathan Goldberg)[5] erected their more sinister portraits.

Hagiography's converse, then, was the spectacle of John Donne the careerist, marked by a devouring ego, acting always from expediency, and obsessed with a desire to replicate his sovereign's status and style in his own life and writings. We were told of the "thwarted, grasping parasitic life that Donne was forced to lead"; that after Donne's ecclesiastical promotion "he grew repressive, as people generally do with age and success"; and that "the egotism manifest throughout his career is what impels the poetry."[6] This form of psychobiography sought to account for everything Donne wrote as the fallout of two fatal decisions,

3. *John Donne: A Life* (Oxford, 1970).

4. *John Donne: Life, Mind and Art* (New York, 1981).

5. Goldberg, *James I and the Politics of Literature* (Baltimore, 1983). Goldberg makes Donne one of the chief exhibits of his thesis that James totally dominated early-seventeenth-century culture by the coercive force of his Word, hypostasized as *Works* in 1616.

6. Carey, *John Donne*, 19, 11.

which in Carey's chronology are melded into one: the decision to abandon his family religion, shortly after the death of his brother Henry while in prison for consorting with a Jesuit priest in 1593; and the decision to seek advancement at all costs. Not only did the bad conscience Donne suffered while practicing the arts of apostasy and ambition produce its symptoms in the imagistic texture of his poems, but, it was argued, Donne embraced the very powers that had driven his family into martyrdom and outlawry. Carey noted (correctly) that James's presence and doings are insinuated into private poems that appear to deny their importance; but he also believed that this denial was always effected, as it is in *The Sunne Rising* or *The Anniversarie*, in terms of the speaker's claim himself to royal status, to monarchical absolutism: "What the real court and the real king may be doing stays at the back of his mind, and as if to counteract this the poem evolves its announcement of personal kingship. . . . Royalty glowed in the depth of his consciousness. . . . In giving his unqualified allegiance to James, Donne answered the need of his imagination";[7] and Goldberg repeated this observation with the statement that "Donne's self constitution is absolutist."[8]

I do not wish to deny this psychological insight. Carey's approach has considerable explanatory force with respect to Donne's fascination by the terms (martyrdom, recusancy, idolatry, canonization) suggestive of his abandoned and outlawed religion; and Carey was particularly acute on the way intelligence is shaped by early repression, on the "sense of perilous trespass" that made Donne an outsider who both despised those whose rules rejected him and longed for incorporation.[9] But about Donne's politics in the stricter sense Carey was both reticent and mistaken, while Goldberg leaped on the mistake and accentuated it. From the records that Donne left us to consider (and from some that he never intended for the scrutiny of anyone except his closest friends), it is impossible to produce a single-minded person, let alone a coherent pattern of behaviors. The story of Donne's politics is one of self-division and self-contradiction; and

7. Carey, *John Donne*, 109, 115.
8. *James I*, 219.
9. Carey, *John Donne*, 21.

we will learn more about both Donne and his culture by noticing the contradictions than by trying to smooth them away.

Before proceeding, however, I must first acknowledge two rather different accounts of Donne's thought and situation. In a study subtitled "Religion, Politics, and the Dominant Culture," Debora Shuger has attempted to replace the over-simple opposition between orthodoxy and its legitimation on the one hand, and opposition and subversive ideas on the other, by a more complex model.[10] Shuger, whose primary topic, despite her subtitle, is theology and ecclesiology (in Lancelot Andrewes, Richard Hooker, and Donne himself), found the *established* religious culture more protean, "probing, and self-critical than has often been assumed" (14–15). Nevertheless, she too sees Donne's sermons as exemplifying his "absolutist theology." In any case, by addressing only an audience that is itself extremely sophisticated in literary theory, the larger political implications of the argument are rendered, by their exclusiveness, innocuous.

The second (though chronologically prior) is Arthur Marotti's account of Donne as a "coterie poet," which begins with the important reminder that Donne's poetry belonged to the world of manuscript circulation and therefore spoke to a self-selected audience in a culturally encoded language.[11] This recontextualization of Donne's work was an important first step in complicating his image and rendering him less amenable to Gosse's confident description. Marotti's able deployment of Inns of Court attitudes and conventions, for instance, led him to pay more attention to the iconoclastic satires and elegies; while his serious investigation of the poetry of compliment, especially as addressed to female patrons, led him to a more subtle account of Donne's relation to the patronage system than Carey's or Goldberg's. In a summary statement poised on the threshold between Donne's youthful and aborted career under Elizabeth and his amazing success under James, Marotti remarked:

> Donne was simply neither the social and intellectual rebel nor the flattering importunate courtier: he contradictorily assumed both roles and his complex behavior changed according to circum-

10. *Habits of Thought in the English Renaissance: Religion, Politics, and the Dominant Culture* (Berkeley and Los Angeles, 1990).
11. *John Donne, Coterie Poet* (Madison, 1986).

stances. To characterize him accurately, one need not accept either the hagiographical pattern laid down by Walton . . . or the model of Donne as the intellectual skeptic-hero who refused to compromise himself for crass worldly ends. The fact is that he was both jauntily, if not self-destructively, *subversive of* as well as contritely *deferential toward* the Establishment. (182)

Yet the fact is also that Marotti's study, like Shuger's, is directed at what is in effect a contemporary coterie audience; if not the relatively small number of intellectual historians who are up-to-date on literary theory, then the equally small world of Donne specialists.

My own argument is both more straightforwardly polemical and addressed, *deo volente*, to a wider audience. It is what Donne has represented in the institutionalization of literature and literary criticism in general that justifies making him a cause, if not a cause célèbre. I too wish to promote a more nuanced account of his work, or, putting it in human terms, to achieve better justice for Donne by demonstrating that he was never so simply the king's man, never so simply careerist or absorptive of absolutist monarchism as twentieth-century literary critics (with the exception of Marotti) have been led or chosen to believe. To this end, I make central the peculiar products of Donne's transitional period, from 1606 to 1615, when he was clearly engaged in an intellectual agon with his environment—works that Marotti passes over in a few suggestive pages. This message is addressed to any reader of literature who has too easily accepted the paradigm for which I unfairly make Lauro Martines responsible. But because the effect of this focus is to highlight political events (including Donne's own brief experiment with active politics as a member of parliament) and to tackle in some detail what Donne actually thought about absolutist monarchy, the argument may be of some interest also to historians of the early modern period. In particular, this view of Donne's career could shed light on current debates about motivation. If the two major competing models of motivation are principle and self-interest,[12] it may be useful to show how difficult it is, in certain complex political careers, to tell which of these is, from moment to moment, speak-

---

12. See especially T. K. Rabb and D. M. Hirst, "Revisionism Revised," *Past and Present* 92 (1981): 55–99.

ing to us from the past through the textual record; which, for this topic, must certainly include literature.

Perhaps more than any other Renaissance poet Donne challenges us to conceive of subjectivity in environmental terms, to see how socio-economic and political circumstances interact with a particular temperament to produce the historical person, who is both partly conscious of the rules by which he must play and partly the director of all his roles.[13] But once we enter the territory where psychobiography and cultural history merge, another Donne legend complicates our task: the myth of maturation and renunciation to which Donne himself contributed. In 1619, putting his life in order before departing for Germany as a member of the embassy James was sending to Bohemia, Donne wrote to Sir Robert Carr, the cousin of the king's favorite and one of Donne's closest friends, and sent him the manuscript of *Biathanatos*, his essay on suicide, along with a letter that, perhaps better than any poem, tells the story of Donne's ambivalences:

> It was written by me many years since; and because it is upon a misinterpretable subject, I have always gone so near suppressing it, as that it is onely not burnt: no hand hath passed upon it to copy it, nor many eyes to read it: onely to some particular friends in both Universities, then when I writ it, I did communicate it: . . . Keep it, I pray, with the same jealousie; let any that your discretion admits to the sight of it, know the date of it; and that it is a Book written by *Jack Donne*, and not by *Dr. Donne*: Reserve it for me, if I live, and if I die, I only forbid it the Presse, and the Fire: publish it not, but yet burn it not: and between those, do what you will with it.[14]

This letter attempts to negotiate a space "between": between "the Presse" and "the Fire," open publication and absolute self-censorship. By the same token, we can imagine a self-

13. Compare the argument of Ernest Gilman, in " 'To adore, or scorn an image': Donne and the Iconoclastic Controversy," *John Donne Journal* 5 (1986), that "the surviving portraits offer a series of shifting, carefully contrived poses that vividly reflect the several different selves Donne would fashion for himself—the resolute 'gentleman volunteer' at eighteen, the fastidious melancholiac at twenty-three, the sober courtier at thirty-four, the august divine at forty-nine" (68).

14. Donne, *Letters to Severall Persons of Honour* (1651), facsimile ed. M. Thomas Hester (New York, 1977), 21–22.

characterization somewhere between Jack and the Doctor, in the sense that neither of the two can exist without drawing on the other's resources; and as Jack's book has been kept by the Doctor in a marginal category strangely described as "onely not burnt," so Donne himself exists in an autobiographical limbo between past and present. Unfortunately, this dramatic act of self-division has also inhibited the project of resituating Donne in the cultural environment that made him, with his own collaboration, what he was. For whatever their motives (polishing or darkening the image), critics and scholars have tended to count on the divide between Jack and the Doctor, in order to save the Donne they prefer from his other self. In addition, the problem of dating posthumously published poems has been bedeviled by Ben Jonson's statement that Donne had written "all his best pieces ere he was 25 years old,"[15] a generalization that begs the question of value. In contrast, I shall argue here that Jack and the Doctor inhabited the same psychic and cultural space—the space between full publication and full suppression—from the time Donne entered Lincoln's Inn in 1592 until his death in 1631; and that reading between the lines of *all* his work (or at least some of the lines of all of the *kinds* of that work) will give us a fairer picture.

Spied Spies and Dark Doubles: The Satires

Nothing he wrote more evidently belonged in that "onely not burnt" category than Donne's satires, which can be roughly assigned to the time when Donne was a law student in London and during his appointment as secretary to Sir Thomas Egerton, the Lord Keeper, in 1598.[16] In another letter, perhaps to Sir Henry Wotton, perhaps in 1600, Donne insisted that "no coppy

15. Jonson, *Works*, ed. C. H. Herford, P. Simpson, and E. Simpson, 11 vols. (Oxford, 1925–52), 1:135.

16. For a dispute about dating *within* this period, compare Bald, *John Donne: A Life*, 77, who spaces the five satires over a five-year period from 1593 to 1598, with John T. Shawcross, who locates them all in 1597–98, when Donne was first in Egerton's employ. See his " 'All Attest his Writs Canonical' : The Texts, Meaning and Evaluation of Donne's Satires," in *Just So Much Honor*, ed. Peter A. Fiore (University Park, Pa., 1972), 245–72. For the only major study of Donne's satires, see M. Thomas Hester, *Kinde Pity and Brave Scorn: John Donne's Satyres* (Durham, 1982).

shall bee taken" of any of the "compositions" he has been and will be sending his friend. "Call not this," he wrote, "a distrustfull but a free spirit":

> to my satyrs there belongs some fear and to some elegies and these perhaps, shame. Against both which dispositions although I be tough enough, yet I have a ridling disposition to bee ashamed of feare and afrayd of shame. Therefore am I desirous to hyde them without any over reconing of them or there maker.[17]

For reasons that will become obvious, none of the five satires was published during Donne's lifetime (though they evidently circulated fairly widely in manuscript). When the posthumous edition of Donne's poems was being prepared in 1633, the satires (and five of the elegies) were excluded from the license to publish, although at the last minute permission was granted for the satires, perhaps because the object of their critique is so evidently Elizabeth's regime that the licenser thought them safely archaic. But for us they can do more to explain the political Donne than any of the more famous "Songs and Sonets," or any of the Jacobean sermons.

The last of the five is the most clearly Elizabethan. Addressed both to the queen herself, "Greatest and fairest Empress," and to an unnamed justicer who is surely Egerton, the poem bears a certain awkward likeness to Spenser's Legend of Justice. Here the satire is pitched at authorized bribery, that aspect of the patronage system which requires all access to the Law to be mediated by state officials, so that the legal world is divided into two populations, officers and their suitors. Officers adulterate the law; suitors are complicit in its adulteration by paying the fees demanded of them. "Th'Iron Age *that* was, when justice was sold," wrote Donne, implicitly aligning Elizabeth with Astraea and Egerton with Spenser's Artegall, but going one better (or worse): "now / Injustice is sold dearer farre" (lines 37–38).[18] For tactical reasons, Donne briefly offers to separate his two addressees from the abuses of the system for which they are responsible,

17. Donne, *Complete Poetry and Selected Prose*, ed. Charles M. Coffin (New York, 1952), 364; from the Burley MS.

18. Donne, *The Satires, Epigrams and Verse Letters*, ed. W. Milgate (Oxford, 1967), 23.

assuming ignorance in the queen and a desire for reform in the minister:

> Greatest and fairest Empresse, know you this?
> Alas, no more than Thames calme head doth know
> Whose meades her armes drowne, or whose corn o'rflow:
> You Sir, whose righteousness she loves, whom I
> By having leave to serve, am most richly
> For service paid, authoriz'd, now beginne
> To know and weed out this enormous sinne.
>
> (Lines 28–34)

But no sooner has he observed the conventional distinction between monarch and government than he drops the pretense of advising his superiors and returns to his real purpose: advising the have-nots to despair of the system:

> If Law be in the Judges heart, and hee
> Have no heart to resist letter, or fee,
> Where wilt thou'appeale? Powre of the Courts below
> Flow from the first maine head, and these can throw
> Thee, if they sucke thee in, to misery,
> To fetters, halters. . . .
>
> (Lines 43–48)

Like Spenser, Donne alludes to the dubious extension of the doctrine of equity, which when viewed negatively could be seen as extending the power of the judiciary, so that law may be seen as residing not in the words of parliamentary statutes, but in "the Judges heart."[19] The topic was particularly germane in a poem partly addressed to Egerton where, more daringly, Donne extends the reign of injustice to the measures taken against Roman Catholics, who (under Kafka's sign of the Goddess of the Hunt) were tracked down by special officers called pursuivants, and sometimes indicted merely for having in their possession ritual objects of the old religion. Donne invites anger from those who never show it (stoic, coward, martyr) at a scene worthy of Kafka:

19. See J. H. Baker, *An Introduction to English Legal History* (London, 1979), 83–95; Baker, ed., *The Reports of Sir John Spelman*, 2 vols. (London, 1978), 2:37–56; *A Discourse upon the Exposicion & Understandinge of Statutes With Sir Thomas Egerton's Additions*, ed. Samuel E. Thorne (San Marino, 1942), 54–67, 76–85.

> To see a Pursivant come in, and call
> All his cloathes, Copes; Bookes, Primers; and all
> His Plate, Challices; and mistake them away,
> And aske a fee for comming. . . .
>
> (Lines 65–68)

And though he momentarily permits the alternative vision of an absolute, allegorical justice ("Oh, ne'er may / Faire lawes white reverend name be strumpeted"), that possibility is never given narrative space. Rather, it is Law as a personification who dictates economic injustice, who "tells us who must bee / Rich, who poore, who in chaires, who in jayles" (lines 72–74). Finally the satirist, it seems, is addressing himself; and the dream of law reform is dissolved in an Aesopian fable about illusion, *The Dog and the Shadow*:

> Thou'art the swimming dog whom shadows cosened,
> And div'st, neare drowning, for what vanished.[20]

The theme of Law as the heart of an oppressive society had been anticipated in Satire 2, directed against a bad poet who becomes a worse lawyer. This epitome is, however, inadequate to the spreading stain Donne envisages in Elizabethan legal practice and beyond. Far from specifying a particular, isolated charlatan, the poem is packed with wide-reaching charges, some deviously inserted as if they were merely metaphors. For instance, the introductory and secondary theme of bad literature includes a playwright who

> (like a wretch, which at Barre judg'd as dead,
> Yet prompts him which stands next, and cannot reade,
> And saves his life) gives ideot actors meanes
> (Starving himselfe) to live by'his labor'd sceanes.
>
> (Lines 111–14)

So the primary theme of bad Law enters surreptitiously, in parenthesis. It also enters ambiguously; for though the comparison between poverty-stricken playwright and condemned criminal sounds contemptuous at the level of epithet ("wretch," "idiot"), at the narrative level it points to a natural generosity among the

---

20. Compare Spenser's use of this fable in *The Shepheardes Calender*, 50 above.

underprivileged, along with the ingenuity that allows them to exploit the absurd and the obsolete in the juridical system (the benefit of clergy and the use of a rudimentary literacy—the "neck-verse"—to claim it).[21]

The body of the satire also entangles legal corruption and the art of writing in a difficult argument, one that spreads across society and subsumes, again through metaphor, most of the supposedly intellectual practices of church and state in a single indictment. The corrupt lawyer, Coscus, is described as accumulating land by sharp practice, deliberately producing flawed legal documents so that he may later profit from his own errors:

> Peecemeale he gets lands, and spends as much time
> Wringing each Acre, as men pulling prime.
> In parchments then, large as his fields, hee drawes
> Assurances, bigge, as gloss'd civill laws,
> So huge, that men (in our time's forwardnesse)
> Are Fathers of the Church for writing lesse.
> These hee writes not; nor for these written payes,
> Therefore spares no length; as in those first dayes
> When Luther was profest, he did desire
> Short *Pater nosters*, saying as a Fryer
> Each day his beads, but having left those lawes,
> Addes to Christs prayer, the Power and glory clause.
> But when he sells or changes land, he'impaires
> His writings, and (unwatch'd) leaves out, *ses heires*,
> As slily'as any Commenter goes by
> Hard words, or sense; or in Divinity
> As controverters, in vouch'd texts, leave out
> Shrewd words, which might against them cleare the doubt.
>
> (Lines 85–102)

Who would be better placed than a lawyer-in-training to recognize the more disreputable aspects of the profession? Assurances, or title deeds to property, have grown so complicated that they

21. For an excellent summary of the legal history of benefit of clergy and its artibrary extension to laymen in the sixteenth century, see Baker, *Reports of Sir John Spelman* 2:327–33. Baker cites an intriguing comment by Sir Henry Hobart, to the effect that the protection of the literate should continue as being "in favour of learning in generall, and in reverence of mankind, and man's blood (which in persons *of use* is not to be shed lightly")" (331; italics added), a comment capable of generating Donne's social cynicism.

can be deployed to cheat those whom they should protect. As Milgate pointed out, the tendency of an over-complex law to defraud the uneducated was already a commonplace of social criticism. In Philip Stubbes's *Anatomy of Abuses* there is a lament for "times past when men dealt uprightly" and "sixe or seven lines was sufficient for the assurance of any peece of land whatsoever," whereas now (in the 1580s) two or three skins of parchment will hardly serve: "Wherein shalbe so many provisoes, particles, and clauses . . . that it is hard for a poore ignorant man to keep halfe of them: and if he fail in one of the lest, you knowe what followeth" (Part II, sig. E7v).[22]

John Lauritsen has rightly observed that the real subject of this satire is not merely the law but the "rather broader matter of the perversion of the word, whether this be in law, theology, or poetry."[23] Donne equates fraudulent legal writing to textual scholarship which avoids precisely the "hard words" that most need glossing, or the dishonest theological controversy which, when citing the text of Scripture, leaves out those intractable passages which cannot be brought into line with the position being argued. But what makes this broader conception possible is the huge territory that "law" covered, virtually synonymous with "society," or "the system," but a system without coherence. Common law, civil law, canon law; all three were competing for jurisdiction in Elizabethan England, a situation creative at least of relativism, at worst of cynicism. The satire concludes by naming a fourth category, statute law, which, though produced by Parliament and including such venerable protections for the citizen as Magna Carta, might well have become the most dangerous of the four, at least for a satirist. Yet in naming the danger Donne defies it: "my words none drawes / Within the vast reach of th'huge statute lawes." The first two treason acts of Elizabeth's reign (1 Eliz. c. 5 [1559]; 13 Eliz. c. 1 [1571]) specifically included words along with overt acts in the definition of treason; four other parliamentary statutes in the sessions of 1571 and 1572 were intended to deal with the new threat posed by the Jesuits and by Elizabeth's excommunication and to further extend the defi-

22. See Milgate, *Satires, Epigrams and Verse Letters*, 127.
23. "Donne's *Satyres*: The Drama of Self-Discovery," *Studies in English Literature* 16 (1976): 123.

nition of treason. In 1585 a new act (27 Eliz. c. 2) covered the mere presence in the realm of a Jesuit or newly trained seminary priest or the act of receiving a traitor into one's house. As John Bellamy has argued, the piling of statute upon statute led to a confusion fortuitous for the government, dangerous for the subject:

> The policy, which was quite apparent later in the sixteenth century, of framing indictments so that they might be said to be founded on several statutes was a deceitful subterfuge to gain procedural benefits, like avoiding the need to produce witnesses. . . . Many of these weaknesses and difficulties might have been resolved if the scope of the treason laws had been open to criticism. Unfortunately, the heightened political and religious tensions tended to make men curb their tongues for fear of being regarded as betrayers of their prince, church and realm. Very noticeably, there was no opposition by the nobility as the fourteenth- and early fifteenth-century kings had met with when they sought to change the scope of the treason laws. The magnates of those times had been great experts on illegal accusations and precedents in general, but in the sixteenth all those with a good knowledge of the law seem to have been in thrall to the crown. With no accepted and organized opposition for much of the period, there was not the same need to observe the letter of the law so strictly.[24]

Satire 2 stands, in effect, as Donne's manifesto for the satiric program, as a writerly exposé of a crisis in Law in the most comprehensive sense; and in its focus on the *textual* nature of malfeasance, the complicity in systemic corruption of writing and the intelligence that drives it, it helps to explain not only the other satires, but also Donne's political poetics.

As Lauritsen noted (117–30), the satires also develop prophylactically the self-division Donne defined in the letter to Carr about *Biathanatos*, and that became, I shall argue, the strongest symptom in his middle years of an inability to decide securely between principle and self-interest, between a dangerous integrity and a prudent clientage. In Satire 1 the division is between the "fondling motley humorist" whose passions are clothes and

24. *The Tudor Law of Treason* (London and Toronto, 1979), 61–82, especially 82–83. And though not a treason statute, the "Act against seditious words and rumors" (23 Eliz. c. 2), sometimes referred to as the "statute of silence," introduced by the Lords in the 1581 Parliament, was another attempt to control discussion of the queen's marriage plans and the problem of the succession.

women, and the scholar who, though wishing to remain "coffin'd" in his study surrounded by his books, is cajoled out into
the streets, without which expedition the satire, it needs hardly be said, would be empty of material. In Satire 4 this scenario
is repeated, as the speaker, having unwisely gone to court, finds
himself trapped, his back against a wall, by a version of himself:
that is to say, one who pretends a commitment to the Elizabethan court ("If of court life you knew the good, / You would leave
lonenesse"), but who in reality wishes only to exchange scandalous gossip:

> he nigardly
> As loth t'enrich me, so tells many'a lie,
> More then ten Hollensheads, or Halls, or Stowes,
> Of triviall household trash he knowes; He knowes
> When the Queene frown'd, or smil'd, and he knows what
> A subtle States-man may gather of that;
> He knowes who loves; whom; and who by poyson
> Hasts to an Offices reversion;
>   . . .
> He like a priviledg'd spie, whom nothing can
> Discredit, Libells now 'gainst each great man.
> He names a price for every office paid.
>   (Lines 95–102, 119–21)

This passage functions as insidiously as the court gossip moves
from the trivial (which, as signified by the Tudor chroniclers, may
not be so trivial after all) to the deeply corrupt; for the focus of
Donne's satire, evidently, is not the gossip but what gives rise
to it. Repeating it, he credits it; while at the same time, by mentioning Burghley's and Walsingham's well-known spy systems,
he warns those like himself who may be tempted to discuss scandalous events and practices that those with whom they share
their outrage may actually be engaged in entrapment.

   And, more profoundly, Donne then proceeds to bring to full
analytical consciousness, and into structural relation, three complex ideas: the problem of complicity inherent in satire as a genre;
the fact that scandal, as an interpretive posture, is actually created by censorship, which transforms social criticism into a dangerous, outlaw activity; and the psychic experience of guilt,
which religion explains as the effect of original sin, but which
may, in this larger analysis, have sociopolitical origins:

I more amas'd then Circes prisoners, when
They felt themselves turne beasts, felt my selfe then
Becomming Traytor, and mee thought I saw
One of our Giant Statutes ope his jaw
To sucke me in; for hearing him, I found
That as burnt venom'd lechers doe grow sound
By giving others their soares, I might growe
Guilty, and he free: Therefore I did show
All signes of loathing; But since I am in,
I must pay mine and my forefathers sinne.

(Lines 129–38)

Indeed, having escaped the physical presence of this alter ego (who is dressed, significantly, in the same black velvet, though shabbier, that Donne wears in his youngest portrait) the speaker of Satire 4 finds that he has caught, as an infection, the scandalous *mentalité*. "At home in wholesome solitarinesse," he finds himself not returned to scholarly serenity, but on the contrary overtaken by a Dantesque vision:

a trance
Like his, who dreamt he saw hell, did advance
It selfe on me; Such men as he saw there,
I saw at Court, and worse, and more.

In the last lines of the poem, the speaker returns, awake and voluntarily, to court, where, feeling inexplicably threatened by the sight of the queen's guards, he "shook like a spyed Spie" (line 135). The merger of innocent and guilty, self and libellous other is complete, but completely ambiguous. And if the writer has become the spy, is it now the reader who should fear entrapment?

Despite Ben Jonson's own gossip about chronology, it seems clear that much of Donne's lyric poetry was staged as a response to Jacobean, not Elizabethan, culture. *The Canonization* distinguishes between the "Kings reall, or his stamped face,"[25] that is to say, his image on coinage, as Elegy 10 speaks of love impressing his heart "As Kings do coynes, to which their stamps impart /

25. Donne, *Poetical Works*, ed. H. J. C. Grierson (Oxford, 1929), 14. I refer to this paperback version of the first volume of Grierson's edition on the grounds of its accessibility. The pagination differs from that of the original two-volume edition (Oxford, 1912) which contains annotation.

The value" (84). More significantly, *The Sunne Rising* and the lesser known *Loves Exchange* refer to the king's hunting, an unmistakable code (shared with *King Lear*) that specifies James as the royal referent.[26] Likewise the speaker in Elegy 15 includes in his maledictions against the man who betrayed the lovers into quarreling the hope that "his carrion coarse be a longer feast / To the Kings dogges, then any other beast" (98). This theme connects erotics to a more sinister account of the Jacobean Hunt (as Kafka allegorically conceived the state's pursuit of offenders). *Pseudo-Martyr* (1610) refers to "any such hunting as [the Jesuits] will call intemperate,"[27] an allusion that on the surface appears to defend the king against his Roman critics, but which could also relate to the activities of the pursuivants. *The Courtier's Library*, a parodic bibliography based on Rabelais, written in Latin, and never published in Donne's lifetime, contains in its preface the following address to the courtly aspirant:

> The engagements natural to your life at court leave you no leisure for literature [sleep, dress, meals, and amusements]. . . . But still you condescend to keep up an appearance of learning, to enable you occasionally to praise with grace and point your fellow-menials, the royal hounds.[28]

In this context the specifically Jacobean clue, "the royal hounds," is unmistakably presented in a contemptuous light, implying the conventional relationship between fawning dogs and flatterers.

This alone might counter the claim that Donne in the reign of James was totally dominated by the personal style and utterances of his sovereign. But the refutation must go deeper. Intricately connected to the workings of James's court Donne certainly was, and he had more direct dealings with James than most of his "literary" contemporaries. Like James, Donne was a learned controversialist, whose intelligence was bent to the king's agenda;

26. If there remains any doubt that the king's passion for hunting was a frontal issue early in the reign, James settled that doubt by issuing, on September 9, 1609, a proclamation against poaching that began: "We had hoped, seeing it is notorious to all our subjects how greatly we delight in the exercise of hunting. . . ."

27. *Pseudo-Martyr*, ed. F. J. Sypher (Delmar, N.Y., 1974), 187.

28. *The Courtier's Library, or Catalogus Librorum Aulicorum*, ed. E. M. Simpson (London, 1930), 40–41.

but he was *equally* connected to the opposition group in the troublesome Jacobean parliaments. His writing is therefore marked by a deep ambivalence about the world of influence in which he both desperately wanted and deeply disdained to participate.

One of the earliest of Donne's verse letters was sent to Sir Henry Wotton as he left for his embassy to Venice on July 13, 1604, and its language reflects, as well as the complimentary function of the poem, the optimism that generally accompanied the opening of the new reign, the political honeymoon. Donne referred there to "those reverend papers" that gave Wotton his commission, "whose soule is / Our good and great Kings lov'd hand and fear'd name,"[29] the symbolic combination of text, person, and office in the royal signature. But by no means all of the Jacobean writings retain this idealistic stance. The *Essays in Divinity,* for example, show Donne in transition between what his son, who published them, called "Civill business" and his later career in the church. They contain (like the fourth satire) gibes at royal favorites and financial mismanagement, which helps to explain why John Donne, Jr., dedicated them to Sir Henry Vane in 1651, suggesting that "the manner of their birth may seem to have some analogie with the course you now seem to steer . . . being so highly interested in the publick Affairs of the State."[30] Donne's anti-Catholic polemic, and even more the products of his deanship of St. Paul's, the majestic sermons that account for Gosse's construction of Donne as a pillar of the "old order," would seem to make him the king's man; between 1623 and 1626 there appeared first *Three Sermons upon Speciall Occasions,* then *Foure,* and then *Five,* their publication and republication indicating the importance Donne took them to have in public affairs, and the title of the volumes indicating the extent to which he had accepted the role of a high priest of public events, if not of public policy. But even in his 1622 sermon to the Virginia Company Donne recorded the ethical dangers of tying the pulpit to secular purpose:

> Birds that are kept in cages may learne some Notes, which they should never have sung in the Woods or Fields; but yet they may

29. *Poetical Works,* 189.
30. Donne, *Essays in Divinity,* ed. E. M. Simpson (Oxford, 1952), 3.

forget their Naturall Notes too. Preachers that bind themselves alwaies to Cities and Courts, and great Auditories, may learne new Notes, they may become occasionall Preachers, and make the emergent affaires of the time, their Text, and the humors of the hearers their Bible.[31]

A Jacobean Satire?

Donne's transitional years, especially, were marked by contradiction and its writerly symptoms: on the one hand a continuation into the new reign of satirical, even subversive and unpublishable writings; on the other, the use of his extraordinary intellect and eloquence for official purposes. For a closer look at the bird not yet in the cage, we might do well to begin with Elegy 14, *A Tale of a Citizen and His Wife*, not least because efforts have been made to excise it from the record. Although it appeared in the 1635 and 1669 editions of Donne's poems and was accepted by Grierson with mild hesitation, John Shawcross defined it as "having generally been rejected" and omitted it from his own edition "in conviction of [its] spuriousness and in hope of helping rid Donne of [its] inferiority."[32] Helen Gardner had earlier discarded it from hers, with a revealing justification:

> Although some students of Donne would not regard it as impossible that he should write an improper poem in 1609, at the time that he was writing *Pseudo-Martyr* and the "Holy Sonnets," it is surely in the highest degree unlikely that he would produce a weak *pastiche* of his earlier style, echoing phrases and lines from his own fourth Satire and Elegies at a time when he had developed a new style.[33]

Gardner's exclusion of Elegy 14 begs precisely those questions the poem demands we answer, and was motivated by a moral

31. Donne, *A Sermon Upon the VIII Verse of the 1 Chapter of the Acts of the Apostles. Preach'd To the Honourable Company of the Virginia Plantation. 13 Novemb. 1622* (London, 1622), 33. For an instance of Donne's resistance to the role of king's man in the pulpit, see my account, in *Censorship and Interpretation*, 97–101, of the sermon Donne was commanded to preach in September 1622 supporting James's *Directions to Preachers*, restraining the pulpit from discussing the affairs of the Palatinate.

32. Shawcross, ed., *Complete Poetry of John Donne* (Garden City, N.Y., 1967), xxiii.

33. Gardner, ed., *The Elegies and the Songs and Sonnets* (Oxford, 1965), xxxix.

and evolutionary theory of Donne's development not so very different, finally, from that of Walton, Gosse, or Bald.

As Gardner was well aware, *A Tale of a Citizen and His Wife* reiterates the strategy of Donne's fourth satire, of sedition-by-proxy. By now placing his satire in the mouth of a discontented Londoner, pretending all the while to be shocked at what is said, and flirting, while it is said, with the citizen's wife behind his back, Donne once again divided himself into two voices, the one asserting its loyalty but demonstrating its frivolity, the other supposedly rejected as treasonous, yet carrying a certain obvious conviction.

The poem is, moreover, saturated with issues contemporary to the first decade of James's reign. As the speaker attempts to make contact with the citizen whose wife is making eyes at him behind her husband's back, he tries to find topics likely to engage a London merchant—to establish (and Donne uses a word fashionable in our own literary practice) the local "discourse":

> To get acquaintance with him I began
> To sort *discourse* fit for so fine a man:
> I ask'd the number of the Plaguy Bill,
> Ask'd if the Custome Farmers held out still,
> Of the Virginian Plot, and whether Ward
> The traffique of the Inland seas had marr'd,
> Whether the Brittaine Burse did fill apace,
> And likely were to give th'Exchange disgrace;
> Of new-built Algate, and the More-field crosses,
> Of store of Bankerouts, and poore Merchants losses.

And the citizen, his tongue finally loosened by the theme of "Tradesmens gaines," launches into a heated critique of the Jacobean economy in its relation to the power structure:

> He rail'd, as fray'd me; for he gave no praise,
> To any but my Lord of Essex dayes;
> Call'd those the age of action; true (quoth Hee)
> There's now as great an itch of bravery,
> And heat of taking up, but cold lay downe,
> For, put to push of pay, away they runne;
> Our onely City trades of hope now are
> Bawd, Tavern-keeper, Whore and Scrivener;

> The much of Privileg'd kingsmen, and the store
> Of fresh protections make the rest all poore.[34]

As Grierson worked through the series of topical references,[35] the poem appeared to situate itself in late 1609 or early 1610. Aldgate was rebuilt by 1609, and on April 11, 1609, "Britain's Bourse," constructed by Salisbury to draw financial business away from the City, was formally opened and so named by the king. The reference to Custom Farmers refers to a transaction initiated by Salisbury in 1604, with Arthur Ingram as his agent, by which the so-called Great Farm of the Customs was leased out to merchant syndicates, who from their profits, so the justification went, would lend money to the crown; but by 1609/10 they were becoming increasingly reluctant to do so. There were two expeditions sent to Virginia in 1609, one in May and one at the end of the year. The reference to Ward, a notorious pirate, though less chronologically specific, also relates to this period. There were numerous complaints from the Venetian ambassador, and the issue of pirate control was raised in the 1610 Parliament. As for the "Plaguy Bill," 1609 was a particularly bad year for plague. There were no theatrical performances at court during the winter 1609–10, and, more to the point, on September 29, 1609, James issued a proclamation further proroguing Parliament until February 9, citing plague as the primary reason.[36] Another proclamation on September 22, this time affecting the legal profession, adjourned part of Michaelmas term, also on account of plague.[37] The fact, therefore, that "the Plaguy Bill" of this poem echoes that of *The Canonization* ("When did the heats which my veines fill / Adde one more to the plaguie Bill?") may rather destabilize the presumed earliness of the lyric than the lateness of the satire; it surely cautions us that the sharp break between "early" and "mature" work posited by Gardner was a wishful critical construction.

Perhaps most tellingly, Grierson discerned in the citizen's complaint echoes of yet another royal proclamation, this time on

34. *Poetical Works*, 95–96.
35. Grierson, *Poetical Works* (1929), 2:84.
36. See James Larkin and Paul Hughes, eds., *Stuart Royal Proclamations*, 3 vols. (Oxford, 1973), 1:232–33.
37. *Stuart Royal Proclamations* 1:230–31.

March 25, 1610. If he was right, Elegy 14 belongs to the late spring of 1610, when many of Donne's friends were convened at Whitehall, protesting, among other things, the publication of John Cowell's *The Interpreter*, a book dedicated to Archbishop Bancroft and devoted to the praise and mystification of the royal prerogative. Phrases from the proclamation seem to have been lifted, not only out of context, but into an opposing "discourse," one might even say, a discourse of opposition. James's strategy in publishing the proclamation had been to preempt the parliamentary attack on Cowell, which had probably been led by Richard Martin,[38] by claiming that he himself was outraged by this unwarranted intervention by an amateur into constitutional theory. Yet the method James chose to discredit Cowell in public was to deliver a broad attack on *all* public discussion of these issues, and to combine this prohibition with a lament for the good old days:

> The later age and times of the world wherein we are fallen, is so much given to verball profession, as well of Religion, as of all commendable Morall vertues, but wanting the action and deedes agreeable to so specious a profession, as it hath bred such an insatiable curiosity in many mens spirits, and such an itching the tongues and pennes of most men, as nothing is left unsearched to the bottome, both in talking and writing. . . . And therefore it is no wonder, that men in these our dayes do not spare to wade in all the deepest mysteries that belong to the persons or State of Kings or Princes, that are gods upon Earth: since we see . . . that they spare not God himselfe. And this license that every talker or writer now assumeth to himselfe, is come to this abuse, that . . . many men that never went out of the compasse of Cloister or Colledges, will freely wade by their writings in the deepest mysteries of Monarchie and politique government.[39]

To counter this "license" of talk and writing, James ended by proclaiming a new campaign for "better oversight of Books of all sorts before they come to the Presse"; in other words, an increase in censorship.

The phrases that Grierson discerned as carried over into the citizen's protest were the lament for "action and deedes," and a

---

38. See Elizabeth Read Foster, ed., *Proceedings in Parliament 1610*, 2 vols. (New Haven, 1966), 1:25.

39. *Stuart Royal Proclamations* 1:243.

complaint against the "itching" of tongues and pens. Yet during the transfer, if such it were, the nostalgia for an "age of action" has become the clearly seditious claim that the only age of action was "my lord of Essex dayes." Donne himself had volunteered for the two expeditions against Spain in 1596 and 1597. Among Donne's friends, Sir Henry Goodyer, Sir Henry Wotton, and Sir Henry Neville all had had connections with Essex. Goodyer was knighted by Essex in Ireland in 1599. Wotton, who had been Essex's secretary and may well have introduced to him his good friend Donne, hastily detached himself when the breach with the queen seemed irreparable, and awaited in Venice James's accession. Which Henry Neville attended with Donne at the Mitre Tavern we cannot be sure. If it was Sir Henry Neville of Abergavenny, he was knighted by Essex at Cadiz; if it was Sir Henry Neville of Billingbear, Berkshire, he was later implicated in Essex's conspiracy, stripped of his offices, and imprisoned in the Tower from July 1601 until James's accession.[40] Sir Thomas Roe, another of Donne's close friends and correspondents, wrote a flaming satire about the Jacobean court that partly corroborates the citizen's complaint in Elegy 14. Roe's speaker, like Donne's in the fourth satire, went to court (but after 1603) and found there "Kings were but men":

> What Treason is, and what did Essex kill,
> Not true Treason, but Treason handled ill;
> And which of them stood for their Countries good,
> Or what might be the cause of so much Blood.
> He said she stunck, and men might not have said
> That she was old before that she was dead.
> His Case was hard, to do or suffer; loth
> To do, he made it harder, and did both.
> Too much preparing lost them all their Lives,
> Like some in Plagues kill'd with preservatives.
> Friends, like land-souldiers in a storm at Sea,
> Not knowing what to do, for him did pray.[41]

40. For a fuller account of the Neville identity problem, and of the "Mitre Tavern Ballad" as an important key to Donne's environment, see my "All Donne," an earlier version of this chapter, in *Soliciting Interpretation*, ed. Elizabeth Harvey and Katharine Maus (Chicago and London, 1990), 37–67.

41. Printed by Grierson in an appendix, *Poetical Works*, 375.

Whoever attributed this poem to Donne, adding it to his satires in the 1669 edition, obviously believed that its tone and opinions were compatible with the five that preceded it;[42] and Roe's Jacobean satire also tells us much about the confusion and guilt, what one might call the survivor complex, that affected those who had looked to Essex as a focus for their own alienation and who, when the mortal danger of their allegiance dawned on them, "not knowing what to do," chose to be ineffectual. Carey berated Donne for apparently abandoning Essex as soon as his fall from favor was apparent, citing a letter of Christmas 1599: "My lorde of Essex and his trayne are no more mist here then the Aungells which were cast downe from heaven nor (for anything I see) likelyer to retourne" (71).[43] I, however, find it impossible to tell from this statement whether or not Donne was of the Devil's party, with or without knowing it. Neither Bald nor Carey mentions Elegy 14, the latter being therefore able to conclude that although "James's court was far more obviously corrupt and degenerate than Elizabeth's, Donne never ventured any criticism of it at all" (64).[44] "I am no Libeller, nor will be any," says the narrator, in introducing his citizen decoy, and dismisses his "harsh talke" as "void of reason." But as he listens, the narrator once again begins to "sweat for feare of treason." From this perspective, Elegy 14 becomes a significant exhibit in the cultural afterlife of the Essex rebellion, a tribute to the role played in that event (or in those that led up to it) by difficult intellectuals like Donne and his friends.

Law versus Prerogative: Constitutional Theory

The issue of the royal prerogative and what, if any, were its limitations was one of the central preoccupations of both James and

42. He may or may not have known that Donne's *Courtier's Library* (ca. 1609) contains two items indicating continued support for Essex after his indictment: "The Brazen Head of Francis Bacon: concerning Robert the First, King of England," an attack on Bacon for his betrayal of Essex; and "An Encomion on Doctor Shaw, Chaplain to Richard III, by Doctor Barlow," which equated Barlow's Sermon at Paul's Cross in 1601, as an attempt to manipulate public sympathy away from Essex, with Shaw's "sycophantic defence" of the murder of the Princes in the Tower (51–52).

43. For the letter, see Bald, *John Donne: A Life*, 117–18.

44. Carey did, however, note that "the thought of government spies and

his parliaments throughout the reign. Revisionist historians have denied that this *was* a preoccupation, at least of Parliament, and claimed that the issue did not become seriously contentious until the subsequent reign. I agree rather with those who perceive a steady development in the House of Commons of a *theory* of political opposition, one that was partly generated by James's own determination to theorize the prerogative, or an unlimited sovereignty, and partly a response to local issues of economics—taxes, monopolies, "the much of privileged kingsmen," and the responsibility of the Commons to monitor the nation's finances.

In *Biathanatos*, his essay on suicide, seemingly an unlikely location for the development of constitutional theory, Donne's thoughts on sovereign power were recorded in a way that is both supremely his own (that is to say, evasive) and specifically Jacobean. A religious case of conscience—the rightness or wrongness of taking one's own life—is to be settled by way of a political analogy, but one, it appears, of the same paradoxical structure as the treatise it supports. The personal liberty of conscience that permits a rational man to take his own life in defiance of the natural law of self-preservation is equated, not, as one might more easily imagine, to the liberty of the subject—that great and contentious topic of Jacobean parliamentary discourse—but to its equally contentious opposite, royal prerogative. The text insists perversely that "mans liberty" can be understood as an illimitable sovereign power of the individual to dispose of himself as he pleases: and (as Donne continues to upend the political analogy) the natural law of self-preservation operates only like those temporary stays on royal prerogative that parliamentary watchdogs attempt to provide:

> as neither the watchfulnesse of Parliaments, nor the descents and indulgences of Princes, which have consented to lawes derogatory to themselves, have beene able to prejudice the Princes *non obstantes*, because prerogative is incomprehensible, and overflowes and transcends all law. . . . so, what law soever is cast upon the conscience or liberty of man, of which the reason is mutable,

---

butchers like Topcliffe . . . never failed to turn his stomach. They are still among the targets in *The Courtier's Library*, which probably received its final form as late as 1611" (36).

is naturally condition'd with this, that it binds so long as the reason lives.[45]

Now it might be possible to argue that Donne was here constituting himself in monarchist, absolutist terms in order to deflect his sense of powerlessness within the system; and/or that the statement that royal prerogative is unbounded is to be taken at face value, as proof of Donne's literal acceptance of the Stuart doctrine of the divine right of kingship. But neither of these meanings seems compatible with the genre of the paradox, whose substance is a profound alienation from commonly accepted belief, and which in Donne's practice elsewhere requires the reader at least to experience the temptation to read every statement in reverse, as a mirror image of itself. Nor, if we suppose that in this major paradox Donne was expressing a real, though controversial and indeed unpublishable, conviction of his own, is it likely that he would so toy with the concept of personal liberty as to *equate* it with precisely that power that was most inimical to freedom of religious practice in his own state. And indeed the language here is slippery. To call the prerogative "incomprehensible" is potentially a subversive pun, combining what can not be understood with what can not be contained.[46] This implication is corroborated by the following statement that the prerogative "over-flowes and transcends all law."

This was a motif of political thought and discourse that was increasingly common from 1604 through 1610, especially among Donne's friends and associates. His reference to the "watchfulnesse of Parliaments" might appear to be evaluatively neutral, but the so-called "Mitre Tavern" ballad tells us that Donne, who himself would soon be returned as a member for Taunton in the truncated session of 1614, belonged to a group that included several members of the House of Commons: Christopher Brooke, Richard Martin, Arthur Ingram, Sir Henry Goodyer, Henry Holland, Sir Robert Phelips, and Sir John Hoskyns. More signifi-

45. Donne, *Biathanatos. A Declaration of that Paradoxe, or Thesis, that Selfe-homicide is not so Naturally Sinne, that it may never be otherwise* (London, 1646), 48–49.

46. Compare *The Courtier's Library*, 24: "Edward Hoby's Afternoon Belchings; or, A Treatise of Univocals, as of the King's Prerogative." This shows that Donne was certainly capable of irony on the subject.

cantly, several of those were already well known, and some
would later become notorious, as Parliamentarians who consistently opposed what they saw as unwarranted extension of the
royal prerogative. On May 16, 1610, for instance, James had sent
a message to the Commons forbidding them from debating any
further his prerogative in the matter of impositions, or additional
taxes levied on imports. John Hoskyns had thereupon challenged
the newly mystified doctrine of the prerogative which Northampton and some of the higher clergy, in their separate ways, were
attempting to place in the category of *arcana imperii*. "Methinks,"
said Hoskyns on May 18, "our answer should be that we may
dispute [the prerogative]. And as to the phrases of infinite and
inscrutable, they be things that belong to heaven and are not
upon earth and he that looks for them here upon earth, may miss
them in heaven." And Christopher Brooke, who had given away
the bride at Donne's secret marriage and himself been thrown
into prison in consequence, added with careful balance: "As I
am always unwilling to argue the prerogative of my sovereign;
so am I not willing to lose the liberty of a subject. The prerogative is great yet is it not endless nor boundless, but justice and
equity are the bounds and limits of it."[47]

In his letter entrusting *Biathanatos* to Sir Robert Carr, Donne
had defined suicide as the "misinterpretable subject." The same
could be said both of the royal prerogative and of Donne's statements about it, which both resembled those of his friends and
were yet not so easy to place in the ideological spectrum.[48] The
fear of misinterpretation was one of Donne's most frequently
expressed anxieties; and while it undoubtedly spoke to an age

47. See *Proceedings in Parliament 1610* 2:94.
48. Among the items in the *Courtier's Library* were "A few small Treatises
supplementary to the Books of Pancirolli; to the Book of Things Lost is added
A Treatise on Virtue and on Popular Liberty, begun by a chaplain of John Cade
and finished by Buchanan." And in another, more economical joke Donne
added, "Tarlton, *On the Privileges of Parliament*" (48, 53). The first item associates
popular liberty both with outright and unsuccessful rebellion, in the form of
Jack Cade's 1450 insurrection, and with James's formidable Scottish tutor
George Buchanan, a name that stood for the theory of contractual monarchy,
classical republicanism, and, if necessary, tyrannicide. The second item associates the privileges of Parliament, which from 1604 onward were consistently
identified with freedom of speech, with a famous theatrical clown. It is impossible to determine, however, from which direction Donne's irony is coming.

of official censorship, it also authorizes us to read his writings as *capable* of misinterpretation, deliberately so. This is no less true of *Pseudo-Martyr*, for all its status as an official text published with the king's encouragement and dedicated to him. We know that Donne had entered the controversy over the Oath of Allegiance at the urging of Thomas Morton, which may have been seconded by James himself. Apparently it was not without internal resistance. His dedication of *Pseudo-Martyr* to James begins, "As Temporall armies consist of Press'd men, and voluntaries, so doe they also in this warfare" (A2), leaving it open to inference which category he himself belonged to. There is certainly evidence here of sycophancy: Donne describes himself as turned into an exhalation drawn upward by the solar influence of the king's "Bookes," a metaphor for his "ambition, of ascending" to the king's presence in some permanent capacity (A2r). Yet prior to the dedication, Donne addressed the ordinary reader in a way that suggests the pressures upon him; for to prove his sincerity he inserted an admission of his Catholic upbringing, transforming a conventional rhetorical gambit into a gamble. "I have beene ever kept awake," he wrote, "in a meditation of Martyrdome, by being derived from such a stocke and race, as, I believe, no family, (which is not of farre larger extent, and greater branches,) hath endured and suffered more in their persons and fortunes, for obeying the Teachers of Romane Doctrine, than it hath done." Although the context is rejection, the language is that of family pride and solidarity.

That Donne refused to include his family in the massive attack he would mount against the Jesuit mission is confirmed by his treatment of Sir Thomas More. It was one of James's own concerns to shatter the More legend and disperse the aura of sanctity it emitted. In his *Triplici Nodo*, the royal reply to the pope's breves and to cardinal Bellarmine, James quoted More's defense before the House of Lords, and concluded that by "his owne confession it is plaine, that this great martyr himselfe took the cause of his owne death, to be onely for his being refractary to the King in this said matter of Marriage and Succession; which is but a very fleshly cause of Martyrdome, as I conceive."[49] To which

49. James I, *Tripli Nodo, Triplex Cuneus. Or an Apologie for the Oath of Allegiance*, in *The Political Works of James I*, ed. C. H. McIlwain, 2 vols. (Cambridge, Mass, 1918), 1:106.

Donne replied in *Pseudo-Martyr* by invoking "Sir Thomas Moore, of whose firmeness to the integrity of the Romane faith, that Church neede not be ashamed" (108). The comment is inserted parenthetically in an attack on the doctrine of Purgatory; yet what Donne destroys with one hand—integrity—he restores with the other as a property of both the Roman faith and the martyr who chose to die for it.

But *Pseudo-Martyr* contains a larger sign than family solidarity of Donne's resistance to his self-assumed role as the king's polemicist. His strategy throughout was to compare the claims made by James and Pope Paul V, respectively, and to assert that those of the pope were more excessive than those of the king; yet the inference remains that those of the king may be *somewhat* excessive. For instance, having stated that when princes assume "high stiles" they "do but draw men to a just reverence, and estimation of that power, which subjects naturally know to be in them," whereas popes "by these Titles seeke to build up, and establish a power, which was ever litigious and controverted," Donne continued:

> And the farthest mischiefe, which by this excesse Princes could stray into, or subjects suffer, is a deviation into Tyranny, and an ordinary use of an extraordinary power and prerogative, of so making subjects slaves, and (as the Lawyers say) *Personas Res.* (43)

It is hard to believe that he intended this to be reassuring!

It was, in fact, the ordinary use (to raise revenue) of an extraordinary power that the opposition group in the Commons perceived as particularly dangerous, not least because absolutist theorists of the law were currently arguing that taxation was *not* an ordinary function of royal power but a legitimate function of the prerogative.[50] If issues like impositions were governed not by *meum et tuum*, the principle at the heart of common law, but rather by *salus populi*, the principle of royal prerogative, the effect

---

50. For a definition of the distinction between ordinary and absolute royal power, as it was articulated in 1606 by Sir Thomas Fleming, a common law judge, see Brian Levack, "Law and Ideology: The Civil Law and Theories of Absolutism in Elizabethan and Jacobean England," in *The Historical Renaissance*, ed. Heather Dubrow and Richard Strier (Chicago and London, 1988), 232. See also Francis Oakley, "Jacobean Political Theology: The Absolute and Ordinary Powers of the King," *Journal of the History of Ideas* 29 (1968): 323–46.

would indeed by, as men like Nicholas Fuller and Thomas Hedley argued, to make subjects slaves. In addition, however careful James had been in his early statements in England to present himself as a constitutional monarch, by early 1610 he had managed to give a contrary impression. On March 21 he addressed the new session of Parliament with a speech that referred to "doubts, which hath bene in the heads of some . . . whether I was resolved in the generall, to continue still my government according to the ancient forme of this State, and the Lawes of this Kingdome: Or if I had an intention not to limit my selfe within those bounds, but to alter the same when I thought it convenient, by the absolute power of a King."[51] Those doubts had been raised, in part, by an excessive reliance on proclamations during a long prorogation, and their publication in a single volume on February 3, 1610,[52] which gave the impression of *codification* just prior to Parliament's opening. At that opening, on February 15, Salisbury referred to those ill-affected persons who, "hearing of a course taken to bind up all the printed proclamations into a book to the intent that there may be better notice taken of those things which they commanded, have been content to raise a bruit that it was intended at this parliament to make the power of proclamations equal to the laws."[53] And especially in his speech of May 21 James exacerbated those doubts and bruits by his sharp and coercive tone. "If a king be resolute to be a tyrant," he said, "all you can do will not hinder him."[54] Although some modern historians have seen this speech as conciliatory, James himself said at the outset that his tone was negative: "I must complain of you to yourselves and begin with a grievance

51. James I, "A Speech to the Lords and Commons of the Parliament at White-Hall, on Wednesday the XXI of March. Anno 1609," in *Political Works*, 306–7.

52. See *A Booke of Proclamations, published since the beginning of his Majesty's most happy reign over England, etc. until this present moneth of February 3. Anno Domini 1609* (London, 1610).

53. See *Proceedings in Parliament 1610* 2:22. And see also Larkin and Hughes, *Stuart Royal Proclamations* 1:v–vi: "The Jacobean proclamations are pointed expressions of attitudes and axioms of the Crown and of its wearer . . . . Constitutionally, these documents are perhaps most significant as a prime source of friction between Crown and Parliament, especially the Commons, which repeatedly advanced them as grievances against the common law."

54. *Proceedings in Parliament 1610* 2:103.

instead of a gratulation" (2:103). And its effect, John Chamberlain reported to Dudley Carleton, was "so litle to theyr satisfaction, that I heare yt bred generally much discomfort; to see our monarchical powre and regall prerogative strained so high and made so transcendant every way, that yf the practise shold follow the positions, we are not like to leave to our successors the freedome we received from our forefathers."[55] "Transcendant," we remember, was the term that Donne used of the "incomprehensible" concept of prerogative in *Biathanatos*, entrusted to Carr as unpublishable, and so, in his own mind, still potent nine years *after* he had published *Pseudo-Martyr*, his partly obedient defense of obedience to the crown.[56]

J. P. Sommerville, in providing us with the clearest account to date of the competing theories of government and sovereignty in the earlier seventeenth century, several times cites Donne, apparently in the belief that he belonged on the side of the theorists of absolutism:

> Many writers—including Donne, Maynwaring, Willan, Rawlinson and Field—endorsed the view that Adam's power had been kingly. . . . If the power of the first fathers had been kingly, it followed that the doctrines of originall democracy and of the contractual origins of regal authority were false.[57]

But in fact the statement in *Pseudo-Martyr* to which he alludes *combines* a theory of original democracy ("if a companie of Savages, should consent and concurre to a civill maner of living, Magistracie, & Superioritie, would necessarily, and naturally, and Divinely grow out of this consent") with the statement that "Adam was created a Magistrate" (83). And Donne's rejection

55. Chamberlain, *Letters*, ed. Norman McClure, 2 vols. (Philadephia, 1939), 1:301. For an immediate response in the House, see James Whitelocke's statement that "he heard the speech yesterday and came ther with great desire and hope but went away exceeding sad and heavy and . . . saw nothing in that speech any way to restrain the power of imposing, even upon our lands and goods"(*Proceedings in Parliament 1610* 2:108).

56. See also the warning of Thomas Hedley in the 1610 debates that those who maintain "an unlimited and transcendent prerogative may peradventure be holden like the lovers of Alexander with Ephestion but never true lovers of the king with Craterus" (*Proceedings in Parliament 1610* 2:197).

57. *Politics and Ideology in England, 1603–1640* (London and New York, 1986), 30.

of the transference theory ("Regall authority is not therefore derived from men, so, as that certaine men have lighted a King at their Candle" [169]) is part of a larger rejection, as "a cloudie and muddie search," of all arguments as to the human origins of sovereignty, "since it growes not in man." Certainly John Donne, Jr., did not think that the belief in Adam's magistracy was automatically a belief in kingship by divine and unlimited right; for when he dedicated the *Essays in Divinity* to Vane, he remarked (as one addressing a revolutionary general):

> And although it bee objected, that the Sword be no good Key to open the Gates of Heaven, yet it was thought fit to protect and defend Paradise, and keep out even ADAM himself, who was the first and lawfull Heir, and who had for ever enjoyed his Prerogative, if he had not exceeded his Commission, in devouring that which he was forbidden to taste.[58]

He evidently intended Donne's readers to apply this reproach to Charles I.

Equivocations

Despite these irruptions into the text of *Pseudo-Martyr* of what look like arguments *with* James I rather than for him, the treatise as a whole was obviously intended to be *taken* as a loyal exercise in Protestant nationalist propaganda. As such, it conflicts with *The Courtier's Library*, where Donne's butts include Protestant spokesmen Martin Luther and John Foxe, anti-Catholic polemicists Edward Hoby and Matthew Sutcliffe (whose voice we have heard against the Martinists in Chapter 3), and Richard Topcliffe, one of the vilest agents of anti-Catholic persecution, whose name appears also in some of the manuscripts of Donne's fourth satire instead of the word "pursuivant." But the *Courtier's Library* also includes a strange item whose contents connect both to the fourth satire, to the troubled speaker "who dreamt he saw hell" at the Elizabethan court, and, more intensely, to the work that immediately followed *Pseudo-Martyr*, the *Conclave Ignatii*, entered in the Stationers' Register in January 1611. For the conclave is described by an anonymous speaker who fell into an "Extasie" and "saw all the roomes in Hell open to [his] sight,"

58. Donne, *Essays in Divinity*, 4.

with Ignatius Loyola as *diabolus in cathedra*. And in the sardonic *Library* (like the *Conclave* written in Latin) the courtier is encouraged to read a book entitled *The Quintessence of Hell; or, The private apartment in Hell, in which is a discussion of the fifth region passed over by Homer, Virgil, Dante and the rest of the papists, where, over and above the penalties and sensations of the damned, Kings are tortured by a recollection of the past* (51–52). It looks, then, as if Donne continued to imagine a court in infernal terms, as much under James as Elizabeth, a fact that destabilizes the contrast drawn in the *Conclave* between a demonic Loyola down below, and the European monarchs, specifically James and Elizabeth, against whom (so the *Conclave* claims) the primary malice of the Jesuits is directed.

But the *Conclave* is in almost every way a radically unstable text. Published anonymously, first in Latin and then in a still anonymous translation by Donne himself, it was in both versions a tiny octavo, self-declared a satire, and mockingly dedicated not to James but to "the two Adversary Angels, which are Protectors of the Papall Consistory, and of the Colledge of Sorbon." Yet the book insists on establishing a mirror relationship with *Pseudo-Martyr*. Continuing the strategy Donne had developed for the fourth satire, where the authorial voice divides itself between the poem's "I" and the seditious courtier who corners him, the *Conclave* pretends in its address "To the Reader" to distinguish author from editor, while insisting that the author's identity is unknowable.

"Dost thou seek after the Author?" asks the preface; "It is in vaine."[59] For the only thing known of him was conveyed to the fictional editor by a friend of the author's, in a letter, as follows:

> The Author was unwilling to have this book published, thinking it unfit both for the matter, which in it selfe is weighty and serious, and for that gravity which himselfe had proposed and observed in an *other* booke formerly published, to descend to this kind of writing. . . . At the last he yeelded, and made mee owner of his booke, which I send to you to be delivered over to forraine

59. The Latin is still more potent: "Autorem quaeris? Frustra." It is worth noting that when Kepler read the *Conclave* and noted its dependence on his own *Somnium*, he was unable to attach a name to it. See Marjorie Nicolson, *Science and Imagination* (Ithaca, 1956), 63, 67.

nations, (a) *farre from the father:* and (as his desire is) (b) his last in this kinde. Hee chooses and desires, that his *other* booke should testifie his ingenuity, and candor, and his disposition to labour for the reconciling of all parts. This Booke must teach what humane infirmity is.[60]

This extraordinary passage tells us more about the motives for returning to the Jesuits than Bald's hypothesis that the later work was a spillover, that Donne "had been unable to use a whole sheaf of the more extreme and ridiculous utterances of his opponents," and therefore published a second work from the cuttings (228). For the father from whose jurisdiction this squib escapes may be either its author or the patriarchal figure who commanded Donne's *other* book and dictated the gravity of its utterance. That second meaning admits the pressures on the self of the domains of law and authority, those territories entry into which Lacanian theory has identified with social and linguistic maturity and subsumed under the Name-of-the-Father. But if Donne intuits the point at which psychoanalysis will merge with sociology, he offers himself and his readers a strategy for self-management that Lacanian theory, with its stress on irreparable bondage, overlooks. Dividing himself between author and editor, reluctant utterer and eager promoter, dividing his utterance between *this* book, written in the alienated voice of satire, and the *other*, written from the "reconciling" perspective of the official propagandist, Donne found a way to speak ambivalence. And though by this strategy Donne may not have been able to reconcile all parts of himself, his appeal to "humane infirmity" is both disingenuous and ingenuous at the same time, demanding for himself the toleration that his project denied to others.

The text of the *Conclave* is no less peculiar than its preface. As Dennis Flynn points out, Donne's marginal citations are almost exclusively from Catholic authors, indicating his access to a library "unusually strong and up-to-date in the areas of Catholic controversial theology, history, and hagiography."[61] In addi-

60. Donne, *Ignatius his Conclave* (London, 1611), A3r-5v; italics added. Succeeding references are to this edition, p. 228.

61. Dennis Flynn, "Donne's *Ignatius his Conclave*," *John Donne Journal* 6 (1987), 170, who surmises that Donne had access to the books of the earl of Northumberland, imprisoned in the Tower on suspicion of complicity in the Gunpowder Plot, and one of the first purchasers of the *Conclave Ignatii*.

tion, the tone of the pamphlet makes it possible to feel that "Donne was not honestly or actively on the King's side," and that his trivialization of the royal arguments reflects adversely upon them. Indeed, as the preface reminds us of Donne's origins ("how hard a matter is it for a man . . . so thoroughly to cast off the Jesuits, as that he contract nothing of their natural drosses, which are Petulancy, and Lightnesse" [5V]), the ironies of the text are so rebarbative that it looks suspiciously as if the author had reserved to himself the Jesuit strategy of "Mentall Reservation, and Mixt propositions," otherwise known, since the trial of Father Garnet, as the "art of equivocation" (55, 33). The *Conclave* consists in a demonic competition, presided over by Lucifer, between all the greatest innovators in contemporary thought, in theology, science, or the "Arts," "or in any thing which . . . may so provoke to quarrelsom and brawling controversies: For so the truth be lost, it is no matter how" (13). Among the contestants, then, are Copernicus, Paracelsus, Machiavelli, Aretino, Columbus, and Ignatius Loyola, who will win; and in the course of putting his own case forward Machiavelli complains that the followers of Ignatius "have brought into the world a new art of Equivocation . . . have raised to life againe the language of the Tower of Babel, so long concealed, and brought us againe from understanding one an other" (27). Conversely, Ignatius, who has argued against Copernicus' claims as insufficiently perverse ("those opinions of yours may very well be true" [17]),[62] attacks Machiavelli (his most formidable rival) on the grounds that his teachings have worked against the kingdom of Rome:

> for what else doth hee endeavour or go about, but to change the forme of common-wealth, and so to deprive the people (who are a soft, a liquid and ductile mettall, and apter for our impressions) of all their liberty: & having so destroyed all civility and republique, to reduce all states to Monarchies; a name which in secular states, wee doe so much abhor. (78–79)

This statement establishes Loyola as a radical republican, discrediting Machiavelli's claims to the throne of Hell by making

---

62. T. S. Healey, ed. *Ignatius his Conclave* (Oxford, 1969), xxx, suggests that Donne did not wish to satirize Galileo and was uneasy with the attack on Copernicus.

him an advocate of monarchical absolutism; but the description of monarchy, which comes into existence by depriving the people "of all their liberty" and "having . . . destroyed all civility," carries its devious thrust. One cannot imagine James I being willing to endorse this description. The irony cannot, in other words, be intended to function by a simple discrediting or inversion of all that Loyola says, for that would nullify his malice and deprive the pamphlet of its point. If other texts of Donne's are slippery, this one is positively glacial; with the author absent and anonymous, there is no place for the reader to set her feet securely.

But equivocation is not restricted to Donne's Jacobean prose, and appears even in poems that would seem to have completely abandoned that territory of personal freedom to which Donne keeps alluding, in however peculiar a tone. We know, for instance, that Donne profited from the greatest scandal of James's reign, in which Frances Howard's divorce from the third earl of Essex and remarriage to the *other* and more famous Sir Robert Carr, now earl of Somerset, was made still more disreputable by the murder of someone who had resolutely opposed it. On September 14, 1613, Sir Thomas Overbury died in the Tower, poisoned, it was later charged, by the countess through her accomplices. Donne, in the meantime, had not only sought out Somerset as a new patron, but had accepted the position as his secretary that Overbury's imprisonment had vacated. By mid-December rumors were circulating that there had been foul play; so that Donne already knew how he had fulfilled one of the most horrible of the charges laid by the seditious speaker in his own fourth satire, where the first-person persona learns unwillingly "who by poyson / Hasts to an Offices reversion."

This may help to explain why Donne was late in contributing his own verse tribute to the Somerset-Howard marriage. He may have been very late indeed. Although the *Ecclogue* that prefaces the epithalamion is dated December 26, 1613, the date of the marriage, we know from his private correspondence that Donne did not begin it until several weeks later. The function of the *Ecclogue* is, in fact, to explain the delay in the poem's completion and delivery; and it provides the most sharply delineated version in Donne's work of that formally divided self to which he apparently had recourse when attempting to deal with ambivalence, here personified as Idios ("one's own," "pertaining to one's self") and Allophanes ("appearing otherwise," or, perhaps, "the face of the Other"). In their dialogue, Allophanes reproaches Idios for his absence from court on this great occasion of the marriage, only to be told that even in the country Idios so reveres the king and his style of government that he is not, in spirit, "from Court."[63] Yet the language in which Allophanes records the virtues of James and Somerset treads that slippery line whereby the claim for good can be rendered only rhetorically, as a denial of the converse imputation. It is a court "where it is no levity to trust, [?]/ Where there is no ambition, but to'obey, / Where men need whisper nothing, and yet may"; and the question of Somerset's own role in that structure is addressed in the most oblique manner possible:

> the King's favours are so plac'd, that all
> Finde that the King therein is liberall
> To them, *in him,* because his favours bend
> To vertue, to *the which they all pretend.* [?]
> (Lines 81–84)

These lines "pretend" to unsay those lines in Donne's second satire which speak of lying "Like a Kings favourite, yea like a King" and which the editor of the 1633 volume of Donne's *Poems* thought too dangerous to print.[64] While the discreetly unnamed recipient of the king's favors supposedly is merely the conduit of those favors to "all" who desire them, and the king's liberality supposedly proven by the favorite's selfless virtue, the mobility of "all" as a qualifier may expand to include suitors, Somerset, king, all. All are then governed by the disabling and concluding verb "pretend," which obviously claimed its innocent meaning of "profess" while admitting the suspicious one, the one that, as the language evolved, drove out the neutral connotation. It is then not entirely surprising that the language Idios himself uses to explain his delayed eulogy is more elegiac than celebratory:

> I knew
> All this, and onely therefore I withdrew.

63. Donne, *Poetical Works,* 118.
64. Donne, *Poetical Works,* 135. For the 1633 omission, see Milgate, *The Satires, Epigrams and Verse Letters,* 135.

To know and feele all this, and not to have
Words to expresse it, makes a man a grave
Of his owne thoughts; I would not therefore stay
At a great feast, having no grace to say.

(Lines 91–96)

If one reads these lines *without* a prior assumption that Donne when he wrote them was utterly cynical, they express rather clearly and painfully the particular version of the inexpressibility topos that actual and self-inflicted censorships had arranged. The crucial "whisper" ("where men need whisper nothing, and yet may"), political opposition or "sedition," is here introduced (through denial) in order to explain the mortal gap between knowing all and telling only part of it; while the powerful and indecorous image of the marriage celebrant becoming a "grave of his own thoughts" reintroduces the necrophilic imagination ("in this standing wooden chest . . . let me lye in prison, and here be coffin'd")[65] of Donne's first satire, and reveals, after all, what generic affiliates this pretended pastoral confesses to.

Undertaking

This brings us to the meaning of Donne's participation in the ill-fated Parliament of 1614; for understanding which, however, we first need to glance back at 1610. As the 1610 Parliament ground its way toward stalemate, it was rumored that efforts were being made by the king's councillors to dismantle the opposition. On December 10, the Venetian ambassador, Marc Antonio Correr, wrote to his employers:

> The business in Parliament has gone from bad to worse. Meantime they will try to win over some of those who have shown most opposition, and if they do not succeed Parliament will be dissolved altogether, so that the constituencies will elect new members. There are those who say that the King will never summon Parliament again, but his need of money is against that, and maybe this rumour is put about to frighten many of them.[66]

In fact, as the dissolution approached, four of the most determined oppositionists, Lewknor, Fuller, Wentworth, and the

65. Donne, *Poetical Works*, 129.
66. *Calendar of State Papers Venetian* 12:100, art. 151.

redoubtable John Hoskyns were sent for by Salisbury for a private conference.[67] On December 31, Correr continued his report:

> Certain persons have been approached with a view to inducing them to bow to his Majesty's wishes and desires (I have information on this point from a good quarter, but it would only weary your Serenity).[68]

And on January 21 Correr reported the dissolution of the Parliament, which, after a series of adjournments, was dissolved by royal proclamation (in the middle of a prorogation) on December 31:

> This step, which is unusual, as Parliament is usually prorogued, and the rumour that the King intends to issue privy seals for the amount of one million six hundred thousand crowns, give rise to some talk. This loan once obtained his Majesty will summon a new Parliament; care being taken that those hostile to him shall not be re-elected. He will all the more readily obtain subsidies to pay back the loan, in that everyone will have an interest in voting it, and all the money will pass into the hands of the nobility. Some cry out that it is not well to exclude those who have forgotten their personal interest in the service of their country; others are unwilling that his Majesty should achieve by indirect ways what was refused him in Parliament. All the same . . . if he gains the Parliamentary leaders he will secure a return of a majority of members that suit his taste.[69]

Diplomatic reports are often, especially by revisionist historians, treated with a certain skepticism, dependent as they were, in Kevin Sharpe's words, "upon information, even rumour, from courtiers, M.P.'s, and newsmongers." Yet Sharpe also admits that "at times their reports may reflect the views of a courtier who spoke his mind but would not commit his opinion to the dangerous permanence of paper";[70] and Correr's report has pre-

---

67. See Foster, *Proceedings in Parliament 1610* 2:344.
68. *Calendar of State Papers Venetian* 12:102, art. 153.
69. *Calendar of State Papers Venetian* 12:110, art. 164.
70. "Parliamentary History 1603–1629: In or out of Perspective?" in *Faction and Parliament*, ed. Kevin Sharpe (Oxford, 1978), 13. It is worth noting that Sharpe (12) cites the Venetian ambassador's report in 1607 that James had "reached such a pitch of formidable power that he can do what he likes," but not the subsequent reports which indicate oppositional behavior in the Commons.

cisely that quality of *talk*, of being part of a discursive formation, that connects it with Elegy 14.[71]

It also helps to explain the Addled Parliament, that *parlamentum inchoatum* (as John Chamberlain called it)[72] for which writs were finally called in the spring of 1614 (even, perhaps, while Donne was finishing his leaden tribute to Somerset). The grease that rendered the political territory unstable was, not surprisingly, self-interest. One of the questions that exercised the Commons in the few weeks between April 14 and June 7, when James dissolved them, was whether their proceedings had been destabilized by bribery.[73] Some modern historians have discounted the invidiousness of "undertaking" and defended the motives of Sir Henry Neville, who attempted to persuade James to call another Parliament on the grounds that the dissolution of the previous one was causing dissent and harming England's reputation abroad.[74] Neville had committed himself to negotiate with the "patriots" in the House of Commons on the basis of his friendship with them, and, in exchange for certain "graces," such as forgiven loans, "protections" against bankruptcy, and a commitment that no impositions should subsequently be levied except through Parliament, to neutralize their opposition. He claimed to speak "as one that lived and conversed inwardly with the chief of them that were noted to be the most backward and know their inwardest thoughts in that business"; and, in a phrase that subsequently entered the language as a new concept in political thought, he added: "So I dare undertake for most of them,

71. Correr's information was, however, wrong as regards the loan. This did not occur until after the abortive session of 1614. In 1611 James and Salisbury instead fell back on a large-scale sale of baronetcies.

72. Chamberlain, *Letters* 1:539.

73. See Maija Jansson, ed., *Proceedings in Parliament 1614 (House of Commons)* (Philadelphia, 1988), xxiii–xxx.

74. This was Sir Henry Neville of Billingbear. See Clayton Roberts and Owen Duncan, "The Parliamentary Undertaking of 1614," *English Historical Review* 93 (1978), 481–98. Roberts subsequently published a second version of his argument (without his collaborator) in *Schemes and Undertakings: A Study of English Politics in the Seventeenth Century* (Columbus, Ohio, 1985). It is worth noting (with some historical irony) that this book, which makes Henry Neville the heroic pioneer of undertaking, seen as a valuable innovation in political practice, concludes with a praise of Margaret Thatcher as the heroic inheritor who brings the practice to perfection: "She, and only she, can undertake to manage the Queen's affairs in Parliament successfully" (251).

that . . . [the king] shall find those gentlemen willing to do him service." But while it was probably true, as Roberts and Duncan argued, that the Commons was capable of distinguishing between such an undertaking and any attempt actually to pack the house by manipulating the election, and while Neville himself, whose "Advice" to the king[75] was subsequently circulated in the House, was cleared of any wrongdoing, there were certainly some who believed that undertaking, as the institutionalization of the deal, was inimical to genuine parliamentary process. As Sir John Holles complained to Lord Holles on April 28:

> a schism is cast into the House by reason of some interlopers between the K. and the Parliament, whom they term undertakers, so named, because they have promised that the Parliament shall supply the King's want to his contentment . . . nor for that they envy these undertakers' reward but that they foresee a perilous consequence by this precedent to the State, when kings heartened by this success shall hereafter practise the like; and sprinkling some hires upon a few shall . . . so by little and little steal away the liberty and at the next opportunity overthrow Parliament itself.[76]

Even before the Privy Council had advised James to issue the writs for the election, Donne himself had written to a friend that "it is taken ill, though it be but mistaken that certain men (whom they call undertakers) should presume either to understand the house before it sit, or to incline it then, and this rumour beforehand, . . . must impeach, if it do not defeat their purposes at last."[77] Despite the cautious neutrality of this statement, its very occurrence shows that Donne was concerned on behalf of the Parliament's success. While we cannot tell from this letter *whose* purposes he supported, Donne, who received his seat through Sir Edward Phelips (no doubt through the request of

75. It was presented to James in July 1612. The full text is printed in S. R. Gardiner's *History of England from the Accession of James to the Outbreak of Civil War*, 10 vols. (London, 1883–84), 2:389–94.

76. Sir John Holles to Lord Norris, 28 April, 1614; H.M.C. Portland MSS 9:27.

77. Gosse, *Life and Letters of John Donne* 2:34. In the second version of his argument, Clayton Roberts mentioned Donne's letter (mistakenly referring to him as the dean of St. Paul's at this time) and claimed that it was the first recorded use of the term "undertaker" in this sense. See *Schemes and Undertakings* x. "Within three months," Roberts continued, "the word *undertaker* was on every man's lips."

his son, Sir Robert, who was one of Donne's personal friends), could well have shared the dilemma of Sir Robert and other opposition leaders,[78] that if they pursued the charge of undertaking too zealously, too many of their own group would be revealed to have benefited in some way from the court patronage system, and so be forced, defensively, into political defection. Sir John Holles himself, who had no patron since the death of Prince Henry, and who despised the Scottish favorites at court, had sometime in 1614 applied for assistance to Somerset.

There is no record of Donne's having spoken in the Commons, though he was named to important committees. One, in May, was to prepare a conference with the Lords so that both Houses could present a joint petition to the king against monopolies. The others were a series of select committees appointed to cope with a constitutional crisis in which Richard Neile, bishop of Lincoln, had declared that the Commons had no business meddling with impositions, that they were a *noli me tangere.* "Proud Prelate," said Sir William Strowde in the Commons; and Sir Edward Hoby, "Woe to that Time, wher an humble Petition of the grieved Gentry of England shall be called an entering upon the King's Prerogative."[79] But both Egerton (now Lord Ellesmere), Donne's former employer, and Sir George More, his father-in-law, defended Neile. The pressures on everyone were evident, and Donne more than others must have experienced those pressures as the pull of divided allegiances.

For Bald, the absence of evidence that Donne participated in the debates meant that he did not, although the official records are, to say the least, elliptical. "*No doubt,*" wrote Bald, arguing from silence, "he judged it the part of discretion not to run the

78. After the session collapsed, the immediate provocation having been John Hoskyns' imprudent attack on the Scottish favorites and the reference to a Sicilian Vespers, John Chamberlain suggested that the Phelipses, father and son, might have been responsible: "for there be many presumptions that his hand was in it, his son being so busy and factious in the House, and Hoskyns one of his chief consorts and minions so far engaged, besides divers untoward speeches of his own." See John Chamberlain, *Letters* 1:540; and Linda Levy Peck, *Northampton: Patronage and Policy at the Court of James I* (London, 1982), 210, who cites Chamberlain's suggestion as part of her argument that the conspiracy theory involving Northampton—that Hoskyns' speech was planted in *order* to abort the session—was merely one of multiple rumors.

79. *Journal of the House of Commons* 1:494, 496.

risk of expressing himself too openly or of giving offence. He seems to have been a good committee-man [and what a derogatory phrase that is] but he *probably* kept out of the debates *quite deliberately,* less he should spoil his chances with the King or the leading members of the Government" (289; italics added). By the time Carey retold the story, that "no doubt" and "probably" had hardened into statement: "Christopher Brooke and other *former* friends of Donne vehemently opposed these abuses of royal power. Donne discreetly held his tongue" (88).[80] But silence is notoriously hard to argue from. Is it merely by coincidence that one of Donne's love poems goes under the title of *The Undertaking* and begins (and ends) as follows:

> I have done one braver thing
> Then all the Worthies did,
> And yet a braver thence doth spring,
> Which is, to keepe that hid?
>
> (9–10)

Between the Lines of the Lyrics

This brings us back, finally, to the poems that made Donne famous in our time, though not in his. When Carey performed his powerful analysis of the image patterns in Donne's love poetry, and noticed how frequently love relations are conducted from a position of monarchical power, he overlooked the fact that these poems are also riddled with a specifically political terminology, by no means all of which situates the speaker on the side of royal absolutism.

It is when one collects these terms into relation with each other, into what one might call a grammar of political consciousness, that the unstable tone of the canon as a whole becomes noticeable. To begin with the question of favorites, between the evidently hostile reference in Satire 2 and the ambiguous epithalamion for Somerset there are a series of references to this problem, more topical for a Jacobean audience than an Elizabethan one. *The Anniversarie* opens with the statement that "All Kings, and all

---

80. When added to the misleading statement that Donne acquired his seat through "court influence" (87), when in fact he owed it to the father of one of the leading oppositionists, Carey's language quite unjustly suggests betrayal of friendship, another form of apostasy.

their favorites . . . [are] elder by a yeare." *Elegy 6* opens by denying in private relations the stance that Donne was willing to adopt
in his public life:

> Oh, let mee not serve so, as those men serve
> Whom honours' smokes at once fatten and starve;
> . . .
> As those Idolatrous flatterers, which still
> Their Princes stiles, with many Realmes fulfill
> Whence they no tribute have, and where no sway.
> . . . Oh then let mee
> Favorite in Ordinary, or no favorite bee.[81]

And the *Essays in Divinity*, certainly a Jacobean text, contain the
following remarkable analogy for the doctrine of election:

> To enquire further the way and manner by which God makes a
> few do acceptable works; or, how out of a corrupt lumpe he selects
> and purifies a few, is but a stumbling block and a tentation: . . .
> will any favorite, whom his Prince only for his appliableness to
> him, or some half-vertue, or his own glory, burdens with Honours
> and Fortunes every day, and destines to future Offices and Dig-
> nities, dispute or expostulate with his Prince, why he rather chose
> not another, how he will restore his Coffers; how he will quench
> his peoples murmurings, by whom this liberality is fed; or his
> Nobility, with whom he equalls new men . . . ? (87)

This passage, with its clear reference to the problems in dispute
between James and his parliaments from 1604 through 1614, is
the *other* side of the untrue compliments in the 1614 *Ecclogue*,
where Donne claimed that "the King's favours are so plac'd" in
Somerset "that all / Finde that the King therein is liberall / To
them."

As for the term *prerogative*, its recurrence in the lyrics is remarkable, and shows how preoccupations developed in Elizabeth's
reign were deepened under James. In his fourth satire Donne had
punned on "the prerogative of my Crowne," the coin he paid to
get rid of his seditious companion, who "like a priviledg'd spie"
he imagined to be drawing him into treasonous thoughts.[82] But
in *A Valediction: of the booke*, using the metaphor of scholarship

81. Donne, *Poetical Works*, 90, 22, 78.
82. Donne, *Poetical Works*, 145.

as a basis for writing the definitive history of his love affair,
Donne gives it institutional or constitutional force:

> Here more then in their bookes may Lawyers find
> Both by what titles Mistresses are ours,
> And how prerogative these states devours,
> Transferr'd from Love himselfe, to womankinde,
> Who though from heart, and eyes,
> They exact great subsidies,[83]
> Forsake him who on them relies,
> And for the cause, honour, or conscience give,
> Chimeraes, vaine as they, or their prerogative.
>
> (28–29)

It scarcely needs pointing out that to speak of the prerogative
as devouring the state, or as a vain chimaera, was not to align
oneself with monarchical absolutism. In *Loves Deitie*, the poet
complains that "every moderne god will now extend / His vast
prerogative, as far as Jove," and calls it a "Tyrannie" against
which his own posture is that of "Rebell and Atheist too" (49).
And in *Love's Exchange* he agrees not to "sue from thee to draw,
/ A *non obstante* on natures law, / These are prerogatives, they
inhere / In thee and thine" (32). The *non obstante*, or "notwithstanding [any statute to the contrary]," was a term foregrounded
in the debates of 1610, when Heneage Finch, insisting that "the
prerogative of the king is not infinite," and that because it had
been augmented in the past through Parliament it could also be
diminished, used the phrase *non obstante* nine times. He concluded, focusing on the issue of protections, that "though a protection were granted in such a case with a *non obstante*, the judges
will not allow such protection, for the king cannot protect him
contrary to the law."[84] This casts a rather different light on the
statement in *Essays in Divinity*, that "Nature is the Common law
by which God governs us, and Miracle is his Prerogative. For Mir-
acles are but so many Non-obstantes upon Nature. And Miracle
is not like prerogative in any thing more then in this, that no body

83. See also the ironic metaphor, in *Loves Growth*, that the relationship expands "as princes doe in times of action get / New taxes, and remit them not
in peace" (*Poetical Works*, 31).

84. See *Proceedings in Parliament 1610* 2:241. This speech took place on July 2,
1610.

can tell what it is" (81).[85] If one suspects a certain irony here (remembering the "chimaeras" of the *Valediction*), one's suspicion is confirmed by the later statement that "multiplicity of laws . . . is not so burdenous as is thought, except it be in a captious, and entangling, and needy State; or under a Prince too indulgent to his own Prerogative" (94); a statement that John Donne, Jr., clearly remembered when he dedicated the book to Vane.

But perhaps the most surprising appearance of contemporary politics in Donne's consciousness is the *Second Anniversary*, a poem we know, along with its partner, *An Anatomy of the World*, to have been published in 1612 in honor of Elizabeth Drury, dead in her teens and not known personally to Donne; an occasion, therefore, for a meditation on what was wrong (everything) with the world that he knew. And in accordance with Donne's plan in these poems to balance his universal critique with extreme idealism, to make Elizabeth Drury, however inappropriately, the epitome of "the best that [he] could conceive," the *Second Anniversary* presents her soul as a perfect form of government:

> Shee, who being to her selfe a State, injoy'd
> All royalties which any State employ'd;
> For shee made warres, and triumph'd; reason still
> Did not o'rthrow, but rectified her will:
> And she made peace, for no peace is like this,
> That beauty, and chastity together kisse:
> She did high justice, for she crucified
> Every first motion of rebellious pride:
> And she gave pardons, and was liberall,
> For, onely her selfe except, she pardon'd all:
> She coy'nd, in this, that her impressions gave
> To all our actions all the worth they have:
> She gave protections; the thoughts of her brest
> Satans rude Officers could ne'r arrest.
> As these *prerogatives* being met in one,

85. J. P. Sommerville, *Politics and Ideology*, 37, cited this passage as demonstrating that Donne supported the concept of free or unlimited monarchy. See also Donne's funeral elegy for Lord Harington, brother of Lucy, countess of Bedford, where, in reference to his early death in 1614, Donne commented: "Yet I am farre from daring to dispute / With that great soveraigntie, whose absolute / Prerogative hath thus dispens'd with thee, / 'Gainst natures lawes" (254). The context here, of course, made the belief in divine absolutism appropriate.

> Made her a soveraigne State; religion
> Made her a Church; and these two made her all.
>
> (237)

It would have been impossible for Donne's readers in 1612 not to notice, in this analysis, one by one, of the categories of the royal prerogative, what is missing: making war and peace, giving pardons, even protections; but not, significantly, impositions. Given this omission, one must also question Donne's *avoidance* of the easier metaphorical alignment between ideal woman and ideal monarch, and its replacement by the personification of a more ambiguous "soveraigne State."

Finally, however, we should consider a love poem in which Donne himself was not sovereign but very much subject to Eros, and in which that relationship was expressed in terms not of prerogative but its counterprinciple in English constitutional theory—personal liberty. In *Elegy 17* the speaker complains that while in the good old days of erotic conquest men were essentially polygamous, now, in an honor culture,

> The golden laws of nature are repeald,
> Which our first Fathers in such reverence held;
> Our liberty's revers'd, our Charter's gone.
>
> (102)

Nevertheless, in this newly restrictive context, "Onely some few strong in themselves and free / Retain the seeds of antient liberty" and continue the old tradition of libertinage. Donne's language here echoes that of the opposition in the 1610 Parliament, which frequently cited Magna Carta as the source of those ancient liberties which the new stress on prerogative looked in danger of abrogating. On June 28, 1610, Thomas Hedley drew his last and best argument against the impositions "from the ancient freedom and liberty of the subject of England, which appeareth and is confirmed by the great Charter of the liberties of England."[86] Yet the poem, as it speaks of "resisting hearts," itself resists solution. From a statement that such a return to the ancient liberty is only a different form of "subjection" to his "Soveraigne" Eros, Donne imagines a time when that liberty/subjection will be discarded also:

86. See *Proceedings in Parliament 1610* 2:164, 190.

For our allegiance temporary is,
When firmer age returnes our liberties.

(103)

And in the last redefinition liberty becomes a patient and contented monogamy. If the poem was a ruse by which to express a residual political independence, its behavior is as inchoate as the public forum in which such principles were debated; more likely it functioned in Donne's own mind as a therapeutic displacement into wit of contradictions that, in their real location, he was quite unable to resolve.

Perhaps the most telling statement was made after the 1614 session was over, when Sir John Holles was deciding whether his constituency should contribute to the forced loan. Holles' advice was yes, lest Nottingham stand out from its neighbor counties in isolated resistance; and, becoming philosophical, he added:

> These foreseeings and cogitations decline me something from that *quod oportet* and draws me with the throng into the broad high way of *quod convenit*, which, though not so honest as the other, yet (as our nowadays wise will have it) more courtly and civil; so as I hold it expedient rather to *errare cum Aristotele*, to give as our fellows do, than to offer with one finger to stay a falling house.[87]

Such troubled testimony in others both has significant implications for parliamentary history[88] and permits in the "literary" arena a more generous view of John Donne that the ambitious apostate to whom we can feel superior. It allows us to recognize that *quod oportet* (principle) is seldom available in its pure form as a political option, and that *quod convenit* (interest), precisely because it can appear more courtly and civil, is that to which the majority of academics themselves aspire. Donne, however, seems to have struggled to permit the sense of what ought to be done and thought to appear between the lines of even his most

87. Sir John Holles, *Historical Manuscripts Commission, Rutland* 9:139.

88. For one thing, it questions Kevin Sharpe's certainty ("Parliamentary History" 19) that in the summer of 1614 "the country gentlemen gave generously to a voluntary contribution which brought in at least as much as a subsidy," a statement intended to support Conrad Russell's position "that the Commons never successfully used, and seldom tried to use, the weapon of withholding supply in order to gain advantages." What one man stated, others may also have felt, imagining themselves also in the minority.

conformist writing, and somehow, always, to put the merely conventional to shame.

It is beyond the scope of this chapter to tackle the enormous topic of Donne's career as a preacher, and to defend the compromise he chose by a close examination of the way he conducted himself, as (in Gosse's words) the pulpit's "most magnificent and minatory clerical embodiment." Yet it is only fair to Donne to end with one of his first sermons, preached "at Pauls Cross to the Lords of the Council" on March 24, 1617, the anniversary of James's accession to the crown, at a time when the king was in progress in Scotland. His audience included, as we know from John Chamberlain, "the archbishop of Canterburie [George Abbott], the Lord Keper [Sir Francis Bacon], Lord Privie-Seal [Edward Somerset, ninth earl of Worcester], the earle of Arundell, the earle of Southampton, the Lord Hayes, the controller, Secretarie Winwood, the Master of the Rolls [Sir Julius Caesar], with divers other great men"; and his sermon "was exceedingly well liked generally, the rather for that he did Quene Elizabeth great right, and held himself close to the text without flattering the time too much."[89] The sermon is, in fact, a defense of Jacobean policy with respect to international peacemaking, union with Scotland, and an aggressive anti-Catholic policy at home; but it is also a defense of Donne's own position. Preached on the text "He that loveth pureness of heart, for the grace of his lips, the king shall be his friend" (Proverbs 22.11), the sermon constitutes a claim that integrity ("pureness of heart") can be reconciled with patronage, that using his eloquence in the pulpit is more honorable than keeping it to himself. "Because thy wit, thy fashion, and some such nothing as that hath made thee a delightful and acceptable companion, wilt thou therefore pass in jest, and be nothing?" Donne asked himself as well as his auditors. "Thinkest thou to eat bread, and not sweat?" "Hast thou a prerogative above the common Law of Nature?" A man of talent who does not employ it in the service of the public is equivalent to a usurer who keeps his money out of circulation:

> It is all as one as if he had no grace of lips, if he never have the grace to open his lips; to bury himself alive, is as much wrong to

89. Donne, *Sermons*, ed. George Potter and Evelyn M. Simpson, 10 vols. (Berkeley and Los Angeles, 1953–62), 1:125.

the State, as if he kill himself. Every man hath a Politick life, as well as a natural life; and he may no more take himself away from the world, then he may make himself away out of the world. (208–11)

The sermons, then, mark not the end but the transformation of Donne's political poetics. The author of *Biathanatos* has redefined suicide as compliance in one's own silencing. And one could even say that Chamberlain's approval of this sermon for not "flattering the time too much" was insufficiently generous. For Donne, at this his first Paul's Cross appearance, came out in front of the privy councillors swinging his political principles. The opening lines of the sermon were as follows:

The Man that said it was possible to carve the faces of all good Kings that ever were, in a Cherry-stone, had a seditious, and a trayterous meaning in his words. And he that thought it a good description, a good Character of good subjects, that they were *Populus natus ad servitutem*, A people disposed to bear any slavish yoak, had a tyrannical meaning in his words. (183)

"Both in politics and theology," wrote Debora Shuger, completing her analysis of Donne's "absolutist theology," "modernity entails the rejection of the absolutist paradigm based on the polarities of power and subjection and therefore of the psychocultural formation which made this paradigm acceptable."[90] This remark comes as the climax of the claim that Donne saw his God as an absolute monarch who greatly resembled King James I, and to whom he related with a mixture of guilt and infantile dependency. In my own view, another thing that modernity entails is an immodesty with respect to the past and an underestimation of the capacity of people who anticipated us in time to anticipate us also in self-knowledge. The psychocultural formation that, in my view, Donne inhabited was not "the whole complex of archaic/infantile emotions" that Shuger finds in his sermons, but a highly developed if unstable world of articulated choices, in which *quod oportet* negotiated with *quod convenit*, Jack with the Doctor, in which there was both a disposition and an equally strong indisposition to bear a slavish yoke.

90. *Habits of Thought*, 203.

7

The Good Old Cause

The Republican's Library

I know too well you and your royal tribe
Scorn the good people, scorn the late election.
. . .
And, though you laugh at this, you and your train,
. . .
Yet wise men know 'tis very rarely seen
That a free people should desire the hurt
Of common liberty . . .
For those desires arise from their oppression,
Of from suspicion they are falling to it;
But put the case that those their fears were false,
Ways may be found to rectify their errors.
For grant the people ignorant of themselves,
Yet are they capable of being told,
And will conceive a truth from worthy men.

This speech bespeaks an ideal relationship between education and democratic involvement in the political life of the nation; it also implies a hostility to monarchy and, in its surrounding narrative, a fully fledged theory of republicanism. It was spoken on the London stage in 1680, for less than a week, before the play that promoted these values was suppressed. Nathaniel Lee's *Lucius Junius Brutus* was performed in December 1680 for either three or six days (the records conflict) and was shut down by order of the Lord Chamberlain, for reasons that are obvious if one recognizes the tensions of the historical moment (at the height of the Exclusion crisis) and the contemporary significance of the ancient history (the founding moment of the Roman republic) that Lee was here resuscitating. The speech with which I begin was delivered by Lee's Brutus to Collatine, and it expands on Livy by making Brutus more consciously populist, more democratic, than the original account of the expulsion of the Tarquins required. As John Loftis remarked, in editing the play for the Regents Restoration series, "Any English play about Lucius Junius Brutus had to be a Whig play."[1] In his own dedication to Charles Sackville, Lord Buckhurst, earl of Dorset,[2] Lee connected Machiavelli's *Discourses on Livy* to "Shakespeare's Brutus," who must surely be the Lucius Junius of *The Rape of Lucrece*, not his successor in *Julius Caesar*, and added that Shakespeare's character "with much ado beat himself into the heads of a blockish age, so knotty were the oaks he had to deal with."[3] I take it his protest is still applicable.

This play is not eccentric. Rather, it is just the tip of the iceberg. Many writers in early modern England, far more than we have been told, shared the convictions of that speaker, or at least would not have found them laughable. They possessed, or, more accurately, developed, an economical vocabulary for representing the central questions of political and social thought—a set of terms that, when any or each of them was introduced, immediately invoked an entire agenda. This agenda was focused on the rights of the subject, the dangers of a royal prerogative overused or overtheorized, the significance of Magna Carta as the document that marked the origins of English statute law and parliamentary government, and even broader concepts of public consent and enfranchisement. I call this agenda "republican" in

1. Nathaniel Lee, *Lucius Junius Brutus*, ed. John Loftis (Lincoln, Neb., 1967), xviii–xix.

2. Dorset was himself a political satirist who by 1688 had set himself in open opposition to James II, and who subsequently was among those who invited William to England. See *Poems on Affairs of State*, ed. George de Forest Lord, vol. 4 (New Haven, 1968), 189–90.

3. Lee, *Lucius Junius Brutus*, 5. His reference to Machiavelli is also interesting: "nothing ever presented itself to my fancy with that solid pleasure as Brutus did in sacrificing his sons. Before I read Machivel's notes upon the place, I concluded it the greatest action that was ever seen throughout all ages on the greatest occasion" (4).

the loose sense in which the term *respublica* was itself used, to denote the public interest or common wealth, on the grounds that it is often supported by allusion to Roman republicanism in the past or to contemporary Venice or the United Dutch Republic; and one of my objectives is to show that within a general understanding of republican values there was considerable, and fertile, range of opinion.[4]

The vocabulary that carried these opinions was not a code, since encoded writing is not transparent, whereas these terms were so fraught with intelligibility that they functioned, in Fredric Jameson's useful term, as ideologemes. But they were developed under cover nevertheless: either in forms of communication that enjoyed some official immunity, such as the parliamentary debates where speakers were supposed to enjoy the privilege of outspokenness; or in locations rendered unsuspicious by their seemingly apolitical nature. The vocabulary that signifies a republican subtext consists of at least the following terms: *liberty* and its cognate *freedom*, especially when qualified as *ancient*; *Charter*, especially when designated "Great," i.e., Magna Carta as the originating mandate of ancient liberty; *absolute*, as a qualifier for monarchy, which could be used both positively and negatively (although James I himself preferred to use the ironic term "free monarchy," that is to say, unlimited); *arbitrary*, as a qualifier for government, as in Andrew Marvell's famous pamphlet *An Account of the Growth of Popery and Arbitrary Government*, published just prior to the Exclusion crisis; *tyrant*, which is self-explanatory; *common*, especially when conjoined with "good," "wealth," or "weal," and its neighborly terms *equity* and *equal*; *prerogative*, especially when complained of as "transcendent" or "stretched"; the group of words alluding to taxation, of which *subsidies* is a neutral example and *exactions* a stig-

4. Intellectual historians might see this lumping together of different strains of republicanism as disreputable. Perez Zagorin, for example, distinguishes between (1) classical republicanism in the strict sense, deriving from the civic humanism of cinquecento Italy, especially from Machiavelli's *Discourses* (which he finds in Harrington); (2) a republicanism based on ideas of natural law, natural rights, and original freedom (which he finds in Milton); and (3) a republicanism based on English antiquarianism and legal history, founded on Magna Carta and the theory of the ancient constitution. I believe that these ideas were, if not interchangeable, mutually reinforcing, and often themselves appear in loose mixtures.

matic one; the group of words signifying a contractual theory of government, *voluntary*, (whose negative version is *wilful*) *election*, *voices*, *suffrage*, *franchise*, and especially, at their center, the term *consent*; and at the extreme end of the argument—at the end where social and political reconstruction is imagined—*popular* and *innovation*. Symbolic persons historical, literary, or in the in-between territory of legend also entered this vocabulary: on the side of the just, Hercules, Lucius Junius Brutus, Marcus Brutus, Martin Marprelate, Robert Devereux, second Earl of Essex; on the side of the tyrants, Tarquin, Nimrod, Rehoboam, Richard II. Also among the heroes were authors who constituted what might be called the republican canon: Livy and the Machiavelli of the *Discourses on Livy*; George Buchanan, François Hotman, Christopher Goodman, the anonymous author of the *Vindiciae contra Tyrannos*, John Milton. It scarcely needs saying that the appearance of these terms in clusters intensifies their significance; and when they appear in clusters it becomes possible to determine their positive or negative valence.

But I also wish to denote the mainframe of "republican" values and the arguments that supported them by a different and differently contentious name—the Good Old Cause. This phrase is usually taken to refer to a specifically English and seventeenth-century phenomenon. By tradition, the Good Old Cause has been taken to refer to whatever it was that motivated whatever it was that happened in England between 1640, when the Long Parliament came into existence, and 1660, when the Stuart monarchy was restored. From the moment when Sir Henry Vane named the Cause both Good and Old in 1656, in his famous pamphlet *A Healing Question propounded and resolved*, it was invoked by seventeenth-century writers in contexts at best nostalgic, at worst contemptuous, always retroactive, but retroactive only to 1640, or perhaps only to 1648/49, when the English republic was formally inaugurated. As the Restoration approached the phrase became ubiquitous. The nostalgic version was then represented by R. Fitz-Brian's tract *The Good Old Cause Dress'd in its Primitive Lustre* (1659), implicitly an argument for support of the Rump as the natural descendant of the Long Parliament: "There was in those virgin (i.e., pre-Cromwellian) daies such a mutuall, strict and lovely harmony and agreement . . . between the Parliament and the honest unbiass'd people of the Nation" (5). The hostile version appeared in William Prynne's *The Re-publicans and Others Spurious Good Old Cause . . . Anatomized* (May 1659), or the anonymous *A Coffin for the Good Old Cause* (1660), or the broadside *An Exit to the Exit Tyrannus*, which claimed that "their Good old Cause / Was only made for a pretence, / To banish all our freedome hence, / and overthrow our Lawes."[5]

Vane's definition of the Cause had been, importantly, bifocal. The Puritan revolution (a term that also asserts two distinct but related motivations for change) had been, Vane declared, the attempt of the English to recover "their just natural rights in civil things, and true freedom in matters of conscience."[6] His sense of the inevitable connection between constitutional government and rights theory, on the one hand, and freedom of conscience (of which freedom of thought is the secular extension) on the other, was correct. His sense of historical perspective, of the longer *durée*, was unduly if understandably limited. I have already shown, in relation to the careers of Job Throkmorton and John Donne ("rebel and atheist too"), how interdependent, sixty years or more before "the Puritans" became the dominant political agency, were the pressures for religious decentralization and political resistance to the expansion of monarchical controls. And these two objectives *still* organized the work of Milton, as also of Andrew Marvell and Edmund Ludlow, in the postrevolutionary period, when the republican experiment was supposed to be dead in the water.[7]

For my purposes, then, the Good Old Cause has considerably more chronological extension than Vane imagined, a still broader meaning, and, in our own environment, valuable side effects.

5. For a full account of the Good Old Cause in 1659, see Austin Woolrych, "The Good Old Cause and the Fall of the Protectorate," *Cambridge Historical Journal* 13 (1957): 133–61; and see also Robert Zaller, "The Good Old Cause and the Crisis of 1659," in Gordon J. Schochet, ed., *Restoration, Ideology, and Revolution: Proceedings of the Folger Institute Center for the History of Political Thought*, vol. 4 (Washington, D.C., 1990), 23–40.

6. See Vane, *A Healing Question propounded and resolved*, in *Somers Tracts*, ed. Sir W. Scott (London, 1809–15), 6:303.

7. For the still later stage, see Caroline Robbins, *The Eighteenth-Century Commonwealthman: Studies in the Transmission, Development and Circumstances of English Liberal Thought from the Restoration of Charles II until the War with the Thirteen Colonies* (Cambridge, Mass., 1959, 1968).

In the first place, its use as an ideologeme problematizes the matter of origins, the antiquity of this way of thinking, and makes it possible to argue that the Cause was very Old indeed; for those who espoused it, the older the better. Second, it foregrounds the vexed relation between causation and motivation—the motives behind past actions—in our reconstruction of historical events; for there is a connection between the way people construe historical causation and their capacity or disinclination to accept the existence of a supervening Cause, in the sense of a group commitment over time to a principled agenda, which in turn becomes the motive for political behavior. Third, it puts squarely before modern readers the question of what political values they themselves espouse, and to what extent our interpretations of the past are an extension of those values. By choosing to argue the importance and extension in early modern England of Good Old Cause values, I, for one, am willing to reveal that they still look Good to me.

I have, of course, distinguished predecessors in the task of recuperating such patterns of thought in the early modern period. Preeminent among these are Quentin Skinner and John Pocock, whose magisterial studies of the European republican tradition, of "ancient constitutionalism," "the common-law mind," and the "Machiavellian moment" might seem to have settled the matter.[8] Yet in "The Ancient Constitution Revisited: A Retrospect from 1986," Pocock not only defended his thesis against charges of overstatement, but alluded to certain developments in the history and historiography of English political thought that, though he did not say so precisely, seemed to threaten the entire edifice that he and Skinner had reconstructed. "There are historians of deserved authority," Pocock wrote, "who would not wish to accept that belief in the ancient constitution took shape as the result of processes accruing over the second half of the sixteenth century and the first quarter of the seventeenth":

> Such an explanation would smack of the currently unacceptable belief that the parliament and the House of Commons became

---

8. Quentin Skinner, *The Foundations of Modern Political Thought: The Renaissance*, 2 vols. (Cambridge, 1978); J. G. A. Pocock, *The Machiavellian Moment: Florentine Political Thought and the Atlantic Republican Tradition* (Princeton, 1975).

steadily more autonomous and assertive over the whole of that tract of time. It is not my concern to argue against wind and tide that this happened after all, but it does seem worth pointing out that the anti-whig reaction in historiography has now reached a point where all processes are to be dissolved into moments and all long-term explanations dismissed in favour of short-term ones. The ideological implications are fairly clear: all history is to be reduced to high politics, to the actions of those close enough to power to disregard change, unless thay are its authors, and act only in the short run. . . . There is much to be said for such a view; actors in history are usually motivated by short-term considerations, and English political history has been a pretty oligarchic affair. It remains a question, however, whether short-term actions are not sometimes undertaken in contexts stabilised by structures having a longer *durée* behind them, and whether changes in such structures are not sometimes slow and continuous enough to merit the name of "processes." All that has been inveighed against, since Butterfield, as "whig history" is simply a mistaken way of identifying the processes.[9]

What Pocock here urbanely deferred to is the so-called "revisionist history" initiated by Sir Geoffrey Elton, who in 1965 disturbed the paradigms of British historiography with respect to the seventeenth-century Revolution, a term he did not use. As I have argued elsewhere, one's attitude to those events is usually signaled by one's chosen terminology.[10] Clarendon, for obvious reasons, preferred to call it the Great Rebellion; contemporary historians, unless they are well to the left, have tended to prefer the Civil War or even the Interregnum. Elton, whose article was entitled "A High Road to Civil War?" doubted generally whether there were any structural or ideological causes for the events of 1640–60, and especially whether there were any signs of approaching conflict in the Jacobean parliaments; specifically he wished to refute the oppositional significance that had been attributed to the Commons' *Apology* of 1604.[11] In a

---

9. *The Ancient Constitution and the Feudal Law: A Study of English Historical Thought in the Seventeenth Century* (Cambridge, 1957; reissued 1987), 278.

10. See Patterson, "The Very Name of the Game: Theories of Order and Disorder," in *Literature and the Civil War*, ed. Thomas Healey and Jonathan Sawday (Cambridge, 1990), 21–37.

11. Elton, "A High Road to Civil War?" in his *Studies in Tudor and Stuart Politics and Government*, 2 vols. (London, 1974), 2:164–82. It is worth noting,

subsequent essay, first delivered in 1978 as the J. E. Neale Memorial lecture, Elton proceeded, with oedipal aplomb, to attack the central hypotheses of Neale's work on the Tudor House of Commons, to deny that "the real significance of the institution's history lay in its political function," and that function was "to provide a counterbalance to monarchic rule."[12] Elton's own perspective was that of an institutional historian whose preferred model of government was an efficient bureaucracy, by which standard the Whig commitment to constitutionalism was irrelevant. And one of the authorities on whom he relied for this depoliticized view of the role of Parliament was Sir Thomas Smith's *De republica anglorum*, itself quite properly intended as a neutral and judicious *description* of English institutions.

Pocock's other project, also obliquely presented here, but intimately connected to the rise of revisionist history, was to clear away the confusions attracted to the term "Whig" by Herbert Butterfield in *The Whig Interpretation of History*, published in 1931 but still working its way into general currency long after Butterfield had thought better of it in the shock of World War II. Pocock usefully distinguished not only between the naive progressivism attacked by Butterfield and the "ancient constitutionalism" on which he himself was the authority, but also between those who supported the Good Old Cause and the so-called "Junto Whigs, Court Whigs, Modern Whigs, or whatever the politicians of the increasingly Whig regimes of 1690–1720 may be called."[13] These people, Pocock continued, "were more anxious than ever to escape regicide and revolutionary (to say nothing of Dissenter) associations, and it is from this time that we may date the appearance of the famous (but little studied) 'Whig interpretation of history', which was based upon extolling the parliamentary

---

however, that Elton, who further doubted whether James had ever received the *Apology*, did not manage to explain away entirely the fact that, in his diatribe addressed to the Commons at the end of the session, "James did say something that sounds like an allusion" to it: "The best Apology-maker of you all, for all his eloquence, cannot make all good. Forsooth, a goodly matter, to make Apologies, when no man is by to answer" (181).

12. Elton, "Parliament in the Sixteenth Century: Functions and Fortunes," *Historical Journal* 22 (1979): 155.

13. *Ancient Constitution*, 364.

oppositions to Charles I while condemning the Independent revolution of 1647-9, and upon condemning the unsuccessful revolutionaries Shaftesbury and Monmouth while extolling the bloodless, preserving and glorious revolution of 1688-9." The intent of clearing away the confusions, evidently, was to clear away the stigma also; but it is perhaps worth noting that Pocock, as himself Butterfield's student, was more inhibited in his rejection of the thesis than I am free to be.

During the 1970s and 1980s, the major architects of revisionism developed Elton's revisionism in a wide variety of ways.[14] Closest to Elton, perhaps, in his premises, Conrad Russell, in his extraordinarily influential *Parliaments and English Politics*, seemed to complete the project of emasculating the early parliaments by extending Elton's premises to the Stuart era. Redescribed as ineffective, archaic in their resistance to the necessary modernization of the state, the parliaments of James I and Charles I came to resemble the British labor unions, perhaps; though tiresomely obstructive, they were deemed incapable of anything as concerted as a cause, a unified and principled opposition.[15] By parliaments, however, I here mean primarily the House of Commons; since one of the objects of revisionism has been to undo the work of Neale and Wallace Notestein in foregrounding the Commons, and to replace them as agents in the causes of the civil war by an emphasis on the Lords.[16]

14. See, for example: Kevin Sharpe, "Introduction: Parliamentary History 1603-29," in Sharpe, ed., *Faction and Parliament* (Oxford, 1973); Sharpe, "An Unwanted Civil War," *New York Review of Books*, December 3, 1982; M. Kishlansky, "The Emergence of Adversary Politics in the Long Parliament," *JMH* 49 (1977), 617-40; Barry Coward, "Was There an English Revolution in the Middle of the Seventeenth Century," in *Politics and People in Revolutionary England: Essays in Honor of Ivan Root*, ed. Colin Jones, Malyn Newitt, and Stephen Roberts (Oxford, 1986), 9-40; J. C. D. Clark, *Revolution and Rebellion* (London, 1986).

15. C. S. R. Russell, *Parliament and English Politics, 1621-1629* (Oxford, 1979). See also Russell's earlier introduction to *The Origins of the Civil War* (1973) and his essay "Parliamentary History in Perspective, 1604-29," *History* 61 (1976): 1-27.

16. See, in particular, the work of John Adamson, as in "The English Nobility and the Projected Settlement of 1647," *Historical Journal* 30 (1987): 567-602; "Parliamentary Management, Men-of-Business and the House of Lords, 1640-49," in Clyve Jones, ed., *A Pillar of the Constitution: The House of Lords in British Politics 1640-1784* (1989), 21-50; and "The Baronial Context of the English Civil War," *Transactions of the Royal Historical Society*, 5th ser., no. 40 (1990): 93-120.

Thus, for example, as part of his claim that the notion of a parliamentary opposition in the earlier seventeenth century had been seriously overstated, Russell cited a 1610 memorandum by Sir Thomas Egerton, then chancellor and Lord Ellesmere, objecting to the activities of the House of Commons in the preceding session. From February through November 1610 the Commons had negotiated with the king, via Cecil and the Lords, as to how the country was to be taxed for payment of the royal debts and continued revenues. As the negotiations gradually broke down for what was to have been a Great Contract, whereby the king in return for a settled income would abandon certain feudal dues, with mutual distrust increased rather than diminished by the exercise, an opposition group within the Commons had articulated a version of the Good Old Cause that was both constitutionally precise and semantically rich, a key to many later documents.[17] "The *popular* state," Ellesmere had written in response, "ever since the beginning of his Majesty's gracious and sweet government hath grown big and audacious"; and he quoted Livy (24.25.8) in support of his advice against conciliation:

> It was long ago observed by Livy, *vulgus aut humiliter servit aut superbe dominatur* [The crowd will either serve humbly or govern imperiously]. And it is daily found true, *Plebis importunitas cedendo accenditur* [the importunity of the plebs is increased by yielding to them]. . . . And grant wilful folly what it desireth, it will never be satisfied.[18]

Apart from the bizarre application of the terms "vulgus" and "plebs" to the members of the House of Commons, there was considerable irony in Ellesmere's invocation of Livy, the most republican of the ancient historians, not least because his quotation is taken, out of context, from the story of the revolution in 214 B.C. against Hieronymus, the tyrant of Sicily, an account marked, in Livy's own words, by "the frequent mention of restored freedom—a word sweet to the ears" ("libertatis restitutae

17. Johann Sommerville, in an important essay entitled "Ideology, Property and the Constitution," shows how the terms of this debate would be repeated in 1628 and into the 1640s. See his "Ideology, Property and the Constitution," in *Conflict in Early Stuart England: Studies in Religion and Politics 1603–1642*, ed. Richard Cust and Ann Hughes (London and New York, 1989), 47–71.

18. See *Proceedings in Parliament 1610*, ed. Elizabeth Read Foster, 2 vols. (New Haven, 1966), 1:276.

dulce auditu nomen crebro usurpatum").[19] And Russell's point, that Ellesmere's fear of "innovation and social insubordination" was widely shared—so widely as to make impossible the ideological differences that his predecessors had discerned in the records of the Jacobean parliaments[20]—is supported by citing one side only of the argument.

Some of the voices on the other side have already been cited in my chapter on Donne. But the importance of the 1610 debates needs to be restated. In beginning the great debate on impositions on June 23, 1610, Nicholas Fuller remarked that these custom duties "appear to be contrary to the laws of the realm and directly contrary to the *great Charter*, which laws having once a settled allowance cannot be altered, changed, or made void by act of prince or people, but by *mutual consent* in parliament of prince and people."[21] He also, naughtily, described an occasion on which, as a lawyer, he had defeated Ellesmere in the courts on an issue of prerogative.[22]

In his own contribution to the debate on May 21, King James, who had himself earlier compared the Commons (unfavorably) to tribunes of the people,[23] had exacerbated the fears of the

19. Livy, *Ab urbe condita*, trans. Frank Gardner Moore (Cambridge, Mass., 1940), 6:240–41.

20. Russell, *Parliament and English Politics 1621–1629*, 24.

21. See *Proceedings in Parliament 1610* 2:164.

22. See *Proceedings in Parliament 1610* 2:156–57. Fuller referred to a suit in the Star Chamber against a London printer "for printing contrary to a monopoly granted to I. S. [John Stow]." Ellesmere, whom Fuller unmistakably referred to as "a learned lawyer (then Solicitor to Queen Elizabeth and after Lord Chancellor of England and ever a great maintainer of the prerogative)," had then taken the position that "the king's prerogative was a matter of so high a nature and so tender and jealous to be treated of, that he durst not meddle therin or speak thereof," despite his warrant under the queen's privy seal. Fuller, however, as counsel for the printer, had stated that if the case involved "the lands, good or liberties" of a subject it had to be fully examined, no matter what the prerogative interest, before competent judges. The case, which was dismissed, was tentatively identified by Foster as Flower v. Bourne, in February 1586.

23. We might add to participants in the 1610 debate the tribune Brutus in Shakespeare's *Coriolanus*, who reproaches the plebeians for having given their voices (votes) to Coriolanus in assent to his candidacy for the consulship:

   Could you not have told him
  As you were lesson'd: when he had no power,

"republicans" by abandoning finesse. James's bark was usually worse than his bite. In the speech I have already cited in connection with Donne's constitutional theory, James declared: "You must not set such laws as make [kings] the shadows of kings and dukes of Venice. . . . You cannot so clip the wings of greatness. If a king be resolute to be a *tyrant*, all you can do will not hinder him."[24] But that the conceptual struggle turned on finer distinctions than these, that both sides were engaged in a struggle over crucial definitions, had been made clear almost from the beginning of the session, when the Commons protested the publication of Dr. John Cowell's *The Interpreter*, a work of political theory dedicated to Archbishop Bancroft and containing definitions of which the Commons heartily disapproved. As a Mr. Martin said in a conference with the Lords on March 2, 1610 (and this was in all probability Donne's friend, Richard Martin, the witty member of the Middle Temple), Cowell had defined "King" to mean "that he is above the law and not subject to law"; "Parliament" as merely a "colloquium," or consultation, for "to bind the king to any law were repugnant unto an absolute monarchy"; and "Prerogative" as "the making of laws which are in the king's power . . . *insigniae summae et absolutae potestatis.*" "This book," he concluded, "is *vocabulum*, the explaining of words, which how he hath overshot himself, we leave to your Lordships' wisdoms."[25]

Martin's concern with "*vocabulum*" is an interesting confirmation of my premise that ideologically freighted words were crucial to the evolution of and traffic between various shades of republican thought, from moderate constitutionalism to outright populist radicalism. A battle over words is never over words

---

But was a petty servant to the state,
He was your enemy, ever spake against
Your *liberties* and the *charters* that you bear
I'th'body of the weal; and now arriving
A place of potency and sway o'th'state,
If he should still malignantly remain
Fast foe to th' plebeii, your *voices* might
Be curses to yourselves?

(2.3.174–83)

24. *Proceedings in Parliament 1610* 2:103.
25. *Proceedings in Parliament 1610* 1:25.

alone. But there is another aspect of revisionism which also threatens *any* concept of political "thought" as such, by proposing a theory of motivation inimical to the rational pursuit of any beliefs whatever. This is exemplified, though perhaps not fully intentionally, by John Morrill's *The Revolt of the Provinces*. Here the turn to social history inaugurated by the *Annales* school—initially a liberating shift in methodology intended to free historians from the duty of rehearsing only the history of kings and battles—has negative consequences Morrill may have not foreseen. Like the revisionists of parliamentary history, Morrill too discarded all previous explanatory factors for the events of the 1640s—religious ideology, republican theory, large-scale economic factors—but he replaced them not with what Pocock called "high politics," but with the study of local interest and personal motives among the country gentry on a case-by-case basis, telling the stories of unheroic and essentially selfish persons.

Central to Morrill's project was the denial of full political consciousness to his subjects. Taking as his exemplar William Davenport, whose commonplace book exists in the Chester public records, Morrill made him "typical of the upper gentry in knowing a good deal that was distasteful and unpleasant about the Court, but knowing and understanding less about the real constitutional issues, leaving that to the experts."[26] The experts, on the other hand, are characterized as "extremists," "activists," or (in parentheses) "those who pushed themselves forward" (47). Our choice is therefore between an uninformed, confused, if not actually stupid gentry (the majority) who fail to understand the constitutional issues underlying ship money, and a minority of brash and dogmatic men like John Pym whose excesses (in defining the constitutional issues) eventually drove some of the passive majority into something resembling a position—namely royalism.

Beyond the problem of what constitutes legitimate generalizations about motives—how we move from the individual case to the group—lies the vexed issues of how people behave over time, the problem of consistency. Morrill concluded his study by citing the case of John Poyer, an early "bullheaded" declarer

26. *The Revolt of the Provinces: Conservatives and Radicals in the English Civil War, 1630–1650* (London, 1976), 23.

for Parliament who became entangled in local rivalries and ended his career by surrendering Pembroke Castle to Cromwell. "Here was a man," Morrill summed up caustically, "praying that the 'lawes of the land and the liberties of the people may be all established in their proper bounds.' The great majority of Englishmen had never asked for any more and had yet to learn that a civil war can only protect such liberties by abrogating them" (131). Such points are easy to score in a period in which political consistency was bought at greater individual cost than it is today.

How soon things change! Whereas Pocock, in 1986, felt unwilling or unable "to argue against wind and tide" that the revisionist account of political thought in early modern England was itself a distortion, a quarter of a century seems to have sufficed to absorb the revisionist paradigm, assess its contributions, and to develop a reaction to the reaction, a revision of the revision. In the work of Richard Cust and Ann Hughes, of Thomas Cogswell and Johann Sommerville, British historiography has already recovered (if not its own procedural innocence) much of what was taken away from the early and mid-seventeenth century in terms of explanatory force.[27] As for the Restoration, revision and counterrevision proceed simultaneously as if ignorant of the other's presence. Mark Kishlansky, for example, canvasses the tracts of the most extreme royalist writers, such as Nalson, Petyt,

27. See Richard Cust and Ann Hughes, "Introduction: After Revisionism," in *Conflict in Early Stuart England: Studies in Religion and Politics, 1603–1642*, ed. Cust and Hughes (London and New York, 1989), 1–46, which provides the clearest manifesto of the counterrevisionary movement. Johann Sommerville's *Politics and Ideology in England, 1603–1640* broadened the issue to constitutional theory. Thomas Cogswell initiated the challenge to Russell on his own territory, the character of the Jacobean parliament, and even foregrounded the dangerous R-word in the title of his book, *The Blessed Revolution: English Politics and the Coming of War, 1621–24* (Cambridge, 1989). Richard Cust's *The Forced Loan and English Politics* (Oxford, 1987) and Ann Hughes's *Politics, Society and Civil War in Warwickshire* (Cambridge, 1987) both challenged the premise that county history revealed mainly private interest as the determinant motive in the war. Conrad Russell's *Unrevolutionary England, 1603–1642* (London and Roncelverte, 1990) begins by admitting that Sommerville's attempt to "go back to a 'two sides' picture of early seventeenth-century political ideas" must imply "either that most men ignored their own ideas when it came to the point of action" or that his own account of the politics of the period must be "fundamentally wrong." "At this point," Russell concluded, "it is right to say only that, as usual, the debate goes on" (xxx).

Bagshaw, and Sir Roger L'Estrange, in order to be able to claim that the nation as a whole experienced such a revulsion away from republican thinking, such a wholehearted acceptance of the return of the monarchy, that all dissident voices were silenced.[28] Yet Jonathan Scott has effectively demonstrated that Algernon Sidney at least was an impenitent republican, whose thinking and motivation had been shaped not by the local Exclusion crisis but by the revolutionary experiment of the 1640s.[29] And Richard L. Greaves, in the first of a three-stage study of the Restoration, closed his description of the radical underground movement with the following commonsense (and Whiggish) conclusions:

> Although the radicals failed to attain their aims, their legacy was nevertheless significant. . . . At root, the radical cause did not die, although some of its more parochial or unenlightened goals . . . mercifully did. But in its broadest principles—government under law, freedom, and toleration—it ultimately triumphed. Viewed in this light, their experience of defeat was only temporary.[30]

My point in presenting this story of internecine warfare among the historians of early modern England is not merely that history is a less objective discipline than used to be claimed. It is also to broaden the concept of reading between the lines one stage further, to show that an openness to the complex political messages of early modern texts must inevitably be accompanied by wariness about the half-hidden political messages delivered by the late modern or postmodern scholars who read the early ones on our behalf. We all have our own stories to tell. A hermeneutics of suspicion must extend to ourselves. Beyond this general caveat, my aim is to show how the challenges that have been posed by revisionist history are antipathetic to the Good Old Cause, all of whose terms might have been thought demolished. As Pocock's "retrospective" indicated in 1986, some defense was then required for the "longer *durée*," the conceptual age of the "ancient constitution" and the *mentalité* that supported it; the

---

28. Mark Kishlansky, in an unpublished paper delivered at the Southeastern Renaissance Society of America Conference, the Huntington Library, May 1991.

29. *Algernon Sidney and the English Republic, 1623–1677* (Cambridge, 1988).

30. *Deliver Us from Evil: The Radical Underground in Britain, 1660–1663* (New York and Oxford, 1986), 229.

goodness, or value, of republican thinking, though not explicitly under attack, had clearly also been undermined; and the notion of an overriding Cause had been scoffed at, along with the belief in any significant ideological divisions in Tudor and Stuart political life (although the strife between the modern historians was itself a sign of ideological divisions). In its place was supposedly established the play of faction, imprudence, and self-interest.

One of the reasons, I contest, that the revisionist argument could seem so persuasive (apart from the attraction of any new paradigm and its mental fit with modern political or professional consciousness) was that certain archives were privileged in making the argument and others were ignored or misread. It was not merely a question of focusing on Sir Thomas Smith's or Lord Ellesmere's view of the Commons and its function instead of on Richard Martin's or Nicholas Fuller's; misapprehension of how the Good Old Cause was constructed and transmitted in *symbolic* forms was equally a factor. The "republicanism" whose presence, longevity, and continuity I assert will naturally not be found in the letters or pamphlets of government spokesmen, and is not only to be found in political tracts or formal political theory. It *can* be recognized, however, in a wide range of writings of different types, some of which we have subsequently decided are "literature." The first part of this chapter begins and ends with literature, and much of it will be focused on an indubitably literary figure, John Milton, in whose political thought the Good Old Cause, in the broader as well as the narrower sense, is a constant though evolving construct. The second part will be devoted to one significant part of the Miltonic canon—*Paradise Lost* itself—that has often been declared either immune from politics altogether or a statement of disillusionment with and abandonment of the Cause.

Milton and the "Republican's Library"

I propose to examine a very different reading list from that of Donne's parodic *Courtier's Library*—the cultural inheritance of the Good Old Cause by way of the paradigmatic case of Milton; not solely because Milton himself was a republican (though for how long is precisely what is most disputed about his remarkable career), but because he has left us, through his writing, an extraordinary record of his reading. With the assistance of the monumental scholarship of D. M. Wolfe and the other scholars who edited Milton's prose works, it is possible to see, reconstituted, the shape of the republican canon as Milton himself had discovered it. And my overall argument, which will extend into the second half of this chapter, is that, like the Cause itself, Milton's involvement with it both began earlier and continued longer than is usually allowed.

Obviously, the most unmediated record of Milton's reading is to be found in his commonplace book. Written for himself alone, free of the careful self-constructions by which Milton offered himself in his published works to the admiration of his contemporaries and posterity, and especially free from the restraints that publishing imposed, the official ones of licensing and the interior ones of natural prudence and second thoughts, the commonplace book should really take precedence over the tracts as a key to Milton's "real" opinions. Before it was edited by Ruth Mohl for the Yale edition, the reigning theory of Milton's development as a political thinker, as articulated by Zera Fink, was that he began, under the influence of Sir Thomas Smith's *De republica anglorum*, as a firm believer in the Polybian theory of the mixed state, and that in the early 1640s, though committed to the principle of popular sovereignty, he still regarded the English monarchy as a viable form of magistracy. Not until he embarked on his defenses of the regicide in 1649, thought Fink, did Milton arrive at a fully fledged theory of republicanism.[31] Yet the commonplace book tells otherwise.

31. Zera Fink, "The Theory of the Mixed State and the Development of Milton's Political Thought," *PMLA* 17 (1942): 705–36. This must also be the place to acknowledge both the similarity of my argument to, and its difference from, that of Fink's subsequent monograph, *The Classical Republicans: An Essay in the Recovery of a Pattern of Thought in Seventeenth Century England*, Northwestern University Studies in the Humanities, no. 9 (Evanston, 1945). Fink did not consider literature a serious component of his archive and, on the one occasion when he quotes a substantial chunk of verse, from George Wither's *Poem concerning a perpetuall parliament* (1653), he introduces it apologetically. Although, for example, he devotes space to Gasparo Contarini's *The commonwealth and government of Venice*, translated by Lewis Lewknor in 1599, he does not mention the fact that Edmund Spenser wrote a sonnet commending that translation, concluding with the statement that Venice "farre exceedes in policie of right." Fink's sources include, after Machiavelli's *Discourses on Livy*, primarily

In the early 1640s Milton was (like Spenser and E. K. in 1579, as the glosses to *The Shepheardes Calender* attest) working with Smith's *De republica anglorum*; but he used it not only as an authority for the theory of England as a mixed state, but as the basis for a comment on the decadence of the Roman republic, and "the error of the noble Brutus and Cassius who felt themselves of spirit to free an nation but consider'd not that the nation was not fit to be free."[32] In fact, Milton's extracts from Smith seem brilliantly, if perversely, chosen to cast doubts on the viability of the mixed state, particularly when they appear in the context of the antimonarchical remarks that surround them. Thus Milton finds that Smith argues against absolute monarchy, and remarks that the act of a king "neither approved by the people, nor establisht by act of parliament" is "taken for nothing" and binds nobody, not even the king himself (1:442); and he notes Smith's definition of a king as one "who by succession *or election* commeth with good will of the people to his government, and doth administer the com[mon]-welth by the laws of the same and by equity," whereas he who operates "without consent of the people, and regardeth not the wealth of the commons," Smith defines as a tyrant (1:443). At roughly the same time Milton cited Machiavelli's *Art of War*, to the effect that "a commonwealth is preferable to a monarchy" (1:421), and a much later scribal entry shows that he has also been reading Machiavelli's *Discorsi* on Livy, gathering from that somewhat slippery text the unambiguous information that "Machiavelli much prefers a republican form to monarchy" (1:477), and, more strenuously, "To cure the ills of the people, words suffice, and against those of the prince the sword is necessary" (1:456).

It is true, however, that Milton attempted to combine his *own* version of the classical theory of a mixed state with the alterna-

---

seventeenth-century political theory in the formal sense: Harrington's *Oceana*, Milton's late tracts, and Algernon Sidney's *Discourses concerning government*, for which, though they remained in manuscript, Sidney was executed in 1683. Because of his focus on the Polybian origins of Machiavelli's thought, Fink puts more emphasis on the theory of the "mixed state," conceivably adaptable to a constitutional monarchy, than on the more threatening sense of a "republic" as a polity in which monarchy has been abolished altogether.

32. Milton, *Complete Prose Works*, ed. D. M. Wolfe et al., 8 vols. (New Haven, 1953–82), 1:420.

tive theory of the "ancient constitution," a set of arguments drawing on English medieval history and privileging common and statute law. Though Fink, according to the protocols of the history of political thought, saw this as a muddle endemic to the period, it did not appear a problem to Milton; nor, in the latitudinarian tradition of English "republicanism," does it seem to be a weakness. Under the heading of "Laws," a series of entries which may date from as early as 1639 all indicate that Milton was particularly interested in the laws that bind monarchs rather than their subjects. Of only two citations that he took from the jurist William Lambarde's *Archeion or a commentary upon the High Courts of Justice in England* (1635), one "saith that laws were first devis'd to bound and limit the power of governours, that they might not make lust thire judge, and might their minister." As for medieval history, Milton was obsessively interested in what could be gleaned from it of a constitutional nature. A series of references from Speed's *Historie*, from John Stow's *Annales*, and especially from the 1587 edition of "Holinshed's" *Chronicles* are consistently suspicious of monarchical motives, protective of parliamentary and other liberties, and alert to the criterion that law should be simple and intelligible to the ordinary man. In particular, we can see an ideological node forming around the reign of Richard II, particularly as recounted by Holinshed. Twice, once under the heading of "Subject [subditus]" and again under the heading of "Tyrant," Milton took note of what Holinshed had drawn to the attention of his Elizabethan readers—the thirty-three articles drawn up by Richard's parliament in 1398, stating why he should be deposed (1:446, 454). These notes would come into their own eight or nine years later, when in *The Tenure of Kings and Magistrates* Milton recalled Richard's deposition in a way that refuted both Filmer and Prynne:

> Whence doubtless our Ancestors who were not ignorant what rights either Nature or ancient Constitution had endowed them, . . . thought it no way illegal to depose and put to death thir tyrannous Kings. Insomuch that the Parlament drew up a charge against Richard the second, and the Commons requested to have judgement decree'd against him, that the realme might not be endangerd. (3:220–21)

However telling the selection and grouping of such quotations may be, it is also important to note that not everything in the commonplace book is merely quotation. Stow's information that Alfred "turn'd the old laws into english" elicited from Milton a personal intervention: "I would he liv'd now to rid us of this norman gibbrish" (1:424). By the same token, the category "King" and Stow's account of the death of William the Conqueror inspired Milton to the reflection that "Kings scarcely recognize themselves as mortals, . . . except on the day they are made king or on the day they die. On the former day they feign humility and gentleness, in the hope of capturing the voice of the people. On the latter, having death before their eyes and in the knowledge of their evil deeds, they confess what is a fact, namely, that they are wretched mortals" (1:441–42).

In addition to the English chroniclers and jurists, Milton was, in the mid-1640s, reading the French Protestant monarchomachs, beginning with the *Historia* of Thuanus (Jacques de Thou), published in Geneva in 1626 (1:445), which celebrated the parliamentary resistance of the Estates General of Holland to the tyranny of Philip of Spain; this book in turn excited Milton's curiosity about Hotman's *Franco-Gallia*, which he would later call into service for his first *Defence* of the English republic.

And, as another minor theme that connects Milton's political thought with that of Spenser and Donne, the commonplace book shows that Milton was interested in and sympathetic to the Essex rebellion. Noting the damage that Leicester had done to Walter, first earl of Essex, Milton added, "Just so another Essex was destroyed by the same deceits" (1:464); and in an early entry under the heading of "Property and taxes," in which Milton throughout takes the position of the parliamentary opposition in 1610 and 1628, he refers himself to Camden's account, in the *Annales*, of Essex's rebellion, and to the popular support for Essex, which Camden attributed to the poverty of the common people (1:484).

These concerns are equally evident in the anti-episcopal pamphlets that Milton produced, in a rush, in 1641 and 1642. It is true, of course, that his primary topic was ecclesiastical government and religious reform, in the direction, as he remarks in *Of Reformation*, that has been "desir'd, and beseech't, yea sometimes favourably forwarded by the Parliaments themselves" ever since the first year of Elizabeth's reign (1:602). Yet the two books of *Of Reformation* divide into the two topics of church and state; and although the pretext of the second book was to dispose of the argument implied in James I's much-quoted aphorism "No bishop no king," and hence widen the support for presbyterianism, its "real" subject is the one to which the commonplace book returns over and over again: the encroachments that have been encouraged, and already taken place, on the ancient constitution. Thus, wrote Milton:

> We know that Monarchy is made up of two parts, the Liberty of the subject, and the supremacie of the King. I begin at the root. . . . Yet these devout Prelates, spight of our *great Charter*, and the soules of our Progenitors that wrested their liberties out of the Norman gripe with their dearest blood and highest prowesse, for these many years have not ceas't in their Pulpits wrinching, and spraining the text, to set at nought and trample under foot all the most sacred, and life blood Lawes, Statutes, and Acts of Parliament that are the holy Cov'nant of Union, and Marriage betweene the King and his Realme, by proscribing, and confiscating from us all the right we have to our owne bodies, goods and liberties. (1:592–93)

This clear reference to a version of anti-Normanism ("the Norman gripe") indicates that Milton was already closer to Coke, at one end of the "republican" scale, and on the other to Winstanley, than he was to Sir Thomas Smith.[33] Likewise, the definition he gave of the mixed state in *Of Reformation* had a noticeably less Polybian than an English parliamentary focus:

> There is no Civill Government that hath beene knowne . . . more divinely and harmoniously tun'd, more equally ballanc'd as it

33. For Sir Edward Coke's assimilation of the Conquest to the theory of the ancient constitution, by way of the claim that William I had sworn to observe the ancient laws, see Pocock, *Ancient Constitution*, 42–45; for his distinction between the "ancient constitution" and the "radical" theory of the Norman Yoke as the belief "that the laws are unjust, Norman and still in force," a belief that the Levellers and Winstanley held for different reasons, see 318–21. Milton's references to William I, however, seem to combine both theories. Like Coke, he puts emphasis on the fact that William I claimed the kingdom not by right of conquest but by swearing to uphold the laws already in force; yet as someone who himself frequently advocates radical law reform and proclaims his dislike of law French ("norman gibbrish") he is closer to Lilburne and Winstanley.

were by the hand and the scale of Justice, then is the *Commonwealth* of England: where under a free, and untutor'd Monarch, the noblest, worthiest, and most prudent men, with full approbation, and *suffrage* of the People, have in their power the supreme, and finall determination of highest Affaires. (1:599)

Unlike Spenser's or Kafka's, Milton's version of "the hand and the scale of Justice" is unproblematically rendered concrete in a political institution; and it is difficult to believe Milton was unconscious of the clash between the beginning of his definition of the English constitution and its end, between the "free and untutor'd Monarch," a phrase which recalls other locutions of James I, and the "finall determination of highest Affaires" which Milton attributes to the English Parliament.[34]

Again, in *Of Prelatical Episcopacy*, while apparently discussing merely the question of whether and why Calvin and Beza could be said to have been temporarily bishops, Milton slips in the secular and more serious analogy that invokes republicanism in its very beginnings:

Brutus that expell'd the Kings out of Rome, was for the time forc't to be as it were a King himself, till matters were set in order, as in a *free commonwealth*. He that had seen Pericles lead the Athenians which way he lists, haply would have said he had bin their Prince, and yet he was but a powerfull and eloquent man in a *Democratie*, and had no more at any time then a Temporary, and *elective* sway, which was in the will of the people to abrogate. (1:640)

In 1642, Milton inserted in his *Apology*, the last of his pamphlets written in support of the presbyterian attack on the English bishops, a digression on the Long Parliament, which at that early stage of the revolution was not yet visibly more enduring than its predecessors, but on the contrary seemed the agent of great beginnings. Here he went out of his way to recall the *last* Caroline Parliament of 1628/29 and the struggles over the Petition of Right. Some of the present members, he observes, now sit, "not without imprisonment and open disgraces in the *cause* of their country" as their qualification; and their present victory over the bishops (their exclusion from the House of Lords of February 1642)

---

34. D. M. Wolfe, editor of *Of Reformation*, notes in this passage Milton's "implicit rejection of divine right."

is a constitutional victory: "With one stroke winning againe our lost *liberties and Charters*, which our forefathers after so many battels could scarce maintaine" (1:924). In other words, from at least 1642 onward, Milton conceived of a Cause that united all those "that lov'd religion, and their native liberty," precisely the binary structure of the Good Old Cause that Vane would articulate in 1656. In addition, although in *Eikonoklastes* he demurred that constitutional law as such was neither his "element, nor . . . proper work," Milton was clearly concerned with "the more Lawyerlie mooting" of his arguments (3:403). If for "true freedom in matters of religion" he relied, obviously, on Scripture, for "just natural rights in civil things" he turned to the history and theory of English law.

If then, as it appears, Milton's republican thinking was fairly strongly developed in the 1640s, we need posit no gap, and certainly not one of self-interest, between the Milton who saw himself as an independent contributor to the reforming moment in the church, and the Milton who became an employee of the Council of State and a defender of its actions before the world. But although there is no conceptual turnabout, there *is* visible in the tracts of 1649 through 1651 (or indeed through 1658, if we take into account that the *First Defence* was revised and reissued in that year) a steady expansion of the republican's library as Milton was taking command of it. In the *Tenure*, many of the texts that Matthew Sutcliffe and Richard Bancroft, attacking the Marprelate pamphlets, had lined up sixty years before as constituting a *combined* political and ecclesiastical threat, now appear as Milton's authorities: Thomas Cartwright; George Buchanan's *Powers of the Crown*; Christopher Goodman's *How Superior Powers Oght to be Obeyd of Their Subjects* (published in Geneva in 1558); Dudley Fenner's *Sacra Theologia* (published in Geneva in 1586); and John Ponet's *Short Treatise of Politike Power* (published semi-anonymously in Strassburg in 1556),[35] which Milton, using an intermediate source, mistakenly attributed to Anthony Gilby. As Bancroft had warned from the pulpit at Paul's Cross in February 1589 ("being the first Sunday in the Parleament,"), "Read the

35. Ponet's tract was published under the initials D.I.P.B.R.W., not too hard to translate into Dr. John Ponet, Bishop of Rochester and Winchester. The tract was republished in London in 1639 and 1642.

writings of the chiefest pillars of these platforms, as the booke *De jure magistratum in subditos*: the book intituled *Vindiciae contra tyrannos*: another *De jure regni apud Scotos* . . . and you shal find in them these most strange and rebellious propositions stifly maintained, dilated and amplified."[36] And Sutcliffe, in his *Answer* to Job Throkmorton, had linked together in a single agenda the Martinist pamphlets, the first and second *Admonitions* to Parliament in 1572, Fenner, Goodman, Buchanan, and Gilby, "tumultuous subscriptions, dangerous meetings."[37]

It is also worth noting how smoothly, by now, Milton conflated the symbolic names and moments in republican history, sacred and profane, and connected them to his own moment. In the *Tenure*, Milton connected the Roman expulsion of the Tarquins with the revolt of the Jews against Rehoboam at Sechem (1 Kings 12):

> As Livy praises the Romans who took occasion from Tarquinius a wicked Prince to gaine their libertie. . . . Nor was it in the former example don unlawfully; for when Roboam had prepar'd a huge Army to reduce the Israelites, he was forbidd'n by the Prophet. . . . And those grave and wise Counselors whom Rehoboam first advis'd with, spake no such thing, as our old gray headed Flatterers now are wont, stand upon your birth-right, scorn to capitulate, you hold of God [and] not of them; for they knew no such matter, unless conditionally, but gave him politic counsel, as in a civil transaction. (3:208–9)

Likewise in the *First Defence*, where the story of Rehoboam is greatly expanded, Ehud who slew the tyrant Eglon, king of Moab, shares a paragraph with Marcus Brutus, and they are followed by "Samson, that renowned champion, though his countrymen blamed him. . . . and whether instigated by God or by his own valor only, slew not one, but many at once of his country's tyrants."

The pamphlet that most clearly demonstrates the breadth and depth, fluidity and catholicity, of the republican archive must surely be the *First Defence*, first published in 1651, under the title

---

36. See Richard Bancroft, *A Sermon preached at Paules Crosse the 9 of Februarie, being the first Sunday in the Parleament, Anno 1588* (London, 1589; rpt. 1636), 78.

37. Matthew Sutcliffe, *An Answere unto a certaine calumnious letter published by M. Job Throkmorton* (London, 1595), 48.

Defension pro populo Anglicano, as an answer to Salmasius (Claude de Saumaise), who was employed by the royalists in exile to proclaim the illegality of the regicides' proceedings against Charles I. One of the least known and least admired of Milton's regicide tracts, the *First Defence* is as rude as it can be to Salmasius and bound by the structural rules of animadversions to follow its opponent's argument step by laborious step. Nevertheless, it can instruct us about the extent to which principles were claimed, and witnesses adduced, to explain the motivation of those who had emerged as the leaders of the new commonwealth. Indeed, as one of Salmasius' claims was that there had been no national consensus in rebellion, but only a small faction of men operating outside the law, one might see him as the first revisionist historian of these events.

In the *First Defence* Milton ransacks Scripture, the Church Fathers, and classical history and literature for statements limiting the power of kings—frequently turning to examples chosen by Salmasius and turning them against him by cleverer logic or better scholarship. There is, however, one new source of authority visible in the *First Defence,* or at least, one less noticeable in the earlier tracts, for the good reason, perhaps, that Milton had not realized how *its* interpretation could change in the light of recent events. Responding to Salmasius' charge that the English revolutionaries have abused the term *populus,* the people, by abolishing the House of Lords, with the result that the *populus* have been reduced to the *plebs,* the common people only, Milton replies:

> And yet this is the very thing that shows that under the word people we comprehend all our citizens, of what order and degree however; in that we have established a single supreme Commons' House only. . . .[38]

And a few pages later, he supports his position by way of what he calls the *Modus habendi Parlamenta* (better known today as the *Modus tenendi*) which "tells us that the King and the Commons may hold a Parliament and enact laws though the Earls and Bishops are absent, but that the King with the Earls and Bishops

---

38. For the translation of this passage of the *First Defence,* I prefer that by Samuel L. Wolff for the Columbia edition (New York, 1932), 7:391.

cannot do so in the absence of the Commons." The *Modus* had been printed by John Hooker in 1572, and attached to his own *Order and Usage of the Keeping of a Parlement in England*, an updating and expansion of the *Modus* which was subsequently republished in the 1587 edition of "Holinshed's" *Chronicles*. The authority of the *Modus*, writes Milton, in his own struggles with revisionist historiography, shows that "the Commons are felt to be present in the name of the whole nation, and in that name to be more powerful and more noble than the Lords, and altogether to be preferred" (7:425). As Coke had done in his *Institutes*, Milton here adduced the fourteenth-century *Modus* as a witness to ancient constitutionalism, along with Fortescue, Bracton and Fleta, and like Coke, he calmly combined it with what Pocock calls "the lavishly fantastic *Mirror of Justices*" to get the results he wanted[39]; but his motives were perhaps closer to those of William Hakewill, whose response to the debates in the 1610 parliament included making a translation of the *Modus* as a preface to his own account of Commons' procedure, published for the first time, by parliamentary authority, in 1641. For Milton, reinterpreting the *Modus* in the light of 1648/49, it functioned as an "ancient" witness to Parliament as the supreme power in the nation, and to the Commons as the crucial element in the parliamentary process; but in the light of 1648/49, the "whole truth" of the debates about balance of powers and the mixed state comes down to this still more radical proposition, that Parliament is the master, and the king merely its servant:

> Parliament is the supreme council of the nation, constituted and appointed by an absolutely free people, and armed with ample power and authority, for this end and purpose: viz. to consult together upon the most weighty affairs; the king was created to take care that there should be executed, obedient to their vote and resolution, all the acts and decrees of those Orders, Estates, or Houses. (7:459)

There is one other aspect of the *First Defence* that is important to my case that Milton himself is important as a witness. It is

39. For the *Modus* and its history of interpretation, see Nicholas Pronay and John Taylor, *Parliamentary Texts of the Later Middle Ages* (Oxford, 1980), 19–114, especially 35, 54. For the *Mirror*, see Pocock, *Ancient Constitution*, 43.

evident in this tract that Milton does not generally discriminate epistemologically between literature and the other activities from which republican thought can be reconstructed; on the other hand, in the case of literature, the protocol of holistic interpretation (not citing individual statements out of context) is peculiarly demanding. Challenging Salmasius' citation of Aeschylus' *The Suppliants*, Milton warned, "We must not regard the poet's words as his own, but consider who it is who speaks in the play, and what that person says; for different persons are introduced, sometimes good, sometimes bad, sometimes wise men, sometimes fools and they speak not always the poet's own opinion, but what is most fitting to each character." And having filled in the gaps around Salmasius' selective quotation, he concludes: "Had I not related the whole thing, how rashly would this smatterer have laid down the law concerning the right of kings among Grecians, out of the mouths of women that were both strangers and supplicants, though both the king himself and the very action of the drama lead us to a far different conclusion!" That is to say, a suppliant will necessarily adopt a more submissive posture to the powerful figure from whom she needs a favor. A few pages later, this elementary warning against uncontextualized quotation receives a supplement. Returning to Seneca's *Hercules furens*, one of the loci classici for the sixteenth-century monarchomachs, Milton remarks:

> That familiar passage of Seneca the tragedian may relate both to the Romans and to the Greeks:
>> There can be slain
>> No sacrifice to God more acceptable
>> Than an unjust and wicked king.
>
> For if this be taken as the sentiment of Hercules, who speaks these words, it shows what was the opinion of the most eminent Greeks in that age; if it be taken as the sentiment of the poet, who flourished under Nero (and poets generally put something like their own opinions into the mouths of their best characters), then this passage betokened what both Seneca himself and all good men, even in Nero's time, thought should be done to a tyrant. . . . (7:327)

As we approach the interpretive puzzle of *Paradise Lost*, these sentences should themselves become part of the context.

"To the end persisting"

I have claimed above that after the republican experiment and Protectorate disintegrated, the Good Old Cause continued to operate, as an ideologeme of sufficient power or capaciousness to unite those who, if they agreed on nothing else, agreed that the Restoration of the Stuarts was a disaster for one or both of Vane's two principles, civil liberties and religious toleration: those, like the regicide Edmund Ludlow, who believed that Cromwell had betrayed the revolution, as well as those who, like Milton and Marvell, had committed themselves to the Protectorate. But my case is at least as well, if not better, demonstrated by the writings of those who, conversely, committed themselves to Charles II and James II, of whom Dryden is the most interesting example. Particularly between 1680 and 1684 there is constantly asserted in pro-Stuart propaganda the threat of a continuous radical tradition whose continuity increased its danger; and by the irony of history this stigmatic view of the Cause helps us at this distance to recognize its survival, however it may have gone underground.

In 1683, for example, Robert Ferguson's *Lamentation for the Destruction of the Association and the Good Old Cause* is actually a crudely ironized attack on Shaftesbury and his supporters, who are made to define their cause as follows: "Interest is our Aim, Rebellion is our Doctrine, Hipocracy is our Cloak, Murder our Intention, Religion we have none, and the Devil is our Master" (3). "For our further proceedings we have the Presidents of the Late uncivil Civil strife from Forty One to Forty Eight, and the same Path was, and is our present Rode" (9). Significantly (if one looks forward to, or back from, United States constitutionalism) Ferguson suggests that the only way to put an end to the Good Old Cause as he has redefined it would be a massive, apocalyptic, enforced emigration to New England:

> Were New England Wall'd round with brass, after our Banishment thither, that no Gate, Part, or any Place of Retreat could be made from it, and the whole Land become (like Mount Ætna) Consuming Flame, that we might pass at one Sacrifice. Then, Quiet, Peace, Union, and Continual Concord might Inhabit the Earth. But till that happens, it is no more in our Power, to Alter our Natures (though the Mercy of the King should forgive us) then to Create our selves Angels of Light. (9–10)

It may be only by coincidence that America is here envisaged in the imaginative terms of Milton's Hell. But is it also a coincidence when Dryden begins in the 1680s to equate the Fall of Lucifer with the Exclusion crisis? Dryden, we know, wanted to rewrite *Paradise Lost* in that "modern bondage" of rhyme, and indeed reproduced it as *The State of Innocence*, an opera (planned in 1667, written in 1674, and published in 1677) with a significantly different title and different effect.

When Dryden's *All for Love: Or, the World well Lost* was published in 1681, it appeared with a dedication to the earl of Danby, Charles's chief minister, and thereby became an occasion to inveigh against republicanism, past and present. "Both my Nature, as I am an Englishman," wrote Dryden, "And my Reason, as I am a Man, have bred in me a loathing to that specious Name of a Republick: that mock-appearance of a Liberty, where all who have not part in the Government, are Slaves." Citing Satan as the source of all rebellion, and clearly thereby alluding to Shaftesbury, Dryden also looked back to those "who began the late Rebellion," and who, when Cromwell emerged as the master mind, "enjoy'd not the fruit of their undertaking, but were crush'd themselves by the Usurpation of their own Instrument."[40] This allusion to Satan as the first rebel, though in one way entirely conventional (it was an opening premise of the Elizabethan *Homily on Disobedience* first published in 1571, and employed against Lilburne in his trial for treason in 1649) was repeated in Dryden's dedication of *Plutarch's Lives* (1683) to the duke of Ormonde. There Dryden wrote of the ingratitude of Shaftesbury and such of his followers who were former Royalists and who had been lavishly rewarded since the Restoration:

40. See Dryden, *All for Love, Oedipus, Troilus and Cressida*, ed. Maximilian E. Novak and George T. Guffey, vol. 13 of *Works* (Berkeley and Los Angeles, 1984), 6–7. This equation of the 1640s and the 1680s is typical of Dryden, whose theory of the *continuity* of the Good Old Cause is the negative mirror image of my own. In 1684, he dedicated the *History of the League* to Charles II and added a "Postscript" creating a genealogy of rebellion from Luther onward. "Calvin, to do him right," he remarked, "writ to King Edward the Sixth, a sharp Letter against these People [the extreme radical sects]; but our Presbyterians after him, have been content to make use of them in the late Civil Wars, where they and all the rest of the Sectaries were joyn'd in the *Good Old Cause* of Rebellion against His Late Majesty." Vol. 18 of *Works*, ed. Alan Roper and Vinton Dearing (Berkeley and Los Angeles, 1974), 398–99.

The greater and the stronger ties which some of them have had, are the deeper brands of their Apostacy: For Arch-Angels were the first and most glorious of the whole Creation: They were the morning work of God; and had the first impressions of his Image, what Creatures cou'd be made: . . . Their fall was therefore more opprobrious than that of Man, because they had no clay for their excuse; Though I hope and wish the latter part of the Allegory may not hold, and that repentance may yet be allow'd them.[41]

My point is that Dryden was here engaged in a reading of *Paradise Lost* that not only implied a straightforward political allegory—the Fall of the Angels as the Puritan Revolution—but also imposed a second level of allegory from subsequent political history—the Fall of the Angels as the Exclusion crisis, with Shaftesbury in the place of Cromwell. The effect of this move was to enroll Milton posthumously in a cause which was the very opposite of that which, I believe, he would at that time have espoused.

In the preface to *Religio Laici* (1682), Dryden had extended the retroactive history of party back to the 1580s, referring to "Martin Mar-Prelate (the Marvel of those times)" as "the first Presbyterian Scribler, who sanctify'd Libels and Scurrility to the use of the Good Old Cause" (b1). He thereby created a centennial loop from the Admonition Controversy of 1572 and its immediate consequence in the Marprelate pamphlets to the Andrew Marvell whom he knew (and despised) as the author of the *Rehearsal Transpros'd* of 1672.[42] In 1672, when Marvell took up the cause of religious toleration against Samuel Parker (for which Dryden equated him with the Marprelate writers), he made it clear that they were indeed engaging in another phase of an ongoing struggle. On the one hand, the Anglican clergy who were now arguing for strict state-enforced conformity were illegitimately invoking the specter of the 1640s to demonize the Nonconformists: "You represent them, to a man, to be all of them

41. Dryden, *Prose 1668–1691*, ed. Samuel Holt Monk and A. E. Wallace Maurer, in *The Works of John Dryden*, vol. 17 (Berkeley, Los Angeles, London, 1971), 233.

42. Marvell himself says there, in response to Samuel Parker, "you would fix upon me the old Martin Mar-Prelate (in one page you do it four times)." See *The Rehearsal Transpros'd and The Rehearsal Transpros'd: The Second Part*, ed. D. I. B. Smith (Oxford, 1971), 294.

of Republican Principles, most pestilent, and, *eo nomine*, enemies to Monarchy . . . onely the memory of the late War serves for demonstration, and the detestable sentence & execution, of his late Majesty is represented again upon the Scaffold . . . to prove that the late War was wholly upon a Fanatical Cause, and the dissenting party do still goe big with the same Monster" (125). On the other hand, much of Marvell's case against Parker consists in aligning him with the Anglican clergy of the 1620s and 1630s, Robert Sibthorpe and Roger Maynwaring, whose published sermons asserted the doctrine of monarchical absolutism and the irrelevance of Parliament (127–33), and whose destructive advice, culminating in the policies of Laud, Marvell holds responsible for the civil war.

This strategy permitted him to speak with inimitable but also inimical tact about Charles II, whose Declaration of Indulgence could certainly have been interpreted as an improper use of the prerogative. Granting both the first and the second Charles a technical immunity from his critique by holding the clergy responsible for all nonconstitutional behavior in the civil sphere and all intolerance in ecclesiastical jurisdiction, Marvell was able to imply both loyalty and respect. Reciprocally, Charles intervened with the licenser, Sir Roger L'Estrange, and the *Rehearsal Transpros'd* and its author were given immunity from censorship.

But one does not have to work very hard to detect, between the lines of the *Rehearsal Transpros'd*, a clear message to the king that if he continues to repeat the mistakes his father made, history may repeat itself. Looking back himself to the 1640s, Marvell wrote:

> Whether it were a War of Religion, or of Liberty [Vane's two principles], is not worth the labour to enquire. . . . but upon considering all, I think the Cause was too good to have been fought for. Men ought to have trusted God; they ought and might have trusted the King with the whole matter. The *Arms of the Church are Prayers and Tears*, the Arms of the Subject are Patience and Petitions. . . . For men may spare their pains where Nature is at work, and the world will not go the faster for our driving. Even as his present Majesties happy Restauration did it self, so all things else happen in their best and proper time, without any need of our officiousness. (135)

At the very least, this statement retains the integrity of the Cause while denying the militancy that supported it. But she who reads suspiciously is certainly permitted to imagine *another* phase of historical development to follow in *its* "best and proper time," a suspicion not diminished by finding in the next sentence a distinct warning: that "the fatal Consequences of that Rebellion . . . can only serve as Sea-marks unto wise Princes to avoid the Causes."[43] Two kinds of Cause are thereby united in Marvell's argument. The first is the Good Old Cause that he still undeniably supported, and to which he would dedicate his *Account of the Growth of Popery and Arbitrary Government*; the second, the arbitrary behavior of monarchs that caused the first revolution of the seventeenth century and that would, in "proper time," also result in the second.

In the second part of the *Rehearsal Transpros'd* there appears an account of Milton during the Restoration, which we should treat with the same suspicion as Marvell's disingenuous manifesto on the Good Old Cause itself. His motive was to protect his friend from the charge of collaborating on the first part of the *Rehearsal*; the strategy, to imply that Milton, in the experience of defeat, had given up writing: having by "misfortune" been "toss'd on the wrong side" in the civil war, and having written "*Flagrante bello* certain dangerous Treatises . . . At his Majesties happy Return, J.M. did partake . . . of his Regal Clemency and has ever since expiated himself in a retired silence" (312). At the very least this was a rather peculiar description of the man who, five years before, had published *Paradise Lost*. For certain readers, Marvell's statement that Milton had been silenced must have clashed with the invocation to book 7 of that poem, where Milton himself declared that his voice was "unchang'd / to hoarse or mute." I believe that Marvell and Dryden were each, from opposite points of view, aware of what Milton was up to in *Paradise Lost*, and that while Marvell assumed a role of protective disingenuity, Dryden, who admired Milton and had even helped to shield him from the punishment inflicted on the leading regi-

43. For a similar conclusion, that Marvell wrote this passage with deliberate irony and ambiguity, see Christopher Hill, *The Experience of Defeat: Milton and Some Contemporaries* (New York, 1984), 249–50.

cides, tried to appropriate and tame the poem whose subversive force he intuited.

The struggle between Milton and Dryden was not only carried out in terms of Dryden's hoped-for containment of *Paradise Lost*. Mock epic or mock heroic had its own statement to make—in Dryden's hands perceived at least by some as a rescue of epic from sedition. Nathaniel Lee, whose experience with *Lucius Junius Brutus* had apparently brought on a prudential shift of allegiance, contrasted Dryden's *Absalom and Achitophel* favorably to *Paradise Lost*: "As if Milton from the dead arose / Fil'd off the Rust, and the right Party chose."[44] By contrast, Samuel Butler attacked epic itself as a locus of value; and while *Hudibras* is resolutely vicious against the Nonconformists, Butler's *Characters* confirm his own understanding of the link between religious nonconformity and republicanism as a category of thought, a category which Butler does his best to empty: "A Republican is a civil Fanatic, an Utopian Senator; and as all Fanatics cheat themselves with Words, mistaking them for Things: so does he with the false sense of Liberty. . . . He is a nominal Politician, a faithful and loyal Subject to notional Governments, but an obstinate Rebel to the real."[45] It appears that Butler was fully aware of the symbolic force of the left-wing vocabulary, though obscuring behind a high-philosophical debate what must have been an equal knowledge that one side's cheating with words is the other side's necessary art of persuasion.

In 1683, in the aftermath of the Exclusion crisis, the University of Oxford passed in Convocation a judgment "against Certain Pernicious Books and Damnable Doctrines," which, like the pamphlets and sermons of government and episcopal spokesmen a century earlier, conveniently outlined for future nonconformists in church or state the central arguments of the Good Old Cause, along with bibliographical suggestions! It takes little imagination to see that what was proscribed was thereby ren-

44. See "To the Unknown Author of this Excellent Poem," *The Works of Nathaniel Lee*, ed. Thomas B. Stroup and Arthur L. Cooke, 2 vols. (New Brunswick, 1955), 2:559. I owe this reference to Alvin Snider, *Origin and Authority in Seventeenth-Century England*, which I have been fortunate to see in manuscript (144).

45. *Characters*, ed. Charles W. Daves (Cleveland, 1970), 55.

dered both coherent and accessible. Under the third "damnable" doctrine, "That if lawful governors become tyrants, or govern otherwise than by the laws of God and man they ought to do, they forfeit the right they had unto their government," the authorities listed were: *Lex Rex*; Buchanan, *De jure regni*; *Vindiciae contra tyrannos*; Bellarmine, *De conciliis, De pontifici*; Milton; Goodwin; Baxter, *H.C.* [*Holy Commonwealth*]. In the case of Milton, whose official entry into the republican canon was thereby noted, no specific text is indicated.[46] As I have indicated above, there were signs that Milton's contemporaries of the opposed political persuasion would have included *Paradise Lost* in that empty space after his name; and in the second part of this chapter I will show that the story of *Paradise Lost* and how it has been interpreted supports that inference.

But to round off this phase of the argument, it is convenient to end, as I began, with the drama. In 1682, when Nahum Tate's melodramatic rewriting of Shakespeare's *Coriolanus* was acted at the Theatre Royal and subsequently published, as an overt contribution on the king's side to the Exclusion crisis, it was preceded by a prologue, as follows:

> Our Author do's with modesty submit,
> To all the Loyal Criticks of the Pit;
> Not to the Wit-dissenters of the Age,
> Who in a Civil War do still Engage,
> The antient fundamental Laws o'th'Stage:
> Such who have common Places got, by stealth,
> From the Sedition of Wits Common-Wealth.
> From Kings presented, They may well detract,
> Who will not suffer Kings Themselves to Act.

This prologue shows with what sophistication the *vocabulum* of political thought could be deployed metaphorically, as literary criticism; or perhaps how deep was the interpenetration of these two ways of thinking, each of them concerned, though conversely, with the effects of orthodoxy (which alone can generate both loyalty and dissent). As Dryden had attempted to tame

46. For the evolution of the later "Whig" canon, thanks to the editorial zeal of John Toland and others, for use in the next century and encompassing Milton, Marvell, Ludlow, Nedham, Harrington, Algernon Sidney, and John Locke, see Caroline Robbins, *The Eighteenth Century Commonwealthman*.

Paradise Lost by turning it into *The State of Innocence*, Tate attempted to turn Shakespeare's study of the Roman republic into an essay on *The Ingratitude of a Common-Wealth* to its monarch, and a recommendation of "Submission and Adherence to Establisht Lawful Power." His play thus symmetrically reverses, with its emphasis on *modest submission, loyalty, dissenters*, and *sedition*, the impulse of Nathaniel Lee's *Lucius Junius Brutus*, played and suppressed two years earlier, with *its* emphasis on *desire, suspicion, fear, ignorance, error,* and the people's capacity to recover from their errors by *being told* the *truth*. The struggle for control over the past—its cultural objects, its symbolic names and moments, its history—will undoubtedly continue to evince these polarities, as well as a series of intermediate positions. But here I do *not* recommend a compromise posture, either between Tate and Lee, or between the revisionist historians and the counterrevisionists. It is time unequivocally to recuperate what for half a century has been stigmatized, thanks to Herbert Butterfield, as the "Whig" interpretation of history, and to remember that the values subsumed under the Good Old Cause are those for which people of principle were persecuted, in pursuit of which the New England settlements were founded, and for which modern democracies may properly congratulate themselves, if such they really are.

"The Civil War is not ended": Milton's Modern Readers

"The Civil War is not ended": Reading Literary Criticism

In early 1660, in desperation at the seeming inevitability of the Restoration, Milton dashed off a pamphlet ironically entitled *The Readie and Easie Way to Establish a Free Commonwealth*. In its final sentences, he wrote:

> What I have spoken is the language of that which is not called amiss "The Good Old Cause" . . . nay, though what I have spoke should happen . . . to be the last words of our expiring liberty. (7:387–88)

These lines have often been taken as support for the notion that *Paradise Lost* was written in a mood of profound political disillusionment, and that it redirects its readers' aspirations to apolitical, interior, and transcendent values. This theory goes back, as does so much else in literary tradition, to Coleridge. "Finding it impossible," wrote Coleridge, "to realize his own aspirations, either in religion, or in politics, or society, [Milton] gave up his heart to the living spirit and light within him, and avenged himself on the world by enriching it with this record of his own transcendent ideal."[47] The critical tradition that installed this account of *Paradise Lost* at the climax of seventeenth-century *literary* history could only have done so, however, by a powerful act of repression. We can begin to see signs of guilty knowledge at the moment—unusual in literary history—of Milton's *removal* from the literary canon, on the authority of T. S. Eliot and F. R. Leavis, who together provoked a controversy among British intelligentsia that spanned two decades. In 1936, by both Leavis and Eliot, Milton was subjected to the "serious charge" of being a bad influence on poets; of indulging in "rhetoric," as opposed to the conversational style which was carried forward by Dryden, to the extent of creating a barrier of style between his meaning and his reader.[48] In 1947 Eliot delivered another statement on Milton, supposedly to correct the misjudgments of his previous one, but in fact to render an apology so peculiar that it may have been more successful than the original sally in rendering Milton an outlaw. Milton was, after all, Eliot conceded, a great poet whose influence might be less noxious than he had supposed.[49] Understandably, modern poets like himself, who had been carrying out "another revolution in idiom," had been biased. Their bias depreciated Milton while contributing to the "taste" for Donne; but a decade later, Eliot felt, "we cannot, in literature, any more than in the rest of life, live in a perpetual state of revolution" (148). This political metaphor was scarcely coincidental. Milton's own language is now to be seen as the source of his greatness; but it is also described as "a perpetual sequence of original acts of lawlessness" (141).

47. Samuel Taylor Coleridge, Lecture X, *Literary Remains* (London, 1836), quoted from James Thorpe, ed., *Milton Criticism: Selections from Four Centuries* (London, 1951), 97.

48. Leavis, *Revaluation* (London, 1936), reprinted from *Scrutiny* (1933); Eliot, "A Note on the Verse of John Milton," *Essays and Studies of the English Association* (Oxford, 1936), cited from *Selected Prose*, ed. John Hayward (Harmondsworth: Penguin, 1953), 123, 130.

49. "Milton," Annual Lecture on a Master Mind, read March 26, 1947, before the British Academy. Cited from *Selected Prose*, 142.

Eliot himself partially admitted to a political consciousness lurking beneath his adjudicatory system; I say partially, because the admission occurs during his reproach of Dr. Johnson for a failure of objectivity with respect to Milton, a failure from which, Eliot implied, he himself was immune. "There is," Eliot wrote in 1947, "one prejudice against Milton, apparent on almost every page of Johnson's *Life of Milton*, which I imagine is still general":

> we, however, with a longer historical perspective, are in a better position than was Johnson to recognize it and to make allowance for it. This is a prejudice which I share myself: an antipathy towards Milton the man. . . . But this prejudice is often involved with another, more obscure: and I do not think that Johnson had disengaged the two in his own mind. The fact is simply that the Civil War of the seventeenth century, in which Milton is a symbolic figure, has never been concluded. The Civil War is not ended: I question whether any serious civil war ever does end. . . . Reading Johnson's essay one is always aware that Johnson was obstinately and passionately of another party. No other English poet, not Wordsworth, or Shelley, lived through or took sides in such momentous events as did Milton; of no other poet is it so difficult to consider the poetry as poetry, without our theological and political dispositions, conscious and unconscious, inherited or acquired, making an unlawful entry. (134)[50]

Given that Eliot wrote this statement two years after the British Labor party took over the government of his adopted country and proceeded to construct a social revolution; knowing what we know from other sources of Eliot's own "theological and political dispositions," we may guess that Eliot was more like Johnson than he believed. Perhaps he too confused his acknowledged "antipathy towards Milton the man" with one only partly acknowledged, toward Milton the hero of the Whigs. "It is now considered grotesque, on political grounds," Eliot had continued with misleading suavity, "to be of the party of King Charles; it is now, I believe, considered equally grotesque, on moral grounds, to be of the party of the Puritans; . . . it is probably beneficial to question the assumption that Milton was a sound Free Churchman and member of the Liberal Party; but I think that

50. Eliot's striking admission was noted earlier by Colin McCabe, in *Teaching the Text*, ed. Norman Bryson and Suzanne Kappeller (London, 1983), 31.

we still have to be on guard against an unconscious partisanship, if we aim to attend to the poetry for the poetry's sake" (134–35). One could profitably rewrite this advice as follows: we still have to be on guard against an unconscious hostility to Milton's political career, which can easily mask itself as the demand that we attend to the poetry for the poetry's sake (whatever that means), or the related demand that what shall count as poetry, or at least as great poetry, shall not make political demands upon us.

Now, one would have supposed that if Eliot was right in believing that "the Civil War is not ended," there would have emerged from the other side an account of Milton that celebrated his twenty years of political activism and made not the style but the argument of *Paradise Lost* its focus. In fact, most of the initiative for *celebrating* Milton's republican career has come not from literary scholars but rather from Christopher Hill, the most prominent Marxist historian of the seventeenth century. Yet there is a powerful irony dictating the shape of Hill's contribution. Although his work as a whole could be said to have been keeping the Good Old Cause alive as a professional project,[51] his own historiographical allegiances to the Levellers, the Diggers, and other sectarians led him to read the Restoration with the same pessimism as caused him to entitle one of his later books *The Experience of Defeat*. Consequently, Hill produced a model for understanding *Paradise Lost* which, although self-contradictory in ways I shall explain, finally differs very little from the Coleridgean theory of political ideals frustrated and hence sublimely transcended. In *The Experience of Defeat* Hill did argue, though primarily from *Samson Agonistes*, that "there is no evidence that Milton ever adopted the post-1661 Quaker position of pacifism and abstention from politics."[52] But his major statement about Milton was already inscribed in the great biography *Milton and*

51. Indeed, one of his earlier volumes carried that very title. See Christopher Hill and Edmund Dell, eds., *The Good Old Cause: The English Revolution of 1640–60: Its Causes, Course and Consequences: Extracts from Contemporary Sources* (London, 1949). There is some evidence that revisionist historiography was motivated by a desire not only to replace an older Whig historiography, but to refute Hill. Elton referred skeptically to Hill in "A High Road to Civil War?" 167.

52. *Experience of Defeat*, 215. Hill points out that "Samson's name was believed in the seventeenth century to mean 'here the second time'" (317).

the English Revolution.[53] Significantly, this appeared in 1977, at approximately the same time as the revisionist paradigm in British historiography achieved dominance. And although in his early chapters Hill fought manfully for the notion that Milton was already a defender of the Good Old Cause in his early poems—an attempt which probably really was a lost cause, given the scantiness of the evidence[54]—when he turned to *Paradise Lost* he saw it as a message about acceptance of a superior wisdom that frustrates human intervention. "I see Milton," Hill wrote, "bitterly—because he must—accepting the Father whose will is Fate, but aspiring more and more to the position of Sonship, to union with the perfect man who becomes God's son by merit. The possibility of regeneration salvages something of man's dignity, freedom and responsibility from the wreckage of 1660" (358). In order to accommodate some version of the Romantic thesis that Satan the rebel is the true hero of the poem, Hill imagined a chronological or compositional split in the poem, so that the early books, in which Satan is "wrong but grandly wrong" (365), were written before 1660, before Milton's despair was confirmed; but in general Hill believed (in a strange alliance with Northrop Frye) that "the character of Satan alludes to some of the ways in which the Good Old Cause had gone wrong" (366).

This interpretation is, however, rendered unstable by Hill's simultaneous belief that Milton was, in *Paradise Lost*, inhibited by the Restoration censorship. He relates the incident of 1686–87, when Milton's friend Theodore Haak, who had translated the first three books of *Paradise Lost* into German, read them aloud

53. *Milton and the English Revolution* (New York, 1977).

54. Hill found relief from the apparent conventionality of Milton's early poetry in his personal associations; for example, his friendship with Alexander Gil, who was imprisoned for libeling Buckingham in 1628 (28). Other crumbs of comfort were found in Milton's commonplace book, where Milton referred to "Junius Brutus, that second founder of Rome and great avenger of the lusts of kings" (35). But the problem of the early poems had to be faced. "A masque," wrote Hill, contemplating the text we now call *Comus*, "appears at first sight rather a surprising thing for a Puritan to write—if we can properly call Milton a Puritan at this time" (45). The solution, which Hill himself evidently found incompletely satisfying, was to focus on the Lady's plea "for greater economic equality" as against "lewdly-pampered Luxury" (47) and to define the spirit of the masque as being in the Puritan individualist tradition of the lonely, heroic ordeal (49).

to the Hanoverian pastor H. L. Benthem, who understood them as a commentary on Restoration politics in England. According to Benthem, when Milton's friends heard the poem's title before it appeared they assumed it would be a lament for the Good Old Cause and feared for his safety. When they actually read it they were reassured and withdrew their objections to the poem's publication. But, continued Benthem, when Haak read the early books to him he realized that "in fact 'this very wily politician' ['dieser sehr schlau Politicus'] had concealed under this disguise exactly the sort of lament his friends had originally suspected."[55] How, precisely, we are not told. But Hill invokes this anecdote in support of one way of reading the poem—a microcriticism that looks for tiny textual details that can be construed as hints of defiance: for instance, the reference to an eclipse which "with fear of change / Perplexes monarchs,"[56] which we know the censor objected to; and also the "parsimonious emmet," the ant which Milton called a "Pattern of just equality perhaps" (7.484–86) and which Hill saw as a gesture toward a future republic, Milton "covering himself by an ambiguous 'perhaps'" (408). Milton, Hill thought, was unable to write with the freedom he would have chosen and so encoded his views. Apparently he did not notice the contradiction between his own two theories—the argument for Christian resignation and that for encoded political defiance.[57]

---

55. Benthem, *Engelandischer Kirch- und Schulen-Staat* (Luneberg, 1694), 58. Cited in Hill, *Milton and the English Revolution*, 391.

56. For easy access, I cite *Paradise Lost* from Milton, *Complete Poems and Major Prose*, ed. M. Y. Hughes (New York, 1957).

57. In an important essay, Mary Ann Radzinowicz argues that, while *Paradise Lost* will support both the theory of "politics abandoned" and that of "politics encrypted," it does so in order to teach its readers to avoid simple solutions. The poem is a textbook in political education. Like Christopher Hill, Radzinowicz cites the "parsimonious emmet" as an ideologeme of Milton's program. Unlike Hill, she continues Milton's statement about the ant, to note that what immediately follows the word "perhaps" (which Hill read as self-protection) is the word "hereafter," which Radzinowicz reads as deferral. A failed revolution is to be replaced by a better-educated future—men progressively (in the tradition of Christian rationalism) "gaining illumination." Fixed meanings and single interpretations are coercive. Radzinowicz's argument must, however, be recognized not as a genuine compromise but as a skilful rewriting of the traditional argument for transcendence; in the last analysis Christian rational-

If Hill's position may be defined as a nontheoretical Marxist history with an anti-establishment edge, it can be clearly distinguished from other kinds of neo-Marxist thinking in the academy, which has flourished particularly in departments of literature. Literary-theoretical Marxists have faced a different sort of dilemma from that encountered by Hill in his struggle with the revisionists. On the one hand, they must necessarily look with favor on Milton for the sake of his twenty-year participation in the English revolution; on the other, his continual assertion of what is generally castigated as the "bourgeois ideology" of individual self-determination must be something of an embarrassment. To continue to admire Milton as the free, speaking, and *hence* revolutionary subject (even after discounting his inconsistencies and self-deceptions) flies in the face of Althusser's pronouncements that such beliefs in self-determination are the greatest self-deceptions of all, imposed on us by ideologies that in turn are constructed by governments. This dilemma was evidently experienced by Fredric Jameson, who offered in 1980 an account of *Paradise Lost* that was clearly an offshoot of his great book *The Political Unconscious*.[58] Motivated by reflection on the rise of a religious politics in Iran, Jameson suggested, via Durkheim, that religion was the "master code" in which class conflict was played out in England in the seventeenth century. This allowed him to posit an "overlap" between the structures of Calvinism and Marxism—both of them, obviously, determinisms. The idea has formidable analytical potential, not least since the unmistakable intent of Milton's theological arguments in *Paradise Lost*, book 3, was to replace the determinism of orthodox Calvinism with an emphasis on personal choice that the his-

---

ism and literary theory merge, to produce a new version of the disengagement theory. Milton, she concludes, "has successfully resisted the temptation himself to appropriate 'the language of that which is not called amiss the good old Cause' for a utopian program." See "The Politics of *Paradise Lost*," in *Politics of Discourse: The Literature and History of Seventeenth-Century England*, ed. Kevin Sharpe and Steven Zwicker (Berkeley and Los Angeles, 1987), 204–29.

58. Jameson, "Religion and Ideology: A Political Reading of *Paradise Lost*, a paper delivered at a conference at the University of Essex in 1980 and subsequently published in *Literature, Politics and Theory*, ed. Francis Barker et al. (London, 1986), 3–56.

tory of Christianity would label Arminianism, but which, if translated into sociopolitical terms, we would probably recognize as liberalism. Jameson, however, avoided this consequence of his argument. Although Milton clearly and intentionally rejects the heart of Calvinist predestination—the doctrine of limited atonement—in his debates between Father and Son in book 3, Jameson argued, following Althusser and Pierre Macherey in *A Theory of Literary Production*,[59] that *Paradise Lost* unintentionally brings out the contradictions inherent in Calvinist ideology, not by conceptual analysis but by giving it literary representation (46). In other words, *Paradise Lost* succeeds because Milton fails, because his poem "ends up by producing the opposite of what it originally intended" (48). Yet Jameson was unable to account thereby for the fact that even figuratively a middle-class revolution (with religion as its symbolic language) nowhere "seems to be present in the text" (49). Although *Paradise Lost* is "the first great monument of bourgeois literature" (49), this, its supposedly central meaning, must somehow have been still further repressed. Instead of an image of class praxis, the figure of Satan resembles more a great feudal baron, so that (by reversing the allegory assumed by Hill) the rebellious archangel is to be recognized not as the republican leadership but as Charles I. As for the second half of the poem, its definition of the paradise within represents, Jameson thought, "the quietistic and anti-political turn of the post-revolutionary period," and the last two books of the poem "open up that privatized and post-political world, to whose disillusionments the mediocrity of *Paradise Regained* is immediately attributable" (50).

Now, it must be admitted that *Paradise Lost* provokes such disagreements. Why? Because Milton, having rewritten the Fall, broadly speaking, in the political language of monarchy and rebellion and so incited the search for contemporary analogies, refused to permit their unproblematic discovery in its details. In 1698 John Toland asserted in his *Life of John Milton* that "to display the different Effects of Liberty and Tyranny, is the chief design of his *Paradise Lost*," a statement whose truth would probably be conceded by all but the most determined transcenden-

59. Macherey, *A Theory of Literary Production*, trans. Geoffrey Wall (London, 1978).

talist, but which does not take us beyond generalities to the vexed question of where the poem locates liberty and tyranny and how it evaluates them. Both Hill and Jameson had to face the fact that Milton's Satan upholds a version of the Good Old Cause which too closely resembles the dark parody offered by Robert Ferguson ("Interest is our Aim, Rebellion is our Doctrine, Hipocracy is our Cloak, Murder our Intention, Religion we have none, and the Devil is our Master"). And the *narrative* message of the first six books is clearly that rebellion is not only an improper expression of the desire for personal autonomy, it is doomed to fail.

There may be other ways, however, of construing the hints that have come down to us of early readers—Benthem, Toland, Lee, Dryden—reading *Paradise Lost* as a poem dangerous to the Restoration settlement. There are two different ways in which we can reapproach the seeming undecidability of the poem's political stance, and consider what directional signs those early modern readers might have noticed that have been subsequently obscured. The first will take us back to the political vocabulary I defined earlier, to the symbolic names and ideologemes that carried the Good Old Cause from at least the 1640s into the Restoration; the second will take us back, surprisingly, to T. S. Eliot and the Milton controversy of the first half of our own century, with its focus on the merits or demerits of the Miltonic grand style.

The Nimrodic Moment

What neither Hill nor Jameson mentions is that in the *second* half of the poem, and especially in the last two books, Milton moved from the representational mode of political analysis, which was necessarily rich with ambiguity, to straightforward political theory, one of the topics of the tutorial conducted by the archangel Michael with Adam as the father of all students. In a brilliant move, Milton here introduced two of the symbolic figures from the political-theoretical debates of his contemporaries and made them the vehicles of an unambiguous counterargument. The first of these is Adam himself. We can now see that Milton's early interest in the story of the Fall must have been intensified by the role played by Adam in the absolutist monarchy theories of Robert Filmer. Although Filmer's *Patriarcha* was not published until 1680, his *Observations upon Aristotle's Politiques* had been in print since 1652, and would therefore have been not only available to Milton, but of great interest to him, as someone who consistently cites the Aristotelian account of the origins of sovereignty, behind which Filmer had imposed another, earlier origin. The preface of Filmer's *Observations* already contains the crucial statement that Milton could not accept: "The first government in the world was monarchical, in the father of all flesh. Adam . . . having dominion given him over all creatures, was thereby the monarch of the whole world; none of his posterity had any right to possess anything, but by his grant or permission. . . . There was never any such thing as an independent multitude who at first had a natural right to a community."[60] It is this version of patriarchalism that Milton's Adam *himself* refutes, without any indirection at all; and he does so by invoking the second figure from early sacred history in whom political debate had invested, the figure of Nimrod.

Nimrod, in Pocock's words, haunted the dreams of English legal and political theorists, because he constituted, by antedating it, the irreducible exception to the theory of the ancient constitution:

> the spectre of the conqueror, Nimrod or Nembroth as Fortescue named him, who won power by the naked sword and used it to constitute a kingdom in which the enforcement and interpretation of the law of nature belonged to him alone. Nimrod is a figure of primeval nature rather than civil history; as builder of the Tower of Babel, he is older than the *jus gentium* which grew up following its fall, and no civil law—not even the law martial—can be traced directly to him. . . . The problem of conquest was part of the problem of the "Machiavellian moment." The "Nimrodic moment" was . . . almost impossible to define in terms of secular time.[61]

Milton had several times confronted the "Nimrodic moment" in his earlier political writings. In *Eikonoklastes*, in particular, he attacked the dead Charles I in language that recalls Donne's satires against James I, by way of the ideologeme of hunting:

60. Cited from *Divine Right and Democracy*, ed. David Wootton (Harmondsworth, 1986), 110.

61. *Ancient Constitution*, 283–84.

the Bishops could have told him, that Nimrod, the first that hunted after Faction, is reputed, by ancient tradition, the first that founded Monarchy; whence it appeares that to hunt after Faction is more properly the Kings Game; and those Hounds, which he calls the Vulgar, have bin oft'n hollow'd to from Court. (3:466)

In *Animadversions* he averred that "our just Parliament will deliver us from . . . your cruell Nimrods, with whom we shall be ever fearlesse to encounter" (1:729); and in the *First Defence* he had acknowledged obliquely that Nimrod was a crucial figure in royalist definitions of sovereignty, by attacking Salmasius' statement that at the origins of civil society some wise and eloquent man gathered the scattered people together that "he might exercise dominion over them." "Perhaps you are thinking" Milton replied sardonically, "of Nimrod, who is said to have been the first tyrant" (4[1]:473).

With this polemical history behind him, the Nimrod of *Paradise Lost* acquires special status in the narrative of book 12. Milton here reworked his earlier scattered allusions into a coherent political narrative, one that takes the starting point of political history behind Nimrod, who is not even dignified by naming, and who is merely one of a series of problems that Adam, our true original, sees as the future consequences of his own actions. Nimrod appears in Book 12 as "one [who] shal rise

> Of proud ambitious heart, who not content
> With fair equality, fraternal state,
> Will arrogate Dominion undeserv'd
> Over his brethren, and quite dispossess
> Concord and law of Nature from the Earth;
> Hunting (and Men not Beasts shall be his game)
> With War and hostile snare such as refuse
> Subjection to his Empire tyrannous:
> A mighty Hunter thence he shall be styl'd
> Before the Lord, as in despite of Heav'n,
> Or from Heav'n claiming second Sovranty;
> And from Rebellion shall derive his name,
> Though of Rebellion others he accuse.
> (12.24–37)

Milton is here invoking the debates that stemmed from Fortescue's double theory of kingship by law and by conquest, and which led through intricate paths from the Norman Conquest to James I (notorious as a hunter) who claimed his inheritance of the English crown from William the Conqueror.[62] Given Milton's own earlier shots at Charles I as Nimrod, this passage could easily have been recognized as a commentary on Stuart theories of monarchy by divine right, articulated by James but acted upon by his son. But here anticonquest theory is firmly integrated with Christian egalitarianism, with its equivalent in modern political principle. Nimrod's destruction of "fair equality, fraternal state" and his arrogation of "Dominion undeserv'd / Over his brethren" constitute for Milton a second Fall of Man, and echo his statement in the *Readie and Easie Way* that no man "who hath the true principles of justice and religion in him, can presume . . . to be a king and lord over his brethren, whom he cannot but know, whether as men or Christians, to be for the most part every way equal or superiour to himself" (7:364). And Adam continues to explain to his Restoration readers how important it is, when doing political philosophy, to understand and limit the significance of words to their original contexts:

> O execrable son so to aspire
> Above his brethren, to himself assuming
> Authority usurped, from God not given:
> He gave us only over beast, fish, fowl,
> Dominion absolute; that right we hold
> By his donation; but man over men
> He made not Lord; such title to himself
> Reserving, human left from human free.
> (12.64–71)

This move preempts the endless disputes over the origins of law (did it antedate kings, or descend from them?) and sovereignty (was it given by God in perpetuity, or temporarily contracted out by peoples initially free?). One could argue that by this *aufhebung* Milton abandoned his secular argument for resisting government by a single person, and adopted instead the position that could so easily lead to passivity, that as a punishment for the Fall "Tyr-

---

62. See Pocock, *Ancient Constitution*, 284–305. Milton in *The Tenure of Kings and Magistrates* had been careful to dispose of conquest theory, "not forgetting this . . . that William the Norman, though a Conqueror, and not unsworn at his Coronation, was compell'd the second time to take oath at St. Albanes, ere the people would be brought to yeild obedience" (3:201).

anny must be, / Though to the Tyrant no excuse" (12.95–96). But such an argument is harder to hold if one sees that Milton invests his clearest statement of political theory in precisely those figures, differently deployed, on whom the apologists for monarchy relied. Milton therefore anticipated in 1667, but from within a *symbolic* vocabulary, the purely *logical* case that John Locke was eventually to make against the Filmerian use of Adam in his *Two Treatises of Government*, published in 1690 though written, if Peter Lazlett is correct, as a support for Shaftesbury's position in the early 1680s: that Filmer had misconstrued the language of Genesis, and misapplied an ontological brand of sovereignty (man is superior to the animal kingdom) to a pseudohistory of political thought.[63]

"*Unchang'd . . . though fall'n on evil days*": The Political Sublime

With these words in the invocation to *Paradise Lost*, book 7, Milton claimed to be "unchang'd to hoarse or mute" in 1667 from the public servant who had written *The Readie and Easie Way*, unsilenced by the Restoration censorship. It seems reasonable to believe him. *Paradise Lost*, while signaling the extreme complexity of political theory and the functional difficulty of founding a better society, nevertheless intimates the indissoluble, ancient connection between that goal and the republican movement, both as valuable in the past and as potentially recuperable. In fact, signs of intentionality usually overlooked appear in the preliminaries to the poem as published in 1674. One of these was Andrew Marvell's introductory poem, which suggested that Milton was a latter-day Samson braced to bring down the pillars of his society upon the heads of its leaders, an act, moreover, of revenge. This reverberates not only with Milton's invocation in the *First Defence* of "the heroic Samson," who "still made war single-handed on his masters, and. . . . slew at one stroke not one but a host of his country's tyrants" (4[1]:402), but also with Coleridge's statement that "Milton avenged himself on the world by enriching it with this record of his own transcendent ideal." In what sense could *Paradise Lost* possibly be conceived as a

---

63. Locke, *Two Treatises of Government*, ed. Peter Laslett, 2d. ed. (Cambridge, 1967), 35–37, 45–66.

revenge, Marvell's poem provokes us to ask, and what connects that metaphor of violence to Marvell's pioneering definition of Milton's style as "sublime," the cause simultaneously of "delight and horror"? Eliot's reference to this style as "a perpetual sequence of original acts of lawlessness" allows us to posit that style might, after all, *stand for* something other than itself.

After Marvell's poem, which concludes by relating the sublime to the choice of blank verse, there appeared (in 1674, and in some of the editions of 1667/68) a note on "The Verse," whose last lines (which would therefore have been the last words a reader encountered before embarking on the poem) were:

> This neglect then of Rime so little is to be taken for a defect, though it may seem so perhaps to vulgar Readers, that it rather is to be esteemed an example set, the first in English, of *ancient liberty* recover'd to Heroic Poem from the troublesome and modern bondage of Riming.[64]

This not only set Milton apart from the royalist poets of the Restoration, who had made rhyme their mark of modernity, with Dryden as the chief exemplar and polemicist, but, by way of the phrase "ancient liberty," placed *Paradise Lost* and its refusal to rhyme firmly in the same political vocabulary that Milton had been developing from the moment he opened his commonplace book.[65] Blank verse, open-ended, is enrolled in the service of the Good Old Cause.[66] It was no accident that Richard Leigh, who in 1673 attacked Marvell and Milton simultaneously, imply-

---

64. There were nine distinct issues of *Paradise Lost* in 1667 and 1668. One of these, printed by Samuel Simmons in 1668, has fourteen pages or seven leaves added, including the prose "arguments" to each book, and the "Note on the Verse." David Masson interprets the differences between these issues as signs of timidity and caution on the part of Milton's printer. See his *Life of John Milton*, 7 vols. (Cambridge and London, 1859–94), 2:14.

65. Compare Sonnet 12, which he wrote about the hostile reaction to his divorce tracts, which begins, "I did but prompt the age to quit their clogs / By the known rules of ancient liberty."

66. Compare Leonard Goldstein, "The Good Old Cause and Milton's Blank Verse," *Zeitschrift für Anglistik und Amerikanistik* 23 (1975): 133–42, who argues that neoclassical literary theory "with its emphasis on restraint, decorum, order, reason, the rules . . . constitutes counter-revolution in the form of literary criticism" (134). Goldstein's analysis is conducted, however, in terms of the history of prosody, not in terms of the political semantics of "ancient liberty."

ing their collaboration in Marvell's *Rehearsal Transpros'd*, registered the metrical challenge. "The odds betwixt a Transproser
and a Blank Verse Poet, is not great," he wrote; though, being
apparently unwilling to grant *Paradise Lost* its fully contentious
force, Leigh added that Milton's poem was in fact derivative of
Davenant's *Gondibert*: "I think this Schismatick in Poetry," he
concluded, "though nonconformable in point of Rhyme, as
authentick ev'ry jot, as any Bishop Laureat of them all."[67]

But there is a connection between the politics of meter and the
politics of style in the broadest sense—a connection made by
Marvell's poem at the very point where it rejects the mode of
Dryden. "Thy Verse, created like thy Theme sublime," wrote
Marvell to Milton, "In Number, Weight and Measure needs not
rhyme." The word "sublime" is not used casually here, and anticipates our subsequent association of the term with "Longinus"
and his treatise on a very different kind of high style from that
defined in the Ciceronian tradition. In fact, we have overlooked
an important aspect of the politics of the sublime as Milton and
Marvell would have understood it.[68] We know that *Paradise Lost*
readily became a source of examples whereby eighteenth-century
critics could illustrate their expanding doctrine of the Sublime.
I argue that Milton himself *intended* his poem to be seen as a demonstration of sublime themes and effects, with the corollary of
summoning up what might be called the Longinian version of
the Good Old Cause, which thereby could be recognized as very
very old indeed.

When Milton mentions Longinus in his list of authorities in
Of Education from whom one may learn "a graceful and ornate
rhetoric," and follows that with the authorities from whom "the
sublime art" of poetics may be learned (2:403–4), he pointed
(though admittedly with no special emphasis) to a treatise that
was available in Greek and Latin in two editions produced by

67. [Richard Leigh], *The Transproser Rehears'd: or, The Fifth Act of Mr. Bayes's Play* (Oxford, 1673), 39–43.

68. I am deeply indebted in this section to the work of Jonathan Lamb, my colleague at the National Humanities Center in 1991/92, whose investiga-
tions into the politics of the sublime in the eighteenth century opened my
eyes to the political aspects of *On the Sublime* and its attribution to Cassius
Longinus.

Gerard Langbaine.[69] In 1652 there appeared an English translation by John Hall.[70] By the time *Paradise Lost* was written, Langbaine and Hall would clearly have emerged on two different sides of the political divide. Langbaine had become provost of Queen's College, Oxford, a defender of his college against the presbyterian visitors, and a royalist pamphleteer. Hall, though having friends and admirers on both sides of the civil war divide (including both Thomas Hobbes and Samuel Hartlib), was employed by Cromwell as a political pamphleteer during the 1650s and handsomely pensioned accordingly.[71] It is perhaps only fair to say that Langbaine could not have anticipated in 1636 the specifically local meaning that accrued to the Longinian sublime in the 1650s and later; and that as a classical scholar he honestly represented the dynamic of the Longinian text within its supposed historical context, the story of Cassius Longinus as minister or secretary to Zenobia, queen of Palmyra.

Hall's translation was, however, inserted into the political conflict in a way that could scarcely have failed to come to Milton's attention. It was dedicated to Bulstrode Whitelocke, one of the most important, though moderate, members of the revolutionary council of state, one of the three holders of the new republic's great seal, who in the early 1650s was engaged in law reform. In February 1652 Milton, as we know from his correspondence with Herman Mylius, the agent for the count of Oldenburg, was in daily service to the council, and in personal contact with Whitelocke. On February 12, 1652, Milton wrote to Whitelocke stating that he, Milton, had been instructed by the council to carry to Whitelocke his Latin version of the safeguard granted to Oldenburg so that Whitelocke could review it (4[2]:846). In 1654,

69. Gerard Langbaine, ed. *Dionysii Longini Rhetoris praestantissimi liber de grandi loquentia sive sublimi dicendi genere* (Oxford, 1636).

70. *Peri hypsous Or Dionysius Longinus of the Height of Eloquence* (London, 1652).

71. It is unlikely that Hall and Milton did not know each other in the early 1650s. To Hall is now attributed *A Letter to a Gentleman in the Country, Touching the Dissolution of the Late Parliament* (1953), which justified Cromwell's dismissal of the Rump. David Masson attributed the tract to Milton, and Don Wolfe, who sees it as too concerned with economics to be Milton's, nevertheless suggests that Milton "may have dictated parts of the tract to Hall or some other friend" (*Complete Prose Works* 4.1:219).

Milton included Whitelocke in a list of persons whom the *Second Defence* commands as "men famous in private life and the arts of peace, and known to [him] either through friendship or by report" (4[1]:676).

In his dedication Hall declares that he could not find a better protector for *On the Sublime* than Whitelocke, who has been "intrusted with the greatest civil employment that this Nation can make use of," since it was "to civil persons Longinus (who I dare say writes to his own rules) tells us he intended it" (A4). Hall hopes that this "great Critick (for even so his own age acknowledg'd him)" will "find acceptance with a person that in the Hurricans of these great Transactions, is serenely pleased to throw off the publick person, and adopt into his tendernesse and protection all that, unto to which worth and letters may make a claim" (A4–A5). But while making this conventional move from the public to the private, from the republican experiment to the republic of letters, Hall actually resituates his Greek rhetorician in the present and makes him accessory to the rhetorical needs of the early modern politician. As Hall puts it, whereas in ancient Greece there was a confusion between advice to the Senate and "Harangues to the people," "for the same men acted both parts," with the result that rhetorical display ("that which was necessary to gain the people") invaded the counsels of state, "now the Scene is changed, and (in Civil matters) we are to speak to the few and not the many":

> For as the corruption of the time hath diseas'd most Governments into Monarchies, so the least of these few populacies now in being, is too great to be included in the same walls, or brought to the hearing of one voice (long studied Orations becoming uselesse). (A7–A8)

In other words, a *printed* rhetoric dedicated to a political leader is now a timely solution to the demand for new media of persuasion. As Hall put it rather bluntly, language or rhetoric is "a way of speech prevailing over those whom we designe it shall prevail" (B1v).

But it is not just the medium that is at stake here. The Longinian rhetoric was associated with a distinctive message, of special import to readers like Whitelocke and Milton. From either Langbaine's edition or Hall's translation, they would have learned, had they not already known it, that *On the Sublime* is the only ancient rhetorical treatise dedicated to the relationship between oratory and political liberty. Especially in sections 15, 16 and 17 of his treatise, where the topic is the role of the orator after the fatal battle of Chaeronea, when Greek democracy fell to Philip of Macedon, Longinus made it obliquely clear that his heroes are those who use every linguistic trick they possess to defend democracy. What on the face of it are offered merely as examples of a sublime rhetoric in fact carry the story—and it is presented as a long story—of Greek democratic principle; and they carry it forward into an era dominated by imperial power and ideology.

So, Longinus wrote, in the *De corona* Demosthenes was vindicating his public policy with respect to Chaeronea. What would have been the most straightforward way to have treated the subject? It would have been to say (and here I will turn back to John Hall, whose translation of the previous sentences is misleading, though interesting),[72] "You were not deceived (Athenians) when you undertook to protect the Liberty of Greece, though with your own hazard nor want ye examples of this at home, nor did they amisse that engaged at Salamis, nor those at Plataea." Instead of taking this natural path, Demosthenes instead,

> as though he had been suddenly ravished with divine afflation, and struck into a Transport, he swears by the gallant men of Greece; By all those (sayes he) that were in danger at Marathon. Now by this figurate oath (which we call here an Apostrophe) does he *intimate* the deification of his Ancestors, calling them though dead to witnesse, to whom as Gods we ought to appeal. Now he recalling this transaction into the memory of his hearers, and raising up his demonstration to such a transcendencie and vigour, . . . so enflames them with praises that they cannot imagine or expect anything lesse from the fight with Philip then victories as signall as those of Marathon and Salamis. . . . The oath wholly levels at them that were overcome, that so the businesse

72. Hall's version offers: "Demosthenes remonstrates concerning the management of the Commonwealth: but what was the naturall use or end thereof?" (36). William Smith's eighteenth-century version is more accurate: "Demosthenes is producing Proofs of his upright Behaviour whilst in publick Employ. Now which is the most natural Method of doing this?" Longinus, *On the Sublime* (1739) (Delmar, N.Y., 1975), 46.

of Cheronaea might be no longer accounted a great misfortune
to the Athenians. (37–38; italics added)

Here is a perfect instance of Longinus focusing on what is *intimated*, rather than transparently articulated, in Demosthenes'
oration; discovering the energy stored in figurative discourse that
would be dissipated if the political point were simply argued.

That sublimity is associated with concealment is also the topic
of the next section (no. 17), in which Longinus raises the rhetorical ideal of self-concealment. For, wrote Longinus (in Hall's translation), an obviously artful discourse carries political dangers,

> but especially if we addresse [ourselves] to a Judge that hath full
> power in his hands, much more to a Tyrant, King or Generalis-
> simo, for they stomack presently if you endeavour to catch them
> like schoolboyes, with umbratil Pedanteries of Rhetorick, and
> interpreting such little Sophistry to be brought in contempt of
> them, disgust the whole, so that though courted with all the blan-
> dishments and graces of speech, they will never be persuaded.
> (39–40)

In other words, since a successful politician is alert to the figurative nature of rhetoric and will regard a too-obvious application of art as a *deficiency* of sophistry, as an insult to his intelligence, a sublime rhetoric must *conceal* its figurative quality. If this
section seems to loop a logical knot around the previous one, by
seeming to argue that the inequalities of power demand the use
of invisible figures only, that conundrum too is typical of
Longinus; and to tie the knot tighter, the example he uses of a
figure that conceals itself is precisely that oath of Demosthenes
cited in the previous section, which would seem, as a device,
to have called attention to itself. "In what has the Orator concealed the Figure?" asked Longinus, undeterred: "Plainly, in its
own Lustre. For as the Stars are quite dim'd and obscur'd, when
the Sun breaks out in all his blazing Rays, so the Artifices of Rhetoric are entirely overshadow'd by the superior Splendour of sublime Thoughts."[73]

That these central sections intimate the thematics of *Peri hypsous* is confirmed by the last section (no. 44), which stages a

---

73. I cite here from Smith, *On the Sublime*, 51, because Hall's version is almost
unintelligible.

debate between an anonymous philosopher and Longinus himself on the sociopolitical conditions of a great rhetorical tradition: more specifically, this final section contains a defense of
political liberty. Into the mouth of the anonymous philosopher
Longinus puts (in Hall's translation) the following declaration:

> 'Tis a great wonder (said he) whence it should come that in our
> age as well as in many others, large capacities, deep judgments,
> clear and searching heads, but especially vigorous and fiery wits,
> made for the enriching of Eloquence, are very seldom or not at
> all found, such a dearth there is of all men constellated for the sci-
> ences: Shall wee I beseech you believe that which hath been in
> many mens mouths, that a Democracie is the best Nurse of high
> Spirits, and under it so many great Oratours have in a manner not
> only flourish'd, but even decay'd with it? For just liberty feeds and
> nourishes the thoughts with great notions, and draws them for-
> ward, and encreases their emulations and the strong desires they
> have to obtain the priority of honour, and that by the rewards pro-
> posed to them in such Republicks the faculties of their minds and
> all their skills are whetted, and in a manner kindled into a flame,
> which commonly shines freely and brightly as the things they deal
> with. But we of this age, said hee, seem to be taught from chil-
> dren to endure slavery, being swath'd as it were in these customes
> and persuasions even from our tenderest years, so that we can-
> not possibly taste of that rich and full fountain of Eloquence, I
> mean, says he, Liberty. So that in the end we become at best but
> excellent flatterers, and from hence, sayes he, these kinds of hab-
> its follow us to our own homes; and 'tis impossible for a servile
> man to be a true Oratour, for presently his Liberty and his bold-
> ness decayes and consumes, and being as it were by custome used
> to buffeting we dare never speake out but onely mutter. Wee lose
> one half of our vertue (sayes Homer) in one day of our servitude.
> And as (if it be true which I have heard reported) they say the cages
> in which Pigmies commonly called dwarfes are nourished not
> only hinder the encrease and growth of them, but can streighten
> them by a muzzle [or band] put about their mouthes: So may we
> say that any slavery be it never so just, may truly be called a cage
> for the soul and a common Gaol of it. (78–80)

To this complaint Longinus records "himself" as replying that
there is a worse subjection than the political, that is to say, the
inner slavery that comes from "our own turbulent Passions,"
especially lust and avarice. It does not take much perspicacity

to see that this stratagem, of placing the more radical doctrine in the mouth of another ("said he" is four times repeated) and countering it with a more conventionally ethical posture attributed to oneself, is a standard move in the tradition of writing between the lines. Indeed, Hall's translation accentuates the theme of censorship slightly by his emphasis on the "dwarfs in cages" metaphor, with its graphic rendering of the "muzzle [or band] put about their mouthes," and its addition of the phrase "we dare never speake out but onely mutter."[74]

If Hall emphasizes the theme of censorship that underwrites the *Peri hypsous*, Langbaine's edition makes it clear that Longinus' disingenuousness was well understood by classical scholars in Milton's day. Langbaine's prefatory material contains a synopsis of *On the Sublime*, including the statement that Longinus was writing obliquely so as to retain Aurelian's good graces. The problem under discussion, wrote Langbaine, was "slippery and dangerous" ("lubricam & periculosam"), and therefore Longinus says that it comes from a certain nameless philosopher "in order to avoid the odium of his earlier explanation, in that he rightly suspected that the Emperor could be greatly offended" ("ut prioris solutionis invidiam declinet, quippe qua non mediocritur Imperatorem offendi posse suspicabatur merito"). According to the nameless philosopher, under the principate, and with the devolution of supreme authority to a single person, slavery, just like the cages which stunt the growth of pigmies, confines the talents of orators, so that in their place are born and emerge famous flatterers. But this political explanation "Longinus" "cautiously avoids" ("cautè eludit") and "rises to thanks of Aurelian who then held supreme power" ("qui tum rerum potiebatur"); and "beginning with the malcontent natures of those who never acquiesce in the present state of affairs he substituted other causes [for the decal of oratory]," such as avarice, lust, arrogance, luxury, etc. (B6).[75]

74. Compare Smith's avowedly democratic or Whig translation, which nevertheless merely refers to "the Cases in which Dwarfs are kept, [which] not only prevent the future growth of those who are inclosed in them, but diminish what Bulk they already have, by too close Constriction of their Parts" (104).

75. Smith also registers this tradition. In his notes to section 44, Smith cites the opinion of Zachary Pearce, bishop of Rochester, whose edition of *On The*

Section 44 might alone have been the reason for the recovery of Longinus for libertarian tradition, especially when, as Hall's preface makes clear, the huge intellectual activity generated by the English revolution threw into question what role language should play in the reconstruction of society. But the importance of this final section to Milton must have been enormously enhanced by the fact that, so long as *On the Sublime* was attributed to Cassius Longinus, it was read in the context of *that* Longinus' biography, itself an emblem of the cause of political liberty and the dangers of espousing it. As the story was reconstructed from Suidas, Longinus became the secretary to Zenobia, the widowed queen of Palmyra, who rebelled against Aurelian and declared her country's independence from the Roman Empire. In John Hall's words, "the glorious and unfortunate Zenobia gave him occasion of bravely dying for her in being her Secretary" (A4). Longinus was instructed to send Aurelian a message of defiance, which he duly did. (The famous letter is reproduced in the introduction to Langbaine's edition.) But when Aurelian successfully defeated the Persian army, Zenobia capitulated and blamed Longinus. In Smith's words, "the Letter which affronted Aurelian was not her own, Longinus wrote it, the Insolence was his" (xvii). Predictably, Longinus paid the price for his employer's temerity. But "he looked upon Death as a Blessing, since it rescued his Body from Slavery, and gave his Soul the most desirable Freedom" (xvii). While I would not wish to overstress the analogy, there was surely some pertinence in the Longinian myth to Milton's own situation in 1667, as an ex-Secretary of Foreign Tongues to the English Republic, "now fall'n on evil days . . . with dangers compast round."[76] It is not entirely a coincidence that when Rhys Roberts edited *On the Sublime* for Cambridge University Press in 1899 and expressed his feeling

---

Sublime was first published in 1732: "The word *dikaiea*, says he, does not signify mild or easy, as some think, but just and lawful Vassalage, when Kings and Rulers are possessed of a full Power and Authority over their Subjects: and we find Isocrates uses arche dikaia (a despotical Government) in this sense. The Doctor then gives his Opinion, that Longinus added this Word as well as some which follow, that his Affection to the Roman Emperor might not be suspected" (185).

76. *Paradise Lost* 7.25, 27.

that the Longinus of the sublime "might well have lived the life of that Longinus of the third century . . . who at Palmyra . . . inspired the defiant reply sent by the queen to the letter of the emperor Aurelian which demanded her submission," he justified his imaginative suture of the link that modern scholarship had severed by calling his author "a man of great moral endowments [who had] *fallen upon evil days*."[77]

It is therefore all the more perverse that, as Jonathan Lamb discovered, contemporary literary theory should have tried to tie up Longinus in a knot that resembles those of his own making, thereby defaming him. Although possibly Gibbon was the first to accuse Longinus of cowardice in hiding behind his anonymous philosopher,[78] the charge has been rendered infinitely more sophisticated by Paul de Man, who was apparently provoked into thinking about the sublime by Neil Hertz. Hertz had argued that Longinus had, throughout his selection of examples but especially in relation to Demosthenes, intimated rhetoric's constant relation to the master-slave dialectic.[79] Hertz brilliantly intuited that the treatise is all about risks and perils, about human challenges to the gods, symbolically represented by Euripides' account of the flight of Phaeton, one of a cluster of examples that leads directly to the topic of Chaeronea. "May one not say that the writer's soul has mounted the chariot," wrote Longinus, "has taken wing with the horses and shares the danger?"[80] This insight is clearly correct and has powerful filiations with my own argument. Langbaine's edition of Longinus appeared in 1636 with a frontispiece engraved by William Marshall, which shows Mercury as one image of sublime flight, side by side with Phaeton and his chariot tumbling out of the sky. And in Hertz's argument such risks and challenges are connected to the act of writing, the sublime turn, in which is simulated "a transfer of power . . . from the threatening forces to the poetic activity itself" (584).

---

77. W. Rhys Roberts, ed., *Longinus On the Sublime*, 2d ed. (Cambridge, 1907), 34–35, italics added.

78. Gibbon, *The Decline and Fall of the Roman Empire*, 3 vols. (New York, 1946), 1:24.

79. "A Reading of Longinus," *Critical Inquiry* 9 (1983): 579–96. The essay appeared previously in *Poétique* 15 (1973), and subsequently in Hertz, *The End of the Line* (New York, 1985).

80. Hertz, "A Reading," 586.

Yet Hertz also reads the accomplishments of Demosthenes as self-negating, "caught in the act of 'enslaving' [his] listeners by drawing attention away from the possible weaknesses [of his argument] with a striking image" (588). And while fascinated by the subtlety of Longinus' stance, Hertz never mentions the anonymous philosopher and the defense of democracy, nor suggests that these enigmatic procedures have anything to do with external constraints. Instead, the passage in which Longinus wrote directly of concealment (necessary when the powerless orator addresses the all-powerful ruler) is coaxed into, first, an oedipal drama, and second, into the deconstructive premise that Longinus' real subject is language's sublime capacity to intimate the inadequacy of language—"the figurativeness of every instance of the figurative" which, "when revealed, is always revealed as false" (594).

But even the first part of Hertz's argument was too much, it seems, for Paul de Man. Although his primary topic was Hegel on the sublime, and his subtext a defense of Deconstruction against the charge that it forgets or denies the politics of writing, de Man delivered in passing an attack on the notion that figures of symbolic risk and challenge, or Longinus' reading of them as such, or Hertz's reading of Longinus' reading, could constitute that crucial transfer of power from its holders to the challengers at any of those three levels. For de Man, the linguistic or aesthetic version of the master-slave dialectic (which for de Man here takes on a theological turn, being most fully instantiated in the struggle of human impotence with divine omnipotence) cannot be solved by the Longinian claim that a writer can ameliorate his servitude, take back mastery, by *quoting* the texts of older defiances. This, though oblique by modern standards of candor, would still be far too direct for de Man, whose abstruse philosophical reasoning in this essay boils down, I believe, to saying that only the utter "experience of defeat" in discussing a topic could render one's discourse "politically legitimate and effective as the undoer of usurped authority."[81]

But de Man's essay does focus, in passing, on one crucial aspect

---

81. De Man, "Hegel on the Sublime," in Mark Krupnick, ed., *Displacement: Derrida and After* (Bloomington, 1982), 151–53. The phrase "experience of defeat" is not de Man's but, of course, Christopher Hill's.

of the *Peri hypsous*, the one, in fact, which most strongly supports my argument that Milton was *thinking* of Longinus when he worked on the grand design of *Paradise Lost*. That crucial aspect—a single illustration of the sublime—is Longinus' citation of the divine Logos, the *fiat lux* itself, which for de Man functions as the verbal sign of divine absolutism. I believe that Milton's attention was caught, and his intention given shape, by discovering that two of the most important examples that Longinus himself gives of the sublime are the battles between the gods in Homer (*Iliad* 20.58–66) and (in the very next breath) the first words of God in the creation scene in Genesis. "See here (friend)," Longinus said (in section 9 and in Hall's translation),

> the earth shaken, broken, and clefted, nay even hell itself laid open, apprehending a turn and dissolution of the whole; nay altogether Heaven, Earth, Mortals, Immortals, equally endangered and concerned in this fight. But these are terrible, and unless allegorically understood, absolutely Atheisticall and indeed improper. . . .
> Thus the Law-giver of the Jews . . . after he had sufficiently declared the power of the Divinity, and acknowledged it, in the very beginning of the Book of his Laws said God spoke: What? Let there be light, and there was light. (16–17)

This extraordinary interpolation of a Hebrew scripture—indeed, of *the* original Word—into a Greek rhetorical treatise[82] could scarcely have failed to catch Milton's attention. It may even tell us something about the internal construction of *Paradise Lost*, where this same juxtaposition appears, though not, of course, with such abbreviation. In the two central books of his own epic, Milton first recounts in book 6 the battle in Heaven, and then in book 7 the creation of the world. "Let there be Light, said God, and forthwith Light . . . Sprung from the Deep" (7.243–45).

When in 1739 William Smith attempted to explain to his audience the sublimity of battles in heaven, he immediately discovered the appropriate passage in *Paradise Lost* to match Longinus'

---

82. This became an issue in later criticism. As William Smith remarked in his notes to this passage, "Some pretend that Longinus never saw this Passage, tho' he has actually quoted it; and that he never read Moses, tho' he has left so candid an Acknowledgment of his Merit" (128).

definition. Stating that "Milton's Description of the Fight of Angels is well able to stand a Parallel with the Combat of the Gods in Homer," he cited book 6, lines 207–19:

> Now storming fury rose,
> And clamor such as heard in Heav'n till now
> Was never, Arms on Armor clashing bray'd
> Horrible discord, and the madding Wheels
> Of brazen Chariots rag'd; dire was the noise
> Of conflict; . . .
> . . .
> So under fiery Cope together rush'd
> Both Battles main, with ruinous assault
> And inextinguishable rage; all Heav'n
> Resounded, and had Earth been then, all Earth
> Had to her Centre shook.

But he also pointed out that in Milton's version there is an epistemological twist based on a different chronology—a "last Thought, which is superlatively great"—that this phase of Milton's poem *precedes* the creation of the world and so antedates both Homer and Longinus. "He seems apprehensive that the Mind of his Readers was not stocked enough with Ideas to enable them to form a Notion of this Battle, and to raise it the more, recalls to their Remembrance the Time, or that Part of infinite Duration in which it was fought, before Time was" (125–26).

With equal perspicacity, Smith supplied the Miltonic equivalent for Longinus' next example of sublimity. Homer's account of Neptune's triumphal chariot ride (*Iliad* 13.17–31) is to be matched by Milton's description of the repairs performed by the Son on the damaged structure of heaven:

> He on the wings of Cherub rode *sublime*
> On the Crystalline Sky, in Sapphire Thron'd.
> Illustrious far and wide . . .
> . . .
> Before him pow'r divine his way prepar'd;
> At his command the uprooted Hills retir'd
> Each to his place, they heard his voice and went
> Obsequious; Heav'n his wonted face renewed
> And with fresh flowrets hill and valley smil'd.
>   (6.771–3,780–84)

The effect is to show that sublimity distributes itself equally "betwixt the world destroy'd and the world restor'd";[83] a distribution of particular relevance, perhaps, to a poem directed to a Restoration audience.

Yet Smith, as I have said, like Addison and Dennis, never raises the possibility that Milton was deliberately reproducing a Longinian effect, and as deliberately outdoing his authority. For him, the quotations from Milton are merely illustrative of what Longinus intended, to be set alongside other examples from the Bible or Shakespeare. In contrast, the Latin poem by S. B. that, alongside Marvell's *On Paradise Lost*, preceded the epic in 1674 assumes that violence in heaven is a major part of Milton's meaning, and indeed devotes twenty-two of its forty-two lines to showing what the war contributes to the sublime effect, or what he calls "grandia magni / Carmina Miltoni."[84] Since S. B. is a lesser poet than either Milton or Marvell, I will omit citation; but it is perhaps important to note that, as Smith's commentary on Longinus foregrounds the relation between sublime destruction and reconstruction, so S. B.'s story of the war continues through the moment where the Son is sent out in his chariot to end the strife and casts the defeated rebel angels into infernal darkness.

S. B. (M. D.) was identified by John Toland in his biography of Milton as Samuel Barlow, who served as medical physician to General Monck's army in Scotland and played, according to Christopher Hill, "a significant part in bringing about the Restoration."[85] His military experience may have had something to do with his interpretive emphases on the wars in Milton's Heaven. If we remember the Longinian caveat that "these bold Representations, if not allegorically understood, are downright Blasphemy,"[86] the possibility of translating the civil wars in heaven into the local space and time of England in the 1640s becomes once again inviting, despite the interpretive problems

83. *Paradise Lost* 12.3.
84. Compare Michael Lieb, "S. B.'s '*In Paradisum Amissam*': Sublime Commentary," *Milton Quarterly* 19 (1985): 71–79. I am indebted to Michael Lieb for drawing my attention to S. B., and for the biographical facts summarized below.
85. *Milton and the English Revolution*, 217.
86. Smith, *On the Sublime*, 21.

that result from that invitation. Since Barlow became physician in ordinary to Charles II, his advertisement for the poem can scarcely have been intended as subversive of the Restoration censorship, let alone of its government; but perhaps, like Dryden, he intuited a good deal of the poem's elusive representational structure and admired it nevertheless. Perhaps his intention was indeed to claim it as a "bold Representation" of the English civil wars, but one that was imaginatively completed by the Restoration of the monarchy.

One need not conclude, however, that Milton, like Barlow, welcomed the Restoration as a reconstructive miracle. If allegorizations of his poem were in circulation, as seems to have been the case, it may have suited Milton's purposes to have some, at least, of his readers believe that the son of Charles I was configured in the Son. Nor, if we can accept that the Longinian sublime was his model, need we take only at face value the pious disclaimer that Milton built into the last book of his poem, whereby it has been possible to argue that he had discarded the defense of external liberty in favor of internal regeneration. Knowing that Longinus was though to have protected himself by substituting moral degeneration for political repression as the cause of oratory's decay, we can see *the exact equivalent of this strategy* in Milton's framing of the Nimrodian moment:

> Reason in man obscur'd, or not obey'd,
> Immediately inordinate desires
> And upstart Passions catch the Government
> From Reason, and to servitude reduce
> Man till then free. Therefore since hee permits
> Within himself unworthy Powers to reign
> Over free Reason, God in Judgment just
> Subjects him from without to violent Lords;
> Who oft as undeservedly enthral
> His outward freedom: Tyranny must be
> Though to the Tyrant thereby no excuse.
>
> (12.86–96)

Indeed, if we infer that one aspect of the Longinian sublime as Milton would have understood it was its mystery, we can see that the sublimity of *Paradise Lost*, too, its persistence as a daunting object of investigation, lies in its resistance to easy ideological unraveling. One of the interpretive anxieties Marvell's poem voiced was that Milton would have, for some readers, "perplex'd the things he would explain." It is in his focus on "perhaps" as the key to the code, then, that Christopher Hill is most helpful, rather than in his own struggles between the poetics of defeat and those of defiance. And one might add that in offering his readers a *choice* of interpretations, arising out of a welter of conflicting textual directions, Milton created the readerly equivalent of Arminianism, hermeneutical free will. Given free will in interpretation, an educated commonality could theoretically find themselves not surprised by sin (that is to say, constantly corrected for their readerly mistakes),[87] but, conversely, increasingly confident in self-determination; a training that should, in the long run, predispose them to Whiggish principles.[88]

The Voice from the Watchtower

The Good Old Cause is the theme of Edmund Ludlow's massive memoirs, written in exile in Geneva after the Restoration and published in an edited version at the very end of the century by John Toland, whose service in the construction of the republican canon has already been mentioned. As for Ludlow, Neil Keeble has summarized the role that he played in the Res-

---

87. I allude, of course, to the reading strategy of Stanley Fish, in *Surprised by Sin: The Reader in* Paradise Lost (Berkeley and Los Angeles, 1971).

88. As an analogy to this argument, compare Suzanne Woods, "Elective Poetics and Milton's Prose: *A Treatise of Civil Power and Considerations Touching the Likeliest Means to Remove Hirelings Out of the Church*," in *Politics, Poetics and Hermeneutics in Milton's Prose*, ed. David Loewenstein and James Grantham Turner (Cambridge, 1990), 193–211; and compare also Carrol B. Cox, "Citizen Angels: Civil Society and the Abstract Individual in *Paradise Lost*," *Milton Studies* 23 (1987): 165–96. Although Cox constructs an orthodox Marxist argument which "does not depend on the validity of . . . attempts to construe the poem's intentional historical references," (195 n. 39) and believes that Milton "may or may not have distinguished sharply between feudal dominion and corrupt republican tyranny" (177), nevertheless for the *modern* reader the poem can, by its very indeterminacy, function as an exercise in judgment. "The action never carries its own meaning. If the narrator has invoked the right principle, and if the reader in turn accepts that principle as the correct basis for judgement . . . then a social relationship of writer and reader—a miniature bourgeois civil society—will have been created where none existed before" (184–85). Setting aside the methodological self-contradictions generated by the word "right," this essay is interesting as yet another testimony to contemporary dissatisfaction with the either/or approach to Milton's Restoration politics.

toration imagination from August 1660, when, after a famous dream that he feared prognosticated his violent death, he escaped from the authorities to whom he had previously surrendered and fled to the Continent. Rumors of his supposed return to lead an uprising continued unabated through 1666. "Not until 1667," Keeble continued, "does his name fade from the state papers and the fevered imaginations of the government and its spies." But what he had actually done was to settle quietly in Geneva, and he refused complicity in all plots against the Restoration government, including those of Algernon Sidney. "He was," Keeble concluded, "engaged not in the seditious promotion of the Good Old Cause but in its literary commemoration and vindication: he was writing his *Memoirs*."[89]

I am not so sure, however, that we ought to draw the distinction so sharply, even though the main purpose of Keeble's study of Nonconformist writings is to argue for a more nuanced version of the experience of defeat by promoting the role of literature in Nonconformist culture:

> nonconformists had need of a voice which would carry far if they were to be heard from the exile—in prison, the provinces, or abroad—to which the Clarendon Code banished them. In their various kinds of seclusion, they could in writing come to terms with the events which had, apparently so finally, overthrown them; and through publication they could declare their continuing, and renewed, commitment despite those events, their willing submission to God's Providence. This commitment could use the printed book to refute the government's presentation of them as seditious rebels and episcopalian caricatures of them as hypocritical dissemblers. And, above all, by the printed word nonconformists could overcome the isolation and separation caused by the Clarendon Code and prevent the disintegration it intended. (83–84)

It may seem carping to disagree with this intelligent formulation; but disagree one must if one recognizes the binary structure of the Good Old Cause, as simultaneously committed to religious toleration and civil liberty. Keeble's account, with its focus on the Nonconformists, emphasizes the former at the expense of the latter, and is therefore more sensitive to Milton's definition of the "paradise within thee, happier far," with its move

89. *The Literary Culture of Nonconformity in Later Seventeenth-Century England* (Athens, Ga., 1987), 71–72.

to the interior, than to his defiance of Filmer and the well-placed attack on Nimrod. For Edmund Ludlow, as for Vane and Milton, the Cause had always had a binary structure, both political and religious. He looked back in his memoirs to "the worke the Lord had upon the wheele in that our day; which to me seemed to be the establishing of such a righteous frame of government under which men may enjoy their civill liberty, and not be imposed upon by the lust of any person or party, and the word of the Lord may be freely published, and the Saints and churches live in the exercise of its ordinances without interruption."[90] Ludlow observed with pleasure the signs, including material ones, that the Restoration government was less secure than it seemed: "that which gave a demonstration of the affection to the *good old cause* was the sympathy that was expressed by an assembly of people . . . in their contributing, towards the supply of the necessityes of those who lay condemned in the Tower for having judged the late King to death, the summe of an hundred and fower score pounds, as they passed out in the publique meeting place; the report of which gave a great allarum to the Court" (285; italics added).

Toward the end of that section of the memoirs that Blair Worden has edited, an address to the reader appears to be counselling patience; but not for long. Both the rhetorical strategy of this argument and the argument itself lead the reader into submission only strategically, in order to prepare him for greater acts of resistance in the future:

> As well therefore from the consideration of prudence, as of duty and conscience (which tells us that we ought to obey the higher powers, and content ourselves with our share in government relating to the outward man, submitting to, or at least not opposing, those in whom the Lord by his providence declares the power to be, who though it may be are not so righteous and just as were

90. Ludlow, *A Voyce from the Watch Tower: Part Five: 1660–1662*, ed. A. B. Worden, Camden Society, 4th ser., vol. 21 (London, 1978), 308. Worden both established Toland's responsibility for the seventeenth-century edition of the *Voyce*, and, by comparing it with the Bodleian manuscript (Eng. hist. c. 487), which, though 400,000 words long, represents only about a third of the total, was able to demonstrate the editorial manner in which Toland worked, compressing, clarifying, but also supressing, as Worden puts it, "the spiritual dimension of the manuscript," in order to reconstruct Toland as a Country Whig (39–55).

to be wisshed, yet by praying for them we may lead quiet and peacable lives, in all godlynesse and honesty, and blessing the Lord for the libertyes and priviledges they permit us to enjoy . . .). Though no one party whilest uppermost would owne so as to practice, the God of this world blynding their eyes, yet now being under a persecuting and AntiChristian power, . . . all may see it their wisedome and interest to submit unto, that they might put it in practice when they have an opportunity so to doe; which who can tell how soone the Lord would give, were we fitted with a spirit for the promoting a forme of government for the uphold-ing of which the interest of all men and Christians would con-center? This would be an happy effect of the hand of the Lord that hath bin upon us, and would soone put us in possession of what is most desirable; it being their great designe of our adversaryes to keep up their *Nimrodian power* by dividing the languages of the people of God. . . . The Lord therefore unite us in his feare, that by suffering we may be fitted for the doing of his will, and give us wisedome to know when to goe forward and when to stand still, that by making hast we may not strengthen the hand of the enemy, nor by standing still neglect the opportunity he puts into our hands, but that, being on our Watch Tower, and living by faith, we may see our duty so plainly, that when the Lord's tyme is come we may up and be doing, and the Lord may appeare to be with us and to owne us. (310)

The voice from the Watchtower here reveals its more than spiri-tual message, to thwart the "Nimrodian power" and to consol-idate the resistance of those both in exile and biding their time at home, by reuniting the languages of the people of God so that they shall understand each other properly. In this context, to be writing was, in effect, to be "up and doing." And the peculiar kind of watchfulness that Ludlow here recommends, knowing "when to goe forward and when to stand still, that by making hast we may not strengthen the hand of the enemy, nor by stand-ing still neglect the opportunity [God] puts into our hands," may also be recognized in the stance of Milton's heroic avenger in *Sam-son Agonistes*, his own version of Seneca's Hercules, and of whose reappearance as the author of *Paradise Lost* Marvell had notified the world. As for *Paradise Regained*, that is another story.

8

Sleeping with the Enemy

Milton Uncouples Himself

This three-part chapter constellates under a title taken from a contemporary popular novel, felicitous for grouping together three of my own responses to the coming-of-age of feminist criticism. In the third of these, Nancy Price's *Sleeping with the Enemy* will appear in its own right, and bring to our attention a very peculiar conjunction between reading between the lines and the social problem of wife beating. Each of my essays, however, deals in its own (I trust) eccentric way with the problem of male-female hostilities, and the extent to which these are acted out in different kinds of writing, sometimes but not always in the interests of truce or pacification. Here I consider John Milton's pamphlets arguing for the introduction of legal divorce in England, concentrating on the first of his series, *The Doctrine and Discipline of Divorce*, in which the terrible idea of sleeping with the enemy is given all-too-concrete representation; since Milton's own young wife, from whom he wished to be legally separated, belonged to a family on the opposite side of the English civil war.

Milton's divorce pamphlets operate as a hinge between the topic of political liberty and that of gender conflict, not only because he himself saw these topics as connected (an unhappy marriage was the domestic equivalent of the Norman yoke), but because they also sharpened his sense of the crucial importance of liberty of speech and publication. His inability to acquire a license to publish the *Doctrine* is registered in another of the divorce pamphlets, *The Judgement of Martin Bucer*; and attempts by the Presbyterian clergy and the Stationers' Company to have his tracts suppressed led directly to his examination before a committee of the House of Lords, and hence (though he does not admit this) to his writing the *Areopagitica*, which remains, for all subsequent qualifications, our preeminent statement of the ideal of a free press and the free circulation of ideas, subject only to the critical judgment of the reading public at large.[1]

The story I shall tell here, however, is not about official censorship, but about a curious and, at moments, touching form of self-censorship; and though I shall use a method of reading between the lines, I shall in so doing be working against Milton's deliberate intentions. With the return of a critical climate in which (given certain formulaic caveats about the social construction of the self) recourse to biography is once again respectable, one may reinspect the motives that led Milton to turn private domestic embarrassment into public polemic. We need not take exactly at face value his claims to objectivity, either within the pamphlets or later in the autobiographical section of the *Second Defence*, where he argued that his interest in divorce was solely as a branch of an overarching Liberty Tree. In this atmosphere of creative suspicion, the focus of inquiry becomes less the arguments for divorce themselves and the dubious logic by which Milton made the biblical texts on marriage serve his purpose, and more the structure of Milton's personality, and its unwitting representation in an all-too-revealing structure of words and metaphors.

By-ends

In June 1643, Milton, a recently abandoned husband, published the first edition of his first pamphlet on divorce, and about six months later the second edition, "revis'd and much expanded." Both title pages declare that the institution of marriage in England at the time demands revision for "the good of both sexes," a claim easily refuted by today's readers of both sexes, who quickly discover the passages of masculinist bias that, no matter what happened later in *Paradise Lost*, cannot be explained away.

But because the explicit bias of the work is only half the story, we can locate the *Doctrine and Discipline of Divorce* at the point

1. See Milton, *Complete Prose Works*, ed. D. M. Wolfe et al., 8 vols. (New Haven, 1953–82), 2:138–45.

of intersection between psychobiography and genre theory. This pamphlet hovers on an undrawn boundary between polemic and narrative, a boundary whose uncertainty Milton himself discerned and attempted to stabilize by declaring, in a crucial passage to which we shall return, that this was "no meer amatorious novel" (2:256). In fact, this statement was made in reference not to the pamphlet as a whole but to the myth of Eros and Anteros that Milton inserted into it as an image of the reciprocal love and need that was central to his redefinition of marriage. Yet in making the defensive comment, Milton showed self-consciousness about the presence of fictional narrative *within* his pamphlet, and used a term (*novel*) whose past and future were both problematic in the emergent poetics of narrative fiction.

As a derivative of the Italian *novella*, the term referred back to the brief erotic tales of the late Middle Ages, as in Burton's 1621 allusion to "Boccaces Novels",[2] and as Milton apparently employed it when, in the *History of Britain*, he related "another story . . . of Edgar, fitter for a Novel then a History" (5[1]:327), a tale of mistaken (though fortuitous) bedding and concubinage. Yet in its own denotation of the new, or novelty, *novel* also had affiliations with the French *nouvelles*, literally news, or scandalous journalism, which by 1663 was so well established as a genre that it produced its own satire, the *Nouvelles nouvelles* of Donneau de Vize.[3] While Milton's own primary term for fiction was *romance* (and this too, as I have argued elsewhere, was an increasingly disturbing category for him),[4] the prophetic ability of *novel* to displace *romance* as term preceded its paradigmatic victory. *Clidamas or: the Sicilian Tale* (1639) was a Heliodoran romance whose semi-anonymous author (J. S.) offered it to the reader as a "little Novel . . . which though in it selfe be nothing yet . . . may prove something" (A2r). And, as Michael McKeon observes in his magisterial *Origins of the English Novel*, "by the time 'the

2. Robert Burton, *Anatomy of Melancholy* 4.2.2.

3. See Erica Harth, *Ideology and Culture in Seventeenth-Century France* (Ithaca, 1983), 174–75.

4. See "*Paradise Regained:* A Last Chance at True Romance," in *Composite Orders: The Genres of Milton's Last Poems,* ed. Richard Ide and Joseph Wittreich, *Milton Studies* 17 (1983), 187–208. See also Barbara Lewalski, "Milton: Revaluations of Romance," in *Four Essays on Romance,* ed. Herschel Baker (Cambridge, Mass., 1971), 57–70.

novel' was beginning to be accepted as the canonic term for prose fiction in the modern age, the epistemological transformation that is vital to its constitution as a genre had already proceeded very far."[5] No one was more alert than Milton to the epistemological dilemmas inherent in storytelling; and, as we shall see, the narrative impulse would drive him up against the frontiers, such as they were, that divided the romantic past from the novel (and novelistic) future.

For the myth of Eros and Anteros is only one of the interpolated narratives that Milton inserted into the *Doctrine and Discipline of Divorce*, and about the others he was apparently less self-conscious. These include a miniseries of allegories with sexual plots ending with the Eros/Anteros myth but beginning with the liaison, added to the second edition of the pamphlet, between Custom, who is female, and Error, who is male; and a disguised autobiographical account of Milton's own courtship and the early days of his marriage, told prophetically in the style of the domestic fiction that would shortly replace the fashionable, pseudo-historical romances imported from the Continent.

These two types of narrative are distinguished both from each other and from the polemical frame by an oblique relationship to truth or the real. The allegories operate by forcing into painful visibility allegory's structural paradox, that it tries to give language incarnational force, to provide imaginary bodies for disembodied abstractions. By their shared sexual emplotment, Milton's allegories in the *Doctrine* reveal the perversity of this enterprise in general, and particularly the unspeakable agenda which required him to resort to allegory when legal or theological vocabularies failed him. In the first two in the series of three, also, the distortions that Milton introduces into familiar symbolic plots anticipate the grotesque family romance between Satan, Sin, and Death in *Paradise Lost*, itself often noted as a problematic shift of generic gears.

The concealed autobiographical novel, by contrast, registers its presence with a naive realism that predicts Defoe or even Richardson in its mundane vocabulary and social setting, but differs from early novelistic technique primarily in reversing the fictional use of personal pronouns. That is to say, where Defoe

5. *The Origins of the English Novel 1600–1740* (Baltimore, 1987), 27.

creates utterly convincing first-person narrators who appear to relate their biographies, Milton conceals his own by the use of the third person. This stratagem is, however, often subverted by the emotional investment that the prose itself candidly registers. And there may be a third story told only, as it were, in occasional slips of the lexicon, a lapsarian tale of Milton's delayed and painful sexual coming of age, visible momentarily in metaphors and euphemisms for sexual process and parts of the body, a form simultaneously of linguistic precision and avoidance.

If so, all three types of narrative are, finally, different versions of the same story, the tale of what Milton called his "owne by-ends." The phrase occurs in the supplementary address to the Long Parliament that Milton added when he also added his name to the pamphlet, and it stands as one of those disclaimers that proclaim the presence of that which is stated to be absent. "Who among ye," Milton wrote to the Parliamentarians, " . . . hath not been often traduc't to be the agent of his owne by-ends, under pretext of Reformation" (2:225). A few sentences later, that "traduc'd," or falsely accused, is *almost* replaced by the notion that there may be something in the accusation, something that can be turned to everyone's advantage:

> Yet when points of difficulty are to be discusst, appertaining to the removall of unreasonable wrong and burden from the perplext life of our brother, it is incredible how cold, how dull, and farre from all fellow feeling we are, without the spurre of self-concernment. (2:226)

This statement certainly encourages us to read Milton in a way that defies the depersonalizing and anti-anthropological premises of postmodernism, denying us for nearly two decades the commonsense categories of author, oeuvre, and intention; yet without such categories we cannot even begin to see how interesting is the *Doctrine and Discipline of Divorce*. It is *most* interesting precisely in the relation between intended and unintended meaning, in the textual presence of those "by-ends" that Milton knew he would be accused (if not traduced) of having allowed into the deep structure of his text.

The Eloquent "He Who"

I start with the suspected presence in the *Doctrine* of the domestic, autobiographical "amatorious novel," as the most conceptually demanding, if not the most shocking, of Milton's narrative modes; and with two recent proposals about the novel's origins in autobiography, specifically the spiritual autobiography associated with English religious radicalism. Each of these proposals abuts on Milton, the first more directly than the second, but the second more richly. In Leopold Damrosch's *God's Plot and Man's Stories*, the claim is made that one of the cultural formations that led to the emergence of the English novel as a distinct genre was the "radical analysis of the self" that minority Protestantism necessitated and for which autobiography was the natural expression.[6] Damrosch's chapter on Milton, however, deals only with *Paradise Lost*, without recourse to the explicit and implicit autobiography that readers of Milton have for years recognized as embedded in the work of the left hand; and it is less concerned with the domestic psychodrama within the poem than with the theological struggles to which it bears witness. For Damrosch, the novelistic moment (which Bakhtin found recurring in many cultures and centuries apart) occurs only at the Fall, when Adam and Eve become the complex characters that the novel demands. Paradoxically, they thereby *lose* the freedom of choice in action that Angus Fletcher regards as the dividing line between the novel's characters and the bound agents of allegorical narrative.[7] They are thereby distinguished from the narrator of *Paradise Lost*, who has supposedly regained that freedom by his superior vision and alignment with providential pattern.

In Michael McKeon's *Origins of the English Novel* there is a similar claim that fiction, as it evolves in this period, demonstrates the tension between "individual life and overarching pattern" (91). But McKeon offers a more complex genetic model for the novel, in which spiritual biography is only one of its progenitors, and he locates the matrix of narrative instability from which the novel emerged as an epistemological problem rather than a theological one. Too subtle to argue that the novel replaces the romance by making a stronger claim to believability, McKeon posits a continuous dialectic between romance and what he calls "naive empiricism," each of which conducts a philosophical

6. *God's Plot and Man's Stories: Studies in the Fictional Imagination from Milton to Fielding* (Chicago and London, 1985), 21.
7. *Allegory: The Theory of a Symbolic Mode* (Ithaca, 1964), 66.

critique of the other. These terms can certainly illuminate Milton's lifelong struggle to evaluate fictionality under the category "romance." But more precisely to the point here is McKeon's account of how spiritual autobiography itself stages a dialectic between different versions and historical phases of the self or writing subject. In this type of narrative, the basic dynamic between individual life and overarching pattern (which Christianity calls Providence) is reenacted, he argues, by the interplay of Character and Narrator, the first by historical, chronological standards necessarily unrepentant, the second possessed of the powers of atonement that will eventually register the autobiography as generically spiritual:

> As the plot unfolds horizontally, the dangerous gap between Character and Narrator gradually diminishes through vertical narrative intrusions, until the two finally are one, the latter consciousness having subsumed the former in what might be seen as the narrative equivalent of atonement. (95)

McKeon compares this narrative principle to Milton's famous description in *Areopagitica* of the process of learning by one's mistakes, or of "knowing good by evil . . . the scanning of error to the confirmation of truth." For McKeon, however, Milton functions only as a theorist of this "scanning of error," not as a writer himself of spiritual or secular autobiography. The insights so brilliantly encapsulated here are worked out not in relation to Milton's poetry or his prose, but in relation to Defoe's *Robinson Crusoe*, whose connection to spiritual autobiography is clear and direct.

I propose that the *Doctrine and Discipline of Divorce* also introduces the "scanning of error" as a narrative principle, in a story in which Character and Narrator have at least as complex a relation. The theme of error in the *Doctrine* was, of course, foregrounded on both title pages. Its symbolic form appears in the allegory of Custom and Error added to the second edition. Its realistic content, or what McKeon would call its grounding in naive empiricism, is found later, in book 1, chapter 3, where Milton seeks to refute the argument that divorce would be unnecessary if people carefully considered the "disposition" of their intended mates beforehand. "But let them know again," Milton responded to this unheard objection, that for all the warinesse can be us'd, it may yet befall a discreet man to be mistak'n in his choice: *and we have plenty of examples*. the soberest and best govern'd men are lest practiz'd in these affairs; and who knows not that the bashfull mutenes of a virgin may oft-times hide all the unlivelines & naturall sloth which is really unfit for conversation; nor is there that freedom of accesse granted or presum'd, as may suffice to a perfect discerning till too late: and where any indisposition is suspected, what more usuall then the perswasion of friends, that acquaintance, as it encreases, will amend all: And lastly, it is not strange though many who have spent their youth chastely, are in some things not so quick-sighted, while they hast too eagerly to light the nuptiall torch; nor is it therfore that *for a modest error* a man should forfeit so great happiness, and no charitable means to release him. Since they who have liv'd most loosely by reason of their bold accustoming, prove most succesfull in their matches, because their wild affec-tions unsetling at will, have been as so many divorces to teach them experience. When as the sober man honouring the appear-ance of modestie, and hoping well of every sociall vertue under that veile, may easily chance to meet, if not with a body impene-trable, yet often with a minde to all the more estimable and superior purposes of matrimony uselesse and almost liveles. (2:249–50; italics added)

Here Milton, rejecting Fielding's thesis in *Tom Jones* that allow-ing a young man to sow his wild oats will unite him at last with his true Sophia, introduces a century earlier a far less allegori-cal story than Fielding's, a story in which the style of naive real-ism is supposedly explained by the phrase added in 1644 (*"and we have plenty of examples"*)—that is to say, social analysis as the basis for generalization. But the sociological force of "plenty," along with "oft-times," "usuall," "many," "often," is undermined by the corrective nature of the argument, which requires the "sober man" to be perceived as the exception to the carnal rule of the double standard. And where is this sober man to be found, the reader may well ask? The answer, along with a corrobora-tive style and certain exact matches of detail, exists in Milton's early biographies.

The extreme specificity of the contrast between a chaste youth and a sudden haste to light the nuptial torch correlates all too precisely with the story of Milton's sudden marriage in the sum-mer of 1642. "After Whitsuntide it was, or a little after, that he took a journey into the country; nobody about him certainly knowing the reason, or that it was any more than a journey of recreation; after a month's stay, home he returns a married man, that went out a bachelor." So wrote Milton's nephew Edward Phillips, who also recorded the temperamental mismatch between the "philosophical life" of the husband, and the young wife who had "been used to a great house, and much company and joviality."[8] These are, of course, the alternatives Milton had explored for himself in *L'Allegro* and *Il Penseroso*, now given a still more realistic and social form.

Let us pause for a moment on the question of social form. Another aspect of coincidence between Milton's supposedly impersonal narrative of failed courtship and Phillips' admittedly personalized one is the role that friends play in the marital negotiations. Milton described how "the perswasion of friends" worked on the sober young man of small experience to believe that a suspected "indisposition" would disappear on better "acquaintance." The phrase reappears in book 1, chapter 12, where he describes those who do not have the "calling" for marriage, "but by the perswasion of friends, or not knowing themselves do often enter into wedlock" (2:274). Edward Phillips mentions no persuasion in the making of the original match; but his account is remarkable for its emphasis on "the strong intercession of friends of both sides" in effecting the reconciliation. Both texts, therefore, read as a gloss on each other, speak to the specifically social, economic, and sociopolitical interests that produced a marriage in 1642 between a royalist and a republican family, since the poor financial circumstances of the Powells (including an uncollectible debt to John Milton, Sr.) and the changing fortunes of the king's party in the war (which worsened in 1645, suggesting the wisdom of recovering a republican protector) were undoubtedly stronger motives on at least one side of the bargain than the emotional argument Milton, in the *Doctrine*, was attempting to make supreme. It need hardly be said that these were the conditions in which social historians of marriage have become increasingly interested, and which have long been posited as the base of the eighteenth-century domestic

8. See John Milton, *Complete Poems and Major Prose*, ed. M. Y. Hughes (New York, 1957), 1031.

novel. It is almost too good to be true that another of Milton's biographers, perhaps John Phillips, perhaps Cyriack Skinner, refers to the campaign for divorce as "the mending of a decay in the superstructure,"[9] a term that perfectly mandates, if mandate were necessary, our reading of these stories in terms of their socio-economic and political coordinates.

But to return to the contest between L'Allegro and Il Penseroso in Milton's story, the *Doctrine and Discipline of Divorce*, itself a severely entitled work, operates solely under the sign of the latter. The would-be divorcé, invariably referred to as male, is not only sober but melancholy to a fault, even to aberrancy. Having mischosen his mate, Milton remarked earlier (book 1, chapter 3), he is far worse off than the single man, for "here the continuall sight of his deluded thoughts without cure, must needs be to him, if especially his complexion incline him to melancholy, a daily trouble and paine of losse in some degree like that which Reprobates feel" (2:247). And in the same passage Milton emphasizes his individuality by arguing that he shall "doe more manly, to be extraordinary and singular in claiming the due right whereof he is frustrated, then to piece up his lost contentment by visiting the Stews, or stepping to his neighbours bed, which is the common shift in this misfortune" (2:247).

One might be tempted to assume, given the actual biography, that the mischosen mate would be represented as a young and hence permissibly joyous Allegra. Not so. Instead, the question of female Character is ambiguated by two alternative hypotheses of feminine unacceptability. One appears in the narrative of unwise courtship, when the "bashfull mutenes of a virgin" conceals the "unlivelines & naturall sloth which is really unfit for conversation" (2:249). The other appears much later in the pamphlet (and in its chronological development), when Milton is confronting the argument made by Beza and Paraeus, that the Mosaic dispensation for divorce was awarded for the protection of wives against the cruelty of husbands. "Palpably uxurious!" exclaims Milton at this point (book 2, chapter 15), in one of the most dramatic utterances of the entire work:

> Who can be ignorant that woman was created for man, and not man for woman; and that a husband may be injur'd as insuffer-

---

9. *Complete Poems and Major Prose*, 1040.

ably in mariage as a wife. What an injury is it after wedlock not to be belov'd, what to be slighted, what to be contended with in point of house-rule who shall be the head, not for any parity of wisdome, for that were something reasonable, but out of female pride. (2:324)

He then inserts a scriptural anecdote from the book of Esther (1.10–22), of "the cours which the Medes and Persians took by occasion of Vashti, whose meer denial to come at her husbands sending lost her the being Queen any longer." It is surely no coincidence that the language of the "divine relater," as Milton here refers to the holy Word, matches that of Edward Phillips, who related how "Michaelmas being come, and no news of his wife's return," Milton "sent for her by letter; and receiving no answer, sent several other letters, which were also unanswered; so that at last he dispatched down a foot messenger with a letter, desiring her return. But the messenger came back not only without an answer . . . but . . . reported that he was dismissed with some sort of contempt . . . [which] so incensed our author that he thought it would be dishonorable ever to receive her again."[10] The hidden autobiography, in other words, here carries the story of Milton's marriage from the hasty courtship through early days of contention "in point of house-rule" and eventually to the repulse that defined the wife as not passively resistant but actively rebellious against her lord and master.

Here, then, both the spoken and the unspoken biography suggest that Milton did not know precisely what he wanted in a wife, docility or liveliness, an ambiguity that his own text records with less candor than that of his nephew, who reported that Milton "found his chief diversion" while his wife was away and *before* her "deniall to come at her husbands sending" in visiting Lady Margaret Lee, "a woman of great wit and ingenuity." Indeed, whether or not he realized the implications of the admission, Edward Phillips remarks of this phase of the marriage that Milton was "now as it were a single man again"! Since the characterization of the female as insubordinate was added to the 1644 edition, as was the biblical anecdote of Vashti's refusal, we might speculate that the intense anger that Phillips reported was still seeking outlet even as Milton was doing his utmost to place his

10. *Complete Poems and Major Prose*, 1031.

arguments in the respectable and impersonal framework of the thought of the continental reformers.[11]

But there is a more intimate part of the story still, which will take us from Character, male and female, back to the Narrator. In McKeon's account of the spiritual autobiography and its successors in the novel, it is the Narrator who supposedly controls the realist or empirical "scanning of error" on the horizontal axis of narrative by exerting the vertical pressure of atonement. One could reformulate this in Milton's own words as the tension between one's own "by-ends" and a genuine, impersonal zeal for "Reformation," a tension which, it should by now be clear, is far from resolved in the *Doctrine and Discipline of Divorce*. This tension is most clearly recorded in the terrain of syntax, which is also the terrain in which Character and Narrator meet at the closest quarters. In the Narrator's attack on feminine insubordination, the exclamation "What an injury is it after wedlock not to be belov'd" seems asymmetrical as to its verb. It should properly read "What an injury is it after wedlock not to be *obeyed*." We may understand it, however, as an uncontrollable echo of Milton's scandalous paradox, that the would-be divorcer is actually the best upholder of marriage: "for to retain still," he wrote, "and not to be able to love, is to heap up more injury. . . . He therfore who lacking of his due in the most native and humane end of mariage, thinks it better to part then to live sadly and injuriously to that cherfull covnant (for not to be belov'd & yet retain'd, is the greatest injury to a gentle spirit) he I say who therfore seeks to part, is one who highly honours the maried life, and would not stain it" (2:253). How could Milton have committed that powerful Freudian slippage from the high-minded "to retain still and not to be able to love" to the elegiac (and soon to be echoed) "not to *be* belov'd & yet retain'd"? Who, this syntax asks, is doing the divorcing, and at what moment does it occur? At the failure of

11. See also book 2, chapter 18, where Milton redefines fornication as a series of obstinacies derived from Theodosius, which included the "lying forth of her hous without probable cause" (2:334), and illustrated it by Judges 19.2, where "the Levites wife is said to have played the whoor against him; which Josephus and the Septuagint . . . interpret only of stubbornnes and rebellion against her husband" (2:335). "And this I shall contribute," added Milton, "that had it ben whoordom she would have chosen any other place to run to, *then to her fathers house*" (italics added).

love, or at the formal separation? Who injures whom? Does the chiasmus indicate a moment of gender parity in Milton's thinking, or rather the hideous recognition that when he thought he was in control (retaining, but unable to love) he was in fact himself to be retained, but not to be beloved.

In a much later passage (book 2, chapter 20), Milton reassumed command over this situation, reworking the paradox about injury so as to apply only to the woman:

> The law can only appoint the just and equall conditions of divorce, and is to look how it is an injury to the divorc't, which in truth it can be none, as a meer separation; for if she consent, wherin has the law to right her? or consent not, then is it either just and so deserved, or if unjust, such in all likelihood was the divorcer, and to part from an unjust man is a happines, & no injury to be lamented. But suppose it be an injury, the Law is not able to amend it, unlesse she think it other then a miserable redress to return back from whence she was expell'd, or but entreated to be gon. (2:349–50)

So "not to be retained" has become, simply, "expell'd," and the story of the wife who refused to return has been exorcised in another, occluded finale, the miserable opportunity imposed by law to "return back from whence she was expell'd," the worst punishment that Milton can imagine.

But there is another syntactic symptom of distress in the passage of revealing chiasmus. The point at which Character and Narrator meet most clearly is in the eccentric use of personal pronouns. "He therfore," wrote Milton, "who lacking of his due . . . he I say who therfore seeks to part, is one who highly honours the maried life." It is in deference to the late Joan Webber that this part of my argument is subtitled "The Eloquent He Who," for it was in contemplating how much was accomplished for the study of seventeenth-century prose in *The Eloquent I* that I realized how much more might still be said, not least because Joan Webber's account of Milton's "I" restricted itself to the pamphlets on church reform.[12] In that context, she was able to argue that Milton's use of the first personal pronoun, along with other syntactical constructions such as passive verbs and ethical datives,

12. *The Eloquent "I": Style and Self in Seventeenth-Century Prose* (Madison, 1968).

indicated a devout striving after impersonality, a wish to express the subordination of his talent to his calling:

> Milton's muting of the "I" in passages wholly taken up with himself makes his desires seem to rest on God. And often where the "I" does make itself aggressively felt, an overarching periodic sentence prevents the collision of personal with impersonal simply by encompassing both in a larger order. (197)

This idealized reading of Milton's egotistical sublime brings Character and Narrator into continuous negotiation; but it could not, I suggest, have been maintained at this ideal level had Webber turned her meticulous investigation to the divorce pamphlets.[13]

For the *Doctrine and Discipline* introduces a new twist to the syntactical device developed in the church reform pamphlets for distinguishing an ideal and disinterested self from a confessedly self-interested author. The ideal "he who" appears as the heroic agent of reform, "hee who shall indeavour the amendment of any old neglected grievance in Church or State" (2:224), or "he who wisely would restrain the reasonable Soul of man within due bounds" (2:227). Both of these are built into the new address to Parliament added in 1644, and contrast with the modest ethical dative: "For me, as farre as my part leads me, I have already my greatest gain, assurance and inward satisfaction to have done in this nothing unworthy" (2:232). More clearly heroic, participating in the structure of epic and chivalric metaphor with which Milton enlivened his attacks on prelacy, is the "He therefore who by adventuring shall be so happy as with successe . . . to light the way of such an expedient liberty and truth as this . . . [and] shall deserve to be reck'n'd among the publick benefactors of civill and humane life" (2:240). Here, in fact, Milton changed the "He that" of 1643 to "He who" in 1644, one of those miniscule alterations that would seem to carry no significance unless perceived as structural.

But alongside these heroic personae exists another, who belongs rather to the world of error and mistaken choice that Milton entered for the first time in the *Doctrine and Discipline*, and for which, paradoxically, the humility of ethical datives could

---

13. Webber actually argues that the intrusion of self into Milton's church reform pamphlets constitutes "the same kind of spiritual autobiography that other Puritans wrote, except that it is translated into literary terms" (217).

not serve because of the need to conceal his "own by-ends." So the new preface introduces also the figure of "He who marries" and "intends as little to conspire his own ruine, as he that swears Allegiance" (2:229). He will reappear as the anonymous "sober man" in the story of unwise courtship, and in the subsequent lament for the failure of love: "He therfore who lacking of his due . . . thinks it better to part then to live sadly and injuriously . . . (for not to be belov'd & yet retain'd, is the greatest injury to a gentle spirit) he I say who therfore seeks to part, is one who highly honours the maried life, and would not stain it." Especially in that remarkable construction, "he I say who," the grammar of self-division is painfully audible.

Grinding in the Mill

The three myths or allegorical narratives differ from the "amatorious novel" we have just been reading by virtue of their uncomfortable blend of high abstraction with an emphatic sexuality, which goes well beyond the incarnational protocols of allegory as a narrative procedure. In Milton's retelling of Plato's myth of the union of Plenty and Poverty (a pagan version of the story of Ruth and Boaz), everything that was happy or high-spirited in the original is erased. In the *Symposium*, Plenty, having overindulged at Aphrodite's birthday party, lies down in the garden of Zeus and falls asleep, whereupon Poverty, "considering her own straitened circumstances, plotted to have him for a husband, and accordingly she lay down at his side and conceived Love."[14] For Milton, Poverty is recognizable in that loneliness of which Adam complained in the garden, but the myth has gone awry; Plenty vanishes from his text, Penury cannot "lay it self down by the side of such a meet & acceptable union . . . but remains utterly unmaried . . . and still burnes in the proper meaning of St. Paul" (2:252–53). An awkwardness about gender, one might suspect, shows in the conversion of Penury from feminine to neuter, and in the revised genealogy. Instead of the birth of Love, "Then enters Hate, not that Hate that sins, but that which is onely a naturall dissatisfaction and the turning aside from a mistaken object." In this version of the myth the sexual engagement (which represents the spiritual or emotional one) either does not occur

14. *Dialogues of Plato*, trans. Benjamin Jowett, 4 vols. (Oxford, 1871), 1:519.

at all, or, if it does, is so unsatisfactory that it leads to that familiar image of the domestic bedroom, the "turning aside."

The myth of Custom and Error with which the 1644 pamphlet begins is also a myth of generation gone askew. Here Custom is the aggressive female ("being but a meer face") and, like Penury, seeking a mate who has what she lacks, namely, a body. She "rests not in her unaccomplishment, untill by secret inclination, shee accorporat her selfe with error, who being a blind and Serpentine body without a head, willingly accepts what he wants, and supplies what her incompleatnesse went seeking" (223). Lana Cable noted in 1981 the sexual content of this striking opening to the *Doctrine*;[15] but possibly the conventions of academic discourse did not then permit her to say what she meant by the "obvious . . . implications" of this representation of Error as male. The appropriate gloss, I think, comes from Yeats's late poem, *The Chambermaid's Second Song*, where the blind and serpentine body is identified as "his rod and its butting head / Limp as a worm, / His spirit that has fled / Blind as a worm."[16] This myth, too, issues in an allegorical birth, although it is emphatically not an offspring of Custom and Error but rather a birth they would prevent, crying "Innovation," "as if the womb of teeming Truth were to be clos'd up" (2:224). Mysteriously (or perhaps we should say carelessly) a few moments later Truth is no longer the rightful mother, but the child:

> Though this ill hap wait on her nativity, that shee never comes into the world, but like a Bastard, to the ignominy of him that brought her forth: till Time the Midwife rather then the mother of Truth, have washt and salted the Infant, declar'd her legitimat, and Churcht the father of his young Minerva. (2:225)

The editors of the *Yale Prose* remark on this "grotesque" mingling of classical myth with the Anglican service of churching women after childbirth, a relic of the Hebrew purification rites and Old Testament emphases on female uncleanness. But still more unsettling is Milton's distortion of the familial structure of several stories at once, so that Time becomes not Truth's male father,

---

15. "Coupling Logic and Milton's Doctrine of Divorce," *Milton Studies* 15 (1981): 147–48.

16. *Collected Poems* (London, 1950), 346.

a commonplace of Renaissance thought, but her female midwife; while the role of the father is now usurped by the author of the *Doctrine and Discipline of Divorce,* who both claims the Olympian privilege of paternity *without* the assistance of a woman (the birth of the brainchild *through* the brain) and confesses, by way of the metaphor of churching, to an uneasy physicality that requires some ritual (verbal) exorcism.

Cable also proposed that the "accorporation" of Custom and Error functions as a grotesque parody of the longed-for union of Eros and Anteros (book 1, chapter 6). Perhaps; but what I notice rather is the peculiar misappropriateness of the Eros/Anteros model, literally a tale of passionately incestuous love between brothers, as an image of human *marriage,* whose oddness in this context is only underlined by Milton's disclaimer that "of matrimoniall love no doubt but that was chiefly meant." Before attempting to erase this problem by recourse to learned commentary, it might be well to ask whether Milton *needed* to invoke this young all-male image of desire, when he might have just as easily remembered the union of Cupid and "his eternal Bride" Psyche that concludes the published versions of *Comus.* *That* myth would indeed have stood in pure contrast to the two distorted unions and genealogies that precede it, not least because in that earlier, ideal moment Milton could contemplate the "blissful birth" of twins, Youth and Joy. Not so young now, he apparently could not bring himself to recall that particular shape of desire, and the myth he chooses belongs rather to the mindset of Adam after the Fall and before reconciliation with Eve:

> O why did God,
> Creator wise, that peopl'd highest Heav'n
> With spirits Masculine, create at last
> This *novelty* on Earth, this fair defect
> Of Nature, and not fill the World at once
> With Man as Angels without Feminine,
> Or find some other way to generate
> Mankind?
>
> (10.888–95; italics added)

Without the "novelty" of the female, there could be, need be, no "amatorious novel." Milton's framing of the Eros/Anteros myth as a divine fiction sung to him by his "Author," and his denial that it belongs in the genre of domestic or romantic fiction, register both a generic and a gendered discomfort.

Such a reading can only be reinforced by the language Milton employs to denote human and heterosexual activity in the *Doctrine and Discipline of Divorce*. In 1978 Edward Le Comte, in two terse pages, collected some of this vocabulary, some of these metaphors, concluded that they registered Milton's "disgust or scorn," and suggested that if the divorce pamphlets "reflect a sexual refusal, they reflect one, or an inclination to one, far more likely to have come from the husband."[17] He noted that Milton equates heterosexual activity not only with animalism, "a bestial necessity," "bestial burning," "animal or beastish meeting," "a brutish congress," but also with physical labor and slavery. Central to this perception is a sentence Milton added to the 1644 edition: "that to grind in the mill of an undelighted and servil copulation, must be the only forc't work of a Christian mariage, oft times with such a yokefellow, from whom both love and peace, both nature and Religion mourns to be separated" (2:258); and Le Comte showed how this image proleptically alludes to the story of Samson, who in rabbinical tradition was doubly enslaved by the Philistines, combining toiling at the mill with enforced service as a stud.[18] The sexual pun derives also from the discourse of common bawdiness. Le Comte cites the couplet from a 1647 popular rhyme:

> Digby's lady takes it ill,
> That her lord grinds not at her mill.

But we can now see more clearly how and why the sexual distress in the *Doctrine and Discipline of Divorce* is entangled with Milton's ideology of work, that it evinces the same intuition of

---

17. *Milton and Sex* (London, 1978), 29–30. This swift-moving and often reckless account of Milton's conscious and unconscious responses to sex and marriage has now been replaced by James Turner's *One Flesh: Paradisal Marriage and Sexual Relations in the Age of Milton* (Oxford, 1987), which judiciously recognizes Milton's concept of sexuality as "many-layered" (203), and places the misogyny of the divorce pamphlets in the context of other seventeenth-century theorists of marriage, as well as the "virginal philosophy" of *Comus* (222) and the attacks on female rule in the political pamphlets and *History of Britain*.

18. The point originated with Samuel Stollman, " 'To Grind in the Mill . . .,' " *Seventeenth-Century News* 29 (1971): 68–69.

social and economic instability, expressed in terms of agricultural practice and the politics of landowning, also found in the
early poems.[19] We should group around the grinding in the mill
the following phrases from elsewhere in the pamphlet: "bond-
men of a luckles and helples matrimony" (2:240); "the work of
male and female" (2:240); "sowe the furrow of mans nativity with
seed of two incoherent and uncombining dispositions" (2:270);
"an improper and ill-yoking couple . . . the disparity of severall
cattell at the plow" (2:277); and especially "God loves not to plow
out the heart of our endeavours with over-hard and sad tasks . . .
by making wedlock a supportless yoke . . . to make men *the day-
labourers* of their own afflictions" (2:342; italics added). This allusion to day labor connects the pamphlet to the crucial sonnet on
the parable of the talents ("Does God exact day-labor, light
denied?"); but here it reveals more sharply its coordinates in a
socio-economic analysis that Milton has and has not completed.
"I spake ev'n now," he wrote on the question of whether the
Mosaic dispensation could possibly be interpreted as a license
or escape clause given to a hard-hearted people,

> as if sin were condemn'd in a perpetual *villenage* never to be free
> by law, never to be *manumitted*: but sure sin can have no tenure
> by law at all, but is rather an eternal outlaw, and in hostility with
> law past all attonement. (2:288; italics original)

In the deep structure of Milton's imagination the socio-economic
consciousness is now inseparable from the erotic drama that the
pamphlet is staging, *because* Milton has now himself entered the
terrain of mistakenness and is no longer luckily excluded from
the curse of labor. Under this curse, which has always connected
agricultural labor with genital pain, Milton cannot distinguish
the body from the body politic, the master from the slave, the
grinder from the ground. He has found himself expected to plow
and "sow the furrow of man's nativity," and, worse still, to spend
in the process, "to be made to pay out the best substance of his
body, and of his soul too, as some think" (2:271), becoming indis-
tinguishable in this metaphoric exchange from day laborers,

---

19. See my "Forc'd Fingers: Milton's Early Poems and Ideological Constraint," in *The Muses Common-weale*, ed. Claude J. Summers and Ted-Larry
Pebworth (Columbia, 1988), 9–22.

villeins, or even oxen and asses. Milton shares the yoke. Sex is hard work when the heart is not in it; and it would be unkind of his readers to give him the same advice that thousands of mothers gave their daughters: "Shut your eyes and think of England."

Yet in a sense he did just that, stylistically. He turned to euphemism. If writing is, as some think, the art of *not* saying what one means, the most profound avoidance, some of Milton's finest writing occurs in the effort to conceal from his readers and probably from himself the precise effect on his psyche of the long-delayed induction into heterosexual experience. Le Comte's formula of "disgust or scorn" cannot account fully for this language, too lapidary either to allow disgust to register on the reader's sensory scale or to permit the moral distancing of Narrator from Character that scorn requires. Especially in chapter 3, where Milton excoriates canon law for its focus on adultery, his language ricochets between what in *Paradise Lost* he would later register as (divine) "distance and distaste" (9.9). The admonitory distance is invoked by archaic moral allegories of the body (complete with alliteration), such as the "vessell of voluptuous enjoyment," or the "fountain" "from whence must flow the acts of peace and love," or "the channell of concupiscence" (2:248–49). But the embarrassing carnal knowledge (which is only half acknowledged) is written in a libidinal narrative that confuses success and failure and is marked by a compulsion to repeat. "The impediment of carnall performance," the "stopt or extinguisht veins of sensuality," and the "disappointing of an impetuous nerve" alternate with the "impatience of a sensuall desire . . . relieved" and the "prescrib'd satisfaction of an irrationall heat." Even the surrounding vocabulary is contaminated by the story of tumescence and detumescence; so the canon law prescribes that "the contract shall stand as firme as ever," however "flat and melancholious" the emotional relationship may be. Above all, in the notorious "quintessence of an excrement" Milton rather highlighted than solved the problem of distance and distaste, as abstract thought and philosophical idealism (expressed in a classicizing and pseudoscientific vocabulary) reveal their connections to a venerable tradition of misogynistic disgust. As Freud observed in his case history of "Dora," "the

Early Christian Father's 'inter urinas et faeces nascimur' clings to sexual life and cannot be detached from it in spite of every effort of idealization."[20]

Each of Milton's allusions to sexual process, then, is a micronarrative, with a different ending, of the search for satisfaction, of the structure of desire, which modern and postmodern criticism, itself responding to Freudian theory, has made synonymous with the novel as a category of thought, as a genre. In Tzvetan Todorov's *The Poetics of Prose* the quintessential novel must articulate the shared paradoxes of desire and narrative, that "we desire at the same time desire and its object." When we get what we thought we wanted we no longer want it. The story is over. And he also suggests that one of the novel's essential moods, in the grammatical sense, is the optative, of which the renunciative is a special case.[21] The *Doctrine and Discipline of Divorce* is, I suggest, a special case of the renunciative novel, announcing its genre through the paradox of Milton's statement: "he I say who therfore seeks to part, is one who highly honours the maried life, and would not stain it" (2:253). If his story remains carnal, for all his attempts to allegorize it, if the individual life breaks through the generalizing and impersonalizing impulse, if the Narrator fails to control the Character and effect the atonement

20. *Dora: An Analysis of a Case of Hysteria* (1905), ed. Philip Rieff (New York, 1963), 47. Compare Turner's argument that it was precisely the extent of Milton's idealization of marriage that produced, by its failure to be realized, the disgust. My reading of Milton's sexual vocabulary, however, differs from Turner's emphasis on "physical particularity" and "medical precision" (*One Flesh*, 198) by attempting to recognize the element of euphemism or self-protective intellectualism that Milton's vocabulary exhibits. All these strategies Milton shares with Freud, whose equally notorious passage in *Dora* about the difficulties of discussing "such delicate and unpleasant subjects" as "bodily organs and processes" asserts the distance achievable by "dry and direct . . . technical names" (65) only to detour into (unintentional) double-entendre. "J'appelle un chat un chat," wrote Freud, which only Jane Gallop has been bold enough to translate. See her "Keys to Dora," in *In Dora's Case*, ed. Charles Bernheimer and Claire Kahane (New York, 1985), 209. And it is worth noting that without the prurience by which genitalia were themselves rendered euphemistically in Viennese culture at the turn of the century (as in the famous *Schmuckkästchen*, "jewelry box"), Freud's repertory of dream symbols would have been much impoverished.

21. *The Poetics of Prose*, trans. Richard Howard (Ithaca, 1977), 105–6, 114.

and they remain yoked together in the ambiguous lexical territory of euphemism, the "by-ends" that criticism is unfairly equipped to notice, we need not, I think, today be embarrassed, either for Milton or ourselves.

The Rape of Lucrece

My last chapter began with Nathaniel Lee's dramatization, for the Restoration stage, of the legendary origins of the Roman republic, a story that, as Lee remarked in his preface, was influenced by "Shakespeare's Brutus"—the Lucius Junius Brutus of *The Rape of Lucrece*. In fact Lee's play, with its almost total lack of interest in Lucrece, hardly resembles Shakespeare's poem at all. But *The Rape* and its subsequent reception deserve consideration in their own right, even though achronologically at the end of this study, as a demonstration of how modern scholars have their own capacity to remake earlier texts according to later needs, prejudices, and fashions. While never entirely avoidable, this tendency is probably one that requires, if not a trial, at least a public audit. Evidently, as I write in the 1990s, rape and its relation to legal process is a topic of social and intellectual concern as never before, and Shakespeare's poem therefore profits from, and may in turn assist, the sharpening of theoretical focus inevitably produced when a shift in social consciousness not only occurs but is marked by institutional debate.

The metaphor of the trial is the opening gambit in *Chaste Thinking*, Stephanie Jed's highly idiosyncratic study of the Lucretia legend and its transmission by Florentine humanist scholars, especially Coluccio Salutati. Opening with the case Lucretia versus Sextus Tarquinius, Jed proceeds to imagine an appropriate set of questions that might be used in jury selection:

> A woman will testify that on a particular night, in or around the year 510 B.C., the son of the tyrant came to her home and forcibly raped her. She will describe the experience of things a man did to her body. Do you think you can be totally unemotional and impartial in deciding the facts of this case?[22]

22. *Chaste Thinking: The Rape of Lucretia and the Birth of Humanism* (Bloomington and Indianapolis, 1989), 1.

While dealing with Shakespeare only in a few parenthetic remarks, this books pertains to my project, not only because of its fascination with the law but because, like all too many of the products of the liveliest intelligences at work in our profession, it has fastened on the wrong enemy. At trial in *Chaste Thinking* are not only men in general, but also all those (primarily men) responsible for the scholarly practices that produce the state desired of the jurors: "Do you think you can be totally unemotional and impartial in deciding the facts of this case?" This is chaste thinking, connected by Jed to the masculinism that determines Lucretia's behavior by constructing for her a myth of chastity, to the philological method that "castigated" a text for its impurities, and, most dangerously, to the republican tradition as embodied in Lucius Junius Brutus, which (and whom) Jed equates both with masculinism and with heartlessness. Since in Livy's account "any emotional involvement we might feel in what happened to Lucretia is quickly displaced by our admiration for Brutus for liberating Rome," Jed takes it as her responsibility to reverse these effects, and to demonize Brutus as the cause, because the stoppage, of all our woe:

> Livy tells us that when Brutus found the Romans grieving over the fate of Lucretia, he "castigated" them for their tears and emotions and urged them to take up arms instead of weeping. This figure of Brutus as a *castigator lacrimarum* functions not only as a cue to the Romans to subordinate their emotions to the cause of liberty, but also as a cue to the reader to consider the rape of Lucretia "objectively"—that is, as a necessary prologue to Brutus' act of liberation. (10–11)

The cruelty that Brutus later used in another legal contest—the trial and execution of his own sons for conspiracy against the new republic—is (at the level of affect, not of logic) a pretext for rendering the entire project of liberal historiography suspect. In this case the attack on "humanism" and "liberalism," which Jed broadly equates, comes from the perspective of radical feminism. Among her authorities is Catherine MacKinnon, herself a steely advocate for a feminist jurisprudence. I myself use the "case" of *The Rape of Lucrece* as one instance of an unfortunate tendency of contemporary feminist *literary* criticism to ally itself with arguments ultimately pernicious to the traditions of sociopolitical idealism which are feminism's best hope of broadening its mandate. My metaphor for that alliance is "sleeping with the enemy."

In *Shakespeare and the Popular Voice* I touched on the *Rape of Lucrece* in a single paragraph, one that didn't begin to do justice to the massive cultural investments that have been made, in both the early modern era and our own, in the story of Lucretia, the Tarquins, and Lucius Junius Brutus. Without this fuller context, a balanced account of the poem's own peculiarities and its still more striking history of reception is unlikely. Ian Donaldson, who has produced the most comprehensive account so far of the legend of Lucretia and its transmission, believed that in the form it had reached in Livy it was a complex story about the interrelationship of public, political, and private, sexual behavior, of "liberty for the state and liberty for the individual," with Lucius Junius Brutus achieving the first on behalf of Rome, Lucretia the second for herself.[23] Yet his analysis showed that those who adopted or adapted the story for their own purposes subsequently tended to ignore this ideological balance and choose either a story of sexual morality, with Lucretia as its heroine, or one of political principle, with Brutus as its hero or villain.[24]

Donaldson surveyed the shaping and deforming of this story in different media over time: by Saint Augustine, who treated the story as a problem in Christian ethics and deplored not the rape but the sin of Lucretia's suicide; by Renaissance painters from Cranach to Titian, who painted Lucretia naked, at both the moment of the rape and that of the suicide, thereby conflating the two events and, perhaps, subjecting her to further humiliation; by various parodists, especially in plays (a category which includes Machiavelli's comedy *Mandragola*) which tended to the notion that Lucrece did or could have enjoyed the rape; and by those who, in their concern for the development of republican thought, saw Lucius Junius Brutus, not Lucretia, as the central figure in the legend. Nathaniel Lee, obviously, was a later member of this group; but he would certainly have known that the Machiavelli of the *Discourses on Livy* was an earlier and influen-

23. *The Rapes of Lucretia: A Myth and Its Transformations* (Oxford, 1982), 9. See also Hans Galinsky, *Der Lucretia-Stoff in der Weltliteratur* (Breslau, 1932).
24. *Rapes of Lucretia*, 9.

tial one. As Donaldson points out, for Machiavelli the cause of the expulsion of Tarquinius Superbus

> was not that his son, Sextus, had ravished Lucretia, but that he had violated the laws of the kingdom and ruled tyrannically. . . . Hence, if the Lucretia incident had not occurred, something else would have happened and would have led to the same result. (104–5)[25]

There is some reason to suppose that Lee was not alone in his time in inducting "Shakespeare's Brutus" into a political agenda. Licensed for publication under Shakespeare's name in 1594, the *Rape* was remarkably popular as a text for readers over several decades. Although it was not quite as much in demand as *Venus and Adonis* with its thirteen editions before 1640, presumably to be accounted for by a demand for high-class pornography,[26] there were eight editions of the *Rape* by that time (1594, 1598, two in 1600, 1607, 1616, 1624, 1632). The two epyllia were not printed together until 1707, when they appeared, the *Rape* first, and the dedication to Southampton prominently mentioned, in a volume of *Poems on Affairs of State*. In this predominantly but not exclusively Whig collection they were preceded by a poem entitled *The Miseries of England, from the growing power of her domestick enemies. 1701*, whose first two lines read as follows:

> Albion, disclose thy drousy Eyes, and see
> The Bondage that surrounds thy Liberty[27]

and followed by *The First Anniversary of the government under his highness the Lord Protector* (1655), attributed to Waller but in fact Andrew Marvell's celebrated poem. *The First Anniversary* is itself fraught with the republican vocabulary, not least because Marvell was adapting it as best he could to the Protectorate; for example:

> Such was that wondrous Order and *Consent*,
> When Cromwell tun'd the ruling Instrument;
> While tedious Statesmen many years did hack,

---

25. Citing Machiavelli, *Discourses*, trans. Leslie J. Walker (London, 1950), 3.5.1.

26. There were editions in 1593, 1594, 1595, 1596, 1599, three dated 1602 (behind which have been detected 1607/8 and 1608/9), 1617, 1620, 1627, 1630, and 1636.

27. The poem was a protest against the demand for new taxes to support the War of the Spanish Succession.

Framing a *Liberty* that still went back.

. . .

'Tis not a *Freedome*, that where All command;
Nor *Tyranny*, where One does them withstand.[28]

This recirculation of Shakespeare's poems in an explicitly polemical context gives some credence to the argument that the *Rape* was popular because of its bearing on political issues[29]. Though quietly discredited by J. C. Maxwell in his Cambridge edition of the poem, in a note to which we shall return,[30] this hypothesis gains ground in the light of the *Rape*'s subsequent critical history and the effort (strain might be a better word) that has gone into *denying* the presence, let alone the dominance, of a republican thematics.

If we accept Donaldson's claim that most subsequent adapters of the legend chose to suppress one of its major themes in favor of the other, we might at first sight assume that Shakespeare was one of those who made Lucretia the center and banished Brutus to the periphery. In purely structural terms, that is certainly the case. The story of the expulsion of the Tarquins is confined to a prose "Argument" at the beginning and seven stanzas at the end of the poem. Although it is almost two thousand lines long, its *narrative* content can be contained in a couple of sentences. Inflamed by desire at hearing Collatine's boasting of his wife's beauty and chastity, the younger Tarquin rides to her house and, as her guest, rapes her at midnight, despite her pleas. In the morning, she sends for her husband from his military encampment and, having told her story and the name of her ravisher, stabs herself with a knife. What delays the reader for 1,855 lines is primarily psychological and rhetorical filler—the debate Tarquin has with himself before the rape and the one Lucrece

---

28. Marvell, *Poems and Letters*, ed. H. M. Margoliouth, rev. Pierre Legouis, 2 vols. (Oxford, 1971), 1:110, 115. Marvell is referring here to the parliamentary efforts from 1604 to 1640 to establish the terms of "ancient liberty." During the Restoration, however, he wrote his own history of the late Elizabethan and early Stuart period, in which he held the Anglican clergy, particularly Robert Sibthorpe and Roger Maynwaring, responsible for preaching monarchical absolutism and ultimately for the civil war. See his *Rehearsal Transpos'd*, ed. D. I. B. Smith (Oxford, 1971), 127–35.

29. This was suggested, though admittedly not very cogently, by E. P. Kuhl, "Shakespeare's *Rape of Lucrece*," *Philosophical Quarterly* 20 (1941): 352–60.

30. Maxwell, ed., *The Poems* (Cambridge, 1969), 203.

has with herself after it—along with twenty-nine stanzas devoted to an ecphrastic account of a painting of the siege of Troy and Lucrece's meditation on this painting while she waits for her husband's return. Disturbingly, the first half of the poem identifies closely with Tarquin, who is always seen from the inside and who, after the rape, is hideously disappointed: "Pure Chastity is rifled of her store, / and Lust, the thief, far poorer than before."[31]

> Hee like a theevish dog creeps sadly thence,
> Shee like a wearied Lambe lies panting there,
> He scowles and hates himselfe for his offence;
> Shee desperat with her nailes her flesh doth teare.
> He faintly flies sweating with guiltie feare.
>
> (Lines 736–40)

This aspect of *Lucrece* looks forward to Philip Larkin's extraordinary poem *The Less Deceived*, in which, although "her mind lay open like a drawer of knives," the victim of a rape is in the deepest sense less damaged than her ravisher.

But this comparison is somewhat misleading. One *can* find psychological complexity in the *Rape*, but it requires probing. What the poem offers on the surface is a shimmering superficiality, a parade of rhetorical conventions and irrelevant or inadequate responses to the act itself. As Lucrece herself remarks, after thirty-eight stanzas of formal complaint:

> In vaine I raile at oportunitie,
> At time, at Tarquin, and unchearfull night,
> In vaine I cavill with mine infamie,
> In vaine I spurne at my confirm'd despight,
> This helplesse smoake of words doth me no right.
>
> (Lines 1023–27)

This complete rejection of realism, the virtual disappearance of the rape as a sexual occurrence, would make it possible to argue that *neither* Lucrece's final act of independence nor Brutus' role as the liberator of Rome is at the center of the poem, which is filled instead precisely with a "smoake of words."

This phenomenon has complicated the task of those who, in recent years, have wished to claim the poem for Lucrece—that

31. Shakespeare, *The Rape of Lucrece* (London, 1594), lines 693–94.

is to say, feminist critics. Both Coppelia Kahn and Nancy Vickers have tried to capitalize on the poem's rhetorical excesses. Vickers builds on Eve Sedgwick's concept of homosocial rivalry to show how Tarquin's interest in Lucrece is created by "men talking to men about women."[32] Kahn has argued that the highly ornate, image-studded texture of the poem carries its own feminist subtext, relating the metaphorical siege of Lucrece's chastity to the actual siege of Ardea in which Tarquin and Collatine were military companions, while images of possession and ownership ("why is Collatine the publisher / Of that rich jewel he should keep unknown / From thievish ears, because it is his own" [lines 33–35]) indict both men as indifferent to women except as commodities.[33] These insights are clearly correct. Yet even so, as a story of gender conflict Shakespeare's poem fails—fails to involve its readers in either Tarquin's postcoital self-flagellation or Lucrece's predicament, so ornate is their expression.

It is not entirely surprising, therefore, that postmodernism has discovered the *Rape*. I refer to Joel Fineman's essay "The Temporality of Rape," in which, a footnote assures us, he was "primarily concerned to establish the *poetics* of Shakespearean rape" by a Derridean wordplay, a Lacanian vocabulary, a focus on rhetorical figures (especially chiasmus), that is to say, the mirror relation of the letters *M* and *W* (men and women) in a literal "cross-coupling copulation."[34] Lurking within Fineman's own rhetorical display is a strain of feminist thought—this poem "attributes subjectivity only to the 'will' of man," (51); but on the other hand his pleasure in close reading produces an effect equivalent to rape in what it does to Lucrece. Commenting on the lines:

> The wolfe hath ceazd his pray, the poor lamb cries,
> Till with her own white fleece her voice controld
> Intombes her outcrie in her lips sweet fold
>
> (Lines 676–79)

32. Vickers, " 'The blazon of sweet beauty's best': Shakespeare's *Lucrece*," in *Shakespeare and the Question of Theory*, ed. Patricia Parker and Geoffrey Hartman (New York and London, 1985), 96.

33. "The Rape in Shakespeare's *Lucrece*," *Shakespeare Studies* 9 (1976): 53–57.

34. "Shakespeare's *Will*: The Temporality of Rape," *Representations* 20 (1987): 25–76, especially 51, 71.

Fineman remarks:

> It is fitting that the rape, when it finally occurs, is figured in and
> as a simultaneously emergent and recessive in-betweenness form-
> ing and informing the "fold" of Lucrece's lips, for the smirky col-
> lation of Lucrece's mouth with her vagina supports the formal
> implication that Lucrece is asking for her rape because her "no,"
> as "no," means "yes." (43)

This is the postmodern equivalent of the reprehensible tradition
whereby it was assumed that Lucrece partially assented to or at
least involuntarily enjoyed her rape. "Is it possible so much can
come of the writing of letters?" Fineman asked rhetorically. Alas,
yes; and one has to admit that the painting on black velvet that
Shakespeare himself produced, in the center of *Lucrece*, can
scarcely be held inviolate from such insinuations.

But like the majority of contemporary critics, Fineman constructed his reading of the *Rape* in oblivion of the frame. Though
quantitatively overshadowed by the verbosity it surrounds, the
frame economically supplies both the political context for the personal crisis and an implied critique of rhetorical self-indulgence.
Both in the preliminary prose Argument and in the seven concluding stanzas, the reader is reminded of the larger significance
of this otherwise undistinguished family tragedy—namely, its
function as a *cause* in the long history of republican thought and
action. In the Argument, we are told precisely what is the content of the "tyranny" of which the rapist's father was guilty:

> Lucius Tarquinius (for his excessive pride surnamed Superbus),
> after hee had caused his own father in law Servius Tullius to be
> cruelly murdered, and contrarie to the Roman lawes and
> customes, not requiring or staying for the peoples *suffrages*, had
> possessed himselfe of the kingdome. (italics added)

It is not just that the siege of Ardea participates in a general lawlessness, of which the rape of Lucrece herself is, literally, the classic example; but that (and here the Argument selects but one of
the long list of abuses listed by Livy) he made himself king without his nation's *consent*, "not requiring or staying for the peoples suffrages." The phrase "peoples suffrages" is, I submit, not
an inevitable translation of Livy's "neque populi iussu neque
auctoribus patribus" (neither by popular decree nor senatorial
sanction). By the same token, the Argument reduces the empha-

sis on Brutus' own oratory, in Lucrece's family circle and later in Rome, shifting his heroic stance against the Tarquins toward a more consensual model for change. In Livy's version:

> Brutus, while the others were absorbed in grief, drew out the knife from Lucretia's wound, and holding it up, dripping with gore, exclaimed, "By this blood, most chaste until a prince wronged it, I swear, and I take you, gods, to witness, that I will pursue Lucius Tarquinius Superbus and his wicked wife and all his children, with sword, with fire, aye with whatsoever violence I may: and that I will suffer neither them nor any other to be king in Rome!" The knife he then passed to Collatinus, and from him to Lucretius and Valerius. They were dumbfounded at this miracle. Whence came this new spirit in the breast of Brutus? As he bade them, so they swore.

And then, when they carry the body of Lucrece to Rome:

> There he made a speech by no means like what might have been expected of the mind and the spirit which he had feigned up to that day. He spoke of the violence and lust of Sextus Tarquinius, of the shameful defilement of Lucretia and her deplorable death. . . . He reminded them, besides, of the pride of the king himself and the wretched state of the commons who were plunged into ditches and sewers and made to clear them out. The men of Rome, he said . . . had been transformed from warriors into artisans and stone-cutters. He spoke of the shameful murder of King Tullius, and how his daughter had driven her accursed chariot over her father's body, and he invoked the gods who punish crimes against parents.[35]

Livy himself indicated a conflict between rhetorical enhancement of a topic and historical responsibility. "With these and, I fancy, even fiercer reproaches," he wrote, "such as occur to a man in the very presence of an outrage, but are far from easy for a historian to reproduce, he inflamed the people, and brought them to abrogate the king's authority and to exile Lucius Tarquinius, together with his wife and children." And there Livy's account of the decision-making process ended.

By contrast, the Argument of the *Rape* offers an example of precisely that practice, "staying for the people's suffrages," that

35. Livy, *Ab urbe condita*, trans. H. B. Foster (Cambridge, Mass., 1954), 1.49.1–12.

Tarquin had abrogated; it subordinates "he" to "they," the clan and the people, and explains the constitutional nature of the change:

> With one consent they all vowed to roote out the whole hated family of the Tarquins: and bearing the dead body to Rome, Brutus acquainted the people with the doer and manner of the vile deede, with a bitter invective against the *tyranny* of the King, wherewith the people were so moved that *with one consent* and a *general* acclamation, the Tarquins were all exiled, and the state government changed from Kings to Consuls. (italics added)

Clustered together, those crucial terms that I previously identified as part of the vocabulary of early republicanism in England (*suffrages, tyranny, general*, and the twice-invoked *with one consent*) support each other and are themselves supported by the aetiological myth of republican origins.

It is perhaps not surprising, therefore, that Shakespeare's authorship of the Argument has been disputed, in a minihistory of reception as suppression. In 1950 James M. Tolbert argued that since the narrative of the Argument was inconsistent with that of the poem and since their styles were markedly different, the Argument was non-Shakespearean and was constructed by someone else from parts of Livy, Bishop Thomas Cooper's *Thesaurus Linguae Romanae et Brittanicae*, and "the unidentified source of the story as told in *Cooper's Chronicle*."[36] A quarter of a century later the Argument was reclaimed for Shakespeare by Michael Platt, in an essay firmly entitled, *"The Rape of Lucrece* and the Republic for Which It Stands."[37] But this recuperative strategy was subsequently challenged by Heather Dubrow, who restated, though more subtly, the Argument's inautheticity. For Dubrow, the Argument and the poem have completely different agendas:

> the Argument . . . implicitly responds to the query, "Why were the Tarquins banished?" while the inquiry behind the poem might be phrased as "What happened to Lucrece?" In short, the con-

---

36. "The Argument to Shakespeare's 'Lucrece': Its Sources and Authorship," *University of Texas Studies in English* 29 (1950): 77–90.

37. *"The Rape of Lucrece* and the Republic for Which It Stands," *Centennial Review* 19 (1975): 57–79, reprinted in his *Rome and Romans according to Shakespeare*, rev. ed. (Lanham, Md., 1983), 13–51.

cerns of the Argument are more political, those of the poem itself more personal.[38]

The more personal, it is implied, is the more Shakespearean. For Dubrow, however, the Argument's inautheticity is a matter not of its authorship but rather of its credibility as a witness:

> As its detached tone would suggest, the Argument at first strikes us as an unimpeachable account of the facts: . . . But this initial confidence in [its] trustworthiness in fact heightens our dismay when we discover unresolvable contradictions between the Argument and the text of the poem, such as their varying accounts of the events before the rape. (161–62)

The "unresolvable contradictions" to which Dubrow is here referring consist solely, so far as I can tell, of the Argument's omission of the first visit of Sextus Tarquinius to the home of Lucrece and Collatine. But more telling still is Dubrow's analogous attack on that part of the poem which provides the strongest testimony that poem and Argument belong together—that is to say, on the last seven stanzas. There, after Lucrece's suicide, when her husband and father fall into her own mode of helpless complaint, Brutus steps forward. We are now told for the first time that he has bided his time during the tyrannical rule of Tarquinius Superbus by pretending lunacy:

> But now he throwes that shallow habit by,
> Wherein deepe pollicie did him disguise,
> And armed his long-hid wits advisedlie.
>
> (Lines 1812–14)

Grasping the truth that Lucrece herself had partially understood, that her name could be made a legend (though from her perspective only a shameful one), Brutus explains to Collatine that mourning in such circumstances is a wretched weakness ("is woe the cure for woe?") that must be replaced by political action. Lucrece's name is to be made synonymous with Rome itself and "all our countrey rights in Rome maintained" (line 1838), as her bleeding body is to provide the emotional drive to revolution. Stephanie Jed's attack on Brutus as the "castigator lacrimarum" therefore misses the point, at least as it appeared to Shakespeare;

38. *Captive Victors: Shakespeare's Narrative Poems and Sonnets* (Ithaca and London, 1987), 160.

that while "helpless" emotion is castigated both by Brutus and by the poet's own process of selection and adaptation, as a cathexis to political action it is both legitimate and essential. The last two lines of the poem return to, and turn on, metrically speaking, one of the central terms in the republican vocabulary:

> The Romans plausibly did give *consent*,
> To Tarquin's everlasting banishment.

One could "plausibly" argue, then, that the republican motive of the poem, its "deepe pollicie," as compared with its "shallow habit" of rhetorical display, is itself represented in the figure of Brutus, "Shakespeare's Brutus," whose disguise was intended only to be temporary. Dubrow, however, reads Brutus' disguise not as a necessary strategy to protect himself against assassination but as a "shrewdness uncomfortably allied to hypocrisy," which makes him "in a sense one of the earliest of Shakespeare's Machiavels" (127); and she later attaches these same characteristics to the Argument's *selection* of topics:

> [our] doubts grow when we recognize the significance of some of the points that the Argument omits; leaving out both Brutus' earlier deceptions and his manipulations of his listeners, for example, casts a more positive light on his rise to power, avoiding the very facts that render the transition to republicanism morally problematic. (162)

Morally problematic to whom, one must ask, in the face of that coercively critical (or royal) "we"? "To avoid the Tarquins' displeasure" seems a disingenuous redescription of Brutus' motives for disguise, given that Tarquinius Superbus had previously murdered Brutus' father and brother and confiscated the family property!

Here, as so often, William Empson strikes to the heart of the matter in his own eccentric manner. In his introduction to the *Rape* in the Signet edition Empson mockingly cites J. C. Maxwell's note on the Brutus section of the poem:

> It is curious that Shakespeare makes no mention here (though the Argument concludes with it) of the historical importance of this, as involving the abolition of the monarchy . . . ; this tells heavily against the view [of E. P. Kuhl] that the popularity of the poem owed much to its bearing on political issues.

"It is curious," Empson echoes sardonically, "that the scholars of our age . . . are unable to imagine living under a censorship or making an effort to avoid trouble with Thought Police; these unpleasant features of current experience were also familiar in most historical periods, so that the disability must regularly prevent scholars from understanding what they read."[39] And Empson implies that the "smoke of words" in the center of *The Rape* is therefore to be understood as a smoke screen, through which the republican intentions of the poem could still emerge when the poem was read by Southampton and, we might imagine, the second earl of Essex. Was it merely by coincidence that two editions of the poem appeared in 1600, the year when Essex was under house arrest and formal investigation for disobedience or worse?

This brings me back to Ian Donaldson, whose own position on the *Rape* straddles the personal/political divide, though with a different twist. While on the one hand claiming that "the entire political dimension of the story" is "very subdued," and that Shakespeare's special achievement is to have opened up "a new interior world of shifting doubts, hesitations, anxieties, anticipations, and griefs," Donaldson also, like Kahn for her feminist purposes, turns to the imagistic texture of the poem for his. Which is to make a *royalist* argument: not that Shakespeare ignored the political dimensions of his story, but that he inserted between the lines of Lucrece's complaints a message of political orthodoxy. Like Empson, Donaldson assumes that Shakespeare would have been inhibited from *"questioning, even in a very indirect way, the system of monarchical government under which he lived and to which he owed allegiance"*; but, most unlike Empson, he believes that Shakespeare would not have wanted to. In some of the metaphors Lucrece uses, and in her appeals to Tarquin to remember that he is a king's son and should therefore be able to rule his libido, Shakespeare managed "not merely to neutralize but actually to reverse the story's traditional significance" (43–44, 116–17).

To explain again (after having written *Shakespeare and the Popular Voice*) why I think this argument is based on a false premise

39. Introd. to *Poems*, ed. William Burto (New York, 1968), xxiv.

would be gratuitous. But in Donaldson's phrase "questioning, even in a very indirect way," there is an interesting reverse echo of Pangle's account of the Straussian principle of reading between the lines of Plato's *Laws*:

> The only direct link between philosophy and the citizens would be the trail the philosophic legislator blazes for a few of the young, who could discern between the lines of his legislation his invitation *to question, in a suitably prudent way, all authority and law*.[40]

Donaldson admitted that "'Democratic impressions' are indeed not easily to be avoided in any retelling" of the legend, and that "the political implications of the narrative are powerful and seemingly ineradicable" (115). Yet he nevertheless tried to eradicate them in his own critical practice, offering an account of Lee's *Lucius Junius Brutus* that discredits the legendary founder of republicanism by way of his feigned madness ("he is not always strictly truthful") and his later commitment to a necessary violence.[41] In the case of *The Rape of Lucrece*, while acknowledging the clear political intentions of the poem's frame, Donaldson searched for tiny textual intimations that Shakespeare had worked *against* the grain of the legend he had chosen.

The *Rape*'s reception, especially in academic criticism (so soon obsolescent, so narrowed in its readership), is of little intrinsic importance. What justifies its rehearsal here, I would hope, is its capacity to inspire meditation on a central predicament of work in the "humanities" as it relates, in fact or in wishful thinking, to real life. What, in fact, do we see when we read, and how can we adjudicate between different claims as to what the object of our inquiry is "about"? This procedural question, once at the center of literary theory, is now seldom asked in the literary-critical marketplace, where in the last decade the *parti pris* has been

40. See 21–22 above.

41. Donaldson, *Rapes of Lucretia*, 133–38. Note especially the impulse evinced in the following: "Is he a liberator or merely another and more subtle form of tyrant? The political sympathies of the play, as the Lord Chamberlain observed, generally run towards the ideas of Brutus and the new Republic. Yet it is not the political ideals (in any simple sense) that remain most vividly in the mind after reading this tragedy. Lee allows us rather to see the cost, in human terms, that such ideals impose, and to feel a genuine hesitation about the wisdom of the man who attempts so single-mindedly to live by them."

taken for granted. Having chosen a stance from which to investigate literary texts, a critic becomes institutionally identified with that stance and indifferent, if not hostile, to any other. And two stances frequently opposed to each other, though they ought to be allied, are the political-economic and the feminist, currently represented by the still cruder terms of "class" and "gender." In literary criticism and theory, "class" stands, abruptly, for the huge complex of issues relating to government, the legal system, and the economy, categories that affect us all. From the perspective of those who study early modern history and culture, an attention to issues of "class" also involves the study of parliamentary history, the franchise, taxation, wages, land ownership and agricultural relations, food supplies or lack thereof, popular protest, apprenticeship, literacy, sumptuary conventions and regulations—everything that served, or attempted, to distinguish people from each other on a vertical scale. Misleading in a different way, since the term is supposed to indicate a constructed rather than a natural or essential relationship, "gender" stands for the huge complex of issues relating to sexuality, in which people relate to each other horizontally, and for the ways in which their sexuality impinges upon the kinds of lives it is possible for them to lead.

I have come to believe that in the real world (and hence in the literature that mimics it) "class" divides us more incisively than "gender," and that there are more intractable problems than the subordination of women, which is often amenable to individual negotiation. Where it is not so amenable, further analysis may well discover such subordination to be a consequence of economic injustice. System-wide economic injustice, produced by governmental policy, of which benign neglect is another form, is one intractable problem; that the "Law" has often been a polite name for the rules protecting the interest of a ruling oligarchy, and that it is always in danger of recidivism, is another. Feminists who forget these huge concerns, whose alliances are forged solely on the basis of "gender" (which often turns out, after all, to be that old, essentialist fact of being female), who may even find themselves making a case (particularly surprising in the United States of America) *against* the ancient republican ideals, against a liberal (Whig) historiography, against "liberalism" and "humanism" as illusions of a "bourgeois ideology," are, I suggest, engaging voluntarily in the act that Lucretia had forced upon her: sleeping with the enemy. Voluntarily or involuntarily, the consequences may be suicide.

"Sleeping with the Enemy"

To explain that metaphor, whose content is *entirely* cerebral, we need to think back to my opening chapter, with its contribution to the debates over Great Books and the literary canon, and its concern about the political resonance of those debates beyond the imaginary walls of the academy. In this third meditation on sleeping with the enemy (and how to avoid it), I shall attempt to gather up the themes of this book as they have hitherto accreted, and show them converging in an unlikely object, a contemporary novel on the topic of wife beating. The convergence here is between the debates on the canon and an appropriate feminist politics: on the one hand, the assumed incommensurability of Great Books and popular culture can be reconsidered, not least by discovering a work of popular culture that relies for its own values and even its plot on the cultural phenomenon of high culture; on the other, I show how a work of contemporary fiction that tried to send a salutary message about the relationship between economic and sexual subordination, between education and women's agency, was itself violated, its message perverted by the consumerist imagination of the Hollywood film. Thus two forms of popular culture can be differentiated, the one friendly, the other hostile to women and their independence, which (as by now most readers will expect me to argue) should be recognized as belonging to the history of emancipation at large.

I began this project by invoking, though only metaphorically, *Thelma and Louise*, the film, directed by Ridley Scott, whose originating premise is the murder of a would-be rapist by one of the protagonists in defense of the other, an event which precipitates the two women into outlawry and ultimately over the edge of the Grand Canyon. The significance of this film in contemporary popular culture is that it has been misconstrued as a radical feminist statement. While conceived by the scriptwriter, Callie Khouri, as a straightforward western for women, perhaps

with corrective allusions to male "buddy" and male-female outlaw films like *Bonnie and Clyde*, it has been widely and negatively
interpreted as indiscriminately hostile to men.[42] It could equally be interpreted as hostile to women, in that the only form of
self-determination it proposes for them is suicidal (the Lucretia
syndrome), the only form of defense against male violence to
pick up a gun and shoot.

In my chapter on "Holinshed's" *Chronicles*, I implied that a balanced account of early modern society, if possible at all, will
emerge only if we pay serious attention to the interplay between
popular (demotic) culture and "high" (established) culture, since
in such interplay we may best discern whether what were then
presented as majority or consensus values were really so. By the
same token, the value systems of Europe and North America in
the late twentieth century are rendered more intelligible if we
ask of contemporary popular culture whether *it* endorses or disputes what are deemed to be established beliefs and behavioral
conventions. Since popular culture today, unlike Spenser's Egalitarian Giant, can not even be imagined as delivering a single,
coherent message, it is worth contrasting the rape-motivated,
suicidal feminism of *Thelma and Louise* (which one has to admit
is nevertheless oddly cheerful, irrationally uplifting) with that
of another supposedly feminist film and its originating script:
Joseph Ruben's cinematographic reduction of the novel by Nancy
Price *Sleeping with the Enemy*, originally published in 1987 but
reissued as "the book of the film," with Julia Roberts on the cover,
in 1991.

Few experiences with contemporary popular culture have so
aroused my despair, causing me to doubt the Utopian hypothesis that film, with its extraordinary access to audiences that literature can never reach, could appropriate to itself literature's
traditional functions of social analysis and critique. Despair was
produced by the contrast—no, the complete *contradiction*—
between the values promoted by the film and those promoted
by Nancy Price's novel, among which, surprisingly, is the value
of "good" literature.

42. See the review by Larry Rohter, " 'Thelma and Louise' Writer Surprised
by Fuss," *San Francisco Chronicle*, June 10, 1991.

The novel's main target, of course, is wife beating, to which it proposes a Utopian alternative. It argues that the violence of men toward women is neither endemic (since there emerges a decent, alternative husband for the battered runaway wife) nor, when it does occur, simply to be borne. Unlike *Thelma and Louise*, the novel *Sleeping with the Enemy* presents female heroism in the form of hardship survived, an unacceptable identity abandoned and replaced by a better. Sara Burney escapes from her husband in Cape Cod and establishes a new life for herself, as Laura Pray, in Cedar Falls, Iowa. While not itself aspiring to the condition of "good" literature, the novel represents that aspiration as admirable. If *Thelma and Louise* alludes to *Bonnie and Clyde*, *Sleeping with the Enemy* has literary antecedents in Defoe's *Robinson Crusoe* (Sara escapes by swimming ashore from a sailboat, her brutal husband presuming her drowned) and in runaway slave narratives from Frederick Douglass to Alice Walker. It is no coincidence that the decent alternative mate is a university professor of drama who produces *King Lear* and *Candide* and can talk about Petrarch's Laura, Christopher Fry, and Shakespeare's androgynous women; nor that Laura Pray, who once passionately studied literature at Boston University but became merely a town librarian, now makes her living in Cedar Falls by acting as nurse-housekeeper to a retired woman English professor, Hazel George Channing, partially disabled from a car accident, who, solely in vocational frustration, refuses utterly to speak.

This act of self-censorship, and its "literary" resolution, are evidently as central to the novel's message as is the problem of wife beating. For while the violence can not, in this hypothesis, be treated, only escaped, the silencing responds to "literary" therapy. Sara/Laura has been reading aloud to Dr. Channing from the professor's *own* author, Henry James, and driving her to distraction by a hostile, *critical* reading of *The Golden Bowl*:

> And now Laura's soft, subtle, inflexible, eloquent voice droned on, indifferent, as if she didn't understand . . . as if she hated the words! . . . A beautiful, raped, insulted chapter came to an end. . . . Finally Laura met Hazel's glare with her own. "Why doesn't he write what he means? Words, words, words."

But the result of *this* rape is an epiphany, a psychological miracle:

The sound she . . . heard was Hazel George Channing's voice yelling, "No! No! He writes *exactly* what he means! He's the only author who does."

Silence came back to the room, a changed silence that made Hazel and Laura look at each other like strangers. "He *can't* say what he means!" Hazel cried. "*It's got to be between the lines!* [italics added] The things we learn about each other are like that! . . . He's got to *represent* those delicate things that are ruining lives."[43]

The yearning for high culture, figuratively represented in the frustrated early ambitions of Sara Burney and the self-imposed silence of the retired Jamesian, proves itself curative; and the miraculous moment turns on the very concept, reading between the lines, to which this book of mine is dedicated. Here, however, it carries a different intonation: a tribute to the hermeneutics of sensitivity, which is also an ethics. The nuances of (more or less) ordinary life, of interpersonal relations, for which, somewhat implausibly, the notorious indirections of Henry James are made to stand, are what "good" literature offers the key to, what it is good for. I cannot resist the observation that if anticanonical impulses were to remove *The Golden Bowl* from courses on the modern novel and replace it with *Sleeping with the Enemy*, the latter's thesis (about the relationship between high and low culture, between education and the chance of a better life) would be rendered unintelligible.

But if this is one of the central concerns of Price's novel, one would never know it from the cinematographic version, from which Professor Channing has vanished altogether. This erasure is symptomatic of the change in values produced by the change in media, which also involves a debilitating shift from the socioeconomic message of the tale. *Sleeping with the Enemy* values small heroisms: scrubbing walls and ceilings, filial loyalty, the patience required for spooning applesauce into the mouth of an invalid, the patience required for reading aloud *The Golden Bowl* in its entirety, the fortitude of being extremely hungry. Because, for a month before her job with Dr. Channing can begin, Sara/Laura must survive on the rations of a secret indigence: beans, oatmeal, and tomato ketchup. In the film, her ability to survive

43. Nancy Price, *Sleeping with the Enemy* (New York, 1991), 271–72.

without a financial safety net is never an issue. There is no semi-starvation, no work required. She simply opens a mysteriously self-renewing wallet. Likewise, the wretched little house from which she escapes undergoes more of a metamorphosis, in terms of size and beauty and ultramodern executive furnishings, than does Sara from Cape Cod to Cedar Falls. Underclass sociology and feminism, however popular, are commodified by the film industry, and reappear as upper-middle-class fairy tale.

And, as if to mark the violence done to *this* raped and insulted story, Joseph Ruben, who censored out almost all the novel's realism, chose to include the African violets. In the original text, the African violets stand, not without a certain banality, for the Robinson Crusoe motif, the ability to make things grow in foreign soil, the capacity to transport one's civilizing instincts. Sara's violets in her old, violent home grow in well-trained, perfect circles; but before she escapes, as a pledge of her determination to do so, she violates her own creatures:

> She had reached out and broken one leaf from one perfect circle. If the plant had cried as it broke, she wouldn't have been surprised. . . . She broke the circle of the next plant, and the next. She cut each leaf stem with a razor and wrapped it in wet cotton in plastic and then packed them with the razor blade in a small box. She filled two sacks with potting soil and vermiculite and put leaves and sacks at the bottom of her suitcase under her clothes, hiding a small, secret garden. Wherever she found a new home, new plants would grow from each leaf. . . . That night when she got into bed with Martin, the last things she saw were the shelves of violets. Their broken rosettes told her that she would leave if she could, that she meant to try, that it might not be a dream. (53–54)

In the Twentieth Century-Fox motion picture version, which substitutes dreams for sober material caretaking, Julia Roberts will have her violets, but without such preparations. There are no violated violets to mark the break between her old life and her new. Having opened her magic wallet and rented a spacious Victorian house (as distinct from the original "four-rooms-and-a-bath"), she simply goes out to the supermarket and buys the plants that she fancies. When popular culture reflects and continues to promote the economic rapacity and carelessness of the

1980s, it *cannot* simultaneously believe in the therapeutic power of reading, still less of reading carefully, between the lines, by which the intransigent facts of class and gender may be mediated and even ameliorated. One scarcely needs to point the moral, or to identify where the enemy is really to be found.

Postscript: The Return from Theory

In my autobiographical preface, I listed some of the intellectual currents that helped to precipitate the Thelmas and Louises of literary studies into the Grand Canyon. Apart from those brief mentions, this book may have appeared oblivious hitherto to the most startling phenomenon of recent academic history: the turn to theory. Although my account of the Good Old Cause distances itself from some literary theory, and although *en passant* I take small aim at poststructural or deconstructive criticism, I avoid confrontation with "theory" per se. The coming of Grand Theory has, of course, enormously energized literary studies and given the most sophisticated wielders of the new conceptual tools an interdisciplinary prestige they had never before achieved; yet it is unfortunately also true that the values I have here tried to recall have been as seriously undermined by the turn to theory as by other, blunter weapons. By values I mean preeminently humanism, which for these purposes entails at least the following: a belief that human beings are educable and may learn from their mistakes; a belief that rational consensus (for which education is some assistance) is possible; a belief that persons are, within certain limits, free to choose their objectives and even, within obviously greater limits, to try to bring their society in line with those objectives.

I must not, then, avoid the confrontation entirely; although I am fully aware that to engage them only in a postscript will result in oversimplification. I take it that there are four major theoretical models that have changed the shape of literary studies: neo-Marxist criticism, which maintains that literature unwit-

318

tingly reveals the cracks and contradictions in the ideological structures of the society that gives rise to it; deconstructive criticism, which accepts the impossibility of grounded meaning and focuses on the inadequacies of the signifier and problems of representation; psychoanalytic criticism, which believes that a writer unwittingly reveals the deep structure of his psyche (usually the workings of his libido) in what he writes and what he omits; and feminist criticism, which believes that the very structure of "literature" as an object of inquiry has been slanted by a deep cultural prejudice in favor of the males of the species.[1]

Between the first three of these models of understanding are similarities as striking as their differences. All three are determinisms, which assume that writers have little, if any, control over what they think and write. All three, though Marxist critics are more explicit on this point, are antirationalist, anti-Enlightenment, and anti-individualist. All three, then, are opposed to or contemptuous of humanism. By contrast, feminism as a theory is not *necessarily* or structurally antihumanist; and although in the previous chapter I took issue with some extensions of feminist argument that lean in that direction, there would have been no point in doing so had I believed that the central premises of feminist theory were illiberal.

I took a quixotic stand against deconstruction years ago, in the matching postscript to *Censorship and Interpretation*, and to return to that topic would be beating a dead horse. Academic Marxism too has been overtaken by history, forced by the amazing political upheavals of the 1990s to acknowledge that its founding doctrines are decayed nineteenth-century constructions made no sounder by renovations performed in the late 1960s. There remains, however, the still potent force of psychoanalysis as a grand theory that, in its merger with linguistics under the charismatic doctrines of Jacques Lacan, has seemed to some to extend the promise that linguistics itself once made and on which it failed to deliver—of being the key to all our mysteries.

1. I do not include the so-called New Historicism as a separate theory, in part because such theoretical moves as its practitioners make are eclectically borrowed from one or more of the four major theories, in part because, being a return to a historical understanding of texts, it is more a renovation than an absolute innovation.

Although it might be claimed on behalf of Lacan that he rescued the workings of the unconscious from Freud's essentialism
and resituated psychic development in a sociopolitical environment, this was scarcely a liberating gesture. Some of Lacan's
statements are as chillingly anti-Enlightenment as those of Louis
Althusser. For Lacan, "the philosophical *cogito* is at the centre
of the mirage that renders modern man so sure of being himself
even in his uncertainties about himself."[2] But while he shared
Althusser's antirationalism, Lacan made no secret of his contempt for historical or applied Marxism. "I shall be content," he
wrote, "for my little jab at the general function of *praxis* in the
genesis of history, to point out that the very society that wished
to restore, along with the privileges of the producer, the causal
hierarchy of the relations between production and the ideological superstructure to their full political rights, has none the less
failed to give birth to an esperanto in which the relations of language to socialist realities would have rendered any literary for-
malism radically impossible."[3] In other words, Lacan's commitment to what Fredric Jameson named "The Prison-House of Language" was so complete that, barring a complete restructuring
of the linguistic bases of society, all attempts at social change
must be seen as hypocritical. Indeed, the essay containing these
statements, "The Agency of the Letter in the Unconscious, or
Reason since Freud," opens with a fable by Leonardo da Vinci
which might, taken out of context, support such a debilitating
metaphysic:

OF CHILDREN IN SWADDLING CLOTHES

O Cities of the sea, I behold in your citizens, women as well as
men tightly bound with stout bonds around their arms and legs
by folk who will not understand your language; and you will only
be able to give vent to your griefs and sense of loss of liberty by
making tearful complaints, and sighs, and lamentations one to
another; for those who bind you will not understand your language nor will you understand them. (147)

On the other hand, if one places Leonardo's fable not only in his
whole collection (which is pervasively interested in the politi-

---

2. "The Agency of the Letter in the Unconscious, or Reason since Freud,"
in *Ecrits: A Selection*, trans. Alan Sheridan (New York, 1977), 165.
3. "The Agency of the Letter," 148.

cal and social meanings of liberty) but also in the documentable history of the fable, from antiquity onward, as a strategy for evading censorship, it stands rather in an oblique and antagonistic relation to Lacan's essay than as its aphoristic essence.[4]

That Lacan's thought stressed the permanent unfreedom of the psyche, in part because he appropriated to psychoanalytic discourse Hegel's master-slave dialectic, with language in the role of the master, is now a commonplace of psychoanalytic criticism. But the extent of his hostility to humanism is less remarked. Lacan argued, for example, that any attempt to reinstall the conscious "autonomous ego" in the center of the human psyche is doomed to failure, "such that presently as always the word humanism is a sack in which there is quietly rotting, piled one on top of another, the corpses of these successive upheavals of a revolutionary point of view on man."[5] And in a footnote to "The Subversion of the Subject and the Dialectic of Desire in the Freudian Unconscious," Lacan showed that these remarks were not runaway metaphors but part of his deliberate iconoclasm:

> The term "a-human" which someone wished to attribute to what I said [in the lecture that became that essay] did not cause me the least distress, since the element of the new that the category implies gave me, on the contrary, a certain pleasure.[6]

If one finds this disarming by its appeal to modernity, what follows should come as a rude shock: "I must admit," Lacan continued,

> that I am partial to a certain form of humanism, a humanism that comes from an area where, although it is not used with any less cunning than elsewhere, it nevertheless has a certain quality of candour about it: "When the miner comes home, his wife rubs him down. . . . "

4. See Patterson, *Fables of Power* (Durham, N.C., 1991). A brief discussion of Leonardo's fables, and an exemplary instance of a fable that speaks to the themes of this book, appear on 11–12.

5. Lacan, *Le Seminaire II: Le moi dans la théorie de Freud et dans la technique de la psychanalyse* (Paris, 1978), 243. Quoted and translated by Jane Gallop, *Reading Lacan* (Ithaca and London, 1985), 99.

6. "The Subversion of the Subject and the Dialectic of Desire in the Freudian Unconscious," in *Ecrits: A Selection*, 324.

The double condescension here, to groups (workers and their wives) in which Lacanian psychoanalysis is deeply uninterested, makes the admission synonymous with the boast from which it is supposed an exception.

My chief reason for ending this book with an attack on Lacan, however, is that he appropriates to his theory of language not only da Vinci but also Leo Strauss. More precisely, he appropriates to the argument that language is destiny a curious version of Strauss's theory of reading between the lines. It is curious in part because it is so *literary*, being first delivered to the philosophy group of the Fédération des étudiants ès lettres at the Sorbonne, and evidently intended, among other things, to deliver a shock to traditional notions of literary interpretation and figuration; and curious also because the discussion always seems just about to subvert Lacan's intentions for it, by reinstantiating the meanings he was determined to empty out. To use his own terminology, "the incessant sliding of the signified under the signifier" undermines his own discussion and, if I read it correctly, beats him at his own game.

The theme of this essay is the slavery of "the subject," that is to say, the human person, to the language system that precedes the construction of his consciousness and "in which his place is already inscribed at birth, if only by virtue of his proper name" (148). Given his general approval of Saussure's theory of the arbitrariness of signs (the psychoanalytic version of the "arbitrary government" to which early modern republicans argued resistance), Lacan thought it necessary to reduce the major tropes of metaphor and metonymy to merely the relation between words in the signifying chain, from which chain human knowledge, the competent reader, and imaginative association have been banished. "For what is important is not that the subject [reader] know anything whatsoever" (155).

But in what follows, Lacan mysteriously slides from talking about readers to talking about a writer (himself), whose practice, insofar as it draws on Lacan's knowledge of literary criticism, seems in conflict with his psychoanalytical dogma. The starting place is the word "tree," which Lacan, who had been reading (and citing) Paul Valéry, knew to be a major literary and philosophical symbol, capable of generating, even by its mention, waves of cultural memory and ontic associations. Lacan found himself arguing that poetry takes place in *defiance* of the unbreakable laws of language and arbitrary signification:

> What this [arbitrary] structure of the signifying chain discloses is the possibility I have, precisely in so far as I have this language in common with other subjects, that is to say, in so far as it exists as a language, to use it in order to signify *something quite other* than what it says. This function of speech is more worth pointing out than that of "disguising the thought" (more often than not indefinable) of the subject; it is no less than the function of indicating the place of this subject in the search for the true.
>
> I have only to plant my tree in a locution; climb the tree, project on to it the cunning illumination a descriptive context gives a word; raise it (*arborer*) so as not to let myself be imprisoned in some sort of *communiqué* of the facts, however official, and if I know the truth, make it heard, in spite of all the *between-the-lines* censures[,] by the only signifier my acrobatics through the branches of the tree can constitute, provocative to the point of burlesque, or perceptible only to the practised eye, according to whether I wish to be heard by the mob or by the few. (155–56; italics original)

This passage is almost unbearably resistant to solution, especially when, as in this translation and the French edition of *Ecrits* (though not in the first English translation), a crucial comma is omitted. No doubt Lacan himself would have enjoyed this ambiguity. On the one hand (when the comma is present) the writer-subject triumphantly proclaims his "cunning" evasion of the rules, his imaginative leap over the notion of language as "official communiqué," his capacity to make the truth heard; on the other (when the comma is absent) it appears that Lacan himself is the censor, that his own linguist acrobatics work between his own lines to prevent this defiant breaking of the rules from occurring. Writing between the lines is therefore locked in a duel with reading between the lines; and to make matters as complicated as possible, we know from elsewhere in this essay that for Lacan the primary meaning of censorship is Freud's; that is to say, the strategies the psyche uses to repress the truths known by the unconscious, which the unconscious in turn reveals by those slidings of the signifier that constitute resistance to repression.

To this psychoanalytic concept of censorship Lacan intends to assimilate poetry:

> In the case of *Verscheibung,* "displacement," the German term is closer to the idea of that veering off of signification that we see in metonymy, and which from its first appearance in Freud is represented as the most appropriate means used by the unconscious to foil censorship. (160)

But this determination has itself been contaminated (in the structure of the essay) by the fact that Lacan has also been reading Leo Strauss, and by his introduction of the Straussian meaning of reading between the lines as an *analogy* to the psychoanalytic process:

> What does man find in metonymy if not the power to circumvent the obstacles of social censure? Does not this form, which gives its field to truth in its very oppression, manifest a certain servitude inherent in its presentation?
> One may read with profit a book by Leo Strauss, from the land that traditionally offers asylum to those who choose freedom, in which the author reflects on the relation between the art of writing and persecution. By pushing to its limits the sort of connaturality that links this art to that condition, he lets us glimpse a certain something which in this matter imposes its form, in the effect of truth on desire. (158)

I take this passage to offer, first, a serious misreading of Strauss's *Persecution and the Art of Writing;* second, a statement that the "obstacles of social censure" that Lacan mentions are the Freudian obstacles of sexual inhibition, rather than the obstacles that society imposes to free discussion; and third, the claim that even as metonymy attempts to circumvent the oppressive laws of language, its very form (an attribute standing in for the thing itself, a part trying to speak for the whole)[7] manifests the inescapability of those laws, the "certain servitude" which, for Lacan, resistance only confirms.

As one also writing from "the land that traditionally offers asylum to those who choose freedom," I resent the use that Lacan

---

7. Technically this latter definition is of synecdoche; but the example Lacan uses of metonymy—"thirty sails" for a great fleet—is really an example of taking the part for the whole.

here makes of that tradition, merely as an analogy for what really interests him. Lacan's well-known contempt for American psychoanalysis, with its emphasis on therapy, and his astonishing statement that that development in the field was a "mental abdication" caused by the decrepitude of the profession due to "the diaspora of the war," a "reduction of distinguished practice to a label suitable to the 'American way of life,'"[8] all this should have disqualified him from *invoking* the republican tradition, let along turning it, too, into just another signifier. I am suspicious of Lacan's elitism, clearly revealed in the opening gambits of "The Agency of the Letter": self-congratulary statements that he *wants* to be "difficult" to understand, invocation of his specialized audience at the Sorbonne and "the collusion of their common training," all these culminating in that perhaps unguarded moment of delight in his own rhetorical expertise, in which he says that he will choose strategies according to whether he wishes "to be heard by the mob or by the few" (156).

Yet there is something deeply interesting in Lacan's desire to include literature and figuration in his system, to try to account for them, and even, apparently, to proffer them as an *exception* to universal unfreedom, even though that proffer is immediately withdrawn. Lacan lists for his literary audience the traditional figures of rhetoric (peripherasis, hyperbaton, ellipsis, suspension, anticipation, retraction, negation, digression, irony, catechresis, litotes, antonomasis, hypotyposis) and calls them the "mechanisms of the unconscious," the agents by which the unconscious tells its story to the analyst through the lips of the passive analysand, the "active principle of the rhetoric of the discourse that the analysand in fact utters" (169). Yet Lacan's own knowledge of rhetoric and desire to display it imply a very different epistemology—one in which education gives analytic mastery—and indeed he proceeds to claim that Freud himself owed his insights to his broad cultural training:

> To interpret the unconscious as Freud did, one would have to be as he was, an encyclopedia of the arts and muses, as well as an assiduous reader of the *Fliegende Blätter* [a German comic book of the nineteenth-century]. And the task [of the analyst] is made

8. "The Subversion of the Subject," 306–7.

no easier by the fact that we are at the mercy of a thread woven with allusions, quotations, puns, and equivocations.

It seems to me that once this concession has been made, it cannot be undone by stating that the relation between elements on the signifying chain is arbitrary. Lacan's fascination by literature is something that should, in these dark days when literary studies is everybody's scapegoat, give us a little comfort. And the question that this essay admits is central to the human condition—the question of agency (*l'instance*) built into his title at least in translation, the question of who or what is in charge of our behavior—remains as unsettled by Lacan's own allusions, quotations, puns, and equivocations as it was before he began.

Index

Index

Abbot, George, archbishop, 208
Actes and Monuments (John Foxe), 134, 141–42, 144, 145, 146*n34*, 147–48
acyron (the uncouth), 51
Addison, Joseph, 270
Adler, Mortimer, 7
Admonitions to Parliament, 31, 32, 69, 233
Aeschylus, 236
Aesop, 49, 50, 51*n18*, 54–56; Aesopian fables, 170
Alfred, king of England, 229
Allen, James Sloan, 6
Althusser, Louis, 4, 17, 250, 251, 320
Anatomy of Abuses (Philip Stubbes), 172
Ancient constitution, theory of, 215
Anderson, Sir Edmund, 72
Aptekar, Jane, 89*n14*
Aquinas, Thomas, 39
Aretino, Pietro, 194
Aristophanes, 35
Aristotle, 11–12, 14, 83, 96, 98
Arminianism, 251, 272
Arundel, Thomas Howard, earl of, 208
Atheism: in "Longinus," 268; in Plato's *Laws*, 25–27, 30, 33; in early modern France, 81–82
Augustine, St., 299
Aurelian, Roman emperor, 265
Aylmer, John, bishop of London, 114

Babington Plot, 117, 119, 128–29, 136, 154–58

Bacon, Sir Francis, 41, 183*n42*, 208
Bagshaw, Edward, 224
Baker, David, 108–9
Baker, J. H., 91*n15*, 171*n21*
Bakhtin, Mikhail, 281
Bald, R. C., 161–62, 179, 183, 193
Baldwin, Stanley, 55
Bancroft, Richard, archbishop, 181, 221, 232–33
Barlow, Samuel, 270–71
Barlow, William, bishop of Rochester, of Lincoln, 183
Bates, E. H., 62
Bathurst, Theodore, 52
Baxter, Richard, 243
Beacon, Richard, 83
Beale, Matthew, 62
Bedford, Lucy, countess of, 205*n85*
Beer, Barrett, 123*n10*
Bellamy, John, 131, 173
Bellarmine, cardinal Robert, 243
Benthem, H. L., 249, 252
Bèze, Théodore de (Beza), 231, 285
Bishop, George, 122
Bledstein, Burton, 4, 5*n2*
Bloom, Allan, 6, 19–22, 24*n16*, 29
Boccaccio, Giovanni, 125, 140
Bodin, Jean, 127
Boiardo, Matteo, 42, 43
Boleyn, Anne, queen of England, 127
Bolton, Edmund, 117, 121, 122, 126
Bonner, Edmund, bishop of London, 147
Bonnie and Clyde, 313, 314
Booth, Stephen, 122, 129*n18*

329